☀ INSIGHT GUIDES

SOUTHWEST France

Discovery CHANNEL

APA PUBLICATIONS
Part of the Langenscheidt Publishing Group

INSIGHT GUIDE
SOUTHWEST France

Editorial
Project Editor
Nick Inman
Consultant Editor
Rosemary Bailey
Managing Editor
Dorothy Stannard
Editorial Director
Brian Bell

Distribution

UK & Ireland
GeoCenter International Ltd
The Viables Centre, Harrow Way
Basingstoke, Hants RG22 4BJ
Fax: (44) 1256-817988

United States
Langenscheidt Publishers, Inc.
46–35 54th Road, Maspeth, NY 11378
Fax: (1) 718 784-0640

Canada
Thomas Allen & Son Ltd
390 Steelcase Road East
Markham, Ontario L3R 1G2
Fax: (1) 905 475 6747

Australia
Universal Publishers
1 Waterloo Road
Macquarie Park, NSW 2113
Fax: (61) 2 9888 9074

New Zealand
Hema Maps New Zealand Ltd (HNZ)
Unit D, 24 Ra ORA Drive
East Tamaki, Auckland
Fax: (64) 9 273 6479

Worldwide
**Apa Publications GmbH & Co.
Verlag KG (Singapore branch)**
38 Joo Koon Road, Singapore 628990
Tel: (65) 6865-1600. Fax: (65) 6861-6438

Printing

Insight Print Services (Pte) Ltd
38 Joo Koon Road, Singapore 628990
Tel: (65) 6865-1600. Fax: (65) 6861-6438

©2004 Apa Publications GmbH & Co.
Verlag KG (Singapore branch)
All Rights Reserved
First Edition 2001; updated 2004

CONTACTING THE EDITORS
We would appreciate it if readers
would alert us to errors or out-
dated information by writing to:
**Insight Guides, P.O. Box 7910,
London SE1 1WE, England.
Fax: (44) 20 7403-0290.
insight@apaguide.co.uk**

NO part of this book may be reproduced,
stored in a retrieval system or transmitted
in any form or means electronic, mech-
anical, photocopying, recording or otherwise, without prior written permission of
Apa Publications. Brief text quotations
with use of photographs are exempted
for book review purposes only. Information has been obtained from sources
believed to be reliable, but its accuracy
and completeness, and the opinions
based thereon, are not guaranteed.

www.insightguides.com

ABOUT THIS BOOK

This guidebook combines the interests and enthusiasms of two of the world's best known infor-mation providers: Insight Guides, whose titles have set the standard for visual travel guides since 1970, and Discovery Channel, the world's premier source of nonfiction televi-sion programming.

The editors of Insight Guides pro-vide both practical advice and general understanding about a destination's history, culture and people. Discov-ery Channel and its website, www.dis-covery.com, help millions of viewers explore their world from the comfort of their home and also encourages them to explore it first hand.

How to use this book

Insight Guides has a proven formula of informative and well-written text paired with a fresh journalistic approach. The books are carefully structured, both to convey a good understanding of each place and its culture and to guide readers through its many sights:

♦ The **Features** section, indicated by a yellow bar at the top of each page, covers the history and culture of the country in a series of inform-ative essays.

♦ The main **Places** section, indi-cated by a blue bar, is a complete guide to all the sights and areas worth visiting. Places of special interest are coordinated by number with the maps.

♦ The **Travel Tips** listings section, with an orange bar, provides a handy point of reference for infor-mation on travel, accommodation, shopping, restaurants, sport, lan-guage, and much more.

The contributors

The book was steered into existence by Francophile **Nick Inman**, a travel writer covering both sides of the Pyrenees. He was advised on the way by **Rosemary Bailey**, author of several Insight titles and other guides to France, who also wrote the chapters on the Southwest Today, the Changing Countryside, the Basque Country, the Ariège, the Aude, French Catalonia, and Hérault and Gard, as well as the Travel Tips section. She also supplied additional new material and updated information for the 2004 edition.

Professor **Colin Jones** of Warwick University, author of *The Cambridge Illustrated History of France* among other works, wrote about the history of the region. Veteran France author **Peter Graham** (whose most recent book is *Mourjou. The Life and Food of an Auvergne Village*) contributed the essay on food, while wine writer **Jim Budd** covered the vintages of the Southwest. **Elsie Burch Donald**, author of the definitive *The French Farmhouse*, provided an overview of rural architecture. **Barry Miles**, biographer of Allen Ginsberg and Jack Kerouac among others, summed up the complex subject of Romanesque architecture. Author and journalist **Clive Unger-Hamilton** wrote the chapters on Bordeaux and the Gironde, and the Dordogne. **Marion Kaplan**, a writer and photographer resident in the Gers, contributed chapters on Gascony and the Pyrenees. Other chapters were written by Nick Inman.

Many photographers provided images for this book but **Jean-Dominique Dallet** and **Bill Wassman** need special citation. Picture research was under the supervision of **Hilary Genin**. **Zoë Goodwin** took charge of the cartography.

Emily Hatchwell and **Dorothy Stannard** oversaw the project. Veteran travel author and editor **Roger Williams** acted as sage and troubleshooter throughout. **Clara Villanueva** and **Siân Lezard** edited the text. The proofs were read by **Sylvia Suddes** and the index compiled by **Caroline Wilding**.

Many people and organisations lent the team invaluable assistance along the way. They include: **Bob** and **Gwen Royston**, **Polly Timberlake**, **Laurence Ibrahim Aibo** (CRT Midi-Pyrénées), **Raphael Nauche**, **Marie Grellier**, **Chantal Fihey**, **Michèle Pozzo**, **Chantal Verdier** (Pyrenees National Park), and the staffs of **Sopexa** and the **French Tourist Office** in London.

Map Legend

▬ ▬ ∙ ∙	International Boundary
▬▬▬▬	Regional Boundary
▬ ▬ ▬ ▬	Département Boundary
▬ ∙ ▬ ∙ ▬	National Park/Reserve
▬ ▬ ▬ ▬	Ferry Route
✈ ✈	Airport: International/Regional
🚌	Bus Station
❶	Tourist Information
✉	Post Office
⊡ † ✝	Church/Ruins
†	Monastery
ℭ	Mosque
✡	Synagogue
◪ ◲	Castle/Ruins
∴	Archaeological Site
∩	Cave
𝟏	Statue/Monument
★	Place of Interest

The main places of interest in the Places section are coordinated by number with a full-colour map (e.g. **❶**), and a symbol at the top of every right-hand page tells you where to find the map.

INSIGHT GUIDE
SOUTHWEST
France

CONTENTS

The Vieux Palais and Pont Vieux at Espalion, on the Lot.

Insight on ...

Information panels

Travel Tips

◆ **Full Travel Tips index is on page 321**

Places

COAST TO COAST

The best of France is packed into the area between the Massif Central and the Pyrenees, the Atlantic and the Mediterranean

There is nowhere on the map officially called "Southwest France". But there is a large and fascinating corner of the country – an area characterised by its diversity, vibrant cultures and wealth of concentrated detail – in need of a name to sum it up. It has three sharply defined natural borders, two of them composed of water: the Atlantic Ocean in the west, and the Mediterranean Sea and River Rhône in the east. The southern extent is unequivocally etched by the peaks of the Pyrenees (which also form the Franco-Spanish frontier). To the north the geographical limit is not so clear, as the uplands of the southwest merge imperceptibly into the Massif Central; but here a line can be drawn around the northern edges of three of France's great local government regions: Aquitaine, Midi-Pyrénées and Languedoc-Roussillon.

Everything within these limits is, as far as this book is concerned, "Southwest France". It covers an area of 114,000 sq km (44,000 sq miles), constituting over a fifth of the total area of France, and has a population of around 7 million, equivalent to 12 percent of the French population. When these figures are put together, the Southwest is seen to have approximately twice as much space per person as the rest of France.

Far from Paris, between two busy seas and abutting a national border (only fixed in its present form 300 years ago), the Southwest has always been an independent-thinking cultural crossroads. A rich mélange of peoples – Romans, Celts, Visigoths, Arabs, British, Gascons, Occitans, Basques, Catalans and latterly settlers from northern Europe looking for the good life of rural France – has settled and resettled this territory, building up incrementally over generations the fascinating heterogeneity seen today.

The backdrop to human life is the extraordinarily varied landscape of the Southwest. It is as if every possible topography had been squeezed in somewhere: there are lushly wooded river valleys, vertiginous gorges, lakes, crags with castles perched upon them, icy mountain tops, beaches, bays, outsize sand dunes, undulating fields of ripening sunflowers and endless vineyards offering the promise of vintages to come. Nameless it may be, but Southwest France lacks nothing else. ❑

PRECEDING PAGES: St-Cirq-Lapopie; beside the Canal du Midi; painting the Girondins Monument in Bordeaux; the Salle Henri Martin in the Capitole, Toulouse. **LEFT:** cyclist in the Corbières.

Decisive Dates

THE EARLY YEARS

450,000 years ago Tautavel Man lives and hunts on the plains of Roussillon.

17,000–15,000 years ago The walls of Lascaux caves are painted by prehistoric artists.

6,000–4,000 BC Farming and pastoral lifestyles are established in Southwest France.

121 BC The Romans control the Mediterranean coast between Spain and Italy.

58 BC Roman Conquest of Gaul begins with the arrival of Julius Caesar. Last resistance to the

invaders is offered by the Gauls at Uxellodunum (at Puy d'Issolud near Vayrac), in Quercy.

406 AD Frankish armies invade northern France from Germany.

416 AD Visigoths conquer and settle the Southwest region.

THE MIDDLE AGES

496 Clovis enlarges the Frankish state and (in 507) defeats the Visigoths near Poitiers.

732 Charles Martel checks the Arab advance from Spain into the rest of Europe at Poitiers.

801 Charlemagne sets up a Pyrenean buffer state centred on Barcelona, later to form part of the trans-Pyrenean kingdom of Aragon.

843 Treaty of Verdun: the Frankish empire is divided between the grandsons of Charlemagne.

878 Wilfred the Hairy takes control of the eastern Pyrenees and founds the dynastic house of the counts of Barcelona.

905 Navarre, straddling the Pyrenees, becomes a kingdom under Sancho I.

c950 Beginning of the pilgrimage through France to the supposed tomb of St James at present-day Santiago de Compostela, in Spain, where his relics had been discovered around 813.

1130 Aimery Picaud, a monk from Poitou, writes the *Liber Sancti Jacobi*, or *Codex Calixtinus*, the world's first travel guide, for the benefit of pilgrims on the road to Santiago de Compostela.

1152 Eleanor of Aquitaine marries Henry Plantagenet. He becomes Henry II of England in 1154. A third of France is ruled by the English crown.

1137 Barcelona and Aragon united by marriage.

THE CATHAR PERIOD

1194 Raymond VI becomes Count of Toulouse.

1208 The assassination of the papal legate Peter of Castelnau triggers the Albigensian Crusade, the first crusade to be fought against Christians.

1209 22 July: Béziers is sacked by crusaders, its inhabitants slaughtered and the town burned. 15 August: Carcassonne surrenders to the crusaders.

1213–76 Reign of Jaume I (James the Conqueror) of Barcelona (Catalonia-Aragon). Born in Montpellier, he expands the loose federation of states he rules over to reach from the Pyrenees to Valencia. He also controls the Mediterranean as far as Sicily.

1217–18 Simon de Montfort besieges Toulouse but is killed by a randomly fired stone missile.

1244 Montségur capitulates to its besiegers on 2 March, but the garrison is left in possession of the castle for a further 15 days. On 16 March, more than 200 unrepentant Cathars are burnt by the Inquisition at the base of the hill.

1255 Quéribus is the last Cathar stronghold to fall to the crusader army.

1258 By the Treaty of Corbeil, Jaume I relinquishes control of Roussillon to Louis IX of France.

THE HUNDRED YEARS' WAR TO THE REVOLUTION

1337–1453 Hundred Years' War.

1348 The Black Death appears on the Mediterranean coast of France.

1453 The English are beaten by the French in the last battle of the Hundred Years' War at Castillon-la-Bataille, in Guyenne, near Bordeaux. They abandon all French possessions except Calais.

1512 Southern Navarre is annexed by the Spanish crown to unify Spain.

1539 French is decreed the legal language by the royal edict of Villers-Cotterets, exacerbating the decline of the Occitan language.

1562 The Wars of Religion start between Huguenots (Protestants) and Catholics.

1589 French (northern) Navarre passes into the possession of the French crown.

1594 Henri of Navarre, having converted to Catholicism, is crowned Henri IV of France.

1598 The Edict of Nantes effectively brings the Wars of Religion to an end.

1659 The Treaty of the Pyrenees ends a conflict between France and Spain. The border between the two countries is definitively drawn, with Spain ceding Roussillon and the Cerdagne to France.

1681 The Canal du Midi opens, connecting Toulouse (and the Atlantic via the Garonne river system) with the Mediterranean near Béziers.

1685 Louis XIV's Revocation of the Edict of Nantes: Protestant worship in France is prohibited.

1702–10 The Camisard uprising in the Cévennes begins in Le Pont-de-Montvert, 24 July 1702. The guerrilla war lingers until 1710.

1789 The storming of the Bastille in Paris marks the beginning of the French Revolution.

1792 Declaration of the First Republic. Louis XVI is tried, and executed the following year.

1804 Napoleon becomes emperor.

1814 Louis XVIII, the younger brother of Louis XVI, enters Southwest France from Spain with the allied armies that have defeated Napoleon.

1844 Architect Viollet-le-Duc begins the controversial restoration of the Cité of Carcassonne.

1848–52 The short-lived Second Republic ends with a coup d'état, establishing Louis Napoleon Bonaparte's Second Empire.

MODERN TIMES

1858 The 14-year-old Bernadette Soubirous sees the first of 18 Christian-related visions of the Immaculate Conception in a grotto at Lourdes.

1868 Phylloxera destroys vineyards.

1870 Proclamation of the Third Republic, which will survive until 1940.

1907 Wine Growers' Revolt in Bas Languedoc.

1939 The Spanish Civil War ends with a mass emigration of defeated Republicans over the border into Southwest France. Outbreak of World War II.

1940 On 22 June, an amnesty allows Nazi Germany to occupy northern and western France. The rest of the country is controlled by the Vichy government under Marshal Pétain. On 12 September, four boys discover extraordinary prehistoric paintings in a cave at Lascaux in the Dordogne.

1946–58 Fourth Republic.

1957 France is one of the original members of the European Economic Community (now the EU).

1958 Fifth Republic is proclaimed.

1967 Creation of the Pyrenees National Park.

1970 Airbus Industrie, a consortium of European

firms, is formed, with one of its headquarters at Toulouse. Creation of the Cévennes National Park.

1972 France's 96 *départements* are grouped into 22 regions, including Aquitaine, Midi-Pyrénées and Languedoc-Roussillon in the Southwest.

1990 Opening of high speed Paris–Bordeaux rail link, the *train à grande vitesse* (TGV) *atlantique*.

1993 Andorra becomes an independent state.

2000 The millennium is celebrated with trees planted along the Paris meridian.

2002 Euros replace French francs on 1 January. Jacques Chirac is re-elected President.

2003 A dramatic year of floods, oil spills, and an unprecedented heat wave causing fires and damaging crops. Concorde flights end. ❏

PRECEDING PAGES: Roman mosaic of the god Oceanus in Musée St-Raymond, Toulouse.

LEFT: *The Siege of Toulouse* by Jean-Paul Laurens.

RIGHT: Henri IV with a seven-headed beast.

CAVE PAINTERS TO CATHARS

Since earliest times, the Southwest has had a sense of cultural separateness from the rest of France, fostering a spirit of independence and a tradition of dissent

Southwest France has always had – and usually prided itself upon having – a good deal of independence from northern France. Its history until the later Middle Ages only sporadically collided with that of the north. The region was subsequently often hostile to creeping integration; and even after full inclusion within the French state, its history has been replete with episodes of resistance, opposition and dissent.

In the 17th century, individuals from the south regarded crossing the River Loire as "going to France", and used the term "Frenchmen" to designate those who lived north of that river. This southern sense of otherness has been fully reciprocated. Well into the 19th and 20th centuries, northerners regarded the south as exotically different – and implicitly inferior and less civilised. "The real France," observed the early 19th-century writer and historian, Jules Michelet, "is northern France." So strong was this sentiment, that the history of France has invariably been told from a northern, often Parisian perspective, which has discounted or ignored key episodes in the development of Southwest France.

Prehistoric man

Historians' neglect is all the more regrettable in that the Southwest has a particularly rich, diverse and complex heritage – as well as a very ancient one. The human skulls found at Tautavel are at least 450,000 years old, making them among the oldest found in Europe. No other region in France can boast the extraordinary vestiges of cave art discovered here, which shows a flourishing hunter-gatherer "reindeer culture" in existence as early as circa 15,000 BC, notably in the Dordogne (most famously at Lascaux), but also in the neighbouring Lot and in the Pyrenean foothills.

LEFT: prehistoric painting of bisons in the Grotte de Niaux in the Ariège.
RIGHT: late-Palaeolithic sculpture of the Dame de Brassempouy.

Symptomatically perhaps, it was only following archaeological excavation in the late 19th century that this became known. The region was also – along with neighbouring Provence – the first area in France to welcome farming and pastoral lifestyles from between 6,000 and 4,000 BC onwards.

Roman rule

When in 55–54 BC Julius Caesar drew all of France into the Roman republic, the southern part of Gaul (as he called it) was more ethnically diverse than the north. The Celtic Gauls who had covered most of the region of present-day France over the previous centuries had failed to supplant the indigenous Iberian peoples in the Southwest. In addition, the Mediterranean coastline had already received the imprint, first of Greek merchants and traders and then, after 121 BC, of the Romans themselves, who annexed the long corridor between northern Italy and Spain. The long coastal strip of "Gallia Narbonensis" became a crucial link in the process of Roman colonisation. Its already cosmopolitan capital, the port-city of Narbonne (now long since silted up), became Gaul's second-largest Roman city (after Lyon), and a flourishing grain-exporting centre with links all over the Mediterranean.

The area to the north of Gallia Narbonensis initially resisted Roman occupation, with local tribes fighting pitched battles against Caesar's legionaries. But the modern-day tourist will notice the extent to which the region abandoned resistance and

ROMAN MOTORWAY

The A9 motorway along the Languedoc coast follows the route of the old Roman road, the Via Domitia, from Provence to Spain.

turies AD. Yet whereas northern France was brought directly under the hegemony of the invading Franks, who effaced much of the area's Roman inheritance, the Southwest received far lighter treatment. In 416, the Visigoths, perhaps the most Romanised of all the so-called barbarians, settled the area, following spells in northern Italy and Spain, and built up an empire which by the 470s extended into Provence and on to the Atlantic coastline. Visigoth numbers were not large and they preferred to compromise with local customs and

embraced cooperation. Its road patterns and the extensive Roman remains still to be seen in many of its cities – not least in Avignon, Nîmes and Arles – show a high degree of Romanisation. The region's distinctive urban network was created in this period, and large-scale agricultural holdings centred on villas also developed, specialising not only in grain but also in wine, whose production has been an integral part of the region's identity ever since.

The legacy of the Roman empire

The Roman imprint was seriously diminished by the break-up of the Roman empire following Germanic invasions of the 4th and 5th cen-

mores rather than seek to obliterate them. They also played a leading part in defending the crumbling Roman empire by defeating Attila the Hun near Troyes in 451.

The region from the western Pyrenees to the mouth of the Garonne was also, between the 4th and 6th centuries, being increasingly settled by the Basque peoples (or Vascones) from Navarre, who brought their own distinctive language and genetic mix. The Basques further amplified the region's cultural diversity and gave the inhabitants of "Vasconia" – or Gascony – a distinctness from the north which is still detectable in eye-colour (fewer blues in the south) and blood group.

If the Southwest thus has a distinct genetic mix and historical record, it also, at an early stage, developed a material culture which marks it off from the north. The region's houses tend to be topped with Roman-style tiles, for example, while northern France prefers slate and thatch; and the customary waterwheels, ploughs and field-systems here also differ strikingly from those which became established beyond the Loire. Olive oil and pig- and goose-fat compose the basics of southern cuisine, as against butter in the north.

Furthermore, whereas northern France in the Middle Ages turned increasingly to customary

The Middle Ages

Although the region was to enjoy a great deal of independence following the break-up of the Roman empire, religion was to prove a weak point in the Visigothic armour. The Visigoths were adepts of the Arian heresy, which had pockets of believers throughout the Mediterranean region. When Clovis, king of the Franks, converted from paganism to orthodox Christianity around 496, he led a religious crusade against the south (presaging the later war against Catharism), defeating Visigothic forces at Vouillé, near Poitiers, in 507 and forcing local populations to renounce Arianism.

law, the south held onto its inheritance of Roman law down to the upheavals of the French Revolution of 1789.

Linguistically, too, north and south tended to diverge. The language of northern France was heavily influenced by its Germanic conquerors, whereas the south retained a form closer to classical Latin, so that by the 9th and 10th centuries contemporaries were distinguishing between northern and southern Gallo-Roman.

LEFT: 4th-century Roman mosaic of Thetis and Triton in Musée St-Raymond, Toulouse.
ABOVE: Charlemagne and his wife, shown in a 9th-century illuminated manuscript.

THE LANGUAGE OF "OC"

North of a line running from the confluence of the Dordogne and Garonne rivers in the west to Grenoble in the east, the word for "yes" was "oïl" (modern-day "oui"), while to the south it was "oc". France could thus be divided into the areas of *langue d'oïl* ("the tongue of oui") and *langue d'oc*. The latter term – written "Languedoc" – came to refer to all of the southern region in which the Occitan language (or *patois*, as its detractors would have it) was spoken.

The tongue remained in current use in most of the region well into the 19th century. Attempts are currently being made to revive the language and Occitan culture in the modern Southwest.

Eleanor of Aquitaine

Eleanor of Aquitaine would have been a remarkable woman had she lived at any time in history. Determined and strong-willed, yet also beautiful, cultured and capricious, she dominated the 12th-century affairs of both England and France. She was born around 1122. At the age of 15, when her father William X of Aquitaine died, she inherited the Duchy of Aquitaine, which extended from the Loire to the Pyrenees. In the same year, 1137, she married Prince Louis, who became King Louis VII of France only a month later.

From 1147 to 1149 she accompanied her husband on the Second Crusade to Jerusalem, where she led her own troops into battle, wearing the costume of an Amazonian warrior.

Disagreements in the Holy Land presaged the end of their relationship and although Eleanor bore Louis two daughters, the marriage was annulled in 1152 because of consanguinity.

Almost immediately, Eleanor married Henry Plantagenet, Count of Anjou and Duke of Normandy, who succeeded to the English throne in 1154 as Henry II. The union of Eleanor and Henry brought together England, Normandy and the west of France in the same powerful Angevin empire which would survive for the next 200 years.

Eleanor bore Henry five sons and three daughters. Two of her sons, Richard the Lionheart and John (surnamed Lackland), became kings of England. Her daughters made strategic marriages: Matilda to Henry the Lion, Duke of Saxony and Bavaria; Eleanor to Alfonso VIII, King of Castile; and Joan first to William II of Sicily and then Raymond VI of Toulouse. Because of her dispersed but influential extended family Eleanor has been dubbed "the grandmother of Europe".

All the while Eleanor took a hand in administering the kingdom and especially her own lands. At the same time she was as versed in culture and poetry as she was in politics and military affairs, and was the patron of troubadours, whose art flourished at the court of Poitiers.

Eleanor's life took a new turn in 1173, however, when her sons Richard and John rebelled against their father. Motivated, it is assumed, by her husband's infidelities, Eleanor gave them her support. The rebellion failed, however, and as a consequence she was imprisoned in England, where she remained until Henry's death in 1189.

She then became even more active in affairs of state. Acting as regent she administered Richard the Lionheart's realm while he was away on crusades in the Holy Land (1189–94), keeping it together in defiance of the ambitions of her other son, John, and of the French king, Philip II Augustus. When Richard was later captured by the Duke of Austria, she raised the money for his ransom and went personally to bring him home.

Richard the Lionheart died in 1199 without an heir and John succeeded to the throne of England. By now Eleanor was nearing 80 but she still strove to keep the Plantagenet kingdom intact, journeying to Spain to fetch her granddaughter, Blanche, from the Castilian court so that she could marry her to the son of the king of France. In 1200 she commanded an army which put down a rebellion against John in Anjou.

At the end of her life Eleanor retired to a convent at Fontevraud in the Loire, where she died in 1204 and was buried with her husband, Henry. The nuns of Fontevraud described her as a queen "who surpassed almost all the queens of the world".

After her death, her ancestral domains continued to be loyal to England, and Aquitaine was only finally acquired by the French crown during the 15th century, during the Hundred Years' War. ❑

LEFT: effigy of Eleanor of Aquitaine at Abbaye de Fontevraud in the Loire.

Eastern influence

The invasion of the Iberian peninsula by the Islamic Moors in the 8th century brought a different type of religious threat, this time from the south. In fact, many local lords found the Islamic yoke more congenial than that of the Franks, and the Arabs were able to make Narbonne the base of their operations throughout the south.

But their defeat in the battle of Poitiers, in 732, at the hands of the Frankish ruler, Charles Martel, led to Arab withdrawal from all of France save, for a time, from "Septimania", the coastal area of lower Languedoc and Roussillon

Franks in the Treaty of Verdun in 843 saw an area of West Francia sketched out which ran from the Low Countries to the Pyrenees, with the Rhône as its eastern frontier. Yet despite these formal arrangements, in practice the Southwest enjoyed a marked degree of autonomy. The power of the Franks diminished even north of the Loire, moreover; Viking and Saracen raiding played a part in this, as did the development of feudalism throughout France.

When, in 987, Hugues Capet, the first ruler in a new ("Capetian") dynasty came to power, the kings of West Francia ruled directly over only a meagre amount of territory, even in the north.

nominally under Visigothic control. In his bid to destroy Arab influence and deter local magnates from supporting the infidel, Charles Martel dealt out exemplary destruction throughout the Southwest, leaving the region, as one chronicler put it, "a horribly devastated wilderness".

In theory, the region had to accept ever closer links with the northern Franks: it formed part, for example, of the sprawling European empire which Charlemagne assembled in the late 8th and early 9th centuries. The division of the Carolingian empire between the east and the west

ABOVE: the 9th-century gold- and jewel-covered reliquary of Pepin, in the treasury at Conques.

LA CHANSON DE ROLAND

The *Chanson de Roland (Song of Roland),* an epic poem in Old French written around 1100, tells the story of the death of Roland, the knight commanding the rearguard of Charlemagne's army as it withdraws from Spain across the Pyrenees. The Battle of Roncesvalles (across the border from St-Jean-Pied-de-Port) in 778 was actually an insignificant skirmish between French forces and the Basques but the poem transforms it into an heroic last-ditch stand against the Saracens.

The work traditionally marks the conception of both French literature and the chivalrous ideal of a *douce France* worthy of self-sacrifice.

The rest of their kingdom was controlled by feudal lords who owed little more than an oath of allegiance to their Capetian overlord.

The Southwest was, however, becoming a battleground for competing local dynasties, notably the counts of Toulouse and of Provence and Barcelona and the dukes of Aquitaine. Each sought to establish his power at the expense both of the others and of minor lords and princelings.

Political in-fighting entered a new phase when, in 1152, the heiress to the duchy of Aquitaine, Eleanor *(see page 24)*, married Henry Plantagenet, Count of Anjou and Duke of Normandy, who two years later became King Henry II of England. A Plantagenet empire formed overnight, running from Berwick-on-Tweed on the Anglo-Scottish border down the western side of France to Bayonne and the foothills of the Pyrenees.

This new power bloc decayed after the death of Henry in 1189, but Anglo-Norman influence continued to complicate the political map of the region. The Southwest came to be one of the operational theatres on which successive English and French kings struggled for supremacy. Guyenne, for example, remained English from 1154 until 1453.

THE TROUBADOURS

Troubadour poetry originated in the Southwest around 1100, and flourished until the early 14th century. At its heart lies witty and lyrical inventiveness, expressed in the subtle and nuanced Occitan language.

It developed in princely court culture – its first practitioner was William, Duke of Aquitaine, then resident at Poitiers. But troubadours came to be drawn from every rank of society (including women, or *trobairitzes*) down to wandering minstrels, known as jugglers (*joglars*) who mixed poetry and song with other forms of performance including acrobatics.

Troubadour poetry included political satires, odes to nature, and works of spirituality, alongside anti-clerical compositions. Roughly half of what has come down to us, however, concerned *fin'amor* – "perfect love", for which troubadour poetry is most renowned.

The idealised love that troubadours evoked was not without hints of sensual passion, but focused on the champion's quest to win his lady: "my lady tries me and tests me so she can know how I love her", as William of Aquitaine put it.

The prestige of the troubadours helped spread notions of chivalry and courtly love in northern France (notably through the patronage of Eleanor of Aquitaine), Italy, Catalonia, Spain, Portugal, Germany and England.

The Albigensian Crusade

Warfare was one of the principal occupations of the headstrong Occitanian nobility. When not fighting each other, or engaged in conflicts with the rulers of France, England and Navarre, they were involved in battling the Saracens in Spain, or else engaging in crusades to the Holy Land. (The port at Aigues-Mortes was built specially to allow embarkation for the Seventh Crusade in 1248.)

This warlike caste was, however, unable to resist a further military incursion from their

> ### ROUGH JUSTICE
> "Kill them all; God will recognise his own." – Arnald-Amaury, leading the siege of Béziers, 1209.

marauding band of northern knights led by Simon de Montfort to attack the count of Toulouse, in whose lands the heresy was rooted. Béziers was sacked with a cruelty shocking even by standards of the time. Carcassonne capitulated before it suffered a similar fate. The siege of Minerve ended only with the immolation of 140 Cathars who refused to renounce their faith.

A war of north versus south ensued, whose final episode was reached in the siege and capture in 1243–44 of the penultimate Cathar

Capetian overlords in the north, which – as in 507 – took the form of a religious crusade.

In the area around Albi, Carcassonne and Toulouse the religious movement of the Cathars (*see page 29*) had developed. The pretext for the crusade was the murder of the Papal legate Peter of Castelnau by unknown assassins in 1208. The papacy formally outlawed the so-called "Albigensian Heresy", and in 1209 the Capetian king Philip II "Augustus" allowed a

LEFT: troubadours performing in a 13th-century noble's court.
ABOVE: seal of Raymond VI, Count of Toulouse.
RIGHT: St Dominic burning Cathar scriptures.

> ### THE SIEGE OF MONTSÉGUR
>
> The Cathars made their last great stand at the fortress of Montségur in the Ariège. They withstood an astonishing 10 months of siege by an army of 10,000 men. Finally, the defenders of the castle were given a stark choice: renounce their faith or go to the stake. Some 205 men, women and children hurled themselves into the flaming pyre built at the foot of the mountain, in the Field of the Burned which today is marked by a Cathar cross.
>
> Legend has it that the Cathars managed to smuggle out their mysterious treasure and it is still sought in the nearby Sabarthès caves by psychics, gold-diggers and members of numerous esoteric cults.

stronghold at Montségur in the Ariège. The religious crusade had, by then, metamorphosed into a forceful dynastic power-play.

By 1229, most of the southwest had been added to areas of direct Capetian rule, and in the treaty of Corbeil of 1258, the kings of France and Aragon further simplified the southern map by partitioning the Mediterranean coast between them. Toulouse and Provence remained in French hands in exchange for Capetian renunciation of claims to Catalonia and Roussillon.

> **VALÉRY ON HISTORY**
>
> "History is the science of what never happens twice." – Paul Valéry (1871–1945), born in Sète.

ranean markets, while the Atlantic ports of Bayonne and Bordeaux moved within the economic ambit of England, notably for the export of the wines of the Bordelais. Toulouse, meanwhile, utilised its midway position between the coasts to become one of Europe's most powerful entrepôt cities.

An economic boom fostered cultural vitality. New cathedrals, churches and religious houses tended to follow the Romanesque style. The Gothic was a northern, Capetian style which had some successes – notably at Limoges, Rodez and Narbonne – but often seemed un-

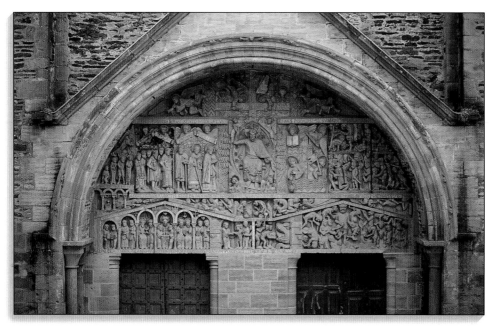

Economic and cultural vitality

Besides suffering a military drubbing at the hands of the Capetians, the Occitan nobility also lost authority within its territories. The frequent absence of nobles on crusades meant that they were never able to submit their peasants to the full weight of feudalism as in the north.

Furthermore, during the 12th and 13th centuries the region's towns rediscovered an urban culture which seemed to have been lost in the overthrow of the Roman empire. They grew progressively strong and independent. The cities participated in the European economic boom which began in the late 12th century. The lower Languedocian port-cities drew on the vitality of Mediter-

welcome and out of place. The Church played an important part in intellectual life, too. And the university of Montpellier drew on Arabic as well as northern learning and became (as it remains) one of Europe's most reputed medical schools.

The local noble class nurtured a more secular culture, however, exemplified by the troubadour style which flourished here in the 12th and 13th centuries. The iron grip which the Church imposed on artistic and intellectual expression following the Albigensian Crusade, however, severely inhibited its progress. ❑

ABOVE: tympanum of the west doorway of Conques, depicting the Last Judgement.

The Cathars

Since nearly all Cathar texts and other records were destroyed after their demise, and most accounts of their beliefs have been written subsequently by their enemies, it is difficult to piece together an accurate picture of the Cathar doctrine. Most experts agree that the Cathars (a name given to them later and not used by themselves) were essentially Christian. They considered themselves to be pursuing a simpler, more authentic version of the faith, advocating a return to the high moral principles of the early Church; in some ways they were precursors of the later Protestants.

They were highly critical of the indulgence and corruption of the established Church (libidinous clergy, bishops who stayed in bed to hear matins, rife nepotism and the like). Their key deviation from traditional Catholicism was their notion of the dual powers of good and evil; Oriental ideas which may have been brought back by the first crusaders to the Holy Land. The Cathars considered the material world to be entirely evil and believed only the world of the spirit to be wholly good. The word Cathar is probably derived from the Greek *catharos*, meaning pure.

They were thus anti-materialistic, advocating simple lives of vegetarianism, pacifism and sexual abstinence. At their most extreme these ideas led logically to rejecting the material world completely and fasting to death to achieve a state of pure spirit.

Their leaders, called "perfecti", travelled the countryside dressed simply in black robes and open sandals, preaching and teaching in the vernacular Occitan, believing that an understanding of the scriptures should not be restricted to the clergy – a further challenge to the power of the established Church, which used only Latin.

The Cathar message found fertile ground in the Languedoc where peasant and nobility alike were determined to maintain their independence from the encroaching French king, and from the taxes of the Roman Church.

But the Cathars rapidly became political pawns, and the Albigensian Crusade was launched in 1209 by Pope Innocent III with tacit approval from the French king who was keen to annex this stubbornly independent territory. It was the first time the "Soldiers of Christ" were used to combat heresy within Christendom itself.

The Crusade was led by the elder Simon de Montfort, an Anglo-Norman baron attracted to the cause by the promised territorial spoils of the heretics. The brutality of the northern crusaders was shown spectacularly at the sieges of Béziers, in 1209, and Minerve, in 1210. Simon continued to pursue the Cathars with relentless barbarism until he was struck down by a stone at the siege of Toulouse in 1218, an event that is depicted in the Siege Stone relief in St Nazaire Cathedral in Carcassonne.

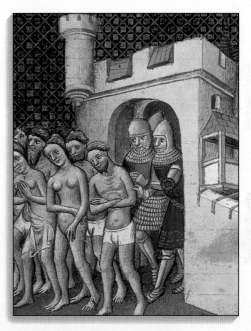

As sieges undermined the resistance of the towns of the Languedoc, the Cathars retreated to the castles of the Corbières and the Ariège, built in easily defended sites on craggy mountains, which provided refuges for the heretics, who were offered sanctuary by sympathetic and rebellious proprietors. These castles were already in existence before the Cathars, many of them defending the much contested frontier between the county of Toulouse and Aragon. They were virtually impregnable and could only be defeated by drawn-out sieges.

The most famous "last" stand of the Cathars was at Montségur *(see pages 27 and 263)*, although Quéribus *(see page 280)* was the last garrison of Cathar resistance to fall, in 1255. ❑

RIGHT: the end of the siege of Muret, 1213, during the Albigensian Crusade.

le diables fai los aimadors fair cortz eiolians e conitz per amor de lur donas.

e diables fai biordar los aimadors p amor de lur do nas.

le diables fai los aimadors seguir taulas redonas e tornei amens p amor de lur do

le diables fai dansar los aimadors ab lur donas. le quals diables meta lur dan sa

le diables fai azorar sa don al aimador gior la imadors el diable portan larma

CENTURIES OF WAR

Plague, protracted wars, religious repression and absolutist royal rule
made the late Middle Ages a turbulent time for the Southwest

The later Middle Ages proved to be a grim chapter in the history of the Southwest. Disease and famine extinguished economic prosperity; persistent warfare wreaked devastation in many areas; and the cultural vitality that had been apparent at the zenith of the Middle Ages was eclipsed. The region's regeneration from the late 15th century onwards was more closely within the aegis of the French state than anything its inhabitants had experienced hitherto.

The plague

The Black Death – bubonic plague – appeared on the Mediterranean shore in early 1348 after an absence from Europe of more than half a millennium. Its impact was catastrophic. There were a few pockets of immunity – notably some remote areas in the Massif Central – but the scourge carried off over one-fifth and possibly more than one-third of the total population, while the disease's frequent reappearances ensured that demographic recovery was very slow. Those lucky enough to survive may actually have improved their living conditions – shortage of manpower drove wages up, and forced feudal lords to lighten the burdens they placed on their peasants as a means of retaining them on the land.

Overall, however, the economy suffered. The cycle of medieval prosperity had seemed to be coming to an end even prior to the Black Death's appearance, moreover: severe famines from around 1310 onwards suggested that population size was running ahead of the economy's ability to support it. Geographical factors also played a part: the Languedoc coast was silting up – the ports of Narbonne and Lattes (near Montpellier) were fatally affected – while the newly created settlement of Aigues-Mortes failed to establish itself.

LEFT: page from a 13th-century manuscript by a monk from Béziers, Matfre Ermengaut.
RIGHT: a public execution in Bordeaux during the Hundred Years' War.

The Hundred Years' War

Warfare made matters worse. The Hundred Years' War between France and England (1337–1453) opened as a dynastic squabble, but soon developed into a chronicle of bitter civil and foreign wars. The wars' destructive impact derived less from the scale of the actual

fighting – battles were few, and armies pretty small – than from plundering committed by the soldiers and their hangers-on. These extracted their livelihoods from the hapless peasantry and citizenry of regions through which they passed. The Black Prince, for example, led a damaging raid through upper Languedoc to Narbonne in 1355. Plunder, pillage and looting became a dreaded currency in the normal life of the region, destabilising markets, triggering shortages, inhibiting population growth, and engendering a mood of constant anxiety and fear.

When the wars went badly for the French kings, local notables were quick to extract concessions from them. In 1345, for example, King

Philip VI was pressurised into convening a meeting at Toulouse of the Estates General of the Langue d'Oc – clergy, nobles, and commoners – which negotiated with the king over taxation. Toulouse was also granted its own *parlement*, or sovereign court of law. Gaston Fébus *(see page 261)*, count of Foix and Béarn, played off both sides to develop a resilient independent state of his own.

A series of revolts and rebellions in lower Languedoc between 1378 and 1382 also highlighted the king's growing weakness. It would not be until the 1430s that the dynasty began to right itself again.

denoted not the whole region in which Occitan was spoken, but merely the province of that name, which made up a fraction of it.

The strengthening of the royal dynasty stimulated the loyalty of many of the local aristocrats in the Southwest. Occitan was losing its place as a political and administrative language even before the royal edict of Villers-Cotterets, in 1539, insisted on the use of French in all public acts. The advent of print played a role in this, too. French and Latin proved the printers' languages of choice and Occitan failed to develop a printed literature, becoming – with brilliant exceptions – an oral means of expression.

Although the last battle of the Hundred Years' War was to occur at Castillon in the Guyenne in 1453, the nobility of the Southwest had shown little leadership or initiative in repelling the English, and the victory belonged to the new standing army of the French king, Charles VII.

The credit that the dynasty derived from expelling the English allowed it to diminish limitations on its powers granted in time of war. The pretensions of the Toulouse *parlement* were clipped, while the Estates General were convened less frequently, retained fewer powers, and had their representative role reduced to the southeastern segment of the Southwest as a whole. The term "Languedoc" henceforth

The Wars of Religion

Political stability proved difficult to establish in the region. The Protestant Reformation brought a new wave of dissension. Despite the attentions of the Catholic authorities, which began to burn heretics, Calvinism developed strongly in a good number of areas within the region and at every level of society.

In the far Southwest, Jeanne d'Albret, mother of Henri, who would become king of Navarre and later Henri IV, made of the Béarn region a stronghold for Protestants (or Huguenots). The new medium of print undoubtedly increased the audience for religious disputation: Huguenots, who staked individual salvation on knowledge of the Bible, were avid to learn how to read. Religious disputes were complicated by dynastic and political issues. A period of regency following the death of Henri II in 1559 ushered in a generation of political instability, as noble families used religious pretexts to achieve preponderance over Queen-Regent Catherine de Medici. A series of wars over the next decades, involving a sickening roster of sieges, plundering raids, brutal massacres and atrocities, severely tested the loyalty of the Huguenot minority.

CRITICAL MASS

"Paris is well worth a Mass." – Henry IV, having converted to Catholicism to accede to the throne of France.

proved to be his decision to convert to Catholicism, a move which attracted him support from Catholics weary of war, yet did not lose him his Protestant followers.

In the Edict of Nantes of 1598, which effectively ended the Wars of Religion, toleration was extended to the Protestant minority, which was thereafter permitted to retain defensible fortifications around those cities in which they held the upper hand.

Although there were important groupings of Protestants to be found north of the Loire –

High hopes of Henri IV

In 1572–73 Nîmes floated the idea of a "Protestant Republic of the South", but it failed to find sufficient backers to become viable.

Huguenot hopes were increasingly pinned on Henri of Navarre, who as scion of the collateral royal line, the Bourbons, stood to inherit the crown should Henri III die childless – which he duly did, in 1589. The new Henri IV had to fight his way to the crown. His strongest card

LEFT: the Siege of Domme during the Hundred Years' War, illustrated in Froissart's *Chronicles*.
ABOVE: students being given a dissection lesson in Montpellier's School of Medicine in 1363.

notably in Paris and in Normandy – the majority of the Huguenot "places of security" were located in the south.

With Henri IV installed in the Tuileries in Paris, Parisians were soon complaining that the palace rang to Gascon dialects and the Occitan language. The way was open for down-at-heel Gascon gentlemen to climb the social ladder in the king's service, as the real-life Gascon musketeer D'Artagnan – immortalised by Alexandre Dumas in the 19th century – was to do from the 1630s onwards.

Yet though he brought a southern temperament and a Protestant sensibility to the throne of France, Henri IV the poacher swiftly turned gamekeeper. He began the work of Catholic reconquest which his son and grandson – Louis XIII and Louis XIV – would continue.

His chipping away at Huguenot rights in his native Béarn was followed by Louis XIII's full-scale attacks during the 1620s on Protestant strongholds there, as well as at Montauban, La Rochelle and Montpellier. Gradually all the military defences of the Huguenot cities were removed, and their other rights eroded. By the 1680s, royal officials were conducting drag-onnades in the Southwest – that is, using military action by dragoons forcibly to convert local populations to Catholicism.

Croquants and Camisards

The Southwest's reputation for violent trucu-lence had political as well as religious dimen-sions. In the 1590s, much of the Périgord had witnessed peasant risings of so-called Cro-quants. The Croquants revolted again in the 1630s, covering the area between the Loire and the Garonne with the most extensive peasant uprising before the Revolution of 1789. Other rural areas and many towns also were involved in riots and revolts through the early decades of the 17th century. The wave of discontent cli-maxed in the civil wars of the Fronde (1648–53), at the close of which the movement

CIVI
TATIS
BVRDE
GALEN
SIS IN
AQVI
TANEA,
GENVI
NA DE
SCRIP.

Revocation of the Edict of Nantes

In 1685, the campaign came to a head in Louis XIV's Revocation of the Edict of Nantes, which abolished Protestant worship within France. Thousands of Huguenots went to the gallows or to jail for refusing to convert: the Tour de Con-stance in Aigues-Mortes in particular became a symbol of Huguenot unwillingness to surrender their beliefs.

In addition, Protestant pastors were hounded down, and their places of worship were either turned over to other uses or razed to the ground. Such was the temper of intolerance that between 200,000 and 250,000 Huguenots fled the country.

of the Ormée in the city of Bordeaux established links with England and declared for republi-canism. A last phase of turbulence was to come in the aftermath of the Revocation of the Edict of Nantes. A guerrilla war *(see box, page 35)* opened up in the Cévennes in 1702 between dis-inherited Huguenot peasants and townspeople, and would-be Catholic converts. It took a mas-sive military presence and appalling scorched-earth policies to bring the area under control.

The Age of Absolutism

The Southwest thus experienced the advent of the new Bourbon dynasty, which had been so solidly rooted in the region, as a grievous disappointment. Louis XIII and Louis XIV undertook a policy of European and overseas expansion, moreover, and expected French society as a whole to provide the wherewithal for massive and long-lasting military campaigns, beginning with engagement from 1635 in the Thirty Years' War (1618–48).

Kings now highlighted the monarchy's allegedly "absolute" character, and sought to remove or stifle any channel of opposition or debate. The tax load sky-rocketed, and a new cohort of royal tax officials – the Intendants – used every means available to break down local immunities and fiscal privileges. Although in

from the 1660s to the 1680s when royal minister Colbert had been at the helm. This was the period in which the Canal du Midi *(see page 83)* was constructed: linking the Mediterranean and the Atlantic, through the Garonne river system, the canal was perhaps the greatest work of civil engineering since Roman times. The Southwest did not immediately derive much benefit from it, however.

In the period following Colbert's death costly warfare combined with natural disasters to make life grim. In 1692–94, and then again in 1709–10, harvest failure caused by bad weather triggered widespread famine.

1659 Roussillon had been acquired from Spain, most of the expansion in the north and east meant little to people in the Southwest.

The region's noble élite was attracted to the patronage on offer in Louis XIV's new palace at Versailles, but anti-court sentiment remained quite strong among other classes. The last years of the reign of Louis XIV in particular were so appalling that the death of the "Sun King" in 1715 left most Southwesterners indifferent. The economy had shown some signs of recovery

LEFT: 16th-century town plan of Bordeaux.
ABOVE: the Beast of Gévaudan, which terrorised the countryside of Lozère in the 18th century *(page 176).*

THE WAR OF THE CAMISARDS

Continuing religious persecution in the years after the Revocation of the Edict of Nantes caused the Protestants of the Cévennes to rise up in revolt in 1702, killing the leader of French forces in the area *(see page 175)*. The rebels came to be known as the Camisards, probably after the peasant shirts *(camisoles)* they wore.

Driven by faith, they held secret religious meetings in secluded mountain locations (called "*déserts*") and would go into battle against superior forces singing psalms.

A century and a half later, Robert Louis Stevenson was inspired to visit the Cévennes by what he saw as the heroic resistance of the Camisards.

Times of prosperity

Though few remarked on it at the time, the absolute monarchy presided over a degree of internal security virtually unmatched in all the region's turbulent history. With very few exceptions, war was conducted henceforth outside French borders. Disease and famine – those other sources of customary dread – also seemed less of a threat: with the exception of a final outbreak in Marseille in 1720, bubonic plague had disappeared by the late 17th century. From the 1730s, the economy began to grow and the population expand. The most dynamic sector of the French economy during the 18th century was colonial trade, in which the Southwest had a very heavy investment.

The Canal du Midi now came into its own, allowing the Languedoc to participate in growing prosperity. Lower Languedoc developed rural manufacturing industry (wool, silk) and some heavy industry (notably mining in the Cévennes), and also gave over more land to viticulture. It could rely on the grain-growing areas of the Toulousain to provide sufficient food swiftly and efficiently even in difficult times, both along the waterway system and along the region's highly impressive road system. The new port at Sète, established by Louis XIV, helped develop Mediterranean trade. A market economy seemed to be trying to break through the restrictive framework of feudalism.

The spread of ideas

The 18th century was an era of communication and exchange in the Southwest – and this extended to ideas as well as commodities. Urban living was increasingly urbane. The book trade boomed, and newspapers increased in numbers and readership. Provincial academies provided a forum for local élites to indulge an interest in science and belles-lettres. Reading rooms, coffee-houses, lending libraries and art schools provided a framework for cultural development. Even quite remote areas benefited from the shift in urban tastes: the mineral spas of the Pyrenees, for example, whose medicinal values were puffed by Montpellier physicians, began to operate for a tourist market for the first time.

Prosperity and well-being also contrived to soften religious divisions – religious indifference and even anti-clericalism were growing, and the crown's adherence to its anti-Protestant legislation seemed increasingly archaic.

The fortunes made in a city like Bordeaux contrasted glaringly with the poverty of less fertile areas. Many townspeople were increasingly aware of the social and economic problems of the region. But in absolutist France it was very difficult for such individuals to make their voices heard and the prosperous middle classes felt shut out from government. The Revolution of 1789 was to provide a golden opportunity for social and political reforms. ❑

BORDEAUX BOOMS

Although it left most of the lucrative slave trade to Nantes, Bordeaux profited enormously through links with the French sugar-producing colony of Saint-Domingue (present-day Haiti). It was also well placed to pick up on growing European, especially English, demand for wines and *eaux-de-vie*. Quality wine-producers – Lafite, Latour, Margaux and others – and producers of cognac, too, were starting to make a durable impact on European palates. The scale of the wealth displayed in the city of Bordeaux – from lush private residences through to public establishments such as the port facilities and the theatre – left even English tourists gasping in admiration.

LEFT: ships in the port of Bordeaux in 1764.
RIGHT: Henri IV (1553–1610).

REVOLUTION AND REPUBLICS

Hopes of the revolutionary era went largely unfulfilled while 19th-century
social and economic development eroded the distinctive culture of the Southwest

Louis XVI's decision to convene the Estates General – the first time this national parliament had met since 1614 – was made under duress. The monarchy was trying to keep under control a financial crisis caused by a century of costly warfare that threatened the state with bankruptcy.

A power vacuum opened up in 1788–89 as preparations were made for the meeting of the Estates. The complex electoral system encouraged all inhabitants to participate, and all the three estates (clergy, nobles and the Third Estate – that is, commoners) were invited to draw up "books of grievances" *(cahiers de doléances)* to present to the king. Third Estate *cahiers* from the Southwest were critical of government taxes and, as well as attacking feudal and ecclesiastical privileges, called for root-and-branch reform of the state. Significantly, they invoked national regeneration rather than the recovery of provincial rights. *La patrie* ("the fatherland") was now French, not Occitan.

The king and his aristocracy were getting cold feet at the prospect of reform when a popular rising in Paris on 14 July 1789, culminating in the storming of the Bastille, forced Louis to accept the call for permanent national representation and a constitutional rather than absolutist monarchy.

Rumours from Paris

Rumours and anxieties about what exactly was happening in Paris caused the provinces, at a time when bread prices were particularly high and social tensions acute, to get caught up in a series of panics. It was believed that bands of brigands had been hired by aristocrats to tour the countryside ruining the crops and denying the country the reforms it craved.

One current of this so-called "Great Fear" started in the Poitou, and within days reached the Pyrenees to the south and lower Languedoc and Provence, leading to the formation of defensive militias. When the "brigands" failed to materialise, peasants and townspeople alike turned their arms against their local oppressors: châteaux were attacked, feudal documents were burned, and a wholesale overthrow of the seigneurial regime enacted.

Reform

The new National Assembly could only bow to the force of peasant revolution, abolishing feudalism even as it passed the Declaration of the Rights of Man and set about establishing a new constitution. The new order implied the dissolution of social privileges from which nobles and clergy in particular had benefited. But it also involved ending many of the liberties and privileges that towns and provinces had enjoyed prior to 1789. This raised some hackles – Languedocian noblemen, for example, protested against the abolition of that province's Estates and convoked an armed camp of ardent counter-revolutionaries at Jalès in the Ardèche

---

LEFT: *French Punishment:* an execution by guillotine, sketched by Goya in the 1820s.
RIGHT: a statue of Danton in Tarbes.

in 1790. In general, however, resistance was attenuated by the considerable degree of decentralisation which the new constitutional arrangements allowed. The old map of provincial privilege was wiped clean, and France was divided up into 83 *départements*. These took on the names of natural features rather than historic precedent: the new one centred on Bordeaux, for example, was named after the River Gironde, while that with Bayonne as its local capital became the Basses-Pyrénées. This new and unitary framework of administration provided a far more extensive degree of election and participation than had ever existed before.

the National Assembly attempted to impose wide-ranging Church reforms in the Civil Constitution of the Clergy. The Pope objected, and around half of the French clergy, often following the prompting of their parishioners, refused a constitutional oath of allegiance. This event opened a fissure that was to prove to have enduring political as well as religious effects.

The Southwest had well above the average number of opponents to the Civil Constitution. The highly refractory areas in the Massif Central and the western foothills of the Pyrenees (where less than a quarter of priests took the oath) were to become counter-revolutionary

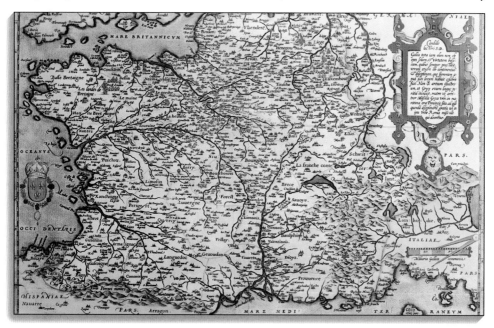

Church and counter-revolution

Local satisfaction in the Southwest at the considerable degree of decentralisation introduced in 1789 was, however, dissipated during the 1790s. Religious conflict, and then, from 1792, the drift towards European warfare and a policy of government-led Terror *(see page 41)* caused widespread disenchantment with the new regime within the region. The granting of religious toleration to Protestants in 1789 was vehemently opposed by some militant Catholics, and there were bloody interdenominational brawls in Nîmes and Montauban in 1790.

An even more contentious religious line of division was opened in 1791, however, when

strongholds throughout the 1790s. They would also – well into the 20th century – be the regions within the Southwest where right-wing political parties had most support.

The Girondins

War against most of the rest of Europe from 1792 onwards exacerbated conflicts, adding new reasons for opposition to the drift that the Revolution was taking. The overthrow and execution of Louis XVI and the declaration of a republic in late 1792 disgusted the old aristocracy, many of whom emigrated from the country. There was a wave of refugees from the Southwest into Spain, and across the German frontier where the king's brothers were organising an emigrant army against the French Republic.

The ranks of the republicans also began to divide. The most radical deputies in the National Assembly had a strong power-base in Paris. They tolerated the sometimes violent actions of the Parisian crowds and fostered support in the country through Jacobin clubs. Deputies from the *département* of the Gironde led the faction within the Assembly that opposed this Jacobin grouping and urged the provinces to form a counterweight to the Parisian *sans-culottes*. From 31 May to 2 June 1793, days of action by Parisian popular

There was a good deal of support for this within the Southwest. Crucially, however, the refusal of Toulouse to enlist made it logistically difficult to join together the rebels in the Bordelais and lower Languedoc. Republican troops mopped up resistance and by the end of 1793 the Federalist Revolt was over. The guillotine worked over-time in areas where rebellion had been most brazen.

White Terror

The Terror proved successful in mobilising France against the united armies of the European powers. But the "mass levy" *(levée en*

activists led to the expulsion and imprisonment of the Girondin faction. The purge of the Girondins excited a national protest, and areas of armed defiance towards the National Assembly opened up in many areas within the Southwest and indeed throughout France. The Jacobins accused their opponents of wanting a federalist system, and indeed some Girondin supporters in Nîmes called for a "Republic of the South" extending from Lyon to Bordeaux.

LEFT: map from 1579 showing the traditional divisions of France.
ABOVE: road map created after the division of France into 83 *départements* by a decree issued in 1790.

OLD NAMES, NEW NAMES

The creation of the *départements* after the Revolution and the organisation of the regions in 1972 have left the Southwest with a confusion of overlapping names.

The *départements* were deliberately artificial creations. But although the old area names seemed at the time to have been banished to history, many are still cherished by locals. Though neither Gascony nor Périgord has any official status both names are still frequently used and invoked by tourist brochures because they are more evocative than the dry departmental names. Some names, such as Aquitaine, disappeared with the Revolution, only to resurface in the 20th century in the name of a region.

masse) instituted in 1793 won less support in the Southwest than in the north and east. Indeed, the region soon became notorious for military desertion and draft-dodging. The Southwest continued to be the theatre for a good deal of fragmentary and uncoordinated opposition to the Revolutionary regime.

From 1795, murder gangs and vigilantes along the Rhône valley and in the southern Massif Central exercised a "White Terror" against radicals who had been involved in the "Red Terror" of 1792–94.

(This often had a religious dimension, in that many urban Protestants had been supporters of the Terror.) The fact that the war was going "better" from 1794 onwards, however, meant that the government was more able to cope with internal dissent.

Napoleon comes to power

The arrival of Napoleon Bonaparte to power, first (in 1799) as consul and then (from 1804) as emperor, strengthened administrative centralisation. Napoleon maintained many of the reforms of the Revolution, but gave them an authoritarian twist. He also took most of the wind out of the sails of the counter-Revolution

NORTHERN PREJUDICE

In the region bounded by Bordeaux, Bayonne and Valence, it was said in the 19th century, "people believe in witches, don't know how to read and don't speak French".

by settling the religious issue in a Concordat with the Pope in 1801.

The Southwest benefited from the political and religious stability that Napoleon brought following the turbulence of the 1790s, but it never warmed whole-heartedly to his reign. The Atlantic seaboard had been among the most economically dynamic areas in the 18th century, but Napoleon's continental obsessions and his failure to win back the seas (and consequently the colonies) from English control caused ports such as Bordeaux, La Rochelle and Bayonne to enter steep decline.

As Louis XVI's younger brother, Louis XVIII, entered France from the Iberian peninsula in 1814, in the baggage-train of the allied armies that had defeated Napoleon, he found the region more welcoming than most.

When Napoleon returned from exile in Elba to try his luck again, Toulouse acted as the royalist headquarters against him and the region witnessed another brutal round of White Terror, as teams of anti-Revolutionary and anti-Napoleonic vigilantes wreaked their revenge on Napoleon's supporters.

Nineteenth-century radicalism

In 1815, following Napoleon's final demise, much of the southwest would pass as "White" – that is, as supporters of royalism and opponents of alternative regimes. Half a century later, the White had turned Red: the area was still critical of central government, but by now from a left-wing perspective. Popular radicalism was apparent in urban milieux from the 1840s, but it was the move in 1851 to create a Second Empire under Napoleon's nephew, Napoleon III, that crystallised discontent.

An insurrectionary movement broke out not only in the towns but also in the countryside of Gascony, lower Languedoc and neighbouring Provence. Pitched battles between peasants and imperial troops took place. Repression was tough, and thousands of rebels were deported to Guyana and Algeria.

The Southwest would also be in the van of the move to institute the Third Republic in 1870 following the military defeats of Napoleon III in the Franco–Prussian war. The "Red South" *(le Midi rouge)* had been born.

The Third Republic

The Southwest had been among the most economically buoyant of regions in the 18th century and boasted a tradition of urban culture dating back to the Romans. Yet by the time of the Third Republic (1870–1940), the contrast between a more modern north and northeast and an archaic and economically backward south and west was becoming increasingly apparent. Inhabitants of the Southwest had worse living standards and poorer levels of literacy. Much of the region underwent de-industrialisation as areas better endowed with coal and steel and better placed in regard to urban and international markets surged ahead. Rural depopulation began as urban and industrial conurbations in the north attracted workers unable to find employment in their villages.

The railway network offered salvation for some, but also hastened de-industrialisation for others, effectively "ruralising" many formerly urbanised areas. The railways brought tourists – Biarritz and Arcachon developed as resorts, while the Marian visions of the Pyrenean peasant girl, Bernadette Soubirous, brought hordes of pilgrims to Lourdes.

Wine-growing and its problems

Conversely, the profits to be made for despatching the wine of the south to Paris and northern markets gave many entrepreneurs in the Southwest the incentive to abandon manufacturing for viticulture. The *vin ordinaire* of the Hérault and Aude *départements* became a staple of northern dining tables, bringing many peasant wine-makers undreamed-of wealth, and endowing many areas with their characteristic appearance of a sea of vines.

Yet the wine boom was not to last. Overproduction, the appearance from the 1860s of phylloxera, which devastated the vines, plus, by the end of the century, competition from cheap Algerian wine, ruined the good times. The Southwest's long-enduring reputation for turbulence was confirmed once again by the Wine-Growers Revolt of 1907, a mass protest movement of almost unparalleled dimensions: nearly one million individuals invaded Montpellier during one demonstration.

LEFT: Napoleon I as emperor.
RIGHT: 19th-century conjugal nightshirt inscribed with the words *"Dieu le veut"* – "God's will be done".

The Felibrige

Opposition was taking literary and linguistic forms too. Since the 16th century, any writer who published in Occitan had probably received his education in French and Latin. Although this remained the case, Romanticism and the growth of folkloric studies triggered a self-conscious Occitan literary movement, known as the Felibrige. Attempts at forging a political identity by Felibrige activists ended up in embarrassing right-wing posturing, however, and the movement failed to link up effectively with the many millions of peasants in the Southwest who still spoke Occitan as a first

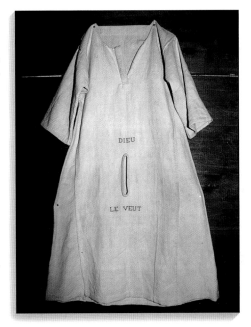

THE CREATIONS OF VIOLLET-LE-DUC

Several ancient buildings in the Southwest bear the indelible and often controversial stamp of Eugène-Emmanuel Viollet-le-Duc (1814–79), an architect with a penchant for the Gothic revival style.

Through his friend, the writer and medievalist, Prosper Merimée, Viollet-le-Duc was asked to restore a string of famous buildings, notably those at Carcassonne, for the Commission des Monuments Historiques. At first he was content to restore the original structures but later he began to add new elements of his own devising. These fanciful inventions have been much criticised by later generations of archaeologists, art critics and historians.

language. Indeed, the period which saw the emergence of the Felibrige also saw the south-west becoming more closely integrated into the national state, culture – and language. The Felibrige was outgunned by the impact made from the 1880s by free primary schooling through the medium of French. Pupils discovered conversing in Occitan were punished severely. School textbooks recounted national, not Occitan history and stressed broader republican values. Education in French prepared the population for a mass culture in that language emerging around the same time: newspapers, the periodical press, cheap novels and, soon,

film and radio. Mass leisure also stimulated involvement in sports such as bullfighting and rugby for which the region became famous on the national scene. An education in national rather than local values was also provided, in a somewhat different way, by the experience of conscription in World War I.

World War II

In 1940, for the first time in its history, the area of Occitan language was given a political form. Inauspiciously, however, it took the shape of the quasi-Fascist regime of General Pétain, following French defeat at the hands of the Germans, and the German occupation of the northern half of France. Vichy failed to unify the region, which came to contain many of the most active and dynamic sectors of the Resistance: national leader Jean Moulin *(see page 123)* was a native of Béziers.

The Resistance utilised the heavy bush cover *(maquis)* in the relatively inaccessible regions of the Massif Central (plus the Alps and to a certain extent the Pyrenees) to form *maquisard* movements which, as the war progressed, became increasingly coordinated and played a significant role in the Liberation of 1944, especially those networks that were run under the aegis of the Communist Party. By then, the region had also witnessed one of the most horrific episodes of the Nazi occupation – the reprisal massacre by German troops of virtually all the inhabitants of the village of Oradour-sur-Glane in the Limousin.

The postwar world

It would be possible to narrate the changes the region has undergone since 1945 as a continuation and worsening of many of the themes implicit in its history since the Revolution: rural depopulation, the decline in the traditional peasantry, the virtual effacement of Occitan as an everyday language. However, this would be to underestimate the extent to which circumstances over the past half century have offered fresh opportunities to the area – opportunities that have been seized with alacrity.

An Occitan cultural movement has made important headway in many areas, and developed a political and, among some, a separatist agenda. Yet the thrust of the movement has been reduced by the development of a mass culture grounded in North American as well as northern French values.

In addition, throughout the 20th and into the 21st century, the regional population became far less homogeneous. The ethnic mix of local populations was already changing radically in the early 20th century, as a result of the arrival of large numbers of immigrant workers from Italy and Spain.

Immigration has been even more marked since 1945. Newcomers include French settlers from Algeria (the so-called *pieds-noirs*), following Algerian independence; immigrants from the developing world (especially North Africa) from the 1960s; and strikingly large numbers of retirees and individuals from other parts of

France and elsewhere in Europe, owning second residences as holiday homes in the area.

After World War II, the strategy adopted by the Fourth Republic and then (from 1958) the Fifth Republic, for economic recovery and development, was centred on a National Plan, which placed a high premium on regional development. As the old *départements* were adjudged insufficiently flexible to manage change, new regional divisions were created that recalled the old pre-1789 provinces – and indeed often laid claim to the nomenclature (if not the actual boundaries) of those bodies. Hence the Southwest saw the reappearance, for

tries gave an additional boost to the regional economy. The aerospace industries in Toulouse – birthplace of Concorde – and the electronics boom in Montpellier, national headquarters of IBM, have made these two cities symbols of the economic renewal of the region as a whole. In post-industrial France, many businesses viewed the attraction of location in the sun-belt south as preferable to closeness to Paris. But in any case, the development of France's superb communications network – highlighted by its TGV trains – was reducing effective distances.

Massive state investment in clearing the low-lying coastal plains of the lower Languedoc of

example, of Languedoc and Aquitaine. The economic vitality of the Southwest contrasted with the more problematic existence of the north and east, whose turn it was now to experience a measure of de-industrialisation as heavy industry went into the doldrums. New energy sources – gas, oil, hydro-electricity and nuclear power – did not require proximity to mineral deposits.

The development of the tertiary sector and of high technology and, later, electronic indus-

mosquitoes allowed the development of the area as a tourist destination for the first time. Natives of the Mediterranean coast still recall when the sprawling ultra-modernistic tourist havens of La Grande Motte and Carnon were nothing more than an assemblage of a few fishermen's huts.

These new cities – together with the exciting experiments in urbanism located in nearby Montpellier – symbolise the extent of the transformation which the region has undergone in recent decades. The Southwest in the early days of the third millennium is a society that is changing fast, and adapting to change both energetically and optimistically. ❏

LEFT: 1930s tourist poster for the Côte Vermeille.
ABOVE: inhabitants of Toulouse watch German tanks entering their city during the occupation of France.

THE SOUTHWEST TODAY

Although they are astonishingly diverse, the peoples of the Southwest are united

by the geographical and psychological distance which separates them from Paris

To the left of the fold in the map dividing France in half lies the Southwest, *la France profonde,* where French and foreigners alike dream of putting down roots and living a perfect country existence away from the stress of modern city life – what Henry Miller called "the Frenchman's Paradise".

There is a change in the landscape as you move towards the Mediterranean and the Pyrenees: vineyards, sunflowers, fields of maize, shuttered villages snoozing in the sun, and everywhere the terracotta tiles of Languedoc roof tops. This is the southern France of people's dreams, not the fleshpots of the Riviera, nor yet the fashionable over-restored villages and glamorous villas of Provence.

This region, which is so attractive to visitors and would-be residents, is at the same time hard to define. Unlike other parts of France – Provence, Normandy, Burgundy – it lacks a name to hold it together. Parts seem familiar to many visitors – the Dordogne and perhaps the Lot – but who could pinpoint either of these on the map? And who could say what or where are the Languedoc, Aquitaine and Gascony? As for the Basque Country and Catalonia: aren't they part of Spain?

At first sight, then, "Southwest France" is a disparate place with no cohesion and little to identify it: what have the slick green tributaries of the Garonne got to do with the vine-clad hills of the Corbières? Or the dockers of Bordeaux with the sheep farmers of the Cévennes?

But take a step back and the Southwest comes into focus. What unites this vast and interesting region, from the Massif Central to the Pyrenees and from the Atlantic to the Med, is its distance from Paris: not only geographical (the Basque Country is as far away from the capital as it is possible to get in mainland France) but also psychological.

PRECEDING PAGES: preparing for a bullfight in Vic Fezensac (Gers); geese for foie gras near Toulouse.
LEFT: relaxing in the book village of Montolieu (Aude).
RIGHT: Ricardo Bofill's Antigone quarter in Montpellier.

Local identities

The Paris-inspired quest to achieve the ultra-centralisation of all things French has influenced the Southwest; but it has always been resisted by people who, often with good reason, feel their existing cultures are better than anything northern France has to offer. People

read their local paper, however bad it is, in preference to Paris-based nationals. In Bordeaux they read *Sud-Ouest*, in Toulouse *Dépêche du Midi*, in the South *Midi Libre* or *L'Indépendant*; all concentrate largely on local news, with relatively meagre coverage of national (let alone international) affairs.

Despite all the efforts of central government through the centuries to undermine the historical independent spirit of the Southwest, there is still a fierce desire for greater autonomy and residual resentment of Parisian interference. Further political reforms with the creation of regional governments in 1981 have devolved power to some degree and granted a certain amount of economic independence, and there is some sign that the Southwest is emerging from its long slumber and at last asserting its equality, or even superiority, to Paris.

Nationalists

Some groups in the Southwest have not regional, but fully fledged national identities to promote. Both the Basques and the Catalans – at opposite ends of the Pyrenees – form strong regional groups, identifying themselves firmly as Basque or Catalan before they are French. Although only

> ### FRENCH OR SPANISH?
>
> There were Catalans in the Pyrenees who did not know whether they were considered French or Spanish till they were called up for World War I.

cross-border affinities of the Basques and Catalans can only grow stronger as differences in economic conditions and living standards between France and Spain harmonise in line with EU policies.

There is a third nationalist group in the Southwest, less well known and less identifiable, but wholly in French territory: the Occitans. There is a significant lobby that would like to revive Occitan, the original *langue d'oc* of the region, a tongue akin to Provençal and Catalan, but today only rarely spoken.

extremists actually seek independence from France, many desire greater autonomy and freedom, especially to use and promote the Catalan and Basque languages.

These allegiances are not contained within France but cross a national frontier. The Pyrenees has always unnaturally divided both the Basque and Catalan peoples, who didn't feel they belonged to either side. In the Basque country they talk about the bull-running festival of Pamplona as if it is their own. For the Catalans, Barcelona is as much their city as Perpignan. Since EU integration has relaxed border regulations, however, the Pyrenees has become more of an integrated frontier region. The

These national groups – Basque, Catalan, Occitan – are very different from one another but all are frustrated by the lack of adequate response from Paris. The French government has yet to ratify the European directive on supporting regional languages, which it sees as a threat to national identity and the French language. However, some efforts have been made to address the problem, and since 1980 it has been permitted to teach regional languages in schools and universities. Both Catalan and Basque are often taught as a second language to schoolchildren. But the French local government system allows nationalist groups no more autonomy than this.

Rural life

One thing that the disparate groups of the Southwest have in common is that their homelands are predominantly rural. The large cities – Toulouse, Montpellier and Bordeaux – are exceptions, albeit important ones, in a mass of fields and mountains.

For the people who have lived their whole lives here, the reality of *la vie en campagne* has been rather different. Until the idea of the countryside as a retreat rather than a place of back-breaking labour took hold in the 20th century, the Southwest was a remote and backward region of France, cold shouldered by cen-

New moves by the government at decentralisation to the regions will mean increased autonomy in many areas from agriculture and tourism to education and transport. There is considerable controversy over these changes, since it remains to be seen whether poorer regions will be able to cope economically.

Traditional industries

Despite technological developments, most people still work in agriculture, from cereal, fruit and vegetable farming to wine production. Unemployment is alleviated by seasonal work, such as picking cherries in April, peaches in

tralised Paris governments. From the mid-19th century onwards, with the advent of the railways, the impact of war and dramatic agricultural changes, the area began to depopulate. As much as a quarter of the population left the land between 1850 and 1950. Some places in the Gers *département*, the hardest hit, lost two-thirds of their population.

Only over the past few decades has the region started to revive economically, with large-scale agricultural reform and massive government investment in industry and tourism.

LEFT: tug-of-war in the Basque Country.
ABOVE: young people relaxing in a park in Toulouse.

McDONALD'S AND LA MALBOUFFE

An activist sheep farmer from the Roquefort cheese area, José Bové, became a hero of the anti-globalisation movement in 1999 when he vandalised a half-built McDonald's restaurant in Millau. He was protesting against *la malbouffe* ("bad food") from abroad, which is widely seen as debasing the French way of life. He accused the French government of killing its own farmers by accepting European agricultural reform and allowing cheaper foreign products into France. Bové served a prison sentence, but the anti-globalisation movement continues to gather force, and 2003 saw a massive protest festival on the plain of Larzac in the Massif Central.

August and harvesting grapes in September.

Most of the successful large-scale farming now takes place on the plain, in the Aquitaine basin, the Aude valley and the coastal plains of Hérault, Gard and Roussillon bordering the Mediterranean. Livestock includes cattle, sheep, goats and poultry, especially ducks and geese, prized for the rich foie gras they produce. The great pine forest of the Landes is an important source of resin, used mainly for turpentine. Languedoc-Roussillon is a hugely important source of fruit and vegetables, especially cherries, apricots and peaches on the Roussillon plain. But agricultural production

Vendres on the Mediterranean or St-Jean-de-Luz south of Biarritz still have their fishing fleets. Both coasts have important oyster and mussel farms, especially around the mouth of the Gironde on the Atlantic and the Languedoc coast lagoons between Sète and Perpignan.

For many in the Southwest, though, it is the ancient industry of wine-making that is their *raison d'être,* and the great success story of the past 25 years. Bordeaux has long been known for the quality of its wine but until relatively recently the wines of Languedoc (the largest wine region of France) were mainly famous for being cheap, supplying much of France with

has been severely threatened by competition, especially since Spain joined the common market (now the European Union). Farmers' protests of peach, apple and tomato dumping have become an annual ritual.

One area of agriculture where European subsidies have been successful is mountain farming. Subisides are paid to encourage hill farmers to move their cows up to higher pastures in the summer – the traditional practice of transhumance.

On both the Mediterranean and Atlantic coasts fishing is also in decline as fish stocks are depleted and foreign competition undermines prices, though ports like Sète and Port

its *vin ordinaire.* Government investment and pressure on recalcitrant wine-growers has finally persuaded them to uproot inferior vineyards and concentrate on growing fewer but better-quality grapes, and today the wines of the Corbières, Minervois, Gard, Roussillon and Hérault are increasingly celebrated. A new generation of trained *vignerons* has sprung up, prepared to experiment and to treat wine-growing as a business as well as a way of life.

The cities

Increasingly the cities of the Southwest are the engines of development, and both Montpellier and Toulouse are developing fast, changing from sleepy southern towns into important cities. Toulouse, the fourth-largest city in France after Marseilles and Lyon, now has its own metro (underground train system) and a city centre which is as sophisticated as any in the country. Montpellier is one of the fastest-growing cities in France, now the eighth biggest, and it has the youngest population – a quarter under the age of 25. It is the centre of high technology; the IBM factory there is the largest in France, employing over 3,500 people. But as the cities expand they gain power and attract more people, creating further potential problems in the delicate balance between city and rural communities.

Tourism

Tourism is one of the major sources of employment in the region. The southwest corner around Biarritz and Pau was Europe's first playground for royalty and other under-employed aristocrats, who came for the balmy climate of the coast and the health-giving properties of the Pyrenean spas. Traditional coastal resorts like Biarritz remain popular, but there have been more recent developments that have made tourism one of the most important sources of revenue for the region.

The new seaside resorts that were constructed with massive government investment along the

Government investment in industrial projects has helped the region a bit, providing jobs for the indigenous population as well as attracting newcomers. There are aerospace and electronics plants around Pau and Bordeaux. Toulouse is a centre of chemicals and electronics, and is the site of the main state aircraft factory *(see page 207)*. The discovery of natural gas deposits at Lacq, near Pau, promoted major new gas-based industries, attracting a new calibre of qualified technicians and engineers.

LEFT: oyster farming in the Bassin d'Arcachon.
ABOVE: a bridge in Auch (in Gascony) serves as an oudoor art gallery.

Languedoc-Roussillon coast in the 1960s, in place of mosquito-infested swamps, now attract more than 4 million visitors a year. Although not everybody approves of the modern architecture, the development undoubtedly benefited from the experiences of older seaside resorts blighting the coasts of Spain and the French Riviera. The beaches have been planned with ecological considerations in mind and stretches of coast have been kept as nature reserves, free of construction.

Increasingly, visitors come not just to enjoy the coastal areas but also the farmlands and mountains, the canals and rivers. They seek peaceful country holidays: walking, climbing, cycling or canoeing. They stay overnight in small *gîtes* and *ferme auberges.* These two new developments – where visitors can stay on private farms, eating local produce, or rent renovated country properties – have been immensely popular.

A place to call home

People don't just want to spend their summer holidays in the Midi; increasingly they want to live here. In the 1990s the Haute Garonne, with the city of Toulouse at its centre, saw a population increase of 1.37 percent per year in contrast to a national average of 0.37 percent.

At the same time, the Languedoc-Roussillon population grew twice as fast as the national average, and it anticipates a population of 3 million by 2020. The sunny south is a popular place to retire to, but increasingly, many of the new settlers tend to be active young people rather than retirees, though this is not without its problems and the region also suffers from high unemployment.

Biarritz is particularly popular for retirees, (16 percent of the population): refined Parisian ladies taking tea in their ancient Chanel suits, their maids waiting outside toting packages or poodles. In Biarritz, however, the annual bridge tournament in the revamped casino is closely followed by the international surfing championships, and a new generation of North American and Australian surfers have become the latest settlers, a burgeoning colony marrying into the local population.

The lure of the good life

All these newcomers are attracted both by economic prospects and by the easy pleasures of the southern lifestyle.

These do not change much: warm weather means life can be lived outside much of the time, with open-air cafés for sipping a cool *pastis,* and houses designed to keep out the heat, sometimes equipped with swimming pools. Life is leisurely, even slow, with two-hour lunches still the norm, and most shops closing for the sacred *midi* break. People still prefer to meet in person rather than discuss business over the phone, and as in the rest of the south, who you know is everything.

The home is a private place, and people are much more likely to meet in restaurants or cafés than in each other's houses. Neighbours may gossip for decades over fences but never actually enter each other's house. Family life is still strong: despite transport problems, a surprisingly large number of people in small towns and villages continue to return home for lunch every day. Throughout the region the family Sunday lunch remains the highlight of the week and Sunday mornings in small towns are full of people shopping for special tarts or *gâteaux* or flowers to take to *grandmère.*

Markets are still a weekly or daily fixture of life in most towns and cities, providing an opportunity for social contact as well as a source of fresh foodstuffs. Everywhere in France people demand high-quality produce, and want to know exactly where their meat comes from – sometimes butchers will even display a photo of the relevant animal. People almost always favour local produce over imports.

The diet is healthy too – it is the Southwest where the much-vaunted French Paradox was identified; despite the fact that a great deal of fat is consumed, people have lower cholesterol levels and far fewer heart attacks than in other areas with a similar diet, a phenomenon which has been attributed to red wine thinning the blood.

LEFT: carnival headdress in the Basque Country.
RIGHT: girls dressed for a festival.

Leisure time

Leisure pursuits have a traditional southern flavour. Bullfights *(see page 317)* remain enormously popular, if politically incorrect, both in public arenas and on television. Country pursuits like hunting, shooting and fishing are still widely followed. Hunting – *la chasse* – in particular is fiercely defended, with a vociferous lobby insisting on the right to shoot anything from small birds to wild boar and even bears. More innocuously, *pétanque (see box below)* is still played everywhere and,

RIGHT TO HUNT

In 1998, 150,000 people, many of them from the Southwest, marched through Paris to proclaim their right to shoot migrating birds.

in the Basque Country the ancient Basque game of *pelota* is followed enthusiastically by young and old. Rugby more than any other sport is a passion *(see page 274)*. The arts are also given their due importance. Bold new cultural centres, concert halls and art galleries are increasingly being opened in the cosmopolitan cities of Toulouse, Montpellier, Nîmes and Bordeaux. The councils of many small towns put on ambitious exhibitions and recitals to present the work of local artists, craftspeople and musicians. ❑

BOWLING IN THE DIRT

Playable almost anywhere and by anyone (both sexes and all ages), the national pastime of *boules* or *pétanque* is as fun to play as it can be to watch – if you know what's going on, that is. It is played with heavy steel balls, each marked with an indestructible pattern and usually scratched from years of use. To begin the game, a line is drawn in the dirt and a small coloured ball, the *cochonnet*, is thrown 6–12 metres (20–40 ft) away. The object is to land your balls closer to the *cochonnet* than your opponents can manage, but the scoring is a little more complicated than that. Even in a friendly game, if it is not obvious whose ball is closest, a tape measure is produced to check exact distances.

It is quite legitimate – laudable even – to knock your opponent's ball out of the way or send the *cochonnet* flying so that it comes to rest close to one of your balls. The slope of the terrain – as long as it is not too extreme – and any stones in the way are the same for all players and merely add variety to the game.

Of course, there are techniques of throwing and a good player will toss his ball high but without excessive force so that when it hits the ground is stops more or less dead where he or she wants it to be. When all balls have been thrown, the scores are mentally recorded and the *cochonnet* is thrown again for the next game.

THE CHANGING COUNTRYSIDE

As the old, arduous, traditional life of the French countryside gradually dies out,

underpopulated villages are being rejuvenated by enthusiastic newcomers

It is 23 June in a small village in the Pyrenees and the community is preparing to celebrate the Fête de St-Jean. Nominally it is the feast of St John the Baptist, but it is probably a Christian adaptation of a festival with earlier, pagan origins connected to the summer solstice and the shortest night of the year. A procession of children dressed in white carrying flaming torches is led by a tall man and his daughter, riding gaily pannired horses. The fire is lit in the village square, sausages are grilled and everyone is offered a drink from a long-spouted jug. Behind the fire is a row of small boys waiting excitedly. When the fire dies down a little they run and leap over the flames.

It is a traditional event that has been taking place for centuries; and though there have been years of plague and of war when the population was so diminished that there were no young men to leap the fire, it has always been resolutely maintained.

But the scene is not quite as immutable as it might appear. The festival may be ancient but the cast has changed. The man frying the sausages is a refugee from Chile. The bespectacled fellow organising the children is Belgian. The over-anxious mother remonstrating over the dangers of fire-jumping is English; and the boys she is worried about are more likely to burn the bottoms of their Nike trainers than their bare feet or clogs. Oh, and girls can now jump the fire, too.

Thus is one small, but not untypical, Southwest village finding a way into the future. Depopulation has reduced its permanent population to just over 200 (to be briefly swelled in the summer months), and the ethnic composition of this population bears no resemblance to 50 or even 25 years ago. An increasing number of incomers, both foreign and French, live in this village all year round, having brought their livelihoods with them or chosen new ones:

there are Dutch potters and gardeners, English writers and artists, and a Northern French family who run the *auberge*, raise cows and ducks and make foie gras. As a result of these incomers the village school has remained open, after closure was threatened when the number of pupils dropped below 20.

The disappearing *paysan*

Although it is not always obvious, the French countryside is near the end of a long phase of transition. Many French people and foreigners still have a rose-tinted image of bucolic, self-sufficient life in rural France; of hard-working but happy people keeping the countryside not only picturesque but alive, while producing the prodigious variety of fresh farm produce for which France is famous.

More than any other Europeans, the French cherish an ideal of rural life and have idealised the *paysan*, struggling for more than a century with agricultural reforms to keep the small farmer on the land. In his classic work, *Rural*

LEFT: view across the countryside of Gers (Gascony) towards the Pyrenees.
RIGHT: hiker on a Southwest byway.

Revolution in France, Gordon Wright observes: "No other industrialised nation has kept so large a proportion of its total population on the soil."

It is true that until the middle of the 20th century the life of the *paysan* had barely changed since medieval times. *Montaillou*, Le Roy Ladurie's classic account of medieval village life in the Pyrenees, based on the Cathar inquisitions *(see page 263)*, details the grim round of back-breaking labour, the social interdependence and petty feuding of one isolated small village.

> **PROUD COUNTRYFOLK**
>
> "...nowhere else do so many city dwellers regard their peasant ancestry as a mark of distinction."
> – Gordon Wright,
> *Rural Revolution in France*

Before the railways and roads were built towards the end of the 19th century, each village had to be self-sufficent. Apart from producing all its own food, and hopefully extra to sell, it would need to be able to build and repair houses, and make its own tools, clothing and footwear. There would be a mason, cartwright, *sabotier* (clog maker), carpenter, butcher, potter, rope-maker, midwife, even a dentist of sorts.

However the reality of the largely rural Southwest today is the inevitable disappearance of the *paysan* (a word which translates poorly as "peasant" with its English connotations of inferiority; "countryman" – or woman – would be closer to its meaning in French). In some small villages you can still see old women in black sitting knitting on doorsteps. You might occasionally glimpse a farmer cutting hay with a traditional scythe. But the days of such people are numbered. Their sons and daughters have already rejected the gruelling country life of dawn-to-dusk labour, and headed for jobs with predictable hours and salaries in the towns and cities.

The long decline of rural France

The decline of the French countryside began in the mid-19th century, after the rural population of France reached an all-time peak in the 1840s. Then the problem was the considerable pressure of population on the land making it hard to feed everyone. In 1846 there were food riots all over Southern France.

People's lives were extremely limited. In 1861, nine out of 10 people were living in the *département* of their birth and had probably never been more than 80 km (50 miles) from their birthplace. Education spread slowly. At the end of the 19th century, a third of the peasant population was still unable to read or write.

By the 1880s better roads were being constructed and the railways began making an impact on remote areas, with secondary rural lines. There was a gradual drift to the towns and cities. Economic crisis exacerbated rural decline; imported grain and wheat eroded traditional markets and when the vine disease, phylloxera, struck in 1875, it destroyed about half the nation's vineyards. New vineyards were planted on the fertile plains of the Midi and the rocky hillsides were abandoned. All over the south traces of the lost terraced vineyards can still be seen.

World War I had a dramatic effect and in every small village today can be seen the war memorial with its grim toll of deaths. Some villages lost as many as half their young men, and when the casualty lists were totalled at the end of the war, 53 percent of the dead or missing were peasants. While many of the young, active male population never came back, life was difficult, too, for the survivors who found it hard to go back to simple country life.

When the Popular Front government established the 40-hour week in 1936, the railways were obliged to recruit 85,000 new employees.

They were deluged with applications from peasants attracted by an unimaginably short working week as well as the appeal of urban life. Over the following three years 300,000 French peasants, many of them under 30, deserted the farm.

It is hard to blame them. As late as the 1930s many farm-workers were still living in appalling conditons. An agricultural survey of 1929 indicated that 250,000 workers were still housed in sheds or barns. And although by the 1950s

VANISHING FARMERS

"Ninety percent of rural households do not contain anybody working in agriculture…what is vanishing is crucial to the nation's idea of its own basic character."

– Jonathan Fenby

abandoned. One valley in the Ariège had a population of 10,000 in 1850, reduced to 1,500 today. It is increasingly difficult to find mayors willing to stand for small communities, many of which number fewer than 700 people. (Mayors are paid according to the number of people they represent and carry a considerable burden of responsibility for local affairs, from unemployment to the state of the roads or the quality of water.) The decline in more remote areas of the Pyrenees and the

most peasant homes had electricity, only 34 percent had running water and only 10 percent had inside toilet facilities. Many were still only a single room with a dirt floor. In most cases animals were still kept on the ground floor and the family lived above, benefiting from the warmth of the animals in the winter. Lighting would have been provided by oil lamps or candles and cooking done over the fire.

Since the 1950s the decline has been even more rapid and many villages were simply

LEFT: farmers at the pony fair in Espelette, in the Basque Country.
ABOVE: shepherd in the Vallée d'Aspe, Pyrenees.

Cévennes is very real. In one small village in the Lozères, La Canourgue, a Foire aux Célibataires is held every spring, to find spouses for single people who live in the region.

Surviving traditions

But, despite all, the country does survive. Agriculture is still the predominant occupation though fewer people are employed than before as the work has become more mechanised. Farmers now drive tractors and use harvesters that can cut and stack a field of hay in a few hours, the equivalent of a few days' work for a team of peasants with scythes. Farming, it must be said, is heavily subsidised, and although the traditional practice of transhumance (taking livestock up to mountain pastures in summer) is still followed it is only because farmers are paid substantial sums for each animal they move.

Despite the decline, rural traditions die hard. For most who still live in the country the rural calendar dominates. They pick wild asparagus in spring and go mushroom hunting in the autumn. Planting is still often done according to the phases of the moon, and St Catherine's day, 25 November, is still considered the best day to plant trees.

Every small village is surrounded by the carefully tended *potagers* (vegetable gardens) of its inhabitants. Many people keep a few animals: chickens, ducks, even a pig. Hunting wild boar and deer is as popular as ever.

Preserving the old ways

Country ways are hard to shake off. Even those who leave the land for a "better" life talk with almost mystical nostalgia of their *pays*; they have a deep attachment to their own bit of country that goes way beyond notions of property. And while the old ways of life are being lost, a new generation is learning to appreciate them and preserve them. The great French cult of *le patrimoine* holds full sway.

FOREIGN INVADERS

The foreigners who have been buying rural second homes here for 20 years or more are turning into a flood, transforming the demography of areas like the Dordogne, now known for its huge British population as the Weetabix belt. Illustrious inhabitants include American singer Madonna and the British ambassador to France.

The Lot and the Tarn are also increasingly popular. According to writer Christoher Hope, author of *Signs of the Heart: Love and Death in Languedoc*, who lives in the Minervois: "Something comforts the English heart in the Tarn. Narrow your eyes and you might be in Gloucestershire. So many migrants from well-heeled London suburbs have

been buying up cottages and farmhouses that they've taken to calling it Kensing-tarn," (Kensington is an expensive neighbourhood in London). One recent estimate calculated that as many as a million Britons had second homes in France, and there may be almost as many Dutch, Germans, Belgians, Swedes and Spaniards.

The Southwest has been invaded by foreigners before but they came with armies to conquer territory by brute force. This latest invasion from abroad is often beneficial for the ailing French countryside. The presence of new families can sometimes make all the difference to the survival of a small rural community.

Work is going on to rediscover the old ways. Ancient festivals are revived and every small village celebrates its fête of garlic, peaches, olives or grapes. Sometimes these are summer events and very popular with tourists, but mainly they are quite genuine expressions of local spirit – some take place in deepest winter – the bear festival at Arles-sur-Tech in Roussillon in February, the Limoux carnival during Lent. Local history and legends are written down and taught to schoolchildren by young teachers with a new awareness of their heritage. Architectural treasures, from small Romanesque churches to Roman bridges, are restored and valued. Museums devoted to local crafts, costumes and tools are lovingly assembled. Eco-museums reconstruct farms and forges and demonstrate traditional crafts and industries.

The rural Renaissance

The *paysan* may disappear but the *pays* will remain. Ironically, the mounting flood of in-comers buying up rural properties that the true country folk have abandoned as the reality of *la vie de campagne* drives them to city jobs, is helping to keep the country alive, if not revive it. Whether the new arrivals looking for something that no longer exists are foreigners or French is all the same to the locals – Paris is almost as alien a place of origin as London or Amsterdam.

A lot of the new countryfolk are Soixante-huitards (as the 1968 generation are termed). They have colonised remote mountainous regions like the Cévennes and the Ariège, bringing with them new ideas about eco-friendly land management and conservation. These so-called "*néo-ruraux*" attempt to cherish and preserve aspects of the *paysan* life that are rapidly disappearing; they struggle to survive – by choice – as basket-weavers, goats' cheese producers or leather workers.

Even in places where outsiders have bought and restored properties it can be difficult to maintain a sufficient infrastructure of schools, shops and restaurants. One excellent initiative is to use the village café to provide school meals for the local children, thus feeding the children and keeping the café open. Increased

numbers of residents also mean that the traditional *boulangerie* and *épicerie*, stocking local produce, have enough customers to keep ticking over from summer to summer, when trade is more brisk. Tourism undoubtedly helps, too, with the popular system of *ferme auberges* and *chambre d'hôtes* providing local employment and supplementary income for farmers.

Such demographic changes are not without friction; in a small village near Aniane in the Hérault, well-meant criticism by newcomers of recent architectural abominations visited on it by locals caused grave offence, dividing the village as bitterly as any medieval feud.

Until recently the French have watched with bemused amusement as thousands of British, Dutch, German and other Europeans rush to buy crumbling ruins in the French countryside, but a recent survey suggested that 44 percent of the French themselves now also dream of a life in the country, away from the city grind of "*métro-boulot-dodo*" ("metro-work-sleep"). In the last decade of the 20th century over 500,000 people left Paris for the provinces.

The combined effect of all these newcomers will be a French countryside unlike that of tradition but at least revived and once again viable, this time with the creature comforts of the modern world. ❑

LEFT: village fête in Mosset, Roussillon.
RIGHT: a family harvesting plums for the famous *pruneaux d'Agen*.

RURAL ARCHITECTURE OF THE SOUTHWEST

The life of country people can be read in the houses they built, adapted over centuries to the climate and the unremitting needs of farming life

The dominant rural house of France was the *maison bloc*, in which everything was included under one roof. The Southwest's rich architectural diversity developed as the result of its soil. This decreed the type of agriculture possible and therefore the type of storage needed, and the building material to be used. What was underfoot thus created the way of life above. In Quercy and the Cévennes, for instance, limestone is available for building; but on the sands of the Landes pine forest half-timbering, of necessity, fitted the bill. Sheep farmers (the Landes and the Cévennes) needed *bergeries* (sheep folds), and cattle farmers, storage for winter forage, accounting for the vast barn-like habitations of the Basque Country. Every house exploited attic space for foodstuffs as seen especially in the steep roofs of Périgord. Man, his livestock and his harvests lived in great intimacy. Animal fodder and the family's own food stores took up most of the space, the average human habitation being limited to a mere two rooms. Families lived and slept in the kitchen warmed by a huge, if inefficient, fireplace, their beds placed against the walls. The spare room housed daughters, while unmarried young men slept in the barn. Self-sufficiency was the key to existence. People produced all that they ate and wore. Every farmhouse had a well, and many had a bread oven. Dovecotes *(see page 188)* abounded because pigeon dung made excellent fertiliser.

(see page 188)

▷ **DRYSTONE CABIN**
The cabin, one of the most ancient forms of shelter, could be built quickly while clearing stones from a field.

▷ **PÉRIGORD FARMHOUSE**
The steeply pitched flat-tiled roofs of Périgord (in the Dordogne) are unique in the Southwest, which has been a land of canal tiles since Roman times.

△ **BRICK BUILDINGS**
Rare in the rest of France, brick is common around Toulouse. Greater wealth there meant people could afford to burn timber to fire the clay.

△ **LANDES HOUSE**
These half-timbered and wattle houses in oak groves have separate outbuildings because of the risk of fire.

▽ **BASQUE *ETCHE***
Typical Basque farmhouses have red-stained timbers (originally using ox blood) and whitewashed walls.

RESTORING AN OLD HOUSE

It may look temptingly gratifying and easy to accomplish, but restoring an old French property is a considerable undertaking which often takes longer, and costs more than estimated. Normally, old country houses have no foundations and the terracotta floor tiles are set directly on the ground. Rising damp and saltpetre can only be contained by re-laying floors on a membrane and doubling walls, leaving a cavity between the old and new. A kitchen and bathrooms must be installed and electricity and plumbing upgraded. Owing to the paucity of traditional living space, attached outbuildings need conversion to equip them for new uses. Despite all the changes around it, the huge fireplace, once a necessity of the daily grind, is usually retained as a focal point of domestic life. Restoration of any building takes attention to detail. But old materials can still be found and artisans still practise traditional techniques, such as installing oak beams and employing mortise and tenon joints.

▷ **CÉVENNES HOUSE**
A tradition of arches and vaults supported by metre-thick walls characterise this windblown region.

▽ **QUERCY HIGH-HOUSE**
This house in the Lot has lodging on the first floor, storage space below and a tower-cum-dovecote.

▽ **LEAVING THE LAND**
Machines and EU-promoted competition have resulted in fewer small farmers. Many old rural houses, having become redundant, are being sold off to outsiders.

ROMANESQUE ARCHITECTURE

France's richest concentration of Romanesque buildings – simple but ingenious and often decorated with exquisite carvings – is to be found in the Southwest

From the great cathedrals, with their enormously high naves and elaborate carvings, to the hundreds of tiny chapels scattered across the countryside, there are always Romanesque architectural treasures to discover in the Southwest. It is rare to find a village that does not house a sculptured capital, a carved doorway, or a fragment of wall painting. Most towns have evidence of grander buildings – sometimes an overlooked cloister or reused monastic barn. Although the Wars of Religion and the Revolution caused tremendous destruction, part of the attraction of these buildings is as a palimpsest of historical layers. They can be viewed not only as objects of great beauty, but also as three-dimensional historical jigsaw puzzles.

The time of Charlemagne

The Romanesque style of architecture emerged in the 9th century during the reign of Charlemagne. His coronation as Roman Emperor at Christmastide, AD 800, marked the beginning of a new age. He saw that the Roman Church was the greatest surviving inheritance from antiquity and forged strong ecclesiastical and political links with Rome, at the same time enlarging the Christian sphere of influence with his military conquests.

The Carolingian period had no distinct architectural style of its own, since many of the buildings simply appropriated portions of the Roman ruins that still dominated the landscape. What we know as the Romanesque evolved out of this borrowing, although true Romanesque was a later phenomenon. Carolingian art – manuscripts, carvings and paintings – was strikingly different from true Romanesque. The buildings from this period, however, often have a strong resemblance to Romanesque, and are thus described as Carolingian Romanesque.

PRECEDING PAGES: figures on the lintel of the church in St-Genis-des-Fontaines (Pyrénées-Orientales).
LEFT: reliquary statue of Ste-Foy (St Faith) in Conques.
RIGHT: the doorway to Moissac Abbey.

The appearance of Romanesque

Scholars prefer to date Romanesque proper from the time of Otto the Great of Germany (936–73). By this time, the three-pronged attacks on France by Normans, Magyars, and Saracens had finally been contained, and a degree of political stability prevailed. The intro-

duction of feudalism, the revival of monasticism and, later, the fact that the world did not end in the year 1000 (though there is no evidence in support of this often quoted reason for the spate of church building around the millennium) all go towards explaining the explosive growth of ecclesiastical construction.

Romanesque architecture was built from the middle of the 10th century until the beginning of the 13th and existed in a number of different national and regional forms. It is the style the British call Norman, and the French confusingly call *Roman*, a term which is frequently mistranslated directly as "Roman" in basic souvenir guides, making unwary tourists think they are viewing something 1,000 years older than it really is. (The French word for Roman, as in the Roman Empire, is actually *Romain*.)

The influences on the church builders of the 10th century were many. One main one was the renewed connections with Rome which enabled scholars to study and learn from the methods of construction of the great buildings of antiquity. Only one architectural manual survived from Roman times: Vetruvius's *The Ten Books on Architecture*, in which he explains how the Romans constructed

> **CHURCHES EVERYWHERE**
>
> "About three years after the year 1000, the earth was covered with a white robe of churches."
>
> – Raoul Glaber, Burgundian monk

or collaterals on either side. The roof was made of wood. The main disadvantage of this structure was that the nave received no direct light. In sunny Italy this was not much of a drawback; but the French winter made the interior very gloomy, even in the Southwest. The solution was to raise the height of the nave above that of the aisles and build a clerestory above the arches with its own row of windows. As long as the roof was wooden, this was not a problem, but French builders, ever conscious of the risk of fire after centuries

their buildings, describes floor plans and gives the background theory on proportion and arches. This, combined with the visual evidence of the existing Roman villas, triumphal arches, amphitheatres and aqueducts that dotted the country, inevitably meant that the new buildings were heavily influenced by the Roman originals. Romanesque has even been described as being nothing more than Roman architecture adapted to the needs of Christianity.

The Romanesque church

Romanesque churches use as their prototype the Roman basilica, that is to say, a building with a central space, or nave, often with aisles

of enemy invasion, wanted to roof their churches with stone. Unfortunately, the large stone barrel or tunnel vaults placed a huge downward thrust on the walls, making the buildings top heavy and causing them to bulge where windows were inserted. The builders compensated by making the walls tremendously thick; these barrel vaults are one of the main characteristics of Romanesque churches.

It is the often elegant solutions that the cathedral builders found to these problems that make Romanesque architecture so appealing: the problem of weight in a stone roof, for instance, led to the development of the pointed arch, which later became a hallmark of Gothic.

The style spreads

The first people to revive Roman building methods were, not surprisingly, the Italians; in fact *Lombardus* became the word for masons in the early period.

Until the monastic centres and towns were well established, stone-masons, bell-founders, glass-makers and fresco-painters worked as travelling bands, spreading out across Europe in answer to the huge demand for skilled craftsmen. Naturally they took their regional interpretation of Romanesque with them, and elements of Lombard style occur throughout France. There are many examples in the South-

ago de Compostela *(see page 75)*. These routes were controlled largely – but not entirely – by the Cluniac order, a vast monastic empire with some 2,000 dependencies, one of the main forces behind Romanesque art and culture of the 11th and early 12th centuries.

The "Pilgrimage Group" of churches: Santiago de Compostela, St-Martin at Tours and St-Martial at Limoges (the latter two demolished), Ste-Foy at Conques, and St-Sernin at Toulouse had a certain homogeneity due to the exchange of architectural ideas resulting from the pilgrimage. They are similar in plan, vaulting systems and in the height of the nave vaults.

west: St-Guilhem-le-Désert has evidence of the Lombard style in its courses of small, rough-hewn stones, in the vaulting of the naves – unusual for that period – and in the decorative pilaster strips and friezes of cogwheel teeth; St-Martin-de-Londres (Hérault) has Lombard pilaster strips and the cathedral of Maguelone (also Hérault) has cross-ribbed segmental vaults in the Lombard style.

Romanesque influences spread along the routes through France that led towards Santi-

LEFT: view of St-Michel-de-Cuxa.
ABOVE: the church of Ste-Foy at Conques, showing the towers added in the 19th century.

SORTING OUT THE REMAINS

Holy relics – bones of saints and pieces of the true cross – were believed in the Middle Ages to have miraculous powers. They could be guaranteed to attract pilgrims (and therefore donations) to a church. These sacred remains were kept in reliquaries of gold and silver embellished with precious jewels.

There was intense competition for the most potent relics. Conques originally stole the relics of Ste-Foy that made its fortune. Not all relics, however, were the genuine article. One story tells of a monk who was sent to find relics but who returned with a third arm of the fragmented saint the monastery already had.

Conques and St-Sernin

Modelled on the earlier St-Martin at Tours, which was destroyed during the Revolution, Conques (*c*.1050–1120) is a wonderful example of form following function: stone honestly used as load-bearing material. There is nothing extraneous in the whole building, even the carved capitals were not merely decorative but were used as picture books by the monks. This accounts for their presence high in the galleries above the aisles where few visitors today can gain access to them. Conques has a tremendous sense of verticality, the nave is 21 metres (68 ft) high, consisting of a barrel vault supported on

Romanesque simplicity

Romanesque is, of course, defined by the round arch – as opposed to the Gothic pointed arch – a direct copy of the Roman originals, using the same classical proportions: multiples or halves of the diameter of circles.

The combination of arches within arches, with crossing barrel vaults, frequently combines to provide an extraordinarily sculptural space, such as at St-Michel-de-Cuxa, near Prades (in French Catalonia, *see page 291*), where the 10th-century arches are Mozarabic – keyhole shaped – influenced by Moorish invaders from the south. Here, particularly in

enormous piers (the western towers are 19th-century additions). With its five tightly curved radiating chapels at the east end, it is a pure example of Romanesque.

The barrel vault over the nave at St-Sernin, Toulouse (11th–12th-century), is the same height as that of Conques, and the plan and exterior also show that Conques was used as a model, though the Toulouse vault is longer. Brick is the local building material here and the builders used it to achieve architectural forms originally conceived in stone at Conques (and earlier at Tours). The piers were covered with plaster and painted to imitate masonry, though the brick exterior has not been disguised.

MEDIEVAL MANHATTAN

New York is almost as good a place to see Romanesque art as Southwest France. The Cloisters Museum, founded by sculptor George Barnard in 1914 and now a part of the Metropolitan Museum, incorporates portions of five medieval cloisters imported from France, most notably those of St-Michel-de-Cuxa and St-Guilhem-le-Désert.

The museum, at Fort Tryon Park in northern Manhattan, is an exquisite recreation of the architecture and cloister gardens of a medieval abbey. It has around 5,000 works of art on display including sculptures, stained-glass windows, altarpieces, frescoes and a set of tapestries called *The Hunt of the Unicorn*.

the large crypt, one literally peers through key-holes at arches within arches surmounted by perfectly smooth, unbroken barrel vaults that are each themselves one continuous arch. There is also an extraordinary circular "palm-tree" chapel with a central column smoothly blending into the vaulted roof and outside walls: literally a circular barrel vault.

The perfect semi-circular apses of Romanesque churches reflect the same proportions on the ground plan, where they are often surrounded by a series of radiating, circular chapels (a feature best appreciated from outside), such as at St-Guilhem-le-Désert.

square bays. The 12th-century St-Étienne-de-la-Cité, in Périgueux, the first to be built in this style, has a row of four domed bays, making it look surprisingly Byzantine. There are a number of other good examples in the Dordogne at Cherval, Trémolat, Grand-Brassac and Agonac.

Story-telling in stone

The great interest and beauty of Romanesque art and architecture is in its rawness, its solidity, its lack of pretension, and nowhere is this more evident than in the carvings in the surviving capitals and portals. The capitals have a vigour and energy unsurpassed in church architecture.

Sometimes the chapels also extend from the transept arms, making a great collection of half circles at the east end of a building, in harmonious contrast to the often austere squared-off bulk of the nave.

The barrel vault was not the only solution to covering a roof in stone: Périgord Romanesque uses domes instead of vaults, which have the great advantage of distributing the weight of the roof so that buttresses are not necessary – the weight is carried on pendentives above

LEFT: St-Michel-de-Cuxa cloister, parts of which are now in the Cloisters Museum, New York.
ABOVE: detail of the tympanum of Moissac Abbey.

The most famous cloister and portal in Southwest France is that of Moissac *(see page 192)*, the subject of many books and monographs. Here, carving in stone was revived in the 12th century after a lapse of over 500 years: the cloister was completed in 1100, the famous tympanum before 1115.

The work is archaic in style, with tremendous disparities in sizes between the figures (seated and standing figures of the same height), and the incised labelling of characters – and even animals – sometimes with the letters S and N reversed, a common mistake of children or the newly literate. The 76 capitals and their associated pier sculptures, on which the salvation of man – a theme of primary significance in medieval times – is dramatically acted out, are alone worth the trip.

Unlike Renaissance carving, the capitals are not designed to be viewed simultaneously, though they are designed as single decorative compositions: they tell a story, often acting like panels in a comic book. We are supposed to read the figures in a sequence of time. In the story of Adam and Eve, Adam appears four times in the relief. Even with no guidelines the work has an unparalleled vitality and freshness.

Size was an important element in Romanesque figure sculpture; small sculptures were

of execution that affords universal human recognition and still speaks to us, albeit with a different message, over the ages.

Exploring Romanesque churches

It is easy to appreciate the soaring height of the naves and the solidity and simplicity of Romanesque churches, but they reveal even more wonders if you explore. These buildings are very old and their most intriguing features are often tucked away: a carved lintel over a blocked-up doorway, an unexpected carved capital in a row of plain columns or fragments of carved work set in walls. Always try to see

never simply reduced versions of large ones. In the adaptation of common themes to a new small scale the thickness of folds is increased and simplified, the features are cut more deeply and given stronger accents.

The capitals are the jewels of Romanesque art and Southwest France is rich in them. From the over-restored, though exquisite, St Guilhem-le-Désert, to the work of the master of Cabestany at the round church at Rieux-Minervois (Aude); from the monumental façade of St-Gilles-de-Gard (Gard) to the mischievous monks peering through doorways on the capitals of the cloisters at Elne (near Perpignan) – all have a directness of vision and a simplicity

the apse, which often shows traces of even earlier churches or actual Roman foundations, sometimes with naive carvings or decorative work, animist carvings or portraits of the villagers from that period when Christianity was just beginning to establish itself in opposition to the old religions of the forest. Often it is the tiny, simple chapels hidden away in the Pyrenees that reveal the most unexpected treasures, such as the 12th-century frescoes only recently revealed at the little church of Vals near Pamiers. ❏

ABOVE: detail of the tympanum of the Abbatiale Ste-Foy in Conques.

French Roads to Santiago

All over Southwest France the symbol of the scallop shell can be seen – carved into stone and wood, in great cathedrals, small chapels, and roadside shrines. The shell is the symbol of the pilgrimage route to Santiago de Compostela in northwest Spain, which was one of the great shrines of the Middle Ages. With Jerusalem so far away and the road to Rome infested by bandits, Santiago grew into the most important destination of western Christendom – Europe's first mass tourist destination.

There were four main pilgrim routes through France, each starting from a holy place. One route began in Paris and led via Orléans, Tours, Poitiers, Saintes and Bordeaux to Ostabat (in Basse Navarre, northeast of St-Jean-Pied-de-Port). Another originated in Vézelay (in Burgundy) and passed through Limoges and Périgueux before joining the first route at Ostabat. The Via Podiensis went from Le Puy-en-Velay through Espalion, Conques, Figeac, St-Cirq-Lapopie, Cahors, Moissac, and Flaran. Today the long-distance footpath, GR 65, follows this route. All three routes met at Ostabat and continued to St-Jean-Pied-de-Port – the last halt before the mountains – and ascended to the Puerto de Cize (Ibañeta), on the other side of which is the town of Roncesvalles.

An easterly route via Arles, the Via Tolosane, included Montpellier, Castres, Toulouse, L'Isle-Jourdain, Auch and Oloron-Ste-Marie before crossing the Pyrenees at Somport to reach Jaca.

In the Middle Ages, between the 12th and 16th centuries, as many as two million pilgrims a year followed the path. Thousands of pilgrims and travellers still follow the routes today, passing through the same towns and villages, worshipping in, or at least visiting, the great churches of Conques or Toulouse, exclaiming at the magnificent cloisters of Moissac or praying at wayside shrines and crosses.

Santiago (or St-Jacques in French) was St James, the disciple of Christ who, it is believed, brought Christianity to Spain, which was then part of the Roman Empire. On his return to Judaea he was executed by Herod, and his followers returned with his martyred body to Galicia in northern Spain. As they approached the shore they saw a man on a horse rise out of the waves, covered in scallop shells, and this became their emblem. The body

was buried but the location of the tomb was forgotten. Then, in the 9th century, a vision of stars (Compostela means "field of stars") is said to have led to the discovery of the tomb. The first recorded pilgrimage to Santiago de Compostela was by the Bishop of Le Puy in 951. Pilgrims were encouraged with the promise of indulgences – forgiveness of their sins and remission of time in purgatory – and pilgrimages became enormously popular.

One of the earliest known travel guidebooks, *Codex Calixtinus*, written in 1140 by Aimery Picaud, a monk from Poitou, details the best places to find sustenance and the best sources of fresh water and points out especially recommended chapels

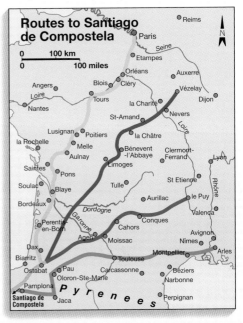

or monasteries to visit. Pilgrims following in his footsteps dressed in a simple, handwoven tunic and carried a staff and water gourd, and always wore the scallop shell to denote their calling.

In 1987 the route to Santiago de Compostela was declared the first European Cultural Route by the Council of Europe, and a system of signposting, using the scallop-shell symbol, was established. The routes through both France and Spain are well organised. There are refuges along the way that accept bona fide pilgrims who have walked, cycled or travelled on horseback. On arrival at Santiago de Compostela, pilgrims receive a certificate in Latin proving they have completed the pilgrimage. ❑

SEA, MOUNTAIN AND RIVER

Southwest France's immensely varied geography makes the
region the ideal setting for a great many outdoor activities

Southwest France, from the Atlantic to the Mediterranean, can be divided broadly into four physical parts. The largest part is one of the great geographical depressions of Europe, the Aquitaine Basin, a plain stretching south from Bordeaux. It is drained by the Garonne (the fourth longest river in France after the Loire, Rhône and Seine), which rises beyond the Pyrenees, in Spain, and empties into the Atlantic Ocean as the Gironde estuary. In most places this plain is heavily cultivated, producing wheat, maize, sunflowers, wine, fruit, vegetables; but its western fringe, along the Atlantic, is a long strip of sand merging into the vast pine forest of the Landes.

To the south the Aquitaine Basin is bordered by the abrupt, serrated mass of the Pyrenees; and to the north by a series of lower mountain ranges comprising the last gasp of the Massif Central – most impressively the limstone plateaux of the Grand Causses and the granite and schist peaks of the Cévennes.

Finally, there is the plain along the Mediterranean coast. This can be subdivided into the Languedoc plain (between the Cévennes and the sea) and, edging up to the Pyrenees, the smaller plain of Roussillon.

At its narrowest, France is only about 360 km (225 miles) across from east to west but the two sides of France could not be more different: the Atlantic seaboard is green, wet and fertile while the Mediterranean is dry and illuminated by a steady, brilliant light.

A land defined by people

Physical geography is only one way of analysing the land. Superimposed on this is another, more human way of surveying territory. The rural inhabitants of France have never thought in terms of mountain ranges and basins; instead they perceive their home area as being

of a more manageable size, with shared customs, crops and other marks of identity: the *pays*. Names for territorial areas larger than the *pays* survive too, despite the post-Revolutionary attempt to rationalise France into *départements*. Thus Quercy and Gascony in a sense still exist, even though they officially became obsolete more than 200 years ago. Such names do not always appear on maps or in travel guide books but it is essential to recognise them to get an understanding of the Southwest as it is perceived by its natives. Other old names survive but have been confusingly put to new uses: Languedoc, once a loose description of a linguistic unit, is now part of the name of one of France's supra-departmental regions, Languedoc-Roussillon.

Whereas man has generally adapted to the world he has found, even shaping villages and towns around outcrops of rock, with the march of progress he has been able to shape the landscape himself. The Romans built aqueducts and

PRECEDING PAGES: a snowboarder takes off from a piste in the Pyrenees.
LEFT: climbing a waterfall, El Portalet.
RIGHT: windsurfer on Lac de Matemale, Capcir.

laid roads. The Middle Ages are sometimes imagined as a time in which man lived in awe and fear of nature but medieval people did their share of rearranging the landscape, clearing forests and building new towns (the *bastides, see page 193*). One of the greatest changes to the landscape occurred in the 17th century when the Canal du Midi, which would be a wonder of engineering even today, effectively connected the Atlantic and the Mediterranean. In the 19th century the distinctive lines of plane trees were planted along the main roads. This was also when the Landes forest was planted on the order of Napoleon III: landscape gar-

dening on an impressive scale. Recently, progress has been faster with the motorway network getting ever thicker and a controversial road tunnel being blasted across the Pyrenees under the Col du Somport, and further plans to construct a rail tunnel right through the centre of the Pyrenees. Most dramatic of all will be the Millau viaduct spanning the Larzac Gorge, which will be the largest bridge in the world when it opens in 2005.

Rivers and coasts

At weekends and in the summer months people bring the landscape to life and at these times it

LONG-DISTANCE WALKING

The Sentiers de Grande Randonnée (GR for short) are marked long-distance footpaths that go through some of the most beautiful parts of the French countryside. The shortest may take five days; the longest will need much longer. Go at your own pace and stay in the many *gîtes d'étape* on the way. The most interesting routes include:
GR6 From the Alps to the Atlantic.
GR7 From the Vosges to the Pyrenees by way of Mont Aigoual and the Canal du Midi.
GR10 goes all along the Pyrenees, from the Atlantic to the Mediterranean. It can take two months to walk the whole way from Hendaye to Banyuls.

GR65, the Chemin de St-Jacques de Compostelle follows one of the routes across Southwest France towards Santiago de Compostela: from Le Puy-en-Velay via Conques, Figeac, Cahors and Moissac to Ostabat.
GR68 is a tour around Mont Lozère (110 km/70 miles).
GR70 is Robert Louis Stevenson's famous route through the Cévennes *(see page 175)* – allow 15 days.

In many areas – particularly nature reserves – there are shorter marked footpaths to follow. When walking in France, take a good map, carry water and wear strong shoes – the latter is particularly important in dry scrubland – in case of vipers.

seems as if all rural Southwest France has become an outdoor pursuits' centre. Few activities seem far removed from water. In between the two coasts run innumerable rivers, into and out of lakes, natural and man-made. There always seems to be somewhere close at hand where you can swim.

Resorts on the coasts vary greatly. At one extreme is the sedate Biarritz, which was welcoming aristocratic visitors long before the days when ordinary working people began to take holidays. Tourism is a relatively new concept further up the Atlantic coast of the Landes, which is particularly known for its surfing.

major river to make its way to the Atlantic but there are several that drain into the Mediterranean: the Tech, Têt, Aude, Orb and Hérault. Somewhere along their length, all these rivers are used for canoeing and rafting. One of the best ways to enjoy the rivers of Southwest France is to hire a one- or two-seater canoe and steer yourself downstream around still, deep meanders and through foaming rapids. Many companies offer a streamlined service to individuals or groups, providing the equipment, advising on safety and picking up wet (but normally cheerful) canoeists and taking them back to the departure point by minibus. A

Many of the resorts on the Mediterranean coast haven't been there long either: development only took off when the marshes were cleared of mosquitoes in the 1960s.

Inland there is plenty of water, too. You don't have to look far for a river with an activity centre beside it. On its way to the Atlantic, via Toulouse and Bordeaux, the Garonne sucks in many lesser but far more attractive rivers: the Dordogne, Lot and Tarn, which are in turn fed by their tributaries. The Adour is the only other

LEFT: a school party sets off on a rafting trip down the River Aude near Quillan.
ABOVE: fishing on one of the rivers of the Dordogne.

THE UNDERGROUND

There is another world to be visited underground. Southwest France is riddled with caves. Some of these are natural marvels. Outstanding among them are the Gouffre de Padirac in the Lot *(see page 153)*, which has to be explored partly by boat; and the vast chamber of Aven Armand, in the Aveyron, which sprouts a stalagmite "forest" *(see page 172)*.

Many caves in the region were decorated by prehistoric painters – most famously Lascaux *(see page 139)*. Gargas *(see page 250)* and Niaux *(see page 261)* are also exceptional. Pech-Merle *(see page 158)*, combines prehistoric art with natural wonders.

10-km (6-mile) stretch can easily be paddled in a morning or afternoon; but it is even more enjoyable if a stop for lunch on a riverside beach is included.

Mountain sports

The Pyrenees are supreme when it comes to skiing, snowboarding and other winter sports, with more than 40 resorts – the older ones generally in the valleys, the more recently created ones on mountain tops. There are smaller resorts, more suited to cross-country than downhill skiing, in the Grand

> ### COASTAL CYCLING
> There are plans to build a 332-km (206-mile) dedicated cycle route along the Languedoc and Roussillon coast all the way from the Camargue to the Pyrenees.

Cycles can be hired in any large town with a modest tourist infrastructure, and also at some SNCF stations. Armed with a good 1 cm=1 km map (IGN or Michelin) you can get right off the main roads and travel through the South-west's thick network of attractive backroads. The Landes is extremely flat. The Gers, the lowland Tarn and the lower Garonne valley offer gentle, uneventful cycling. The Lot and Dordogne are more attractive but they have more ups and downs as soon as you leave the valleys. The

Causses and the Cévennes. The same highlands are good for other sports in the summer: rock climbing, hang-gliding (*deltaplane* in French) and para-gliding *(parapente).*

Getting around on two wheels

The thought of any hill, let alone a mountain, is enough to put many people off cycling altogether. However, Southwest France is excellent cycling country. Keen cyclists may even head for the best hill climbs, the gruelling *cols* of the Pyrenees – Tourmalet, d'Aspin, Soulor – that form part of the bike race, the Tour de France. The arduous climb is rewarded by the prolonged freewheeling down the other side.

Ariège and Pyrenean foothills also take effort but the scenery can be rewarding.

The Grand Causses and the Cévennes have some splendid freewheeling descents into the gorges but they are, of course, matched by tough ascents back on to the plateaux. The plains of Languedoc-Roussillon, beside the Mediterranean, are best not tackled in the summer months, when it can be very hot. If you want the easiest of days out there is a cycle path from the centre of Toulouse to Port Lauragais along the Canal du Midi. ❏

ABOVE: Tour de France competitors on the Col du Tourmalet in the Pyrenees.

The Canal du Midi

The idea of connecting the Atlantic Ocean and the Mediterranean Sea, along the ancient trade route between Aquitaine and the Languedoc, is thought to date back to the Romans.

It took the energy and sacrifice of one man to achieve this dream in the 17th century. In 1662 Pierre-Paul Riquet (1604–80) of Béziers persuaded Colbert, Louis XIV's Comptroller-General of Finances, to back the project and, with royal approval, work began on what became known at court as "Riquet's ditch" in 1666.

There were many problems to overcome, not least of which was how to finance the project. Riquet himself put in a third of the total cost, going into debt and forgoing his daughters' dowries. An estimated 12,000 workers took 14 years to excavate the channel and build the 328 locks, bridges, aqueducts and other constructions necessary.

Riquet's greatest challenge was the Seuil de Naurouze, the raised watershed between the Massif Central and the Pyrenees. It may not look much today but this 194-metre (636-ft) "pass" had defeated the plans of would-be canal builders before Riquet. An 1827 obelisk (on the D218) commemorates Riquet's achievement in crossing it. It is at this point that the canal is supplied with water from the Montagne Noire.

Having devoted himself and all his money to the project, Riquet died in 1680, six months before work was completed.

The 240-km (150-mile) long Canal du Midi runs from the Port de l'Embouchure at Toulouse to Les Onglous on the Étang (or Bassin) de Thau, a lagoon opening on the Mediterranean to the south of Sète.

It originally connected with the River Garonne at Toulouse but since the 19th century it has met the Canal de la Garonne, which follows the banks of the river to Castets-en-Dorthe southeast of Bordeaux. Together, these two canals are known as the Canal des Deux Mers.

The canals of Aquitaine and the Languedoc lost their commercial importance in the early 20th century but have been maintained and restored for leisure sailing. Passenger boats depart from Langon, Marmande, Escassefort, Agen, Malause and Moissac on the Canal de la Garonne and Toulouse, Port Sud, Port Lauragais, Mas-Stes-Puelles, Homps,

RIGHT: boats on the Canal du Midi at Fonserannes locks near Béziers.

Béziers and Agde on the Canal du Midi. Canal boats can be hired in Fourques-sur-Garonne, Le Mas d'Agenais, Damazan, Buzet-sur-Baise, Agen, Toulouse, Ramonville-Ste-Agne, Négra, Castelnaudary, Bram, Trebes, Homps, Argens, Minervois, Le Somail, Colombiers, Béziers, Port Cassafières and Agde. Alternatively, you can walk or cycle alongside the canals, or merely stop your car and admire the elegant architecture of locks, aqueducts, curving basins, and avenues of plane trees, cypresses and pines.

The highlight of the Canal du Midi is the flight of eight locks at Fonserannes, outside Béziers, and the adjacent canal bridge.

The Garonne Canal, meanwhile, has a unique technical installation. The Pente d'Eau de Montech (outside the village of Montech, southwest of Montauban) is an ingenious device for raising or lowering commercial barges without them having to negotiate a series of locks. Two engines resting on fat rubber tyres are used to drag each barge up or down a 400-metre (1,300-ft) "slope" of water.

An exhibition on the Canal du Midi can be seen in the Centre Pierre-Paul Riquet beside the pretty canal basin at Port Lauragais, which has been incorporated into a service area on the south side of the A61 motorway between Toulouse and Carcassonne, close to the Seuil de Naurouze (by the Rugby Museum, *see page 274*). ❏

WILDLIFE

*The region contains two national parks and a host of other nature reserves,
which protect some of the rarest plants and animals of southern France*

The natural world is still held in some reverence by the French, although often taken for granted. "One still gets the impression that nature reigns and man simply harvests," writes Douglas Botting in *Wild France*.

Nowhere is nature more conspicuous and abundant than in the Southwest, where habitats cross every spectrum: from arable plain to the bleak high mountain; fast-flowing river to still, silent lake; lush meadow to parched Mediterranean hillside; windswept Atlantic beach to Dordogne chestnut woods. There is every kind of landscape you could desire, even coral formations underwater.

Few places are totally wild. Most have been "managed" somehow or other, but often in a sustainable way. Traditional patterns of land use have favoured wildlife. Farms are generally not large and small woods and hedgerows – essential havens of wild animals – still separate fields as they have done for centuries. Streams, rivers, lakes and ponds have been left intact, serving as oases for wild creatures.

But for all the French love their countryside, there are threats from every side as traditional agriculture declines. The very best wildlife sites, scientifically speaking at least, are now protected as nature reserves.

Nature under your nose

There is space to breathe in the countryside of Southwest France and enough land without someone living on or even near it, to get comfortably lost in and there's always something interesting to observe. France has around 7,000 species of wild plant, 400 birds, 110 mammals 63 reptiles and amphibians, and innumerable species of insect. A disproportionate number of them occur somewhere in the Southwest.

The real joy of the French countryside lies not in tracking down some conservation corner barricaded off from the modern world, where

there is a remote chance of seeing some endangered species; but in the ordinary, everyday treats. There is plenty to see, day or night, without special equipment but with an eye and an ear always open.

It can be satisfying merely to stroll in an expanse of unmolested chestnut or oak wood, or survey a stand of plane trees planted along a main road or around a square – so typical of small-town France.

Buzzards can frequently be seen wheeling over the fields beside a main road, in search of prey, or sitting defiantly on a fence post. Swallows swoop in and out of barns and house martins race around villages, their nests packed into the eaves of the houses as if these birds could not exist far from man. A hoopoo – exotically decorated for a relatively common bird – may be disturbed on a suburban walk. Or the song of an unseen nightingale, blackcap or golden oriole may cheer up an otherwise dull afternoon. What looks like wasteland next to a car park

---

PRECEDING PAGES: grey heron hunting.
LEFT: barn owl.
RIGHT: mountain goat in the Pyrenees.

can, on closer inspection, turn into a patch of pyramidal orchids. Locally common in season are butterflies like the red admiral, Camberwell beauty, scarce swallowtail, and the humming-bird-lookalike bee hawkmoth. An outdoor meal on a warm summer's night may be punctuated by the silent passing of a bat or the screech of a barn owl as its ghostly white silhouette passes overhead.

The most common species of plants, birds and mammals can be identified with a set of carefully chosen English-language guides. Any good bird book will cover the whole of Europe; but for wildflowers, look for a guide covering the Mediterranean region, not northern Europe. It can be helpful to pick up leaflets about nature in tourist information offices or buy a local booklet, but check that Latin names are given or it can be impossible to cross-refer between books – translations of French common names into English are often inaccurate.

Protected areas

Three main kinds of nature reserve exist in France (and a host of smaller ones). The highest protection to wildlife is afforded by the *parcs nationaux* (national parks; www.parcsnationaux. fr.com), which have a wide-ranging brief to

THE RETURN OF THE GRIFFON VULTURE

Until 1900, the griffon vulture (*Gyps fulvus; vautour faue* in French) was plentiful throughout the south of France, from the Pyrenees to the Alps. But numbers declined drastically over the next few decades, largely due to human activity, including hunting and poisoning, and intervention was necessary if the griffon vulture was to survive here.

In 1974 a conservation scheme began, which has boosted the vulture population of the French Pyrenees from 50 to around 500 breeding pairs.

The situation was worse in the Grands Causses where the griffon vulture had become extinct. In 1981, after considerable preparation, five pairs of vultures were released into the wild in the Gorges de la Jonte and over time a colony successfully established itself.

In 1991 the then mayor of Aste-Béon *(see page 251)*, in collaboration with the Pyrenees National Park, came up with an extraordinary idea to involve and inform the public. He had a video camera discreetly installed on a cliff near the vultures' nests so that live pictures of the birds' movements could be transmitted back to a giant screen in a visitors' centre below.

A similar arrangement was later introduced the Gorges de la Jonte *(see page 171)*. A visit to either place is a memorable experience.

safeguard endangered species (and sometimes to reintroduce them) at the same time as making the area accessible to the public. Each national park has a central zone of high protection and a *zone périphérique*, in which attention is given not only to protecting wildlife but also to managing the area to preserve its scenery and its economic and cultural way of life. Of France's seven national parks, two fall within our area: the Parc National des Pyrénées and the Parc National des Cévennes. Both have visitor information centres *(maisons du parc)* and marked walking trails, and produce a range of informative publications.

Naturel Régional du Haut-Languedoc covers a large area that includes the Montagne Noire, the extraordinary rock formations of the Sidobre, the Monts de Lacaune and the Monts de l'Espinouse.

Even bigger is the Parc Naturel Régional des Grands Causses (in Aveyron, adjacent to the Cévennes National Park). The Parc Naturel Régional des Landes de Gascogne covers part of the forest of the Landes. The Parc Naturel Régional Périgord-Limousin, to the north of the Dordogne, stretches far into the Massif Central. Newly created is the Parc Naturel Régional de Causses de Quercy in the Lot.

There are now 39 *parcs naturels régionaux* (regional natural parks; www.parcs-naturels-regionaux.tm.fr) in France, covering vast areas but with less conspicuous infrastructure than the national parks. Protection for the wildlife within them is less strict than in a national park as they combine conservation with managed ecomomic development – which in these days of declining agriculture usually means creating facilities for eco-friendly tourism. There are five such parks in the Southwest. The Parc

LEFT: buzzard perched on a fence post.
ABOVE: pyramidal orchid in the country near Toulouse.
RIGHT: mistletoe growing on a tree in the Ariège.

The Southwest also includes 27 *réserves naturelles* (natural reserves; www.reserves-naturelles.org), created by state decree to protect small areas important for wildlife. They tend to cluster in the mountains of the eastern Pyrenees, and along the two coasts.

Mountains

Inevitably, the most interesting plants and animals are to be found in the remotest places, away from the disruptions to the natural world caused by humanity.

The Pyrenees are incomparable for wildlife at almost any level *(see pages 254–55)*. The best place to learn about the mountain wildlife is the Parc National des Pyrénées, which is 70 km (43 miles) from east to west but sometimes less than 1 km (½ mile) north to south; and the associated Réserve Naturelle de Néouvielle.

The east and western arms of this mighty range are markedly different because of the influence on climate of the Mediterranean and Atlantic respectively. And there are clear divisions of vegetation the further up the slope you go. These conditions create diversity. In the tiny Pyrenean country of Andorra alone – one of the best plant-hunting regions – 1,000 species of wildflower have been recorded. The Pyrenees makes for good natural history statistics: 160 *naicus)*, the newt-like Pyrenean brook salamander *(Euproctus asper)* and the midwife toad *(Alytes obstetricians)*.

The Cévennes and the Grands Causses, the Massif Central's southeastern buttress, can't compete with the Pyrenees in scale, but they are more accessible. This area is particularly good for birds of prey and for orchids. The Parc National des Cévennes has 2,200 plant species (48 of them endemic) in its deciduous and evergreen forests, sub-alpine meadows, rocky valleys and other ecosystems. There are 70 kinds of mammal and 195 bird species (including reintroduced vultures) living here.

endemic species of plant (those that occur here and nowhere else), 75 of France's 110 species of land mammal; 300 kinds of butterfly and 1,000 varieties of beetle.

Of course, it is the large, rare animals that exert the most pull on the naturalist but they are unlikely to be seen. The number of brown bears left in the Pyrenees is down to single figures. There are only 23 pairs of the great bone-sucking bearded vulture or lammergeier. But thanks to a conservation programme there is a healthy breeding population of the more common griffon vulture *(see box, page 88)*. The Pyrenees has a number of interesting smaller species too, notably the desman *(Galemys pyre-*

Wetlands

Along the Mediterranean coast is a series of saline lagoons, *étangs*, cut off from the sea by sandbars. Not all are attractive places to linger but several have rich birdlife. Flamingos and herons are the most conspicuous species; seabirds, divers, waders and a variety of other waterfowl can also be seen.

There are also wetlands on the Atlantic coast, including the unique Réserve Naturelle du Courant d'Huchet, an 8-km (5-mile) overflow channel connecting the Lac de Léon with the ocean. At La Teich, on the Bassin d'Arcachon, there is an ornithological reserve with 80 resident species and 200 migratory visitors.

Garrigue

The characteristic scenery of Mediterranean France is *garrigue*: dry, open country of shrubs (tree heath and broom), small trees (holm oak, pine, strawberry tree, juniper) and drought-resistant undergrowth. *Garrigue* is found wherever the existing vegetation has been removed by man, or burnt by fire, or the soil is too shallow or stony to cultivate. It dominates hillsides and pokes between vineyards and fields.

The plants of the *garrigue* are adapted to survive the hot, dry, Mediterranean summers. Some, like the varieties of cistus, or rock-rose, have showy flowers. Many are aromatic plants

France. A fragile and diverse ecosystem within the reserve is kept as safe as possible from fishing and pollution, and carefully managed for tourism. An "underwater footpath" has been laid out on the Plage de Peyrefite.

Private shows

France being so geared up for tourism, its wildlife is in many places commercially packaged in private menageries. Birds of prey are the most common subject matter: they can be seen in trained flight at Rocamadour, Carcassonne, Argelès-sur-Mer (near Perpignan), and Arreau and Beaucens (both in the Pyrenees).

that are familiar in any kitchen: sage, thyme and rosemary. These plants attract insects and the summer sound of the *garrigue* is the loud, chirping "song" of the cicada.

The underwater world

The 6.5 km (4 miles) of the Côte Vermeille between Banyuls-sur-Mer and Cerbère – from Ile Grosse to Cap Peyrefite (just north of the Spanish frontier) – are protected as the Réserve Marine Naturelle de Banyuls-Cerbère, the first underwater nature reserve to be declared in

Wolves live in "semi-liberty" (i.e. large enclosures) at Ste-Lucie, in the Gévaudan (to the north of the Cévennes) and in Orlu, near Ax-les-Thermes (Ariège). Bison roam the range at Ste-Eulalie (Lozère) and Lapenne (Ariège). St-Faust (west of Jurançon) has a "Bee City" and Rocamadour has its "House of the Bees". Almost every other living creature in the Southwest similarly has its own sanctuary.

Some of these specialised zoos carry out conservation work and open their doors to the public only to raise awareness of conservation issues. Whatever their credentials, they all enable the wildlife enthusiast to get close to otherwise reclusive animals.   ❑

LEFT: wild boar.
ABOVE: praying mantis.

FOOD IN THE SOUTHWEST

Eating is one of the pleasures of being in France – the restaurants of the Southwest, and the market stalls brimming over with fresh local produce, will not disappoint

ew would dispute that France is blessed with some of the most varied cooking in the world. In no part of the country is the spectrum of ingredients and culinary styles as wide as in the cuisine of Southwest France. This is due in large part to the area's varied climatic conditions and terrain, which range from baking plains and fertile rolling countryside to lush hills and high mountain pastures. All these environments produce different vegetables and fruits and suit different types of farm animals. Cooks are also able to draw on the bounty of two distinct marine ecosystems, the Mediterranean and the Atlantic.

Soup

As peasant food is the bedrock of Southwest cuisine, soup – the staple that enabled people to keep going when times were hard – looms large in the local diet.

Soups range from the most basic possible *(aïgo boulido)* to the sumptuous *(garbure)*. *Aïgo boulido* (literally "boiled water") consists of water, a large amount of garlic, a bay leaf and/or sage with, sometimes, an egg or two beaten into it. *Garbure* is a meal in itself, consisting as it does of potatoes, cabbage, haricot beans, broad beans and *confit d'oie* (goose paté) all cooked with a ham bone to provide extra flavour and served on top of brown bread and, often, crumbled Roquefort.

Charcuterie

The better the ham, the better the soup will be. The most renowned ham of the Southwest is *jambon de Bayonne*, which is not only eaten on its own but used extensively in stuffings and garnishes. In the Basque Country it is added, lightly sautéed, to *pipérade*, a tasty concoction of eggs, tomatoes, peppers and onions. Fine raw ham is also produced in the Aveyron.

The *charcuterie* of the Southwest is, on the

PRECEDING PAGES: drying garlic in Gascony.
LEFT: ingredients for a fish soup.
RIGHT: a chef in Perpignan.

whole, excellent. It includes pâté (often given an extra dimension with Armagnac), *saucisses de Toulouse* (sausages made of pure pork and seasonings), *andouille béarnaise* (dried chitterling) and *boudins* (black puddings) of various shapes and sizes. Lacaune, in the mountains of the Tarn, is known for its somewhat spicy

charcuterie (cold cuts). A rarity well worth trying, from the region of Albi and Carcassonne, is *fetge*, salted and dried pork liver, which is diced and lightly sautéed with radishes.

Foie gras

Gastronomically speaking, one of the best-known products of the Southwest is foie gras. That of the Gers *(see page 220)* and the Dordogne is particularly highly regarded. There is much heated debate over the question of whether duck liver is superior to goose liver, or vice versa. When properly cooked (*mi-cuit*, literally half-cooked, which in fact is more than half-cooked), the pinkish-buff, complex-tasting foie gras is indeed one of the glories of French cuisine. Normally served cold, with toasted brioche or, better, half-rye bread, it can also be flash-fried (it requires some skill to seal the pieces and prevent the fat from seeping out). Foie gras in tins or jars has necessarily been sterilised and is only a pale shadow of the *mi-cuit* version.

The Southwest also produces some exceptionally good poultry: the Landes and the Lauragais (near Castelnaudary) are famous for their capons, while ducks and geese throughout the Southwest are often turned into delicious confits.

lamproie à la bordelaise (lamprey with *jambon de Bayonne*). Locals will pay astronomical prices to get a chance to sample *pibales* (elvers which, although weighing less than a gramme each, have already swum across the Atlantic from the Sargasso Sea).

In the Gironde *département*, farmed *esturgeon* produces both sturgeon steaks and nearly 200 kg (440 lbs) of caviar a year (there is a ban on the fishing of wild sturgeon). The Basque dish, *ttoro*, is a kind of fish stew that differs from the Provençal *bouillabaisse* in that it includes langoustines and a good whack of dried chillies from the village of Espelette.

Fish and seafood

Cooks on the Mediterranean and those on the Atlantic coast do not treat seafood in at all the same way. Fine oysters are produced both in the Étang de Thau, a seawater lagoon behind the large fishing port of Sète, where people usually eat them in the traditional way (with rye bread and lemon juice), and in the Bay of Arcachon, near Bordeaux, where they are accompanied by a shallot-flavoured vinaigrette and thin sausages (the idea being that each bite of sausage clears the palate for the next oyster).

In Bordeaux, red wine is – as one might expect – used as a cooking medium for *anguilles à la médocaine* (eels with prunes) and the rare

While it is true that *bouillabaisse* is eaten as far west as Narbonne, the best-known fish dish on the Mediterranean coast of the Southwest is a speciality of Sète: *bourride*, a rich stew of monkfish with lashings of *aïoli* (garlic mayonnaise) and, usually, saffron. Traditional Sunday lunch in Sète consists of stuffed squid or stuffed mussels, the distinctive feature of which is the minced pork and veal that goes into the stuffing on top of the egg, bread, garlic and parsley.

France's finest anchovies are deemed to come from Collioure, a small port on the Catalan coast near the Spanish border.

A speciality of Nîmes, *brandade de morue*, is a controversial dish. According to the canons of Nîmois orthodoxy, neither garlic nor potatoes should be included in this purée of salt cod and olive oil; yet the *brandade* that is served in restaurants all along the coast will almost certainly include those two "banned" ingredients. It has to be said that, without garlic to jazz it up or potato to lighten its texture, *brandade* tends to be a cloyingly rich dish.

Wind-dried cod goes into what is possibly France's most mysterious dish, *estofinado*, which is eaten in a small pocket of the northern Aveyron around Decazeville. Wind-dried cod from Norway (stockfish) is as hard as wood and will keep almost indefinitely. It has long been eaten in Portugal, Nice and Venice, usually in stews with tomatoes and garlic. In its uncooked state, stockfish has a smell reminiscent of rotten fish. But in *estofinado*, where it is combined with mashed potato, eggs, cream, garlic and parsley, it is magically transformed into a delicate, complex and notably moreish dish. Of the numerous theories about how stockfish came to be consumed in such a tiny part of the Aveyron, one of the most plausible is that it was introduced there by English troops, who were present in the Rouergue, on and off, for decades during the Hundred Years' War, and who included stockfish – a perfect preserve – in their provisions.

> **SACRED CASSOULET**
>
> "*Cassoulet* is the God of Occitan cooking: the *cassoulet* of Castelnaudary is God the Father, that of Carcassonne God the Son, and that of Toulouse the Holy Spirit." – Prosper Montagné

Cassoulet

Probably no other French dish arouses the degree of passion, if not acrimony, of *cassoulet*. It is a calorie-packed casserole of various meats and haricot beans whose paternity is claimed by three Southwest towns, Toulouse, Carcassonne and Castelnaudary, and whose "authentic" ingredients are the subject of much heated (and confused) debate between the inhabitants of those areas.

The original and simplest version of the dish would seem to come from Castelnaudary (where earthenware dishes called *cassoles* are made) and contains haricot beans and plenty of garlic along with pork rind, pig's trotter, pork fillet, *saucisse de Toulouse*, and confit of goose or duck. The Carcassonne version adds to those ingredients leg of lamb and, in season, partridge. In Toulouse, they pull all the stops out,

LEFT: farmed Siberian sturgeon in the Gironde, the source of La Caviar d'Aquitaine.
ABOVE: cassoulet.

combining pork rind, neck and shoulder of lamb, pork fillet, pork spare ribs, raw ham, confit of goose or duck and *saucisses de Toulouse*.

Other meat dishes

A speciality of the Aveyron is *tripous* (or *tripoux*). These highly seasoned bundles of calf's and/or lamb's tripe are traditionally eaten as a *casse-croûte* (snack) very early in the morning at markets. While straightforward roasts (pork, veal, beef, lamb) are nowadays commonly eaten all over Southwest France, the more trad-itional way of dealing with meat used to be to put it into a slowly cooked stew that would turn the toughest flesh tender. In the Basque Country, shoulder of veal and *jambon de Bayonne* are given zip by the fiery Espelette chillies in a ragoût called *hachua* (or *axoa*). Nîmes is famous for its *estouffade de boeuf* (*estouffade* can also be made with veal or rabbit), in which the meat is simmered for hours over an extremely low heat with tomatoes, olives and garlic in a sealed casserole.

The lamb of Barèges-Gavarnie is particularly celebrated. Its flavour is preserved through raising livestock in the traditional mountain way on open pastures, and in 2003 it was awarded an AOC (Appellation Origine

GARLIC GALORE

The Southwest is the place to buy that archetypal, health-giving French vegetable of flavour, garlic. The Gers *département* is France's leading garlic-producing area, with two towns, St-Clar and Beaumont-de-Lomagne, informally competing for the right to be regarded as the garlic capital of France. In St-Clar's annual summer fair, works of art created entirely from heads of garlic are put on display. The town of Lautrec near Albi, meanwhile, produces *l'ail rose* (pink garlic), which is said to be easier on the digestive system and more delicately perfumed, making it suitable for dishes in which garlic predominates, such as *soupe à l'ail* and *aïoli* sauce.

Contrôlée), a rare distinction for meat, thus far only attained by the bulls of the Camargue.

Truffles and other fungi

No survey of the meat dishes of Southwest France would be complete without a mention of that marvellous summer dish from Périgord in which truffles *(see page 143)* give of their best: *enchaud à la périgourdine*. It consists of boned loin of pork larded with garlic and truffles, gently cooked, with its bones, in Madeira and water, and served cold surrounded by chopped aspic. The most sought-after variety of truffle (*Tuber melanosporum*) comes mainly from Périgord, where the biggest truffle markets are held early each year. From there they find their way to the finest tables in the world, lending their incomparable flavour to terrines, foie gras, *poularde demi-deuil* (chicken with truffles) and countless other *haute cuisine* dishes. They can even be eaten – at a price – on their own, cooked *en papillote* (in parchment) or in a salad. That other great mushroom, the cèpe, thrives in many parts of the Southwest and is the subject of keen, if not literally cut-throat, competition between amateur and professional gatherers. It is used chiefly in omelettes, in potato dishes, with poultry and in *tartelettes*.

Fruit and vegetables

The Southwest is home to a wealth of fruits and vegetables. There are several varieties of haricot beans *(cocos, tarbais, michelets, lingots)*, all with slightly different properties. If you're lucky, you might find a restaurant menu that offers a subtly flavoured rarity – *gesses*, or grass peas *(Lathyrus sativus)* – as a garnish.

Some regions have a particular forte. France's biggest walnut-growing area covers part of the Dordogne and the Lot. The renowned *pruneaux* (prunes) *d'Agen* come from lower down the Lot river, north of the town after which they are named. Céret in the Catalan Pyrenees harvests France's first cherries (in mid-April). And Moissac, best known for its Romanesque abbey, is also famous for its sweet, white, table grapes, Chasselas de Moissac, which are protected by their own *appellation d'origine contrôlée* (AOC)

Garlic *(see panel, page 98)* is omnipresent in the cooking of the Southwest and Gascony is a leading centre of production. The less-pungent green shoots of garlic, *aillets*, are used to flavour omelettes in Aquitaine. *Aligot,* a very basic dish (mashed potatoes, garlic and melted cheese), is a speciality of the Aveyron.

Cheese

The cheese used in *aligot* is *tomme fraîche de laguiole*, which is somewhat similar to mozzarella. *Tomme fraîche* is either eaten when it is still fresh and unsalted, or salted and matured until it turns into Laguiole (similar to Cantal).

Much of the stony terrain of the Aveyron and the neighbouring Lot is congenial to goats. The goat's cheeses they produce – Cabécou, Rocamadour – are best when creamy and just beginning to develop a rind after two weeks. The same is true of another goat's cheese, Pélardon, which is produced in the Cévennes and in the Corbières region. Ewe's milk cheeses with a similar texture – Brique de Brebis, Pérail – are found in the Aveyron.

The most famous cheese of the Southwest is, of course, Roquefort *(see page 170)*, a ewe's milk blue cheese. It partly owes its extraordinarily distinctive flavour to the *fleurines*, the cool, draughty and humid caves in which it is matured. Bleu des Causses, a cow's milk blue

LEFT: a box of freshly picked cherries.
RIGHT: making *aligot*.

MEET THE CHEESE

"Je vous présente le fromage," your waiter or waitress will say when the cheese course arrives. You will be welcome – almost expected – to ask questions before choosing what you want from the selection. You may recognise a familiar, mass-produced cheese imported from somewhere else in France, but the most interesting choice will always be a lesser-known local cheese – if there is one. In the north of the region this is likely to come from cow's milk *(vache)* but elsewhere it will be from the milk of sheep *(brebis)* or goat *(chévre)*. *Fort* means strong-tasting; the opposite is *doux* (mild). *Gras* is full fat, while *maigre* means low-fat.

cheese matured in a similar environment, bears a marked resemblance to Roquefort, though it does not have the same tang.

Curiously, the area between the Lot/Aveyron and the Pyrenees is a cheese desert unparalleled elsewhere in France. Many restaurants in Gascony, for example, simply dispense with a cheese platter altogether.

The Pyrenees, on the other hand, produce some of the finest ewe's milk cheeses in the world – Abbaye de Belloc, Ardi-Gasna, Cayolar, Ossau, Laruns, Iraty. With their combination of sweetness and saltiness, they make an ideal accompaniment to a really big red wine.

THE "MINCE PIES" OF PÉZENAS

An English connection is invoked for the origin of *petits pâtés de Pézenas*. These little pies are shaped like cotton reels and filled with a mixture of lamb, lamb suet, brown sugar and finely chopped crystallised citrus peel. Legend has it that Lord Clive of India spent the winter of 1766 in Pézenas and introduced English mince pies (which were originally made with meat) to the local bourgeoisie, who liked them so much they got local *pâtissiers* to make their own version of them. However, sweet meat pies were already being eaten in the region in the 17th century. As with much other culinary mythology, the truth is less interesting than the myth.

Sweets and desserts

The Southwest may not boast a great number of different cheeses, but it certainly makes up for that with the wealth of desserts and sweetmeats in its shops and on its menus.

Perpignan is famous for its *touron*, which usually takes the form of nougat. At the other end of the French Pyrenees, in the Basque Country, there is a different *touron*, made of marzipan, which comes in all colours, shapes and sizes.

Bayonne is noted for its excellent chocolate, a speciality taken there by Jews who had been expelled from Spain and Portugal, and for its *gâteau basque*, a firm sponge cake filled with cherry jam or *crème pâtissière*.

Pastis is a deceptive word: not only can it mean an aniseed-flavoured apéritif like Ricard or Pernod, but it also denotes two completely different types of dessert, depending on their location. *Pastis bourrit* of the Landes is a sponge cake traditionally eaten at weddings and fêtes. *Pastis estirat*, a feather-light Strudel-like accumulation of crisp filo-pastry layers interleaved with apples, is made, as befits its Gascon origin, with goose fat rather than butter. To confuse matters further, *pastis estirat* is also known as *croustade* in Gascony, and is called *tourtière* in the Landes.

Gâteau à la broche dates from the time when people still cooked in the hearth. A rich batter is very slowly dribbled, for a minimum of two hours, on to a wooden cone up to 80 cm (30 inches) long as it turns on a spit in front of a fire. The batter solidifies and cooks as it comes into contact with the heat. The end result looks appealingly knobbly. *Gâteau à la broche* is made across a broad swath of the Southwest, from the Aveyron to the Basque Country.

In French Catalonia they make a wonderfully aromatic *crème brûlée* called *crema cremada* (or *crème catalane*), which is flavoured with aniseed, cinnamon and lemon zest. The dish existed well before the first appearance of *crème brûlée* in the kitchens of Trinity College, Cambridge, where it is frequently alleged to have been invented.

Pézenas (Hérault) and the neighbouring town of Béziers are known for their sweet meat pies *(see panel on left)*. ❏

LEFT: croustade.
RIGHT: chef Michel Guérard *(see page 223)*.

FINE WINES

The high-quality wines made around Bordeaux are known all over the world, but

there are many smaller, individualistic vineyards to discover in the Southwest

There are some 400,000 hectares (1 million acres) of vineyards planted in a broad arc from the Médoc on France's Atlantic coast round to the Rhône delta. The vineyards divide into three contrasting regions: Bordeaux, Southwest France and Languedoc-Roussillon.

Classifying wines

Wines in France are ordered in a strict hierarchical structure based upon quality. The lowliest category is *vin de table,* or plonk in plain English. These wines are anonymous as their labels cannot include where they were made, the grape varieties used or the vintage. There are, however, no restrictions on yield.

The next step up is *vin de pays*, which is an increasingly important category although it was only created in 1973. These are wines that come from a specific region. Many are often sold as varietal wines, for example Chardonnay *vin de pays d'Oc*. Growers have greater freedom of choice over what varieties of grapes they can use.

The top category is the *appellation d'origine contrôlée* (AOC). Such wines are governed by strict rules covering such aspects as the grape varieties that can be planted, the way the vines are trained and the amount of grapes that can be produced.

There is also an intermediate category, the *vin délimité de qualité supérieure* (VDQS). This was introduced as a stepping stone to full *appellation* status. Many such wines have now been promoted to AOC status, although a number remain in the Southwest.

The massive and complex Bordeaux wine region has its own further hierarchy within the *appellation contrôlée*. At the base is plain Bordeaux AOC, which covers the whole region. A step up are sub-regional appellations like the Médoc or the Entre-Deux-Mers. At the top are the communal appellations such as

Pomerol, Pauillac and Sauternes. It has to be said that this official hierarchy of quality is often notional in practice. There are plenty of *vins de pays* that are better than supposedly superior *appellation contrôlée* wines. The most crucial information on any wine label is the name of the producer.

Bordeaux

Despite the emergence of new quality wine-producing countries and regions, Bordeaux remains the largest and most important quality wine-producing region in the world. A number of the world's most famous wines, such as Château Lafite, Château Latour, Château Pétrus and Château d'Yquem are made here. These wines, however, represent only a small fraction of the some 6–7 million hectolitres (15 million gallons) of wine that are produced in Bordeaux annually from the 115,000 hectares (285,000 acres) planted.

Around 90 percent of the wines are red. The chief red grape varieties are Cabernet Sauvignon,

LEFT: the Château de Crouseilles in the Madiran appellation, part of the Southwest France wine region.
RIGHT: testing a new wine in St-Émilion.

Cabernet Franc and Merlot. These grapes are invariably blended together, the proportions varying from district to district and between individual estates.

On the right bank (St-Émilion and Pomerol) Merlot is the dominant variety with quite a high proportion of Cabernet Franc used. On the left bank, especially in the Médoc, Cabernet Sauvignon is dominant, with Merlot playing a secondary role. Some producers also use a small amount of Malbec and Petit Verdot. The classic Bordeaux blend of Cabernet and Merlot

WINE REGIONS

For a map of the wine regions of Southwest France see inside back cover. See page 129 for a map of the wine regions of Bordeaux.

Regional Bordeaux wines

With an annual production of around 3.6 million hectolitres (750,000 gallons), the regional appellations account for half of the wine made in Bordeaux. As well as plain Bordeaux, these are Bordeaux Sec (white), Bordeaux Rosé, Bordeaux Clairet (a slightly deeper-coloured style of rosé), Bordeaux Supérieur (a red with slightly more alcohol than plain Bordeaux) and the small production of sparkling wine, Crémant de Bordeaux. There are some good regional wines made, but they need

has been copied around the world for many top reds, especially those in California, Chile and South Africa. Cabernet, especially Sauvignon, gives structure to the wine, while Merlot softens the tannins and often angular fruit of Cabernet.

For the white wines, Sémillon is the most widely planted grape followed by Sauvignon Blanc, which has been gaining in popularity over the past 15 years, especially in the Entre-Deux-Mers region. It is rare to find a pure Sémillon, while a pure Sauvignon Blanc is increasingly common. Muscadelle is also planted and is mainly used as one of the components in the sweet wines from the regions of Sauternes and Barsac.

searching out, for much of regional Bordeaux is made to a price that encourages over-production and the tendency to pick before the grapes are properly ripe, especially in difficult years.

Graves and Sauternes

Bordeaux can be divided into four sub-regions: Graves and Sauternes; the Entre-Deux-Mers; St-Émilion and Pomerol with its various satellite appellations; and the Médoc.

The vineyards of the Graves begin in the suburbs of Bordeaux – the original Haut Brion winery is now totally enclosed by housing developments. Vines continue intermittently for 40 km (25 miles) southwards along the western bank of the Garonne. They are mainly planted on gravel, hence the name Graves. Bordeaux's best dry white is made here, especially in the superior appellation of Pessac-Leognan. Even so, red wines are in the majority in the Graves. At the southern end are Sauternes and Barsac, their sweet wines made with the assistance of noble rot which concentrates the grape's juice. The Château d'Yquem here makes one of the most expensive wines in the world. On the other side of the Garonne at the southern end of the Premières Côtes de Bordeaux are the three small, sweet wine appellations of Cérons, Cadillac and Ste-Croix-du-Mont.

than those of the Médoc because of the higher proportion of Merlot used. These wines have become increasingly fashionable recently because of their soft appealing fruit and the fact that they are ready to drink earlier than the more tannic wines of the Médoc.

The various satellite appellation groups around St-Émilion, such as St-Georges-St-Émilion, offer similar wines at lower prices and are good value, as are those from nearby Lalande de Pomerol, Fronsac and Côtes de Fronsac. The vineyards of the right bank continue northwards up the Gironde with the Côtes de Bourg and Premières Côtes de Blaye.

Entre-Deux-Mers and St-Émilion

The Entre-Deux-Mers, the land between the Garonne and the Dordogne, provides an interlude between the Graves and the St-Émilion area. This is rolling country and its rich soils are devoted to mixed farming. Red, white and rosé wines are made here but the appellation Entre-Deux-Mers is reserved for white.

Much of Bordeaux is not very picturesque. However, the pretty little town of St-Émilion is an exception. The wines here and from neighbouring Pomerol are softer and rounder

LEFT: a vineyard owner harvests his grapes.
ABOVE: barrel making.

The Médoc

Although, with Château Lafite, Château Latour, Château Margaux and Château Mouton-Rothschild, the Médoc (the land stretching north from the city of Bordeaux, along the Gironde estuary) has four of the most important estates, it is the youngest vineyard of Bordeaux. Until it was drained by the Dutch in the 17th century much of this region was marshy. The best properties here are on gravel beds close to the Gironde. The communes of Margaux, St-Julien, Pauillac and St-Estèphe form the quality heart of the Médoc. Because of the high proportion of Cabernet Sauvignon used, the top wines can age for 50 years and more.

Southwest France wine region

Unlike the large concentrations of vineyards in Bordeaux and Languedoc-Roussillon, the vineyards of the Sud-Ouest wine region are widely scattered. The approximately 32,000 hectares (79,000 acres) under cultivation are spread among some 30 appellations. Within the region there are marked topographical differences and considerable variations in climate from the wetter Atlantic coast to the semi-Mediterranean climate around Toulouse. Many of the wines produced in this region are very individual, using grape varieties that are not seen elsewhere in France.

Buzet; those of Gascony and the Pyrenees; and those of the interior such as Cahors and Gaillac.

The vineyards close to Bordeaux make very similar wines to their large neighbour. Bergerac and its 12 associated appellations is the largest area of vines in the Southwest. Its annual production is about 10 percent of that of Bordeaux. The vineyards lie either side of the Dordogne and are really an eastwards extension of those of St-Émilion and the Côtes de Castillon. This area is in the midst of a revival and there are some very good reds, dry whites and particularly sweet wines, especially in the Monbazillac and Saussignac appellations.

Because of its geographical position at the head of the Garonne, Bordeaux has frequently been an obstacle to the success of wines of the Southwest. In the Middle Ages the Bordelais imposed a toll on wine passing down the Garonne and refused to let any wine pass until they had had a chance to sell their latest vintage. This was a significant advantage in an age when, before the advent of glass bottles, wine travelled in barrels and did not keep. Nowadays consumers judge the quality of a vintage by what it is like in Bordeaux, unaware that the Sud-Ouest may have very different weather.

The region divides into three: those appellations close to Bordeaux, like Bergerac and

The wines of Bergerac now often offer better value than the wines of Bordeaux.

In Gascony and the Pyrenees, with the exception of the largely white wine-producing Côtes de Gascogne, there are small pockets of vines. The two most dynamic appellations are Madiran and Jurançon. The often fascinating whites of Jurançon come from around the town of Pau and can be either dry or sweet. They are made from Petit Courbu, Petit Manseng and Gros Manseng. The wines have a quite high natural acidity and can be very long lived. Madiran is made from a high proportion of the grape, Tannat, which gives an often robust and powerful red. They can be excellent but need several years in the bottle first to soften. A white appellation, Pacherenc du Vic Bilh, covers the same area as Madiran. The wines are similar to those of Jurançon. The VDQS Côtes St Mont come in three colours and can offer very good value.

Down on the Spanish border in the Basque country is the small appellation of Irouléguy with its spectacular hillside vineyards. Cahors and Gaillac are the two most important appellations in the interior. AOC Cahors is for reds only with Auxerrois, known in Bordeaux

> **SOUTHWEST SUPERWINE**
>
> "The past 10 years have seen a transformation that's every bit as impressive as Clark Kent's cape-and-underpants switch in a phone box."
>
> – Tim Atkin, the London *Guardian*

Languedoc-Roussillon

With some 250,000 hectares (620,000 acres) planted, Languedoc-Roussillon remains the largest vineyard in the world with vines stretching from the Rhône delta to Banyuls on the border with Spain. In contrast, Australia has just over 100,000 hectares (250,000 acres) planted despite very rapid expansion over the past ten years.

This region is the most exciting and dynamic in France. Twenty-five years ago Languedoc-Roussillon had some 400,000

and elsewhere as Malbec, as the dominant grape, with Merlot used to soften the powerful Auxerrois. Cahors was famous for its "black" wine, which no longer exists. It is thought that the must was boiled to permit the wine to travel. The best wines age well and are good value. Production in Gaillac is more diverse using some grape varieties, such as Duras (red), Len de l'El and Mauzac that are rarely found elsewhere.

The Côtes de Frontonnais, close to Toulouse, is the only other significant appellation, making soft, juicy, reds from the Negrette grape.

LEFT: operating an old wine press in Bordeaux.
ABOVE: rows of Bordelais vines.

hectares (1 million acres) of vines and was known for the production of enormous quantities of *vin de table*. It was the arrival of the railway link to Paris and northern France that ushered in 120 years of bulk wine production, which could be produced more abundantly and more cheaply here than in other parts of France. However, as French lifestyles changed in the 1970s and 1980s the demand for cheap plonk collapsed. Annual per capita consumption in France has declined over the past 35 years from around 120 litres of wine to about 60 litres today. Languedoc-Roussillon had to find a new market and the only option was to go for quality. The past 25 years have seen an extraordinary transformation. Yields have been reduced, many vineyards have been replanted and there has been big investments in modern equipment.

Languedoc-Roussillon has the best climate in France for grape growing. Indeed, in parts of Languedoc the vine and the olive are the only commercial plants that can survive. The region has a Mediterranean climate with most of the rainfall in the late autumn and winter and heat in July and August. The summer months are often very dry.

There is a wide range of grape varieties. Some are of Mediterranean origin, such as Carignan, Cinsault, Grenache and Mourvèdre

for red, and Bourboulenc, Clairette, Grenache Blanc and Muscat for white. Syrah and Viognier from the Rhône Valley are increasingly being planted, as are several international varieties such as Chardonnay, Cabernet Sauvignon and Merlot.

The Languedoc plain

The vineyards on the plains of Languedoc have changed dramatically over the past 15 years. They are mainly given over to the production of *vin de pays* and, in particular, varietal wines – Chardonnay, Merlot, etc. The most interesting wines in Languedoc, almost invariably red, come from the vineyards in the hills away from the plains. They come from appellations such as Coteaux du Languedoc, Corbières, Fitou and Minervois. Faugères and St-Chinian are two high-quality zones within the Coteaux du Languedoc. The wines from Pic St-Loup have also established a high reputation. In general the best white and sparkling wines come from the cooler Limoux area, south of Carcassonne.

Roussillon: French Catalonia

Roussillon, dominated by the eastern Pyrenees, has significant orchards of cherries, peaches and apricots as well as vineyards. Although it produces similar reds and dry whites to Languedoc, it is more famous for its *vin doux naturel* or fortified wines from the appellations of Banyuls, Maury and Rivesaltes. The best of these have very complex aromas and flavours including coffee, chocolate and nuts, and are among the world's great fortified wines.

The appellation Côtes du Roussillon covers the whole of the region and all three colours. Côtes du Roussillon Villages is for red only and applies to the vineyards around Perpignan and up the Agly Valley. Caramany and Latour de France are supposedly the two *crus* of the Villages appellation.

These distinctions bear no relation to reality. Latour de France has for many years made disappointing wines and there are producers outside the Villages AOC who make wines every bit as good as those within. This only shows how misguided French wine bureaucrats were in rushing to codify a rapidly changing region like Languedoc-Roussillon. ❏

WINES WITHOUT SOUL

The Languedoc wine-growers were recently up in arms at plans by Mondavi, one of the giants of the California wine industry, to plant vineyards in the Hérault *département*. Part of the problem was that Mondavi wanted to clear virgin woodland to plant new vines rather than replanting old vineyards, but a lot of it was also resentment of new methods being introduced, and of Americanisation. One local wine-grower, Aimé Guibert, who once dismissed all American wines as yoghurt, was quoted as saying: "It's cretinous. Their wines are made by computers, they have no soul. It's not poetry any more, it's an industrial product."

LEFT: the cellar master, Château Belair, St-Émilion.
RIGHT: grapes ripening on the vine.

PLACES

*A detailed guide to the entire region, with principal sites
clearly cross-referenced by number to the maps*

Southwest France is composed of 18 *départements*, many of them sharing the names of well-known rivers (Dordogne, Lot, Tarn). These *départements* are officially grouped into three regions – Aquitaine, Midi-Pyrénées and Languedoc-Roussillon – names which are frequently seen on signs and in tourist publications but which do not trip off the tongue, even of their inhabitants. This book has to steer the visitor through this maze of overlapping geographies somehow and the 13 subsequent chapters largely follow the divisions of the *départements.*

It isn't possible to survey Southwest France without being struck by the sheer diversity on offer. To begin at the historical beginning, there are exceptional prehistoric cave paintings at Lascaux in the Dordogne (access to the original is difficult but next door is a replica, Lascaux II), Pech-Merle (Lot), Gargas (High Pyrenees) and Niaux (Ariège). Outstanding natural subterranean features can be seen at Padirac (Lot) and Aven Armand (Aveyron).

Among remains from Roman times are the great monuments of Nîmes, especially the nearby Pont du Gard.

The Middle Ages left many remarkable structures. Carcassonne's restored Cité is in a league of its own but there is also the fortified bridge at Cahors and the shrine of Rocamadour and the ruined castle of Monségur (Ariège) of Cathar fame. The Dordogne and Lot have splendid châteaux. Romanesque art and architecture is in abundance almost everywhere: at Moissac, Conques, St-Michel-de-Cuxa, St-Bertrand-de-Comminges and St-Guilhem-le-Désert.

As for cities, Bordeaux, Montpellier and rose-coloured Toulouse would all be in a French urban top twenty. Many smaller places have outstanding museums of art, including Montauban, Albi, Ceret and Castres.

To list all the beautiful villages in the Southwest corner would mean adding more pages to the book. But the *plus beaux* of the *plus beaux* towns and villages must include St-Émilion (Gironde), Sarlat-la-Caneda (Dordogne), St-Cirq-Lapopie (Lot), Cordes-sur-Ciel, Albi (Tarn) and Collioure in Catalonia, the inspiration of artists.

As for natural scenery, the Cévennes has the stunning Gorges du Tarn. In the Pyrenees are the summits of La Rhune and Pic du Midi de Bigorre, and the remarkable Cirque de Gavarnie. At the other end of the range is the sacred mountain of Canigou. On the Atlantic coast are Biarritz's beautiful beaches and Europe's largest sand dune, the Dune du Pilat. Like a thread winding leisurely through the centre of Southwest France is the Canal du Midi. ❑

PRECEDING PAGES: vineyard above Vinça with the Massif de Canigou behind; the Landes forest; the Dune du Pilat, near Arcachon.
LEFT: plane-tree lined main road near Béziers.

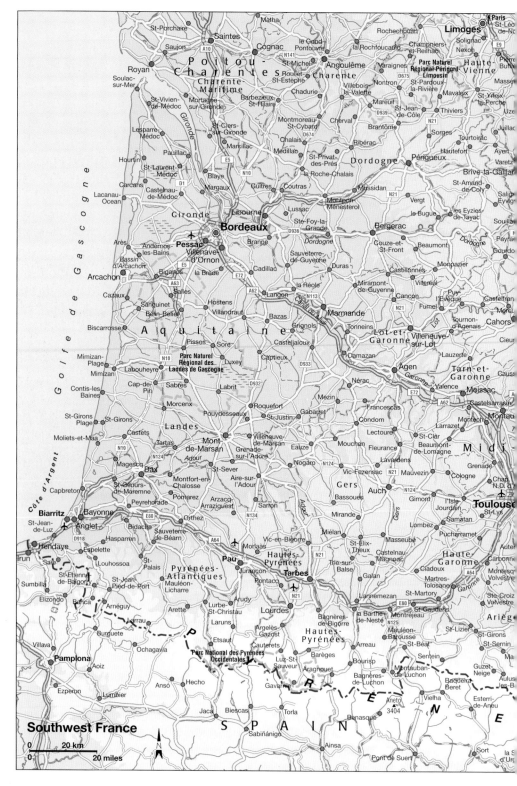

Southwest France

0   20 km

0   20 miles

N

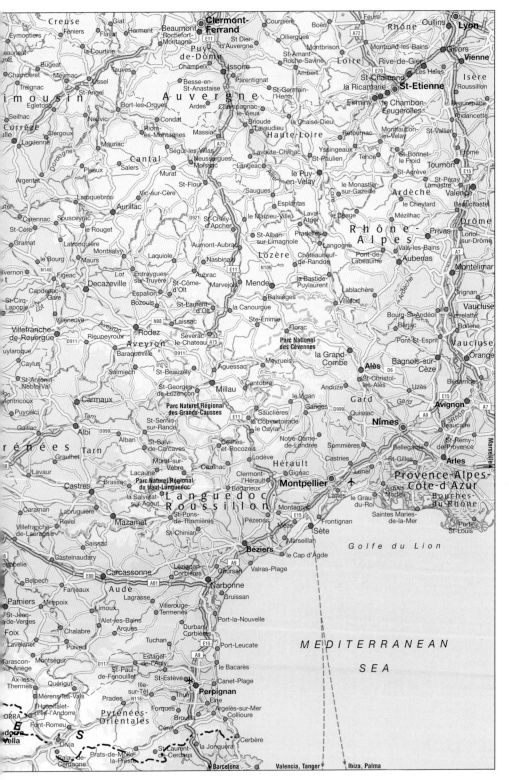

BORDEAUX AND THE GIRONDE

Maps:
Area 122
City 124

Bordeaux grew wealthy from its wine industry, as its many fine buildings show. The countryside is largely made up of vineyard estates, many dominated by magnificent châteaux

The largest of France's 95 *départements*, the Gironde is situated to the west of the Dordogne and the Lot, and bounded on its western edge by the Bay of Biscay. It gets its name from the Gironde River, which is fundamentally the estuary formed by the confluence of the Dordogne and Garonne.

The west side of the Gironde consists mostly of sandy moorland *(lande)*, planted with pines to minimise drift and interspersed with large lakes. The climate is delightfully warm and sunny in summer, and the vast Atlantic beaches are magnificent. The most important industry is, of course, wine: Médoc, Graves, Sauternes, St-Émilion and Entre-Deux-Mers are world-famous regions and their produce is shipped out of Bordeaux, the capital of the *département* and the third-largest port in France. Many of the tourists who come to this region are here predominantly to visit the wine châteaux.

The Gironde River abounds with fish, which are a prominent feature on local menus, especially lamprey *(lamproie)*, shad *(alose)*, elvers *(pibales)* and caviar from farmed sturgeon. The estuary and the coast are likewise famous for their oysters, particularly the *gravettes* from around Arcachon which are traditionally served with grilled local sausages.

LEFT: Château Pichon-Longueville at Pauillac.
BELOW: oyster farmer in Gujan-Mestras.

Bordeaux

Grandiose old **Bordeaux ❶**, the fifth-largest city in France, has been undergoing a major face lift. An urban renewal project has created new parks, landscaped quays and pedestrian promenades, and a clean-up of its many elegant buildings, especially along the banks of the River Garonne, has produced stunning results. A new tramway should be completed by 2007, and as a result of the city's regeneration, even the nightlife has gone from staid to stylish.

To understand the story of this ancient city visit **Bordeaux Monumental** (28 rue des Argentiers; open daily; free admission; tel: 05 56 48 04 24), a permanent exhibition of its history and buildings. The historic sights are for the most part conveniently situated in one compact part of town. This is the **Quartier St-Pierre** to the east of the city centre, reaching down to the elegant quays of the Garonne River. Its fine houses and public buildings reflect the delight in grace and symmetry that was taken in the 18th century by the wealthy burghers of the city who laid out many of its well-proportioned streets and squares.

Bordeaux has been a thriving commercial centre since Roman times. In the 14th century it became the seat of the Black Prince (later crowned King Edward III of England), and a busy trade developed between

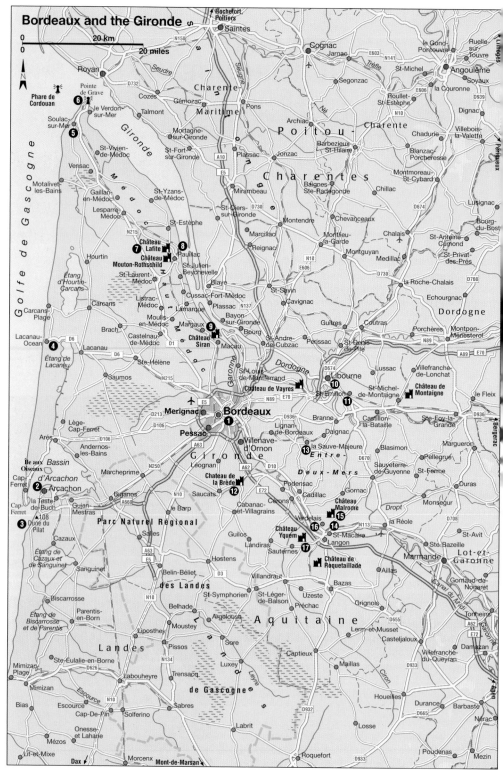

Bordeaux and the Gironde

the city and the great ports of England that continues – albeit on a more modest scale – to this day. The imposing **Esplanade des Quinconces** , which overlooks the Garonne River, is said to be the largest square in Europe. In it stands the **Monument aux Girondins**, erected in memory of the Bordeaux *députés* guillotined during the Revolution *(see page 39)*. Just off the square are the **tourist information office** and the **Maison du Vin** **B** (1 Cours du 30 Juillet; open daily; tel: 05 56 00 22 88; www.vins-bordeaux.fr). The headquarters of the Bordeaux Wine Council (CIVB) *occupy an 18th-century building in the form of the bow of a ship. It makes a good starting point if you are intending to visit vineyards in the region or are interested in the modern wine industry. *The Cours du 30 Juillet leads to the Place de la Comédie and the magnificently colonnaded **Grand Théâtre** **C**, completed just before the outbreak of the Revolution. The theatre marks the northern end of the **Rue Ste-Catherine**, which is the city's principal shopping centre.

A short walk to the east, the handsome **Place de la Bourse** overlooks the river and contains the **Musée des Douanes** **D** (open Tues–Sun; entrance fee; tel: 05 56 48 82 82), which gives a thorough and entertaining overview of the city's commercial and maritime past. Half-way down to the museum from the square is a 15th-century gateway, the **Porte de Cailhau** **E**, named after the piles of pebbles *(cailloux)* stored here for use as ballast by seagoing traffic. Now it houses an interesting exhibition of the city in bygone days. From the riverside here can be seen the brick-built **Pont de Pierre** **F**, constructed on the orders of Napoleon during his protracted war in the Spanish peninsula. Near the bridge is **St-Michel church** **G** and tower. Another distinctive monument and one of the landmarks of Bordeaux is the **Grosse Cloche** **H**, an arched gateway-cum-bell tower.

On the other side of the Rue Ste-Catherine, the twin towers of the **Cathédrale St-André** **I** dominate the skyline. Inside, the elegant, lofty nave is more than 800 years old, crossed by a fine, late Gothic transept. But the Cathedral's most famous feature is outside: its free-standing bell tower, the **Tour Pey-Berland**, which was built in the 15th century and named after the then archbishop of Bordeaux. During the Revolution, this graceful building was turned into a shot tower but it has since been meticulously restored.

Museums and gardens

The **Centre Jean Moulin** **J** (open Tues–Sun; tel: 05 56 79 66 00), facing the north side of the Cathedral, deals with France during World War II. Its displays and mementoes of the Resistance, and of its nominal leader Jean Moulin, provide a poignant insight into the work of the brave men and women who worked to save their country's honour from the shame of the Vichy regime. Moulin himself was captured in 1943 and died while being tortured by Klaus Barbie, the so-called "Butcher of Lyon".

Art lovers will now head for the **Musée des Beaux-Arts** **K** (20 cours d'Albret; open Wed–Mon; entrance fee; tel: 05 56 10 20 56). The collection contains works by Titian *(Tarquin and Lucretia)*, Jan Brueghel the Elder *(The Wedding Feast)*, Rubens, Veronese, Delacroix, Matisse and other masters. North of the

Map on page 124

Map on page 124

INFO

Tourist information office, Bordeaux: 12 Cours du XXX Juillet; tel: 05 56 00 66 00; www.bordeaux-tourisme.com

BELOW: Cathédrale St-André.

TIP

For boat trips from Arcachon ask on the sea-front or at the tourist information office on Esplanade Georges Pompidou (tel: 05 57 52 97 97; open Mon–Sat and Sun morning in summer).

Beaux Arts (rue Bouffard; open Wed–Mon; entrance fee; tel: 05 56 00 72 50) is the **Musée des Arts Décoratifs**, evoking the opulence of past Bordeaux life in a magnificent 18th-century mansion.

To the north of the Esplanade des Quinconces is the striking **Musée d'Arts Contemporains** (7 rue Ferrère; open Tues–Sun; entrance fee; tel: 05 56 00 81 50) housed in a converted spice warehouse, its stone arches an attractive setting for modern works by European and American artists. Not far away is the **Jardin Public** , a beautiful formal park containing the city's botanical gardens.

The coast

The **Côte d'Argent** is a long, straight strip of coastline extending south of the Gironde estuary towards Spain and facing out towards the Golfe de Gascogne. The best-known resort in its northern stretch is **Arcachon** ❷. In summer it is likely to be crowded with holidaymakers from the city enjoying its superb beaches of white sand. The old town (**Ville d'Hiver**) has fantastically decorated villas, thermal baths, forest walks and formal gardens. On the sea-front, look out for the remarkable **Casino**, an architect's fantasy that resembles a fairy-tale castle more than a gambling den.

On rue du Professeur Jolyet, the **Musée Aquarium d'Arcachon** (open daily; entrance fee; tel: 05 56 83 33 32) holds a collection of local marine wildlife, with its upper floors dedicated to other local fauna and flora. Excursions by boat depart from Arcachon to visit the **Bassin d'Arcachon**, an immense bay of 250 sq km (100 sq miles), the **Île aux Oiseaux**, and the extraordinary **Dune du Pilat** (also Pyla) ❸, the biggest sand dune in Europe, with marvellous views from its summit.

BELOW: Bordeaux's Musée d'Arts Contemporains.

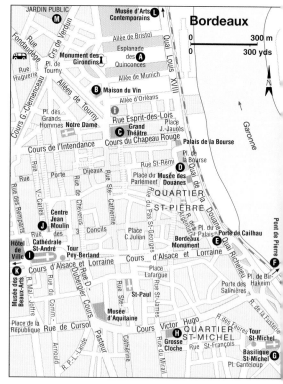

A 20-minute drive from the town is the attractive **Étang de Lacanau**, well equipped for watersports. From the northwest corner of the lake a short walk leads to the pretty seaside village of **Lacanau-Océan ❹**, another popular beach resort but smaller and altogether less hectic than Arcachon.

Maps:
Area 122
City 124

The Médoc

Continuing north and following the sandy coast, a 40-km (26-mile) drive past another lake, **Étang d'Hourtin-Carcans**, and through endless stretches of vines leads to **Soulac-sur-Mer ❺**, a small old-fashioned town with a lovely 14th-century church, a popular spot in summer for seaside family holidays. A couple of miles further on lies the tip of the peninsula that forms the southern end of the vast Gironde estuary (the biggest in France), the **Pointe de Grave ❻**, with glorious views. There is an impressive war memorial here as well as an interesting little **museum** (open daily, afternoons only at weekends) devoted to the history and the working of the **Phare de Cordouan** lighthouse (trips available May–Sept; tel: 05 46 39 05 55), which stands 9 km (5½ miles) out at sea to the northwest. For the intrepid visitor there are also boat trips out to this astonishing lighthouse, which was completed in the early 17th century and is the only one left in the country still to be manned by a keeper. The round trip takes about four and a half hours, and can get choppy.

This is **Médoc** country, and the flat landscape is broken up everywhere by impressive, often opulent wine châteaux. Heading back towards Bordeaux from the Pointe de Grave along the Gironde estuary, shortly before the town of **St-Estèphe**, the region of the **Haut-Médoc** offers an opportunity to visit some châteaux and taste the often superb wine.

"These pleasant Bordelais lead a wholly physical, carefree, out-of-doors life, admirable at a time when hypocrisy is polluting the moral life of France."

– STENDHAL,
Travels in the South of France, 1838

BELOW: oyster beds at Arcachon.

Some of the most important estates, unfortunately, can only be visited by appointment, either through the retail outlet at the château or by telephone. **Château Lafite ❼** (tel: 05 56 59 34 32; www.lafite.com), the most famous of the *grands crus classés*, 5 km (3 miles) south of St Estèphe on the D2, is one such. Almost next door, the **Château Mouton-Rothschild** (tours every hour Mon–Fri and also weekends in summer; entrance fee with optional supplement for tasting; tel: 05 56 73 20 20) has guided tours, also by appointment. Across the road from the château is a splendid panorama over the Gironde estuary, which is more than a mile wide at this point.

The pretty little port of **Pauillac ❽** is the largest town in the Médoc, though its beauty is marred by the presence of a particularly unattractive oil refinery. The tourist office on the waterfront is a mine of information about wine châteaux in the area and will even make appointments for some of them. Stendhal arrived at Pauillac by steam boat from Bordeaux in 1838 and found a new town: "One would say that three quarters of the town was not thirty years old."

Continuing south towards Bordeaux, where the Gironde splits into the Garonne and Dordogne rivers, is the village of **Margaux ❾**, world-famous for its claret. The **Château Margaux** (open Mon–Fri; entrance fee; tel: 05 57 88 83 83; www.chateau-margaux.com), which produces the claret, is far and away the most beautiful in a region of beautiful châteaux. It is open for most of the year (apart from harvest time), and again reservation by telephone is essential. About a mile further south at the village of **Labarde**, the **Château Siran** (open daily; entrance fee; tel: 05 57 88 34 04) has sumptuously furnished apartments and gardens to visit in addition to its cellars, and is open throughout the year.

Libourne

With its proximity to the Dordogne, this lovely, rugged area of the Gironde was much affected by the Anglo–French troubles that changed the face of the neighbouring region in the Middle Ages. The countryside is enchanting, and planted everywhere with vines that produce the important wines of **Pomerol** and **St-Émilion**.

Libourne ❿, the largest town in the region, was originally built in the 13th century as an English stronghold. Now it is a thriving commercial centre with an imposing market square, **Place Abel-Sur-champ**, which is lined with exquisite Renaissance and baroque houses. On its eastern side is the **Hôtel-de-Ville**, which dates back to the 15th century and whose second floor contains the town's museum and art gallery. Chiefly of interest here is an unusual collection of sporting and hunting scenes painted by René Princeteau, an artist friend of Toulouse-Lautrec. The quayside of this little riverside port is an ideal setting for a drink in the sunshine, and from which to admire the **Grand Pont,** an arched stone bridge almost 220 metres (720 ft) from end to end.

A short drive west of Libourne (9 km/5 miles), and on the opposite side of the Dordogne River, stands the splendid **Château de Vayres** (open daily in summer, afternoons only; Sun and public holidays only out of season; entrance fee; tel: 05 57 84 96 59), which was once the

TIP

To visit the vineyards around St-Émilion ask at the tourist information office or at the Maison du Vin (tel: 05 57 55 50 55; open daily), which is next to the bell tower in the town centre.

BELOW:
Château Margaux in the Médoc.

property of King Henri IV and was rebuilt in the 16th century by Louis de Foix, mastermind of the great lighthouse at Cordouan. Its elegant classical gardens that reach down to the river offer a refreshing, shady walk, while the interior apartments are stocked with beautiful furniture and fine tapestries. Also at Vayres, the wine château of **L'Hosanne** (open Mon–Sat; tel: 05 57 74 70 55) offers tastings of some excellent wine *(petite appellation)* in a much more friendly and informal atmosphere than many of the bigger and better-known châteaux.

Map on page 122

St-Émilion

The medieval citadel of **St-Émilion** ⓫ was built by the English King John at the end of the 12th century and is now the commercial centre of one of the world's favourite Bordeaux wines. Standing on a south-facing rocky outcrop, St-Émilion is a jewel of a town, a maze of old-fashioned steep little streets and squares whose walls are clustered with vines. By day the village is thick with tourists at the height of the season, but it recovers its peaceful equilibrium in the evening. Watch out, by the way, for rows of vines that are planted with rose bushes at each end; this is an old custom to show if any disease is likely to attack the valuable vines: it was reckoned that the roses would catch the sickness up to three days earlier and give the growers time to deal with the problem.

Old advert for St-Émilion wines.

Some of St-Émilion's most exciting sights are underground. The subterranean **Église Monolithe** (open daily; guided tours only: apply to the tourist office in the Place des Creneaux at the centre of town; tel: 05 57 55 28 28), in the ancient Place du Marché, was hewn out of solid rock by Benedictine monks between the 9th and 12th centuries. It is an extraordinary achievement, and houses the supposed tomb of the 8th-century eponymous hermit Émilion. Above it stands the

BELOW: rooftops of St-Émilion.

*Charles de Secondat,
Baron de la Brède et
de Montesquieu.*

romantic ruin of the **Trinity Chapel**, the hermit's cave, and the entrance to the **catacombs** that were used as a burial place in the time of St-Émilion. At 1 rue Guadet, a few steps to the east of the place du Marché, is a delightfully old-fashioned shop where macaroons are still baked according to a 17th-century recipe invented by Ursuline nuns.

The southern Gironde

Almost due south of the city of Bordeaux, in the Graves wine region, the **Château de la Brède** ⓬ (open Easter–Nov weekends, July–Sept afternoons; entrance fee; tel: 05 56 20 20 49; www.labrede-montesquieu.com) is reflected in its broad moat. This was the home of the philospher Charles de Secondat, Baron de la Brède et de Montesquieu (1689–1755).

The region to the southeast of Bordeaux, stretching away in a triangle between the Dordogne and Garonne rivers, the **Entre-Deux-Mers**, is perhaps the loveliest in the Gironde, with softly undulating hills and valleys, elegant châteaux and ancient villages. It is renowned for producing excellent white wines.

At the heart of the Entre-Deux-Mers, southeast of Bordeaux, is the village of **La Sauve-Majeure** ⓭. At the centre of this is the miraculously well-preserved 11th-century abbey of **La Grande Sauve** (open daily; closed Mon in winter; entrance fee; tel: 05 56 23 01 55), of key importance once to pilgrims on the road to Santiago de Compostela and a sight that visitors to this area should try not to miss. The "Abbey of the Great Forest" *(Silva Major)* is a haunting and evocative place to visit, best of all for the superb carved stonework in the chancel, depicting fabulous beasts and dramatic scenes from the Old Testament.

BELOW: Château de la Brède.

The delightfully picturesque village of **St-Macaire** ⓮, south of La Sauve-Majeure at the edge of the Garonne River, seems to have changed little since the Middle Ages. The white wine produced here has its own AOC of Côtes de Bordeaux St-Macaire. The ramparts and the huge medieval church are fascinating places to explore, and there is a good choice of excellent local restaurants too.

Château Malrome ⓯ (open daily in summer; spring and autumn Sun and public hols pm only; entrance fee; tel: 05 56 76 44 92) to the northeast is a good place for art lovers: it was the residence of the mother of painter Toulouse-Lautrec (1864–1901) and he often took refuge from Paris here. The apartments are open to the public, including the room where he died in 1901. The artist's tomb is in the church at the nearby village of **Verdelais** ⓰. The novelist and Nobel Prize winner François Mauriac (1885–1970) adored his native Gironde. His former country house, **Malagar** (open June–Sept Wed–Mon; Oct–May Wed–Sun; entrance fee; tel: 05 57 98 17 17), near Verdelais, is now a museum full of his souvenirs.

A few minutes drive to the southwest is the tiny wine region of **Sauternes** and **Barsac**, two names renowned for their sweet white dessert wines. The most famous domaine here, the beautiful renaissance **Château d'Yquem** ⓱ (tel: 05 57 98 07 07; www.chateau-yquem.fr), requires prospective visitors to make postal applications at least one month in advance.

A satisfying alternative is the 17th-century **Château de Malle** (guided tours Apr–Oct; entrance fee; tel: 05 56 62 36 86), west of the small town of Langon. Its apartments and Italianate gardens are the last word in baroque luxury, and the wine (*second cru classé*) is deliciously rich. To the south of Langdon is the fine 14th-century **Château de Roquetaillade**, embellished by the architect Viollet-le-Duc in the 19th century. ❑

Map on page 122

"Happy the people whose annals are boring to read."
– MONTESQUIEU

BELOW: Château de Roquetaillade.

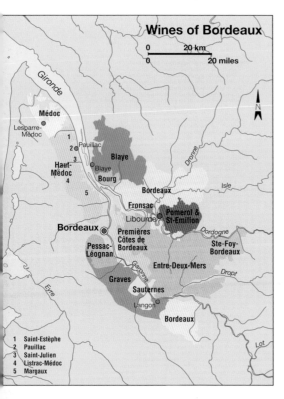

Wines of Bordeaux

0 — 20 km
0 — 20 miles

N

Gironde

Médoc

Lesparre-Médoc

1 Pauillac
2
3
Haut-Médoc
Blaye
Blaye
Bourg

4
5

Bordeaux

Fronsac
Libourne
Pomerol & St-Emilion

Isle

Dordogne

Bordeaux

Premières Côtes de Bordeaux
Pessac-Léognan

Ste-Foy-Bordeaux

Entre-Deux-Mers

Dropt

Graves
Garonne

Sauternes

Langon

Bordeaux

Eyre

Dronne

Lot

1 Saint-Estèphe
2 Pauillac
3 Saint-Julien
4 Listrac-Médoc
5 Margaux

THE DORDOGNE

With its thick woods and beckoning rivers, quaint villages and charming market towns amid fertile fields and vineyards, the Dordogne is the quintessence of rural France

Map on page 134

Henry Miller, the North American writer, left no doubt about his feelings for the Dordogne: "Just to glimpse the black, mysterious river at Domme from the beautiful bluff at the edge of the town is something to be grateful for all one's life." The fascination that the Dordogne has always held for visitors is largely due to its diversity: no other part of provincial France offers such an extraordinary variety of sights for the tourist.

Châteaux, caves with prehistoric art and Roman remains abound in its noble, rugged landscape laced with broad and peaceful rivers. Add the simple fact that the Périgord (to give the Dordogne its traditional name) is a gastronomic heaven upon earth, and it is no surprise that the area has long been the favourite destination for many thousands of tourists. Above Périgueux, the green and wooded region known as the Périgord Blanc is pierced by the valleys of the Dronne and Isle rivers. Its landscape is for the most part a patchwork of heavily cultivated farmland and dramatic forests of oak and chestnut.

Périgueux and the north

Périgueux ❶ is the capital of the Dordogne and stands almost at its centre. It is an ancient and beautiful city, with some fine archaeological remains dating from the Roman occupation of Gaul. The most impressive of these is the **Tour de Vésone**, a 2nd-century AD temple that is dedicated to the goddess Vesunna. She was the guardian of the tribes known to the Romans as Petrocorii, from which the city derives its name. The temple has a fine circular tower and is set in an attractive garden.

Next door is the new **Musée Gallo-Romain** (open July–Aug daily; Sept–June closed Mon; entrance fee; tel: 05 53 05 65 65), a modern structure designed by French architect Jean Nouvel to showcase the excavated Roman villa of Vesunna and its precious wall paintings. A series of walkways reveal the villa, and archaeological artefacts explain the history and lives of its Roman inhabitants.

Near the church of St-Étienne stand the remains of **Les Arènes**. This was a 1st-century amphitheatre, formerly the scene of brutal "games" and human sacrifice. Nearby are extensive sections of the **Gallo-Roman wall** that surrounded the settlement, including **La Porte Normande**, a beautifully preserved Roman gateway dating from the same period.

The **Église de St-Étienne-de-la-Cité** was built in the 12th century on the site of an ancient temple dedicated to Mars. It was St Front who dedicated the building to the martyr Stephen, and it was the first Christian church in the city. The **Cathédrale St-Front**, 300 metres/yards to the east of St-Étienne along the ancient

PRECEDING PAGES: canoeing on the Dordogne. **LEFT:** Cathédrale St-Front, Périgueux. **BELOW:** woman with Périgord ham.

Traditional basket-making is still practised in the Périgord region.

rue des Farges, is an enormous building topped by no fewer than five cupolas, and although heavily restored in the 19th century, makes an unforgettable impression upon visitors. Its vast, bare interior conceals some magnificent paintings and carvings, many taken from other churches.

The **Musée du Périgord** (open Wed–Mon; closed public holidays; entrance fee; tel: 05 53 06 40 70) in the Cours Tourny is another essential destination for anyone interested in the region's history, with rooms devoted to prehistory (don't miss the mammoth tusks), and Roman and medieval artefacts (including some exquisite jewellery, sculptures and pictures).

A short walk back along the Rue des Farges, the **Musée Militaire** (open July–Aug daily; Sept–June afternoons only; entrance fee; tel: 05 53 53 47 36) is an impressive collection of some 10,000 weapons and uniforms from the Middle Ages to the present day. Around the Cathedral are many ancient streets and alleyways to explore, with all manner of traditional and exotic restaurants and cafés for the hungry tourist.

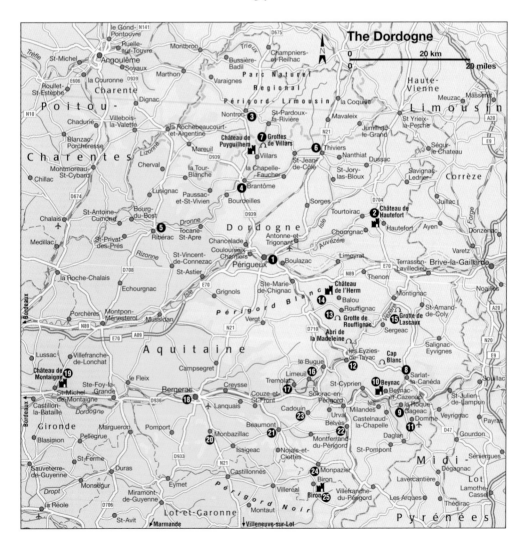

Just over 20 km (12 miles) to the east of Périgueux stands the **Château de Hautefort** ❷ (open Apr–Oct daily; Sun afternoons only; entrance fee; tel: 05 53 50 51 23), one of the most magnificent homes in Southwest France. It was built in the 17th century for a wealthy *seigneur* (lord) and remains in private hands today. Inside, the château has a fine collection of pictures, furniture and tapestries. The gorgeous formal gardens fully merit their classification as an historical monument in themselves.

The town of **Nontron** ❸ is some 44 km (27 miles) north of Périgueux, and is set among attractive lakes that provide ideal sites for a picnic. It stands high up on a rock fortified by massive ramparts. Sadly the Château de Nontron is now closed, having been the victim of a massive burglary of its entire collection, including a museum of antique dolls and toys. Such thefts are an increasingly common problem in France, with its many rich repositories of art and antiques.

A short drive south is the delightful medieval town of **Brantôme** ❹, with a remarkable and ancient **abbey** founded by Charlemagne (742–814). With its soaring campanile, this is one of the most elegant medieval and Renaissance buildings in the Dordogne, complete with caves used by the monks as kitchens and cellars. The town sits on a bend of the Dronne, and a stroll along the riverside here is a fascinating experience. Boat trips are also available. The pretty village of **Bourdeilles**, its château packed with a remarkable collection of furniture, is only 10 km (6 miles) downriver.

To the southwest, the little town of **Ribérac** ❺ has one of the most important markets in the region, which is at its busiest on Fridays. Ribérac appears to have changed little since King Charles IX and Catherine de Medici enjoyed a stop here in the 16th century. Northeast of Brantôme is **Thiviers** ❻, a prosperous and pretty village where Jean-Paul Sartre spent his early childhood. The medieval church here is outstanding, with a collection of superb Romanesque statuary. There is also an intriguing little museum of foie gras and truffles, the **Maison de l'Oie et du Canard** (open July–Aug daily; Sept–June closed Sun; entrance fee; tel: 05 53 55 12 50).

A short distance north of the town of the same name are the **Grottes de Villars** ❼ (open Apr–Oct daily; entrance fee; tel: 05 53 54 82 36), with some impressive stalactites, and paintings more than 17,000 years old; watch out for the picture of the galloping blue horse. Nearby is the **Château de Puyguilhem** (open daily; closed Jan; entrance fee; tel: 05 53 54 82 18), a Renaissance masterpiece that fell into disrepair but was carefully restored after World War II. Like most of the châteaux of the Loire, Puyguilhem was essentially a residence rather than a stronghold. Inside are some superb Aubusson tapestries and fine furniture. The great hall on the first floor has an exquisite carved frieze depicting the Labours of Hercules, and several fireplaces that are carved with exceptional beauty.

Sarlat and the eastern Dordogne

The eastern side of the Dordogne, where it borders on the *départements* of Limousin and the Lot, is the Périgord Noir, which gets its name from the thick and

 Map on page 134

TIP

Cycling is an ideal way to explore the woods and villages around Ribérac. Bicycles can be hired at 19 rue Jean-Moulin.

BELOW: gardens of the Château de Hautefort.

Gosling in a field in the Dordogne.

shady woods that darken the landscape and line the valleys of the Dordogne and Vézère rivers. It is also the region most thickly clustered with interesting and historic sights for visitors to enjoy.

**Sarlat **, some 40 km (25 miles) to the southeast of Périgueux, is one of the most famous and fascinating of them all. An ugly main street (rue de la République, known locally as the Traverse) was driven through Sarlat in the 19th century to ease traffic congestion, but the rest of the little town is one of the most perfectly preserved in France. Parts of it may even look too good to be true, almost like the set for a costume drama, but Sarlat-la-Canéda (to give it its full name) is a thriving commercial centre, and heavily dependent upon tourism.

The **Cathédrale St-Sacerdos** (dedicated to the saint born here about AD 515 and later bishop of Sarlat) dominates the town centre. The present structure dates from the 16th and 17th centuries, and is at the centre of an interesting complex of buildings. Facing the entrance to the south is the **Ancien Évêché**, formerly the bishop's palace, now a theatre, designed in Florentine style and constructed in the 16th century by an Italian bishop of Sarlat. On the opposite side is a sumptuous Renaissance townhouse, the **Maison de La Boétie**, birthplace of the political writer Étienne de La Boétie in 1530.

Sarlat's strangest building stands behind the east end of the cathedral in the old cemetery. The **Lanterne des Morts** (Lantern of the Dead) is a domed stone tower built at the end of the 12th century. What it was for, no-one knows; there is no access to the circular room on its first floor, and even from the outside the narrow windows are too small for a man to penetrate. It is an imposing structure, with an ossuary in the basement from which it derives its name, and the mystery only adds to its attraction. A little to the north of the cemetery is a very grand building: the **Présidial** was built in 1552 by Henri II as the local seat of royal justice, and is now in private ownership.

BELOW: Place des Oies in Sarlat.

La Place de la Liberté is the town's main square where there are lots of cafés and where Sarlat's famous market is held, its stalls groaning with truffles, walnuts and foie gras – all the riches of the region. Nearby is **Place des Oies** (Goose Square) where a goose fair is held throughout the winter. **Rue de la Liberté** is the main shopping street.

The tiny village of **La Roque-Gageac ❾**, 8 km (5 miles) south of Sarlat, nestles on the banks of the Dordogne River beneath a lowering cliff. This is an enchanting place in which to stop and relax, and there are boat trips available, too.

Approximately 8 km (5 miles) downstream, standing high above the river, the forbidding **Château de Beynac ❿** (open daily; entrance fee; tel: 05 53 29 50 40) dominates the landscape. Beynac was originally one of the four baronies of Périgord, and at the end of the 12th century England's King Richard the Lionheart presented it to one of his courtiers, a brutal ruffian named Mercadier who laid waste the surrounding countryside in order to fill English coffers with gold. Though the castle was sacked by Simon de Montfort in the 13th century, it remained in French hands throughout the Hundred Years' War (1337–1453); today it is a fascinating place to visit.

The castle has a formidable adversary just across the river. This is the **Château de Castelnaud** (open daily; entrance fee; tel: 05 53 31 30 00), which was an English stronghold during the Hundred Years' War. Before then it was a Cathar castle, and woe betide any Catholic who fell into the hands of the Lord of Castelnaud. Later on the château became a refuge for Huguenots after the St Bartholomew's Day Massacre, and then fell into decline. Now open to the public, the castle provides superb views over the river from the terrace, and there are interesting video displays demonstrating the art of medieval warfare.

Some 6 km (4 miles) west along the riverbank from here, the fairytale **Château des Milandes** (closed Nov–Mar; otherwise open daily; entrance fee; tel: 05 53 59 31 21; www.milandes.com) has an intriguing story to tell. Originally built in the 13th century by the Lord of Castelnaud as a gift for his wife, after World War II it was bought in a dilapidated condition by the North American cabaret artiste Josephine Baker. She spent every centime she had on restoring it and converting it into a home for what she called her "rainbow tribe" – her many adopted children – but sank hopelessly into debt and was forced to leave. Part of Les Milandes is now an exhibition devoted to the star. There is also a wax works museum, and there are demonstrations of falconry at certain times.

The fortified town of **Domme** ⑪ is, like Sarlat, a miracle of survival and restoration, an exquisite balance between art and nature and known as the "Acropolis of the Périgord Noir". It was fortified against the English forces by Philippe III of France in 1281; it is built on the edge of a high precipice overlooking the Dordogne River and beyond. To say that the view is spectacular is something of an understatement. Its walls have three massive gateways, the main one being the imposing **Porte des Tours**. The central square (Domme is

Map on page 134

Josephine Baker spent many years restoring Château de Les Milandes.

BELOW: setting out from La Roque-Gageac.

When the first examples of prehistoric art were discovered in the late 19th century most experts dismissed them as forgeries. The artistic skill evident on cave walls contradicted the very notion of "primitive" man. Only when similar works of art had been found in caves as far apart as Southwest France and Northern Spain did the evidence of their authenticity become overwhelming.

BELOW: the valley of the River Vézère.

still only a village of 1,000 inhabitants) houses the entrance to some fascinating **caves**, replete with stalactites (closed weekends Nov–Mar; otherwise open daily; entrance fee; tel: 05 53 31 71 00).

Approximately 20 km (12 miles) northwest of Domme and across the river, the town of **Les Eyzies-de-Tayac** is an essential visit for anyone interested in prehistory; it is the place where Cro-Magnon man was discovered in 1868. Also here is the **Musée National de la Préhistoire**, housed in the château (tel: 05 53 06 45 45; closed Tues; entrance fee). The collections and displays here are probably unrivalled; there can be nowhere else in the world so well equipped to give visitors a real understanding of the life and development of early man.

On the edge of Les Eyzies, on the road towards Sarlat, is the cave of **Font-de-Gaume** (open Sun–Fri; afternoons only in winter; advance booking essential; entrance fee; tel: 05 53 06 86 00), containing the most important prehistoric paintings in France after Lascaux, and one of the few where the original paintings are still visible.

Another important cave, the **Grotte de Rouffignac** (open Apr–Oct daily; entrance fee; tel: 05 53 05 41 71), lies 10 km (6 miles) to the north of Les Eyzies, just off the road to the village of Rouffignac. Visitors here travel about a mile into the cave in pitch darkness on a small train to see some extraordinary carved and painted likenesses of mammoths, bison and horses. There is also a souvenir shop, and there are great places for a picnic in the woodland surrounding the entrance.

Outside the village of **Balou**, 8 km (5 miles) northwest of here, stands a sinister ruin. This is the **Château de l'Herm** (open July–Sept daily; Sun afternoons only; entrance fee), the scene of some brutal murders in the 16th century, which eventually led to this fine, moated, Renaissance manor house being abandoned and left to decay. The château is well worth a visit to see what remains of its exquisite architecture – and for its spooky atmosphere. The neighbouring farm sells very good home-made foie gras.

Some 20 km (12 miles) east of here is the little town of **Montignac**, the northernmost point of the Périgord Noir, which has prospered greatly since four boys looking for their lost dog stumbled upon the extraordinary cave paintings of nearby Lascaux in autumn 1940.

The original caves at **Lascaux** ⓕ (now known as Lascaux I, *see pages 144–45*) have been closed to the public since 1963 because of deterioration. But in the 1980s an exact replica, **Lascaux II** (obtain tickets from the tourist information office in Montignac; open daily; closed Jan; booking advisable; entrance fee; tel: 05 53 51 96 23), was constructed nearby. The paintings in it were recreated using the same materials and techniques as the originals. Lascaux may be only a copy of the real thing but a visit remains a stunning experience: the famous **Hall of the Bulls** will still take your breath away.

A short drive to the southwest, where the Vézère and Dordogne rivers meet, is the fortified town of **Limeuil** ⓖ, originally a Gallo-Roman fort, which was later captured by the English in the late 12th century. Its impressive ramparts and gateways are still identifiable, and the view is magnificent. Boat trips and canoeing are available at the old port.

Close by is the pretty village of **Trémolat** ⓗ, which the director Claude Chabrol used as the setting for his 1969 film *Le Boucher,* and where the Dordogne River makes a spectacular loop. The fortified 12th-century church here is a marvel, its interior walls painted with late medieval frescoes.

Map on page 134

IL YA DES GENS QUI FERAIENT N'IMPORTE QUOI POUR POUVOIR RIEN FAIRE

"Some people would do anything in order to do nothing."

BELOW: visitors in Lascaux II.

Bergerac and the West Dordogne

The western side of the Dordogne, the region around **Bergerac ⓲**, presents a gentler landscape than elsewhere. A high proportion of the land here is arable, producing substantial crops of tobacco, grapes, maize and other cereals. The busy town of Bergerac, set in the broad valley of the Dordogne River, is a thriving centre of trade in the agricultural produce of the region, as its imposing commercial buildings show.

The old quarter of town, down near the old port, is the site of the most interesting buildings, such as the **Cloître des Recollets**, a romantic convent built over the centuries in many different styles. It houses the **Maison des Vins** (open summer daily, rest of year closed Sun and Mon; entrance fee; tel: 05 53 63 57 56).

Bergerac is the capital of the French tobacco industry and the **Musée du Tabac** (place du Feu; closed Sun am and Mon; entrance fee), in the elegant 17th-century Maison Peyrarède, presents a fascinating survey of the evolution of tobacco smoking, beginning with its introduction to Europe from South America. The collection features a huge variety of snuff boxes and pipes including Amerindian peace pipes. There are also displays on the cultivation of tobacco in the Bergerac region. Also worth visiting is the **Musée du Vin et de la Batellerie** (5 rue des Conférences; closed Mon; entrance fee; tel 05 53 57 80 92) which explains the history of river transport and wine traffic on the Dordogne.

West of Bergerac is the **Tour de Montaigne ⓳** (open July–Aug daily; Sept–June closed Mon and Tues; entrance fee; tel: 05 53 58 63 93), the home of the writer Michel de Montaigne *(see box opposite)*. It was badly damaged by fire in the 19th century, but has since been carefully restored. The magnificent library in which Montaigne wrote his *Essays* fortunately escaped damage.

Bergerac's "most famous son", the swashbuckling, long-nosed philosopher Cyrano de Bergerac, in reality has no connection with the place except for the shared name. That doesn't stop the town trading on the bogus association, with a statue of Cyrano standing in the place de la Myrpe.

BELOW:
tobacco fields
near Bergerac.

The southern Dordogne

The south of the region, with one or two exceptions, is the area least visited by tourists. This is strange, for it is no less fascinating and beautiful than the better-known parts described above, though the scenery is on the whole less dramatic. Gently rolling hills and valleys are scattered with woodland, crops and pasture: this is ideal walking country, and there is much to explore.

Across the river to the south of Bergerac is **Monbazillac ㉔**, famous for its romantic **château** (open daily mid-Feb–mid-Jan; entrance fee; tel: 05 53 61 52 52) and even more so for its sweet white wine that is the classic accompaniment to foie gras. The château is also home to the most important wine cooperative of the area, a perfect setting in which to taste the different types of the region.

The massive defences at **Beaumont ㉑**, about 30 km (19 miles) east of Monbazillac, were built in the late 13th century on the orders of the English King Edward I. Even more impressive here is the huge fortified church, whose west wall is of a less war-like cast than the other three and is decorated with delicate Gothic ornament.

Belvès ㉒, another 30 km (19 miles) to the east, is a beautiful fortified town perched on a rocky outcrop above the Nauze River. Its castle has a 12th-century keep, and there are many lovely houses of great antiquity. Beneath its walls are cave-dwellings that were in use until well into the Middle Ages. There is an excellent market here on Saturday, which in autumn specialises in walnuts, mostly for the wholesale trade.

The sleepy village of **Cadouin ㉓**, 12 km (7½ miles) northwest of Belvès, is worth a visit. The lay settlement here grew up around its important monastic

> Map on page 134

"As if to drive a final nail into the coffin of English puritan objections to good wine, it is this Protestant château that today houses the wine tasting centre of the Dordogne's largest cave coopérative."

> – JAMES BENTLEY ON MONBAZILLAC

BELOW: Michel de Montaigne.

MICHEL DE MONTAIGNE

One of France's greatest writers, Michel Eyquem de Montaigne (1533–92), was born and died in the château at St-Michel-de-Montaigne. Even as a boy he was something of an intellectual heavyweight: until the age of six he spoke only Latin. He went on to study law, and later spent some years as a city councillor in Bordeaux, eventually becoming its mayor in 1581.

On the early death of his two older brothers, Montaigne succeeded to the family estate and spent the rest of his life there, writing the *Essays* for which he is best remembered. Although he meant the word "*essai*" in the sense of "attempts" (as in "trying out" ideas), he is regarded as having created the literary form of the essay.

As a writer, Montaigne has no equivalent in the English language and is venerated in France with the reverence reserved for giants such as Socrates or Shakespeare (the latter, his contemporary, read him in translation).

His moral *Essays* are by turns wise, trenchant, funny and often fearlessly sceptical of the Catholic Church ("Our religion is meant to eliminate vices; instead it disguises them, nurtures them, and feeds them!"). He was a passionate individualist. "The greatest thing in the world," he wrote, "is to know how to be oneself."

Map
on page
134

TIP

If you're visiting the
Dordogne in late
summer or early
autumn, pack a field
guide to mushrooms
as the woods abound
with cèpes and
chanterelles.

BELOW: truffle
experts at work.

centre, and nothing much appears to have changed since then. The former **Cistercian Abbey** is now open to visitors (open mornings only for guided tours; closed Tues; entrance fee) and the adjacent church, built of glowing yellow stone, contains a 15th-century stone Virgin with a subtle, Gioconda-like smile.

At the back of the church is an enchanting museum, the **Musée du Vélocipède**, devoted to the history of the bicycle; among others it includes the bicycle that once belonged to Jules Verne (open daily; entrance fee; tel: 05 53 63 46 60).

Monpazier ㉔, about 15 km (9 miles) south of here along the D2, is another perfectly preserved medieval *bastide* town built by Edward I of England, and is perhaps the finest of them all. Except for a couple of later houses, its magnificent market square, the **Place des Cornières**, appears not to have changed over the past 700 years. One feature in Monpazier is its narrow alleyways that were built into the medieval plan as fire-breaks. The adjacent lofty church is of white stone: a building of simple and haunting elegance. Monpazier is a popular tourist centre, and accordingly has numerous restaurants.

One candidate for the title of the finest castle in the Dordogne is the **Château de Biron ㉕** (closed Mon, winter closed Fri and Sat; entrance fee; tel: 05 53 63 13 39), 8 km (5 miles) south of Monpazier. It was built originally in the 11th century as a fortress, but rebuilt in several different styles over the centuries. It remained in the same family for no fewer than 24 generations, until just before World War II. To visit this remarkable building, complete with a 24-metre (80-ft) long kitchen and a torture chamber, is to step back in time. The view from the terrace is splendid: it includes Monpazier, which also belonged to the lords of Biron. ❑

Black Diamonds

It may only be a dark-coloured fungus, but Périgord's most famous crop, the truffle, holds an almost mystical allure for anyone of a culinary bent. "If you love her, pay her ransom regally, or leave her alone," wrote Colette. A local saying puts the warning more strongly: "Those who wish to lead virtuous lives had better abstain."

In *The Cooking of Southwest France*, Paula Wolfert describes the sensation of tasting one for the first time: "I felt at one with nature, that my mouth was filled with the taste of the earth. There was a ripeness, a naughtiness, something beyond description. A gastronomic black diamond, it was utter luxury and earthiness combined."

Périgord remains the most famous region in France for truffles, although even here they are now relatively rare and hard to find. Small underground mushrooms *(tuber melanosporum)* no bigger than a walnut, with a distinctive and penetrating scent, these precious delicacies are hunted like gold by the Périgourdains. They are found mostly under the roots of oak trees, and trained truffle hounds (or pigs) are often used to detect their distinctive aroma and grub them out from a few inches below the surface. An animal skilled at its job will cost a great deal of money; virtually all Périgord truffles on the market are found in the wild. They are in season from September until Christmas.

As recently as 50 years ago, truffles were much more common than they are now. Whole handfuls of them would be roasted in the ashes of a wood fire, much as boy scouts cook potatoes, and eaten with nothing more than a sprinkling of salt. Pesticides and deforestation are largely responsible for the increasing rarity and cost of truffles today.

As well as feasting upon this expensive delicacy in local restaurants, if you find a truffle in a local market you may like to try your hand at cooking it yourself. (Avoid the tinned variety.) Simply wipe the surface of the truffle clean of earth and chop it finely, then mix it in and scramble with some fresh free-range eggs, and a simple camp-fire supper quickly becomes a banquet.

Grated truffles are also good stirred into creamy mashed potatoes, or tossed with a green salad dressed with rich olive oil. Fresh chopped walnuts would be an ideal addition to a salad like this: add a bottle of crisp white wine from nearby Bergerac, and who could ask for anything more?

Colette goes on to give cookery advice of her own: "But, having bought her, eat her on her own, fragrant, coarse-grained, eat her like the vegetable that she is, warm, served in sumptuous portions. She will not give you much trouble; her supreme flavour scorns complexity and complicity... As you crunch this jewel of impoverished lands, imagine, those of you who have never been there, the desolation of its realms. For it kills the wild rose, saps the strength of the oak, and ripens beneath barren rocks..."

"Something so magnificent must, inevitably, corrupt," concludes Paula Wolfert. "Well – truffles will ruin your bank account; as for your virtue, they may ruin that too..." ❑

RIGHT: the ultimate gourmet temptation: a crop of newly harvested truffles.

PREHISTORIC ART OF THE CAVE DWELLER

The ancestral paintings and etchings that adorn the walls of many caves in Southwest France are among the wonders of the world

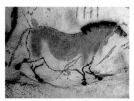

Perhaps 35,000 years ago, early man found parts of Southwest France to be ideal places in which to settle. There was a temperate climate, cliffs and caves for shelter, an abundance of fresh water and thick forests containing the animals he hunted for food. Prolific traces of his existence remain, and the most important of these are the hundreds of paintings he left behind.

These are so marvellously executed and so well preserved that when the first ones were discovered in the 19th century, they were believed to be forgeries. Since then, dating techniques have shown that the oldest paintings appear to come from the region around Les Eyzies, and that the art spread from there to the centre of France and also southwards, into northern Spain. In all, about 100 caves containing prehistoric art have come to light in these regions.

Most of the work was produced between 10,000 and 30,000 years ago, reaching a peak of activity between 15,000 and 17,000 years ago. The most famous example is Lascaux *(see page 139)*, discovered in 1940 by four boys and soon known as the Eighth Wonder of the World.

Exactly why the paintings were produced remains a mystery, though a religious or ritualistic significance appears most likely. The most important paintings were executed predominantly in the most inaccessible places, deep in pitch-black caves and often on the very edge of chasms. A third puzzling fact is why almost all the paintings are of animals: there are very few representations of the human body, and these are crudely drawn by comparison with the sophistication of line and colour in the animal paintings.

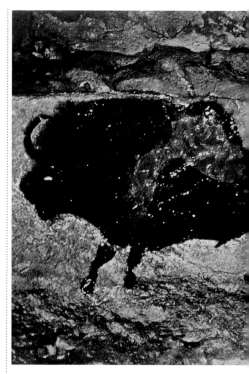

◁ **NIAUX IBEX**
This cave in the Ariège *(see page 261)* is considered to have some of the finest cave art in Europe. Unlike at Lascaux, it is still possible to see the original paintings.

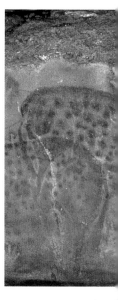

◁ **HENRI BREUIL**
Known in France as the "Father of Prehistory", Abbé Henri Breuil (1877–1961), an expert on Palaeolithic art, wrote over 600 publications on the subject. He was one of the first people to see the paintings of Lascaux and to recognise their significance.

▽ **PECH-MERLE**
The head of this "dotted" horse in the caves at Pech-Merle, in the Lot *(see page 158)*, is formed by the natural shape of the rock. Around the horse are stencils of hands.

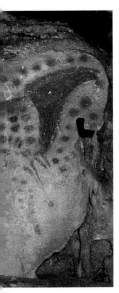

◁ **LASCAUX ANIMALS**
The walls of this famous cave are like a field guide to the animals of prehistoric France. Bulls, aurochs, horses, bears, reindeer, bison, ibexes and rhinoceroses are all depicted.

△ **GARGAS HAND PRINT**
The Grottes de Gargas *(see page 250)* in the Pyrenees are known for their 200 prints of human hands – some of them missing fingers – which are of unknown significance.

△ **HORSE FRIEZE**
The Abri du Cap-Blanc is a small cave in the Dordogne containing a carved relief frieze of horses which makes use of the natural contours of the rock.

▷ **LAUSSEL VENUS**
This female figure holding the horn of an animal in her right hand was carved from limestone around 22,000 years ago, possibly as a symbol of fertilty.

TECHNIQUES OF THE CAVE ARTISTS

The artists would have had to work by artificial light, most probably a torch or lamp burning animal fat, held by an assistant. They learned how to exploit the natural contours of the chosen surface to accentuate the animals' shapes, and used for the most part three different techniques of applying paint. A pencil of pigment or a finger was used for line drawing; balls of hair or fibre filled in the colours; while larger areas were shaded with a hollow bone used as a spray. Outlines were also sometimes carved into the rock. For their subjects (generally bears, bison, horses, bulls and deer, though there are others), the painters had three basic colours at their disposal. Black came mostly from manganese oxide and sometimes from charcoal; red and ochre from mixtures of iron oxides; and white from either haematite or kaolin. With such basic equipment at their disposal, masterpieces like the Great Bull at Lascaux are even more of a testament to the genius of the first artists.

THE LOT

Map on page 150

One of France's most important shrines, two extraordinary caves, an impregnable bridge, quaint medieval villages, formidable châteaux – all are contained within the territory of old Quercy

hree slow, green rivers flow through the *département* of the Lot: the Dordogne (to the north), the Lot itself (in the south) and its tributary, the less well-known Célé. All three form picturesque valleys as they wander and loop eccentrically between densely wooded slopes, limestone cliffs and fertile riverbank farmland. Bridging points and defensive positions are patrolled by medieval towns, imposing châteaux and seigneurial villages. "It is not me that has chosen to live here, it is the land that has chosen me," said the film director Louis Malle of the Lot.

Only when you climb out of the valleys do you realise that the Lot is a transitional zone between the Massif Central and the Aquitaine Basin. The highlands of central France have not quite been left behind: between the seductive river valleys are limestone *causses*: the Causse de Martel north of the Dordogne, the Causse de Gramat (between the Dordogne and the Lot) and the Causse de Limogne (south of the Lot). These great, dry plateaux are mostly given over to sheep-rearing. Although undeniably dreary in places, in others they have impressive natural features, such as the caves of Padirac and the gorge of the Alzou River, which provides a unique emplacement for Rocamadour *(see page 151)*.

Like the Dordogne to the north, this is an area with a prehistoric presence attested to by cave paintings, most remarkably those at Pech-Merle. Later, the industrious and resilient tribe of the Cadurces (or Cadourques) held out obstinately against the Romans as the invaders swept through Gaul. Much later, in the Middle Ages, the Albigensian Crusade, the Hundred Years' War and the Wars of Religion ravaged the area.

PRECEDING PAGES: farmland in the Lot valley near Cajarc. **LEFT:** ballooning over Rocamadour. **BELOW:** boating on the river at Cahors.

The Life of Quercy

Until France was divided up into *départements* in the wake of the Revolution, this area formed part of the ancient administrative district of Quercy (which in its entirety covered the areas occupied by the present-day *départements* of the Lot and Tarn-et-Garonne). The name Quercy is still often used, sometimes synonymously with the Lot *département*.

There is no large industry to speak of in the Lot. Farming – intensive cultivation wherever possible, rather than the small-scale, traditional variety – and the processing of its products is still a staple of the economy. Flocks of geese yield foie gras and confit. The sheep of the *causses* provide meat and cheese. Orchards of fruit trees in more sheltered places have made the Lot the largest jam-producing area of Europe. In the south there are large vineyards (particularly in the valleys of the Lot and its tributaries) producing the very dark red wine of the Cahors *appellation d'origine contrôlée* (AOC).

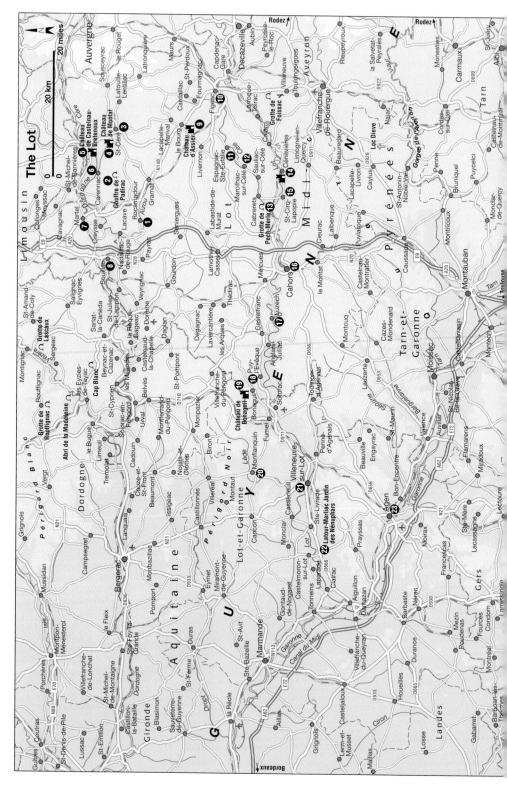

Tourism is also an increasing economic force, especially as communications have improved with the completion of the A20 motorway, bisecting the *département* on its busy way between Toulouse and Northern France. The Lot has also become something of an overspill area for the Dordogne for foreigners and second-home owners.

The Lot flows out of its eponymous *département* into the neighbouring, less definable Lot-et-Garonne, where, as the name suggests, the river ultimately merges with the all-consuming Garonne. The most interesting region to visit here is the fertile, fruit-bearing **Agenais,** particularly famous for its plums.

The ups and downs of Rocamadour

The northern part of the Lot revolves around one sacred spot. **Rocamadour ❶** is France's second most visited place of pilgrimage (after Mont St-Michel) and one of the most extraordinarily sited places in France, its several sanctuaries being built half way up a cliff.

The places of interest at Rocamadour are arranged vertically on a steep slope and you have either to visit them from the top or the bottom. The easiest way to approach them is via **L'Hospitalet**. The site of a hospital founded in the 11th century (of which little remains), L'Hospitalet now acts as a visitors' service centre for Rocamadour. Here you have shops, restaurants, hotels and the tourist information office. This is also the spot to get the famous view of Rocamadour so that you can put the jumble of buildings you are about to see in context.

A road from L'Hospitalet leads to the 19th-century château and a large (free) car park. From here an **inclined lift** (operates daily; fare payable; tel: 05 65 33 67 79) takes you painlessly down to the level of the sanctuaries.

Map on page 150

Divine guidance for finding a hotel from an old tin sign.

BELOW: the Black Madonna of Rocamadour.

THE DRAW OF ROCAMADOUR

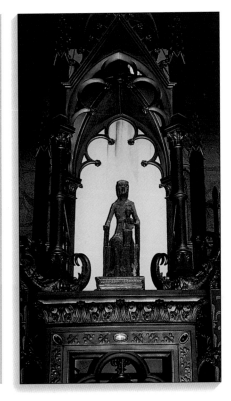

Rocamadour is thought to be named after St Amadour, a mythological hermit who found shelter beneath the rocks of the remote Alzou valley. Since the 15th century it has been believed that St Amadour was actually Zaccheus, husband of Veronica, the woman who wiped the blood and sweat from Christ's face as he walked to Calvary. The couple are said to have fled Palestine and to have reached France by divine guidance. When Veronica died, Zaccheus came here to live as a recluse.

From the 12th century, there were reports of miracles occurring at Rocamadour by the grace of its Black Madonna, and the shrine attracted ever larger crowds of pilgrims, among them many saints and kings. Henry Plantagenet, St Dominic, St Bernard, Philip IV (the Fair) and Louis XI all visited. Rocamadour was at the height of its fame in the 13th century but thereafter fell into decline. The shrine was plundered during the Hundred Years' War and again during the Wars of Religion.

Its churches were rebuilt in the 19th century and it has once again become a place of pilgrimage, although it receives just as many tourists or undecideds as devotees and now includes an infrastructure that takes some of the penitential arduousness out of a visit.

*Monsieur Bibendum
in Rocamadour's
museum of old toys.*

BELOW: the
Parvis des Églises.

That's the easy way, but not the most satisfying. Approaching from the bottom (where there is another car park) and walking up to the sanctuaries gives more of a sense of how it must have been in the Middle Ages.

From the valley floor you come first to **La Cité** – a generous description for what is no more than a road of souvenir shops and restaurants between the two gates of **Porte Basse** and **Porte du Figuier**. Medieval pilgrims probably found a host of sundry, profane entertainments on offer before climbing to the shrine. Modern Rocamadour has several incongruously secular attractions, notably the **Musée du Jouet Ancien** (place Ventadour, outside Porte du Figuier; open daily; entrance fee; tel: 05 65 33 60 75), a museum of old toys.

Beyond the Hôtel de Ville (Town Hall) and near to Porte Hugon, the **L'Escalier des Pèlerins** (Pilgrims' Staircase), a flight of 197 steps, takes off for the sanctuaries above. In the Middle Ages penitents would climb these steps on their knees, wearing only a shirt and with chains wrapped around them. A **lift** (operates daily; fare payable; tel: 05 65 33 62 44) saves the walk, although it seems like cheating for the able-bodied not to walk up the steps, with or without chains on. Towards the top of the staircase you can catch your breath in **rue de la Mercerie**, Rocamadour's oldest street.

Everything of religious importance at Rocamadour is arranged around the **Parvis des Églises**, a small enclosed square. Doors from here lead into the seven sanctuaries, the largest of which is the **Basilique St-Sauveur** (open daily), an 11th–13th-century Romanesque-Gothic church with one wall formed by the bare rock. A door leads from it into the most important sanctuary, the **Chapelle Notre-Dame** (Chapel of Our Lady, or Miraculous Chapel; open daily), Rocamadour's most sacred place, where the diminutive walnut statue of the Black Madonna is

venerated. Above her hangs an iron bell (thought to be 9th-century) which would, allegedly, in less agnostic times ring out by itself to announce miracles.

On the facade of the chapel are the remains of a 13th-century fresco showing the dance of death: three skeletons and their supposed victims. Sticking out of the cliff face above the doorway is Durandal, the sword of Roland (one of Charlemagne's knights), which St Michael miraculously placed here for safe-keeping, far from infidel hands.

The other five sanctuaries off the Parvis – **L'Église St-Amadour** and the chapels of **St-Jean-Baptiste**, **St-Blaise**, **Ste-Anne** and **St-Michel** – are usually kept locked but can be visited on a guided tour (tel: 05 65 33 23 23 or ask at the tourist information office). Also on the Parvis is the **Musée d'Art Sacré** (open June–Aug daily; Sept, Oct, Apr and May Mon–Fri; entrance fee; tel: 05 65 33 23 30), a museum of religious art dedicated to the memory of the composer Francis Poulenc (1899–1963). The exhibits give an inkling of what the sanctuary's treasury must once have contained. See particularly the Limoges enamel-work reliquaries.

The Gouffre de Padirac

With so many hotels and restaurants around it, Rocamadour makes a convenient base for exploring the northern Lot *département,* up to and across the Dordogne. The next most visited sight in the area after Rocamadour is the **Gouffre de Padirac ❷** (open Apr–Oct daily; entrance fee; tel: 05 65 33 64 56). You have to be selective with caves in this region of France or you'd spend most of your time underground, but this one is an exception because of its sheer size and extent. The visit doesn't properly begin until you've made a lengthy trek to the

Map on page 150

Notre-Dame de Rocamadour is one of at least 150 dark-skinned Virgins venerated in France. Some authorities maintain these statues have merely been blackened by candle smoke; others suggest that the images may be the last vestiges of pagan goddess worship.

LEFT: Rocamadour's Pilgrims' Staircase.
BELOW: Gouffre de Padirac.

bottom of an enormous round pothole dripping with foliage. An elegant wrought-iron lift and stair structure has been built on one side of the pothole. Ramps and slippery stairs at the bottom of the lift take you down into the cave proper, 103 metres (338 ft) below ground level. A sinuous tunnel, the Galerie de la Source, leads you past an incongruous shop-counter selling souvenir photographs to departing customers. At last you come to a wharf and board a flat-bottomed boat to be rowed down the Rivière Plane into Lac de la Pluie, passing a huge stalactite called the Grande Pendeloque. Here you disembark and continue the visit on foot down Pas de Crocodile and up steps to Lac Supérieur and the Salle de Grand Dôme, the largest of the chambers in the cave, before returning to the boat and retracing your steps out of the cave.

On the banks of the Dordogne

Several smaller rivers converge on the Dordogne near the town of **St-Céré ❸**, which has a core of old houses and where, it has been said, you always have your "eyes in the air". This comment refers mainly to the Tours de Saint-Laurent, two stray towers left over from the château of the viscounts of Turenne, which preside over the town from a hill top. Not far away are the delightful villages of **Loubressac**, from which on a clear day there are good views over part of the Dordogne valley, and **Autoire**.

Two very different châteaux stand on opposite sides of the Bave River in the Pays de St-Céré. From the outside, the **Château de Montal ❹** (open Apr–Oct Sun–Fri; entrance fee; tel: 05 65 38 13 72), sited on a low wooded hill, looks like a forbidding castle, but another aspect of it is revealed by stepping into the inner courtyard (the *cour d'honneur*), formed by the two wings of the house (the

"The Styx must have been like this ice-dark river; the boatman might easily be Charon; and the French girls crying in delicious terror, 'O mon Dieu! O la la!' in their high treble are like the bird-like twittering of the souls of the dead."

– FREDA WHITE
Three Rivers of France

BELOW: place du Mercadial, St-Céré.

Map on page 150

other two sides of the courtyard were never completed). The facade of the château is a masterpiece of Renaissance decoration with a frieze running above the ground-floor windows. Seven busts on the level of the first floor show members of the Montal family. The main tower, at the junction of the two wings, encloses a Renaissance staircase, a model of its kind.

You wouldn't guess at the tragic history of the building. In 1523 Jeanne de Balsac d'Entraygues, an aristocratic widow, ordered the Château de Montal to be built for her beloved son, Robert, who was fighting in Italy for François I. The château was finished in 1534 but Robert was killed before he could return. The grieving mother had the bleak legend *Plus d'espoir* – "There is no longer hope" – carved on the walls.

Unlike Montal, the **Château de Castelnau-Bretenoux ⑤** (open Apr–Sept daily; Oct–Mar Wed–Mon; guided tour obligatory for the furnished rooms; entrance fee; tel: 05 65 10 98 00) was obviously built not to flatter its owners but as a defensive structure. Despite the name, it is closer to the village of Prud-homat (at the confluence of the Cère and the Dordogne) than to the *bastide* town of Bretenoux. It was built for the powerful barons of Castelnau but given to the Viscount of Turenne in 1184. The oldest surviving part is the keep, which is 13th-century; the rest of the fortifications grew up around it in the Hundred Years' War. Abandoned in the 18th century, ravaged by the Revolution and victim to fire in 1851, it was subsequently restored by the singer Jean Mouliérat.

One of the prettiest villages on the banks of the Dordogne is **Carennac ⑥**, a pleasing jumble of old houses around an old priory. The Île de Calypso in the river is so named because Fénelon (1651–1715), author of *Télémaque* (about the son of Ulysses) spent time at Carennac Priory as a young man.

A late 19th-century owner of the Château de Montal sold off its carved gables and friezes, dispersing them around the world. But in the 1900s a wealthy new owner spent many years and large amounts of money tracing and buying back these treasures to restore the château to its original glory.

BELOW: the historic village of Carennac on the Dordogne.

The 311-metre (1,020-ft) summit of the Puy d'Issolud, 10 km (6 miles) northeast of Martel, is now generally agreed to be the site of Uxellodonum, the fort where the Gauls made their last stand against the invading Roman army under Julius Caesar in 51 BC.

The doorway of the priory church has a sculpted 12th-century Romanesque tympanum but the cloisters were restored in modern times. Carennac's 15th-century château contains the **Maison de la Dordogne Quercynoise** (open Apr–Oct daily; entrance fee; tel: 05 65 10 91 56), an exposition of the Lot's section of the river, the people who live on it and its wildlife.

On the other side of the Dordogne from Carennac is **Martel ❼**, which styles itself as "the town of Seven Towers". Today it is a pleasant enough place with few signs of its former importance apart from these towers and the small cluster of medieval buildings around its 18th-century *halle* (covered market).

The abbey church of **Souillac ❽**, 15 km (9 miles) southwest of Martel, has the interesting remains of its old doorway inside it, including a pillar stunningly carved with snarling animals.

Making a mint in Figeac

There's not much of interest to relieve the landscape of the Causse de Gramat, which separates the Dordogne and Lot valleys, except perhaps the **Château d'Assier ❾** (open July–Aug daily; Sept–June Wed–Mon; entrance fee; tel: 05 65 40 40 99). This was erected between 1520 and 1540 by a Grand Master of Artillery to François I as a large quadrangle of buildings, but only the west wing remains.

Finally, the Route National 140 reaches the handsome town of **Figeac ❿**, which stands on the banks of the Célé River. According to legend, the 8th-century King of Aquitaine, Pepin I, was travelling across Quercy when he saw a flock of doves draw the shape of the cross in the sky. He founded a monastery on the spot beneath this celestial cross. In the 9th century an abbey was built in

BELOW: one of the towers of Martel.
RIGHT: the church in Souillac.

Map on page 150

the same place and Figeac grew up around it. The town prospered in the 11th and 12th centuries, being on the pilgrimage route to Santiago de Compostela and to Rocamadour. In 1302, when the elected merchant consuls who governed it came into conflict with the local abbot, Philip the Fair took the opportunity to add Figeac to the possessions of the French crown.

To appease the townsfolk, Philip granted them the right to mint their own money. The tourist information office is housed in the so-called **Hôtel de la Monnaie**, a restored 13th-century Gothic building, but despite the name the actual mint was elsewhere. The top of the building is a *soleihlo*, an area of open loft characteristic of Figeac architecture, which was used to dry laundry or store vegetables and fruit.

The Hundred Years' War slowed the pace of Figeac's development and its siding with the Calvinists during the Wars of Religion resulted in its fortifications being dismantled. Many of the houses that can be seen today are reconstructions of 14th- and 15th-century stone and half-timbered buildings that survived 19th-century alterations to the town.

A marked walking route, starting from the tourist information office on place Vival, takes you around the highlights of the town centre: Figeac is best taken at a leisurely stroll. The main street of old Figeac is **rue Gambetta**; but the oldest street is **rue Émile Zola**. The **Église St-Sauveur**, parts of which date back to the 11th century, is all that is left of the abbey, the other monastic buildings having disappeared. Since the French Revolution, it has stood on the very secular-sounding place de la Raison. The monastery's former chapterhouse, off the south transept of the church, is now the **Chapelle Notre-Dame-de-la-Pitié**, which is adorned with 17th-century carved, painted wooden panelling.

"It is always a surprise to find degraded modern architecture side by side with an excellent traditional idiom; one would suppose that the architects would revolt at the sight of their own blue-prints and the masons strike rather than build."

– FREDA WHITE
ON FIGEAC,
Three Rivers of France

BELOW:
mural of a medieval village in Figeac.

But it is a combination of old and new that provides Figeac's *pièce de résistance.* The town was the birthplace of Jean-François Champollion, the son of Figeac's first bookshop owner, who eventually deciphered the Rosetta Stone *(see box).* Although the original stone is in the sober confines of the British Museum in London, Figeac has something much better. **Place des Écritures** (near place Champollion) is enclosed by medieval buildings but since 1991 has been paved with an enormous replica of the Rosetta Stone, sculpted in black African granite by Joseph Kossuth. It is best seen from the small garden above the square. Nearby is the **Musée Champollion** (rue des Frères Champollion; open July–Aug daily; Sept–June Tues–Sun; entrance fee; tel: 05 65 50 31 08), which has ancient Egyptian artefacts.

The prehistoric galleries at Pech-Merle were discovered by two youths, aged 15 and 16, in 1922 and the caves opened to the public in 1926. Pech is the French word for the Occitan puèg, *a hill.* Merle *is of unknown origin – it may have been someone's name.*

Pech-Merle

From Figeac to Cahors you have a choice of picturesque river-bank routes: either along the Célé or the Lot. The Célé road leads past the appealing village of **Espagnac-Ste-Eulalie** ⓫, built around a 13th-century priory, and the ruined Benedictine abbey of **Marcilhac-sur-Célé** ⓬.

In the hills above **Cabrerets** is the **Grotte de Pech-Merle** ⓭ (open Easter–Oct and winter by reservation; visit by guided tour only; tel: 05 65 31 27 05; www.quercy.net/pechmerle). The Lot does not have as many painted prehistoric caves as the Dordogne but Pech-Merle counts as one of the special caves of France for its combination of art and natural beauty. The best-known painting in the cave is the frieze of two "dotted" horses, which has several interesting features. The right-hand horse is drawn using a natural shape in the rock. On its back is a red fish – a rare motif in prehistoric art. Around the two horses

BELOW: pondering the inscriptions of the Rosetta Stone.

DECIPHERING THE ROSETTA STONE

The Rosetta Stone, discovered in Egypt by the French in August 1799, proved to be the key to deciphering the ancient Egyptian hieroglyphic writing system that had long baffled Europeans. An irregular block of black basalt, the stone was carved in 196 BC with the same inscription repeated in three writing systems: hieroglyphs, demotic script and Greek.

An English physicist, Thomas Young (1773–1829), was the first to establish that the cartouche (an oval figure drawn around a hieroglyph), which occurs six times on the stone, was the name of Ptolemy V Epiphanes (205–180 BC).

Jean-François Champollion (1790–1832) of Figeac, an expert linguist, built on Young's pioneering work. At the age of 17 he resolved to make the decipherment of the hieroglyphs' code his life's work. With Egypt now in British hands, however, he had to work from copies of the stone rather than the original.

In 1822 he made an important breakthrough when he showed that some of the symbols were mere letters while others stood for syllables (sounds), and that others expressed whole ideas. He also proved that the hieroglyphs on the stone were a translation of the Greek text, not vice versa.

Map
on page
150

are stencilled negative hand prints. Another intriguing drawing is that of "the wounded man" – hard to distinguish unless pointed out by a guide – which shows a human figure apparently wounded by arrows. In the Hall of the Discs, so-named because of circular calcite formations, are a dozen footprints left by a prehistoric adolescent boy. They are known to be genuine because the entrance to the cave was sealed at the end of the last ice age.

There are two other remarkable natural wonders in the cave. The "cave pearls" and "spinning top" both look as though they are man-made but they were formed by sand and gravel particles becoming coated with calcite and polished under water dripping into the cave during heavy rain. In the last part of the cave on the tour, the Combel Gallery, the root of an oak tree descends from the roof to the floor in search of moisture. The tree is still alive and can be seen on the surface (daubed with a white question mark).

The other route between Figeac to Cahors, along the Lot itself, goes through Cajarc and past the 15th–16th-century **Château de Cénevières ⓮** to reach one of the most beautiful villages in France, **St-Cirq-Lapopie ⓯**, a pleasing cluster of old stone houses sited on the top of white cliffs high above the meandering river. There is a splendid view of the valley from the ruined castle at the top of the town (to get there take the path to the right of the town hall).

In June 1950, André Breton – the poet, critic and essayist, best known as the theorist of the Surrealist movement – attended a conference in nearby Cahors and during his visit he disovered St-Cirq-Lapopie. He bought the old inn from the heirs of the painter Henri Martin and from then on spent his summers in the village. In 1966 he was taken ill while staying there and was rushed from St-Cirq-Lapopie to Paris, where he died on 28 September.

The Surrealist André Breton owned a house in St-Cirq-Lapopie.

BELOW:
St-Cirq-Lapopie.

The fortress-bridge

Cahors , built on the inside of a tight loop of the river Lot, was a prosperous university and commercial city in the Middle Ages and the capital of Quercy (the area between the Massif Central and the plains of Aquitaine). It is now the prefecture of the Lot *département*. An influx of commercially savvy Lombards and Templars led to Cahors becoming the banking centre of Europe in the 13th century, lending money to popes and kings. The town duly prospered. Pope John XXII, a native of Cahors, established a university here in 1331, which survived until 1751. Times were not so good during the Hundred Years' War when the city held out for a long time against the English, despite its population being ravaged by the plague.

The republican statesman Léon Gambetta (1838–82) helped bring down Napoleon III and set up the Third Republic in 1870. When Paris was besieged by the Prussians he escaped in a balloon, floating over enemy lines, to organise the French defences.

Its main street, cordoning off the old town (Vieux Cahors), is **boulevard Gambetta**, named after the town's most famous son, statesman Léon Gambetta, who is remembered in street names all over France. In the middle of the old town is the **Cathédrale St-Étienne**, which has Renaissance cloisters. The Romanesque north doorway has a carved tympanum of the Ascension.

The image always associated with Cahors is that of the 14th-century **Pont Valentré**, one of the finest examples of medieval defensive architecture in France. With six Gothic arches, three towers (the central one for observation, the outer ones to control gates and portcullises), honed cutwaters and crenellated walls it is as much a castle as a bridge. Its reputation was enough to deter the English in the Hundred Years' War and discourage Henri IV in 1580 when he besieged Cahors. It has never been tested under attack.

BELOW:
the fortress-bridge
of Pont Valentré
at Cahors.

A legend has it that the architect made a Faustus-like pact with the devil which he then wheedled his way out of. The devil, in frustration, snapped off the top stone of the middle tower. During 19th-century restoration of the bridge the stone was cemented in place and a carved figure of the devil added, but it is difficult to see from below. For the best view of the bridge cross over it from the town to the west (left) bank. Against this bank, upstream from the bridge, is moored an old millboat, the **Moulin à Nef**, which once used the power of the river current to grind grain. Also worth visiting is the **Musée Henri Martin** in the old bishop's palace (rue Emile Zola; open Wed–Mon; entrance fee; tel: 05 65 30 15 13), which as well as local archaeological finds has works by the eponymous 19th-century neo-Impressionist and other regional artists.

Downriver from Cahors

Leaving Cahors behind, the Lot River wanders through the *causses* of Quercy in a series of meanders. **Luzech** straddles the neck of one such meander where only 100 metres (330 ft) of rock keep the river from forming a tear-shaped island out of the Promontoire de la Pistoule. The hill above the town, Impernal, was the site of a Roman city. **Puy l'Évêque** ⓲ is arguably the most picturesque spot on these lower reaches of the Lot.

Away from the river is the **Château de Bonaguil** ⓳ (northeast of Fumel; open daily Feb–Nov, Dec and Jan school hols only; entrance fee; tel: 05 53 71 90 33). This was the last of the great war-minded château-forts to be built in France – as opposed to the effete residential leisure châteaux of later centuries, which were not intended to scare anyone. Its builder, Bérenger de Roquefeuil, wished to deter civil insurrectionists as much as foreign invaders. He was not taking any chances and the castle is unusual in that it was built to deal with the new technology of its day: firearms.

Map on page 150

"I will build a castle that my vile subjects won't be able to attack; nor the English – if they are impudent enough to return, nor the strongest soldiers of the King of France."

– BÉRANGER DE ROQUEFEUIL ON THE CHÂTEAU DE BONAGUIL

BELOW:
Puy l'Évêque, on the lower Lot.

Map on page 150

Roadside sign for the bastide museum in Monflanquin.

BELOW: the Latour-Marliac water-lily garden.
RIGHT: window in Villeneuve-sur-Lot Church.

Bonaguil was never attacked, and it survived in good shape until the Revolution, when it was partially demolished in an attempt to eradicate the old order.

Across country you come to **Monflanquin** ⑳, an attractive 13th-century *bastide* founded in 1256 on a hill above the River Lède by Alphonse of Poitiers, brother of Louis IX. It is arranged around a handsome square, place des Arcades. The most imposing building on this square is the so-called House of the Black Prince, the original use of which is not known. Adjacent to it is the tourist information office, with, above it, the **Musée des Bastides** (open daily; entrance fee; tel: 05 53 36 40 19), explaining the origin and development of these characteristic Southwest towns *(see page 193)*.

Running downhill from the place des Arcades are two medieval alleyways, or *carrétots*. Three recreated medieval gardens can be visited by arrangement with the tourist office.

The Agenais

The *bastide* town of **Villeneuve-sur-Lot** ㉑ was founded in 1253. Its streets still conform to the original grid pattern, and some of them are faced by half-timbered houses. **Place la Fayette**, at the centre, is an arched square. On Wednesday the oldest organic market in France outside Paris is held here.

The town's red-brick church, the **Église Ste-Catherine**, built in 1909 to replace a Gothic predecessor, is oddly oriented north to south. It has restored 14th- and 15th-century stained-glass windows (from the original church) attributed to the school of Arnaud de Moles.

Two city gates, the **Porte de Paris** and **Porte de Pujols**, are all that remain of the ramparts which were dismantled at the end of the 18th century. They stand on either side of the Lot but at some distance from the river. The **Pont des Cieutats** (also known as Pont-Vieux), one of three bridges in town over the Lot, dates from the 13th century. Near Villeneuve is the attractive, medieval hilltop village of **Pujols**.

Further down the Lot is the **Latour-Marliac Jardin des Nénuphars** ㉒ (Le-Temple-sur-Lot; open Mar–Sept daily; entrance fee; tel: 05 53 01 08 05), the oldest water-lily nursery in the world. It was started in 1875 by Joseph Bory Latour-Marliac, the first man to hybridise hardy water lilies (which inspired, among others, the painter Claude Monet).

Agen ㉓, the prefecture of Lot-et-Garonne, lies midway between Bordeaux and Toulouse. It is a centre for vegetables and fruit, especially peaches, Chasselas white grapes and plums (*pruneaux d'Agen* are the best plums of France; dried, they are also the best prunes). The city centre is a collection of uninteresting streets, although there are a few timber-framed houses in rue des Cornières and rue Molinier.

The attraction most worth visiting in Agen is the **Musée des Beaux Arts** (place Docteur Pierre Esquirol; open Wed–Mon; entrance fee; tel: 05 53 69 47 23), which is housed in 16th- and 17th-century mansions. Its best-known exhibit is the Venus de Mas, a 1st-century AD Greek marble statue, but it also has some other good archaeological pieces and a handful of paintings by Goya. ❑

AVEYRON AND THE CÉVENNES

Map on page 168

Impressive natural features – rock formations and deep gorges separated by bleak, grand plateaux – are what attract visitors to this remote but beautiful corner of Southwest France

Sandwiched between the Massif Central, the Lot valley and the plains of Hérault and the Languedoc, are four high limestone plateaux, the Grands Causses: Causse de Sauveterre, Causse Méjean (the "middle" plateau), Causse Noir (named "black" after its forests) and, in the south, the largest of them, the Causse du Larzac. These flat, often featureless, expanses of land were stripped of their tree cover by grazing in the Middle Ages; they can be fiercely hot in summer and freezing cold in winter, with strong winds blowing at any time.

The sparse vegetation makes the *causses* natural country for sheep, which traditionally have provided wool, skins (used in glove-making in Millau), droppings to fertilise the fields and milk for cheese – outstandingly, the blue cheese of Roquefort. Transhumance is still practised by some farmers, with flocks herded along trails in June to the highland pastures for summer grazing until the cold weather begins in September.

Rainwater easily erodes the dolomitic limestone to leave extraordinary rock formations above ground, notably those of Montpellier le Vieux, and water seeps quickly out of sight down swallow holes to gouge out marvellous caverns such as that of Aven Armand.

But what makes the Grands Causses particularly appealing are the spectacular gashes in the landscape which separate them. Just as you are getting used to the almost monotonous lack of relief and the unchanging horizon, the road you are travelling on suddenly dips into one of the immense gorges that separate the *causses* one from another, most famously the Gorges du Tarn. Much of the life of the Grand Causses region congregates in the villages in these sheltered corridors.

East and west of the *causses*

The Grands Causses are bordered to the east by the granite and schist mountains of the Cévennes (in the sparsely populated *département* of Lozère) where slopes are often cloaked in chestnut woods, which until modern times provided the hardy inhabitants with their staple food. Together, the Causses and the Cévennes have become a great outdoor leisure centre, with marked walking trails through beautiful countryside and canoes for hire on the river banks. The roads and towns in the gorges can get choked with tourists in summer, but once you get up onto the *causses* you can usually get away from the crowds.

To the west of the Grands Causses, the landscape softens as the River Lot flows out of Aveyron *département* past several attractive old towns and, in the hills above, the preserved medieval shrine of Conques.

PRECEDING PAGES:
La Couvertoirade.
LEFT: the Vieux Palais and Pont Vieux, Espalion.
BELOW: canoeists on the Tarn.

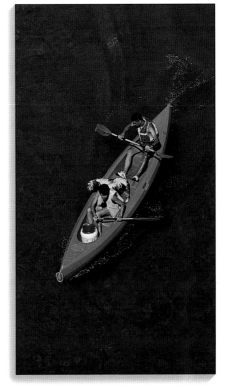

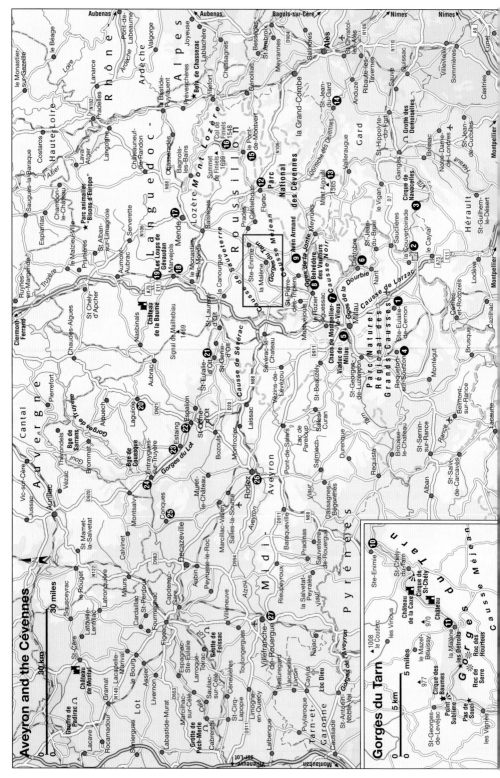

Aveyron and the Cévennes

Gorges du Tarn

The Templars of Larzac

Map on page 168

Approaching this region from the Languedoc and the Mediterranean coast you come first to the Causse du Larzac, between Millau and Lodève, part of which came into the possession of the Knights Templar in the 12th century. The Templar Order was founded in 1119, during the First Crusade. Their headquarters was at **Ste-Eulalie de Cernon ❶**. When the Templar Order was suppressed in 1312 their lands passed to the Knights Hospitallers. Their Commandery, altered later by their successors, can be seen.

La Couvertoirade ❷ is the best preserved Templar town. If you are driving, park outside the town and enter via the main gate, the Portail d'Amont. Steps to your right, beside a Renaissance house, lead up to a parapet around the ramparts (open daily; entrance fee; part of the walk is unprotected and not suitable for small children). The churchyard here contains some unusual gravestones.

Stone face on the wall of the church at La Couvertoirade.

On the doors of some houses of La Couvertoirade, and indeed all over the Grand Causses, you will see pinned up a dried specimen of thistle, *Carlina accanthifolia*. It acts as a kind of barometer, its centre closing when the air is moist and rain expected and opening up on the approach of fine weather.

Southeast of La Couvertoirade is the **Cirque de Navacelles ❸**, a natural bowl in the landscape between the Causse du Larzac and, to the north, the much smaller Causse de Blandas. It was created by a wide and deep meander of the River Vis, since cut off by the River Vis. A road winds down into the *cirque,* to the village of Navacelles, and out again on the other side. There are spectacular viewpoints from the rim of the valley to both north and south.

Roquefort-sur-Soulzon ❹, at the base of a cliff on the southwestern edge of the Causse du Larzac, is the source of France's famous ewe's milk blue

BELOW: the Cirque de Navacelles.

cheese *(see panel below)*. The caves of two cheese-producing companies can be visited: **Caves Société** (open daily; entrance fee; tel: 05 65 58 58 58; www.roquefort-societe.com) and **Papillon** (open daily; entrance free; tel: 05 65 58 50 08). Visitors are advised to wear warm clothes.

Millau ❺, the headquarters of the Parc Naturel Régional des Grands Causses (71 boulevard de l'Ayrolle; tel: 05 65 61 35 50), is traditionally a glove-making town, using the skins from the sheep raised for wool and cheese. The **Musée de Millau** (Hôtel de Pégayrolles, place Foch; open Apr–Sept daily; Oct–Mar Mon–Sat; entrance fee; tel: 05 65 59 01 08) has exhibitions on glove making and of Gallo-Roman pottery from the nearby archaeological site of **Fouilles de la Graufesenque** (open daily for guided tours; entrance fee), one of the main industrial potteries of the Roman empire. Millau is also the location of a massive engineering project, the **viaduc de Millau**, the last link in the A75 *autoroute* linking Clermont Ferrand and Montpellier, due to be completed in 2005. The spectacular viaduct (designed by British architect Norman Foster and engineer of Pont de Normandie, Michel Virlogeux) will be 2,460-metres (8,000-ft) long and span the Tarn valley at an astonishing height of 343 metres (1,125 ft). It will be the biggest bridge in the world with support towers taller than the Eiffel Tower. Weekend visits to the site by minibus are arranged by the Office de Tourisme in Millau (tel: 05 65 60 02 42).

Causse Noir and Causse de Méjean

The smallest of the four *causses*, the Causse Noir, separates gorges formed by the Dourbie and Jonte rivers. Each gorge in this area is different and it is worth driving along them all, as long as you save the Gorges du Tarn *(see page 172)* till last.

British novelist Ian McEwan's haunting story Black Dogs *(1992) about a couple's traumatic encounter with savage dogs, is set around St Maurice-Navacelles, and the Causse du Larzac.*

BELOW:
Roquefort cheese.

ROQUEFORT CHEESE

A ccording to legend, a young shepherd was tending his flock one day near the mouth of a cave in the Combalou, the great cliff that dominates Roquefort. Absent-mindedly, he put down his lunch – a hunk of bread and a morsel of sheep's cheese – in the cave and promptly forgot where he had left it. Sometime later he rediscovered his uneaten lunch and found that the cheese was covered with greeny-blue veins. He tasted it, liked it, and an industry of world renown was born.

In 1666 Roquefort was protected by one of the first *appelations d'origine* in France. Today, the process by which it is made is still strictly controlled. The raw ingredient of Roquefort is full-fat, untreated ewe's milk from flocks within a defined area. The milk is seeded with a natural mould, *penicillium Roqueforti*, made from well-aged bread; the cheese is made into rounds that are matured for a minimum of three months in the caves under the town.

It is the peculiar natural structure of these caves which provide the secret of Roquefort. They are ventilated by natural fissures or tunnels in the rock called *fleurines*. Air blows through the *fleurines* into the cave, creating optimum conditions of temperature and humidity for making the famous blue cheese.

The most picturesque village in the **Gorges de la Dourbie** is **Cantobre ❻**, which peers over the edge of a rock. Just beyond it is **Nant**, a pleasant town with a remnant of an old covered market *(halle)* in its square.

On the plateau above the Dourbie valley is the **Chaos de Montpellier-le-Vieux ❼** (reached by a private road off the D110; open Mar–Nov daily; entrance fee). The road takes a circuitous route to get to the entrance but it is well signposted. This group of rock formations in a wooded setting is thought to be so named because the shepherds who discovered it thought they had stumbled across a ruined city. Allow a couple of hours to explore the site, whether you go on foot or take the tourist road train (additional charge). A series of colour-coded footpaths make for easy and enjoyable walking.

Gorges de La Jonte

The road from Montpellier-le-Vieux brings you down into the **Gorges de la Jonte** at **Le Rozier**, near the start of the Gorges du Tarn. The high cliffs along the gorge are populated by vultures, but they haven't always been, as is explained in the **Belvédère des Vautours ❽** (on the D996 between Le Truel and Le Rozier; open mid-Mar–mid-Nov daily; entrance fee; tel: 05 65 62 69 69) where real-time images from a video camera trained on one of the vultures' nests is projected onto a large screen.

An ornithologist adds the commentary and then takes visitors out on to an observation deck where there are telescopes. Downstairs is an exhibition on vultures and the efforts made here to reintroduce and protect them.

Follow the Gorges de la Jonte to Meyrueis which, with its hotels and restaurants, is something of a service centre for the gorge. From here a road climbs

Map on page 168

Roadside warning against the dangers of forest fire.

BELOW: sheep for milking to make Roquefort cheese.

"Caves, after all, are not for the sophisti-cated, who will find them boring or absurd; they are for children and for those of us who have not lost a child's sense of mystery."

– FREDA WHITE,
Three Rivers of France

out of the gorge to reach **Aven Armand** (open Mar–Nov daily; guided tour only; entrance fee; www.aven-armand.com). There seems to be a visitable cave almost everywhere you turn in France but even if you can't face another drip-ping stalactite, you should give this cave a try. In 1897 the eponymous Louis Armand, a local locksmith, lowered himself through a natural chimney into an extraordinary cavern where he found a petrified subterranean "forest" of weirdly shaped stalagmites. Since Armand's visit, an inclined tunnel has been built and access is now via a short funicular railway. The "Forêt Vierge", a collection of tree-like concretions sprouting from the bottom of the cavern, is like a prehistoric rock jungle. One stalagmite is 30 metres (98 ft) tall.

If you continue along the Aven Armand road you come to the Ferme Causse-narde d'Autrefois at **Hyelzas** (open Apr–Oct daily; entrance fee; tel: 04 66 45 65 25), a museum of life on the *causses* in a traditional 18–19th-century stone farmhouse, where period tools, furniture and costumes can be seen.

Gorges du Tarn

The most impressive of all the canyons (and inevitably the most touristy) is the **Gorges du Tarn**, which carves a deep diagonal northeast–southwest line on the map between the Causse Méjean and the Causse de Sauveterre. In places the gorge is 600 metres (2,000 ft) deep and across the top at its narrowest it is no more than 1,200 metres (3,900 ft). When driving along the road that runs along the bottom of the gorge, it is difficult to gauge the scale of this great natural fea-ture; it is much better to enter it via one of the roads which snake down the cliffs from the plateau to Ste-Enimie, La Malène (roughly in the middle of the gorge) and Les Vignes. There are viewpoints over the gorge on the south

BELOW: Ste-Enimie nestles in the Gorges du Tarn.

bank of the river above La Malène, at the **Roc des Hourtous** and the **Roc de Serre** (which requires a half-hour walk) and on the northern lip of the gorge at **Point Sublime**.

But the drive down the gorge itself, along the road that follows the right (north) bank of the river, is also well worthwhile. Arriving from Florac in the north, the gorge begins at **Ispagnac**. The largest town in the gorge, **Ste-Enimie ❿** is a beautiful cluster of medieval streets beneath an abbey. A small museum, the **Vieux Logis** (open Apr–Sept daily; entrance fee; tel: 04 66 48 50 09), gives an idea of what it was like to live in the Gorges du Tarn in the past.

A short way further down the gorge, cross the river to visit the pretty village of **St Chély du Tarn**, which has a Romanesque church and a communal bread oven in the square. Back on the north of the river you soon come to the **Château de la Caze**, built in the 15th century and now a hotel (not open to non-residents), in which, allegedly, once lived eight beautiful girls known as the "Nymphs of the Tarn".

La Malène ⓫ is a pretty town at a bridging point with another Romanesque church. From here boat excursions (Bateliers des Gorges du Tarn; boats for charter Apr–Oct; journey takes about 1 hour; charge per boat of 4–5 people, reservation essential; tel: 04 66 48 51 10) depart for the most interesting part of the gorge downstream. The 8-km (5-mile) trip follows the river to its narrowest point at **Les Détroits** and ends at the wider but also scenic **Cirque de Baumes**.

The Cévennes

Florac ⓬, at the northeast entrance to the gorge, houses the **Parc National des Cévennes** in its château (6 bis place du Palais, Florac; tel 04 66 49 53 01; www.cevennes-parcnational.fr). The Cévennes is unusual among French

Map on page 168

"Ste-Enimie...was a Merovingian princess suffering from leprosy. She was miraculously cured by the waters of the Fontaine de Burle, but her recovery lasted only if she stayed by its side."

– JOY LAW,
The Midi

LEFT: the River Pêcher on its way through Florac.
BELOW: rustic tower on a back road.

Kilometre stone on the road ascending Mont Aigoual.

BELOW: the observatory on Mont Aigoual.
RIGHT: Le Pont-de-Montvert bridge.

national parks in that it aims not just at strict conservation of endangered species but also at the conservation and understanding of an "agro-pastoral" way of life. To further study and preserve the unique interaction between humanity and the environment, the Cévennes has also been classed by UNESCO as a biosphere reserve. Three *ecomusées* (ecomuseums), spread out on a variety of sites, seek to explain the landscapes and traditional life of the Cévennes. Over 2,200 plants are found within the boundaries of the park, 48 of them endemic and a further hundred rare or endangered species.

One of the prettiest areas of the national park, the Massif de l'Aigoual, is south of here (it can also be accessed via Meyrueis in the Gorge de la Jonte). This is good walking country but it is also possible to drive to the summit of **Mont Aigoual ⓭** (1,565 metres/5,135 ft) where there is a stoutly built meteorological observatory. Climb the spiral staircase on the outside of the tower to a windy viewpoint from which the view encompasses a quarter of France on a clear day, from the Alps to the Pyrenees, and to the Mediterranean. An orientation disc optimistically points out the directions to Tangier and Istanbul as well.

From here it is possible, with a reasonable map, to navigate the lanes across some picturesque Cévennes countryside to strike the **Corniche des Cévennes**, a ridge-top road built in the 18th century between Florac and St-Jean-du-Gard.

Until World War II the Cévennes was an important centre of silk production. The **Musée des Vallées Cévenoles** (open Apr–Oct daily; Nov–Mar closed Tues, Thur and Sun pm; tel: 04 66 85 10 48) in **St-Jean-du-Gard ⓮** has exhibitions on silk-making, as well as other crafts and traditions of the Cévennes.

A steam train travels the 13 km (8 miles) between St-Jean-du-Gard and **Anduze** (four trains each way per day Apr–Oct; fare payable; tel: 04 66 85 13

17; www.citev.com). There is an intermediate station at **La Bambouseraie** (Prafrance; open Mar–Nov daily; entrance fee; tel: 04 66 61 70 47; www.bambouseraie.fr), a stand of giant bamboos, which was planted in 1855.

The Cévennes reach their highest point in the north, in the granite massif of **Mont Lozère**, although the slopes are less severe and the views less good than from Mont Aigoual to the south.

Map on page 168

The Florac to Mont Lozère road passes through **Le Pont-de-Montvert** ⑮, which has a quaint old toll house at the end of an innocent-looking humpback bridge. On this bridge on 24 July 1702 a group of Protestants murdered the Abbot of Chaila, who was in charge of operations against their religion in the Cévennes region, and threw his body into the river. The incident sparked off the War of the Camisards, a bloody guerrilla conflict which left around 14,000 people dead.

One person who later became fascinated by the Camisards and their struggle for the right to enjoy freedom of religious expression was the Scottish writer Robert Louis Stevenson. He passed through Le Pont-de-Montvert on his 12-day trip from the Haute-Loire to St-Jean-du-Gard during the autumn of 1878. When he published an account of his journey as *Travels with a Donkey in the Cévennes* the following year he drew the world's attention to the region. The GR70 long-distance footpath follows Stevenson's route.

From Le Pont-de-Montvert the road climbs gradually to the **Col de Finiels** ⑯, at 1,548 metres (5,080 ft). To reach the 1,699-metre (5574-ft) summit of Mont Lozère, called **Sommet de Finiels** – the highest point in the Cévennes – requires a lengthy hike. Coming down the north side of the mountain you pass by the ski resort of **Chalet du Mont Lozère**.

The Scottish novelist, Robert Louis Stevenson (1850–94) travelled through the Cévennes in 1878.

BELOW: landscape on Mont Lozère.

The Gévaudan and Aubrac

"...there are people who are causse-addicts; who love them as hillmen love their hills. Nothing will do for them but the Great Causses with their silence, their solitude, their thin, high air and long empty vistas. For they are spiritual children of the desert; and the causses *are desert country."*

– FREDA WHITE,
Three Rivers of France

BELOW: an 18th-century depiction of the Beast.

Mende ⑰ is what passes for an urban nucleus in this, one of the most peaceful parts of France. It is the *préfecture* of Lozère, the least-populated *département* of France, in which there are no more than half a dozen sets of traffic lights, most of them in Mende itself. This diminutive and agreeable city has a 13th-century Gothic bridge and, thanks to Pope Urbain V, who was born in the Cévennes, a fine Gothic cathedral (with a Romanesque crypt).

Northwest brings you to **Marvejols** ⑱, a town with three handsome fortified gateways. Further north, near Ste-Lucie, is **Les Loups du Gévaudan** ⑲ (open daily; entrance fee; tel: 04 66 32 09 22), a sanctuary created by Gérard Ménatory, and now maintained by his daughter; more than 100 wolves live in spacious pens in the sanctuary. The animals are not always active but there is an exhibition describing their life-cycle and exploding some of the myths surrounding this almost legendary creature.

The countryside has already changed from that of the Grand Causses, the Gorges du Tarn and the Cévennes to the south; here the landscape is softer and more undulating. But head westward towards the Lot valley and you are in different country again: the bleak, cattle-rearing grasslands and moors of the Aubrac volcanic highlands, one of the least populous areas of France. From late May to autumn, these pastures are grazed by the distinctive Aubrac breed of cattle, which has slender horns and a honey-coloured coat.

It is an unlikely setting for one of France's best restaurants but many people are content to make the trek to **Laguiole** ⑳ to eat the creations of chef Michel Bras in his restaurant *(see page 349)*. Laguiole is also famous for its pocket knives and some of the knifemakers' workshops can be visited, especially Le

THE BEAST OF GÉVAUDAN

For three years, between 1764 and 1767, the area of the Gévaudan was terrorised by a wild animal that attacked and killed children tending flocks in the fields. The "Beast of Gévaudan" has never been positively identified but it has often been suggested that it was a crazed or enraged wolf. Gérard Ménatory, creator of the wolf sanctuary near Ste-Lucie, pointed out that the Beast's behaviour does not square with that of any known wolf. The culprit, he argued, was more likely to be an animal that had escaped from captivity, probably a hyena.

Whatever the truth, the Beast is part of Gévaudan folklore. Robert Louis Stevenson was enchanted by the tale of the Beast: "...this was the land of the ever-memorable BEAST, the Napoleon Bonaparte of wolves...he ate women and children and 'shepherdesses celebrated for their beauty'; he pursued armed horsemen for months; he has been seen at broad noonday chasing a post-chaise and outrider along the king's high-road...He was placarded like a political offender, and ten thousand francs was offered for his head." When the locals wouldn't give him directions, Stevenson turned sardonic: "The Beast of Gévaudan ate about a hundred children of this district; I began to think of him with sympathy."

Couteau de Laguiole (place du Nouveau Forail, 8 rue de la Vergne; open summer Mon–Fri and Sat; tel: 05 65 48 45 47) and Forges de Laguiole (route de l'Aubrac; open daily; tel: 05 65 48 43 34). The main street of the town is lined with shops selling all kinds of knives and some of the craftsmen work in public view. The town also produces the cheese for the characteristic dish of this region, *aligot*, a combination of mashed potatoes, garlic and melted cheese.

Map on page 168

The Pays d'Olt

A string of attractive towns marks the Lot's course through the *département* of Aveyron. **Ste-Eulalie-d'Olt ㉑** has a Romanesque church and an old mill. The spire of the church in **St-Côme-d'Olt** twists in an unusual spiral. **Espalion ㉒** has an 11th-century bridge, the Pont Vieux, with old houses along the banks beside it, their balconies hanging over the water. But its most curious attraction is its museum. Housed in an old church, the **Musée Joseph Vaylet** (Église St-Jean; open July–Aug daily; May, June, Sept and Oct Wed–Sun; Nov–Apr weekends only; entrance fee; tel: 65 44 09 18) has two discrete sections. Most of the museum is an eclectic display of what is described as "folk art and traditions", which includes a nightshirt for puritanical, utilitarian love-making *(see page 43)* and German helmets from World War II. The rear of the building houses the **Musée du Scaphandre** (same opening times), a museum of underwater diving equipment. (The first self-contained breathing apparatus, it is claimed, was invented by two men from Espalion in 1864.)

On the hill above Espalion is the 11th–15th-century **Château de Calmont d'Olt** (open Apr–Sept daily; entrance fee; tel: 05 65 44 15 89), which has been turned into an original museum of medieval siege warfare. You can

Chef Michel Bras, owner of a famous Aubrac restaurant.

LEFT: diving suit in Espalion.
BELOW: siege engines at Calmont d'Olt.

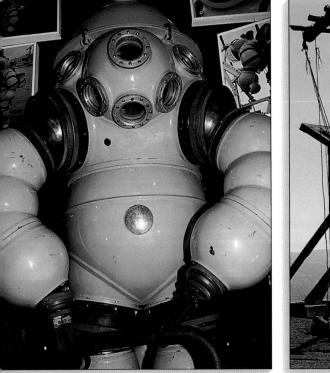

Typical roof and window in the medieval town of Conques.

watch demonstrations of working siege engines daily in July and August.

Estaing ㉓ is built around a 15th–16th-century castle in a clutter of styles. **Entraygues-sur-Truyère ㉔** is sited at the confluence of the Lot and the Truyère, with a Gothic bridge over the latter. The River Truyère forms thickly wooded gorges upstream from Entraygues, which have been transformed into reservoirs to generate hydroelectric power, arguably without detracting from the beauty of the landscape. The workings of the hydroelectric scheme are explained in a visitor centre at the Couesque Dam. Between Espalion and Entraygues the Lot also flows through a gorge but it is not nearly as impressive as those that divide up the Grands Causses to the east.

Conques

In wooded hills above the Lot valley stands the quaint village of **Conques ㉕**, which looks, apart from the addition of the odd *crêperie*, as if it has been in mothballs since the Middle Ages. The stone-built houses arranged on steep narrow streets gather around the **Abbatiale Ste-Foy**, a Romanesque abbey church dedicated to Sainte Foy (St Faith), who was martyred in Agen in about AD 303. Around the 9th century her relics were brought here – some say by subterfuge. The building of the church began in the 11th century but most of it dates from the 12th century. It was a principal stop between Le Puy-en-Velay and Moissac on the route to the shrine of Santiago de Compostela.

The tympanum over the west door – best appreciated in the afternoon with the sun illuminating it – is a famous masterpiece of 12th-century Romanesque art. Even in our agnostic age, it is easy to imagine the impression this depiction of the Last Judgement must have made on the countless pilgrims who passed

BELOW: the Abbatiale Ste-Foy. **RIGHT:** detail of the tympanum of the Abbatiale Ste-Foy.

through the village. It offers mortals a stark choice. The left half of the scene (on Christ's right) represents those who have attained paradise while the right half depicts what happens to the damned when they reach hell. Christ presides in the middle.

The other essential place to visit in Conques is the **Treasury** (open daily), housed on two sites. "Part Two", which can be ignored if time is short, is in a room reached through the tourist information office. The treasure of treasures is displayed in "Part One", a small chamber round the corner. At the end of this room, in a glass case to itself, is the unique 10th-century Statue-reliquaire de **Ste-Foy**. The other exhibits include several exquisitely decorated portable altars.

Rouergue

Rodez ㉖, the *préfecture* of Aveyron *département*, stands on top of a hill and is dominated by the Cathédrale de Notre-Dame – built of red sandstone between the 13th and 15th centuries – and especially by its elegant bell tower. The exterior is ornamented with twisting gargoyles. Inside, the choir stalls, rood screen and organ are worth seeing.

At the confluence of the Aveyron and Alzou stands the *bastide* town of **Villefranche-de-Rouergue** ㉗. Here a Carthusian monastery, the **Chartreuse St-Sauveur** (Avenue Vézian-Valette; open July–Sept daily; at other times of year by arrangement; entrance fee; tel: 05 65 45 13 18) was built between 1451 and 1459 in Gothic style. The smaller of its two cloisters – Flamboyant Gothic with its unglazed tracery – is exquisite and well worth seeing. In the monastery chapel, look out for the menagerie of mythical beasts carved on the 15th-century choir stalls. ❑

Map on page 168

TIP

Look closely at the outer edge of the archivolt (the arch around the tympanum) to see the *curieux de Conques* – inquisitive little faces peeping over the stone rim.

BELOW: misericord in Chartreuse St-Sauveur.

ANTONIN ARTAUD IN RODEZ

The tortured inventor of the Theatre of Cruelty and sometime Surrealist Antonin Artaud (1896–1948) spent three years confined in a mental asylum in Rodez during World War II.

By 1943, Artaud had already spent almost six years in institutions in northern France and lost all but eight of his teeth through poor diet. He was transferred to Rodez because it was felt that he would have a better chance of stability and nourishment in the unoccupied zone of France. Artaud was diagnosed as suffering from "a chronic and extremely intense delirium characterised by persecution..." In a misguided search for a cure, his doctors at Rodez subjected him to 51 unanaesthetised electro-shocks: a controversial form of treatment used to alleviate the symptoms of mental illness, by which electrodes were fixed to the patient's temples and an electric current was sent through his brain.

In May 1946 Artaud was released from his incarceration at Rodez, crippled, emaciated and prematurely aged. The last 22 months of his life, until his death in March 1948, were his most productive period. Some of his vitriolic correspondence from inside the asylum were published as a book, *Letters from Rodez*.

THE TARN

The gentle, green countryside of the Tarn is enlivened by medieval towns and villages and museums housing the work of three artists: Ingres, Goya and, most famously, Toulouse-Lautrec

Map on page 184

The territory covered by the *département* of Tarn has been compared to the palm of a hand: a corrugated bowl of farmland sloping gently southwest, with a swelling of higher ground to the south and east, and three principal rivers – the Tarn, Dadou and Agout – forming lines across it. Geographically and climatically, the Tarn is something of a crossroads between the Massif Central, the Aquitaine basin and the Mediterranean region.

Although easily accessible from Toulouse, the Tarn is not generally as well known as the more distant Lot and Aveyron. This is perhaps because it has few famous sights – only the red-brick *préfecture* of Albi is likely to be known outside the area, let alone outside France, and then only for Toulouse-Lautrec, an artist born in Albi but who lived much of his life in Paris.

History has linked Albi's name with the Cathars, often referred to as the Albigensians. The name is more of a convenience for historians than a precise term, as the heresy was neither centred on nor confined to this area. But the Tarn did suffer at the hands of Simon de Montfort and his northern knights, who besieged Lavaur in 1211 and subsequently massacred many of its inhabitants.

The Wars of Religion spelled further trouble. While Albi stayed true to the Catholic Church, Castres was defiantly Protestant and Cardinal Richelieu himself came to supervise the dismantling of the town's defences, which had been built with stones from demolished churches.

Conflicts aside, the Tarn has been a prosperous place: for a brief time in the 14th and 15th centuries the Lauragais area was supplying most of Europe (via Toulouse) with blue dye from its woad plantations. In the 19th century wool, mining and metallurgy all took off in the Tarn.

The northern border of the Tarn *département* roughly follows the River Aveyron, which flows through a forested gorge on its way to its confluence with the Tarn. The Tarn itself passes through the *bastide* town of Montauban, once a hotbed of Protestantism and now the *préfecture* of the somewhat amorphous *département* of Tarn-et-Garonne. Just before the Tarn merges with the River Garonne, it skirts Moissac, which has grown up around the abbey, one of the wonders of Romanesque architecture.

PRECEDING PAGES: houses beside the river, Castres. **LEFT:** medieval fête in Cordes-sur-Ciel. **BELOW:** field of sunflowers, Tarn.

Albi and Toulouse-Lautrec

Most people are drawn to the city of **Albi ❶** because of Henri Toulouse-Lautrec, who was born here in 1864. In the 1920s, Toulouse-Lautrec's friend Maurice Joyant founded the **Musée Toulouse-Lautrec** (open Apr–Sept daily; Oct–Mar Wed–Mon; entrance fee; tel: 05 63 49 48 70) in the 13th-century Palais de la Berbie, a former episcopal residence. The Count and

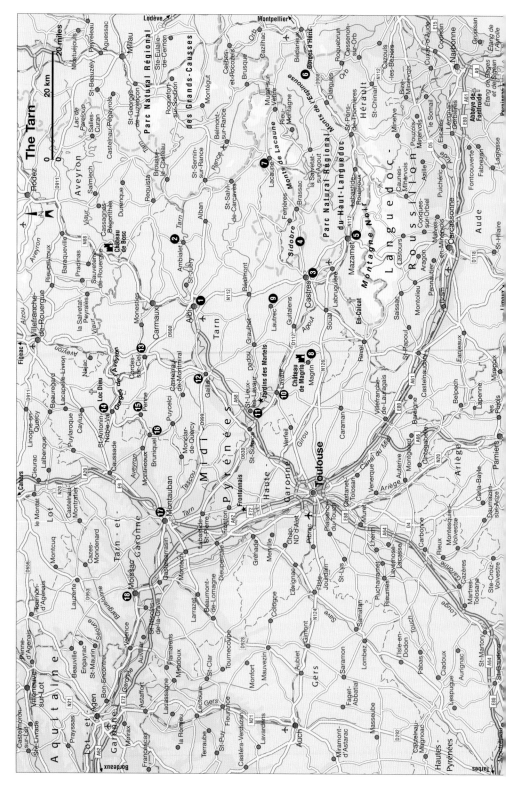

The Tarn

Map on page 184

Countess of Toulouse-Lautrec donated the contents of their son's studio and the result is the best collection of the artist's work in the world.

The museum has three floors of galleries, although the top floor is not marked on the free plan you are given with your ticket. Turn left at the top of the main stairs to see a narrow gallery of archaeological finds, of which the best piece is the Vénus de Courbet, dating from around 20,000 years ago. Also on this floor is the 13th-century Chapelle Notre-Dame. The rest of the first floor is devoted to Toulouse-Lautrec, beginning with portraits of him by other artists. These are followed by his early works. A series of interconnected rooms contain many of his famous works, notably *Au Salon de la rue des Moulins*.

The second floor is usually less crowded and gives more of an insight into the work of Toulouse-Lautrec. Here you can see his drawings, lithographs and posters. Among the other exhibits is his hollow walking cane, which contains a small glass from which he would surreptitiously drink brandy.

The top level of the museum is given over to a light chamber containing modern and contemporary art. The grounds of the Palais de la Berbie, elevated above the River Tarn, are open to visitors.

Albi's huge **Cathédrale Ste-Cécile** (open daily), an acknowledged masterpiece of Southern Gothic, is often compared to a fortress. In the aftermath of the Albigensian Crusade, in which the power of the Church was tested, if not actually much shaken, it was felt that Albi's new Cathedral should be built not just to impress but to overawe the faithful. Begun in 1282, it took a century to build and was altered in the 19th century. An exterior staircase leads up to the canopied porch. To your right as you step inside is a magnificent Flamboyant Gothic rood screen shielding the choir. Originally the screen had almost 100 statues

The artist Henri Toulouse-Lautrec.

BELOW: *La Revue Blanche* (1895) by Toulouse-Lautrec.

HENRI TOULOUSE-LAUTREC

The artist Henri-Marie-Raymonde de Toulouse-Lautrec-Monfa was born into a wealthy family of impeccable lineage in Albi on 24 November 1864. Two accidents in his teenage years atrophied his legs and made it difficult for him to walk. As he convalesced he used art to help him while away the hours of enforced solitude.

In 1872 he visited Paris for the first time. On passing the baccalaureate in 1881 he finally decided to become an artist. At first he studied under professional teachers but in the mid-1880s he rejected the stifling rules of formal art and began to depict the bohemian life of Montmartre using lines free from anatomical accuracy and the laws of perspective. The work of Toulouse-Lautrec goes beyond the merely superficial to reveal something of the inner personality of his subjects. He is especially renowned for his 1896 series portraying life in a brothel, of which *Au Salon de la rue des Moulins (At the Salon)* is considered his masterpiece. But by this time, Toulouse-Lautrec was drinking heavily and in 1899 he was committed to a sanatorium following a mental breakdown. In 1900, after leaving the sanatorium, he resumed his heavy drinking and on 9 September, three months before his 37th birthday, he died at Château de Malromé, near Bordeaux.

Self-portrait by
Francisco de Goya.

BELOW: regional
puppets and home-
made jams on sale.

but all but a few were removed during the Revolution. Against each pillar round the outside of the choir (entrance fee) are polychrome statues of Old Testament characters. There are more statues inside, including dwarf-like figures of Charlemagne and the Emperor Constantine. The five stained-glass windows in the apse are 14th-century, but were restored in the 19th century.

All the while you will be aware of the vaulted ceiling above you, the work of 16th-century artists from Bologna in Italy: a visual version of the Bible almost 100-metres (325-ft) long, with a preponderance of blue and gold. The other wonder of the Cathedral is a sombre, incomplete painting of the *Last Judgement* across the wall of the west end, dating from 1484.

The museum and the cathedral are enough to fill a morning or afternoon and between them overwhelm the city. But the narrow streets on the other side of place Sainte-Cécile have several half-timbered red-brick houses and are worth strolling around.

At **Ambialet ❷**, upriver from Albi, an old priory stands on a picturesque site on an almost circular meander of the Tarn. You can also visit another Toulouse-Lautrec château, the **Château de Bosc** (guided tours all year; tel: 05 65 72 00 19), where he spent much of his childhood – indeed you can see the artist's childhood books and crayons. To get there, head north of Albi towards Rodez, take the D10 south-east to Canjac and follow signs to the château.

Goya and the Black Mountain

Another artist is celebrated further south in **Castres ❸**, but this one is Spanish, not French. The **Musée Goya** (open Tues–Sun; entrance fee; tel: 05 63 71 59 27) on the second floor of the Hôtel de Ville specialises in Spanish painting and has

a renowned collection, as the name suggests, of works by Francisco Goya y Lucientes (1746–1828), bequeathed to the town in 1893 by a local collector. The paintings include a self-portrait of the artist wearing glasses, a portrait of Francisco del Mazo and the big, gloomy canvas of *The Junta of the Philippines.* The adjacent room displays Goya's etchings, which observe the failings of humanity critically but with compassion, including the series *The Disasters of War, Caprices, Tauromaquia* and *The Proverbs.*

Castres, a wool town, stands on the River Agout. During the Albigensian Crusade it survived by submitting to Simon de Montfort but in later centuries became a stronghold of Protestant dissent and consequently embroiled in the Wars of Religion. The modern town is assembled around the place Jean Jaurès, named after the Socialist politician who is Castres' most famous son. From Pont Neuf and Quai des Jacobins there are views of the old, wooden weavers' and dyers' houses overhanging the banks of the river.

To the east of Castres is the granite plateau of **Le Sidobre** ❹, which is much quarried but also much visited for its curious natural rock formations. Chief among these is La Peyro Clabado, a 780-tonne granite boulder precariously balanced on a small pedestal. Several giant stones rest in such a way that they could be set in motion. The best example is the Rocher Tremblant de Sept Faux. In the middle of the Sidobre is the dark, glassy Lac de Merle (lake).

A short way south from Castres is **Mazamet** ❺, a pleasant town with Visigothic roots and an interesting case of industrial specialisation. In 1851 Pierre-Élie Houlès had the idea of importing sheepskins (a cheap commodity) from Argentina, stripping them of their wool, and passing both wool and skins on for processing. Thenceforth Mazamet's textile industry has excelled in *délainage.*

TIP

A trip on the wooden riverboat, *Le Miredames*, will give you a slightly different view of Castres. There are 3–5 sailings a day, depending on season, from the quay in front of the tourist information office; tel: 05 63 59 72 30 to reserve a place.

BELOW: caricature of Jean Jaurès.

THE POLITICS OF JEAN JAURÈS

The controversial pacifist, socialist and humanist Jean Jaurès was born in Castres in 1859. After teaching at a school in Albi and the University of Toulouse he was elected as the deputy for Tarn in 1885.

He was a republican of conviction, a reforming Socialist never afraid to express views unpopular with his fellow left-wingers, a prolific author (notably of the *Socialist History of the French Revolution*) and a powerful orator.

Short and overweight (he was once described as looking like "a fat merchant who overeats"), his scruffy appearance made him an easy target for his enemies to ridicule and he was often caricatured in cartoons of the day. In 1898 he lost his seat in parliament for defending the wrongly accused Captain Alfred Dreyfus. In 1904 he co-founded the newspaper *L'Humanité*.

His last few years were spent passionately working for international brotherhood and the limitation of conflicts. As World War I approached, he attracted the hostility of French nationlists who saw him as promoting a reconciliation with the vilified enemy, Germany. Tragically, he was assassinated in Paris on 31 July 1914, three days after the declaration of the war which he had worked so hard to prevent.

M. Jean JAURÈS
Le Rescapé de l'"Humanité"

"In the past when Lacaune was a spa, it advertised the fact by erecting, in 1559, the Fontaine des Pisseurs, where four young men are immortalized in the act of demonstrating the diuretic nature of its waters."

—JOY LAW,
The Midi

The road out of the south side of Mazamet climbs steeply up the Montagne Noire ("Black Mountain"), the last gasp of the Massif Central and part of a barrier of mountains which cuts off the rest of the Tarn from the plains of the Languedoc. The **Parc Naturel Régional du Haut-Languedoc** (headquarters: 13 rue du Cloître, St-Pons-de-Thomières; tel: 04 67 97 38 22) rounds up a vast sweep of country covering the Montagne Noire, the Monts de l'Espinouse (abutting the Grands Causses) and the Monts de Lacaune to the north where the Tarn *département* reaches its highest point at 1,267 metres (4,157 ft).

On the other side of the Montagne Noire from Mazamet is Carcassonne. There is a marked contrast between the steep north slope, which is darkly forested because of the higher rainfall, and the drier, gentler southern slope with its farmland and Mediterranean vegetation.

Between them, these uplands have many unfrequented places but one well-known beauty spot is the **Gorges d'Héric ❻**. **Lacaune ❼**, in the mountains of the same name, is known for it *charcuterie* (cold-cuts).

The Tarn and the Agout

The middle of the Tarn, west of the Albi–Castres axis, encompasses rolling farmland of cereals, maize and sunflowers, with only isolated pockets of interest to a tourist. The southern part of this area, stretching around the end of the Montagne Noire to the Canal du Midi, is the Lauragais. It was here that woad *(Isatis tinctoria – pastel* in French) was grown intensively in the 15th and 16th centuries, to provide Europe with its blue dye, building the fortune of Toulouse, which administered the trade. So prosperous was the Lauragais that it still likes to call itself the Pays de Cocagne, the Land of Cockaigne, that is, the Land of Milk

BELOW: dovecot *(pigeonnier)* in a field in the Tarn.

ORNITHOLOGICAL ARCHITECTURE

There are *pigeonniers* – dovecotes – all over France, but the Tarn has the highest concentration and the widest variety. Some are merely extensions to farm or village houses – a few holes into a loft protruding from the upper storey. But the finest of them are round or square towers standing apart from a farmhouse, alone in the fields.

Pigeons have been kept at least since Roman times and were highly valued in medieval France because they were easy to rear, breeding quickly and producing meat for the table and droppings to be used as fertiliser for the fields.

The oldest surviving *pigeonniers* date from the 16th century but they hark back to earlier, feudal times when the tower would have been a symbol of privilege. Their architecture is often out of proportion to the utilitarian purpose. Many *pigeonniers* are stone-built with tile roofs, dormer windows containing the entrance/exit holes for the birds, and decorative filials. They stand on arcades or pillars, which are topped with mushroom-shaped caps to prevent predators climbing into the nesting space above.

Some of these quaint buildings have been restored and turned into storage areas or even extra rooms. Others have been left to decay attractively and are now occupied by flocks of wild pigeons.

Map on page 184

and Honey. All that is left to see of the woad industry is in the disjointed-looking **Château de Magrin ❽**, which contains the **Musée de Pastel** (open daily, afternoons only; entrance fee; tel: 05 63 70 63 82). **Lautrec ❾**, off the road between Castres and Albi, still has its agricultural speciality, *l'ail rose*: pink garlic. The town has a lovely medieval quarter with half-timbered brick houses around a small square with arches supported by wooden beams.

The **Cathédrale de St-Alain** in **Lavaur ❿** occupies an unusual site. Built of brick in 1254, it stands apart from the rest of the town with its apse creeping up to a cliff over the River Agout. Note the clock mechanism that has a painted figure to strike the hour. **St-Lieux-les-Lavaur ⓫**, 10 km (6 miles) north of Lavaur, is the starting point for steam trains running along the Chemin de Fer Touristique du Tarn (trains run on Sun and public holidays Easter–Oct, and on most other days during July and Aug; fare payable; tel: 05 61 47 44 52).

Gaillac ⓬ stands in one of France's most ancient wine-growing areas. Vines were often planted around abbeys in the Middle Ages and Gaillac owes its wine industry to the **Abbaye St-Michel**, which was doing good business in wines at least as early as the 10th century. Apart from the vineyards, the abbey church, the brick tower of the **Hôtel-maison Pierre de Brens** and the **Château de Foucaud** and its gardens are the main points of interest. Another popular tourist sight in the Tarn is the **Jardins des Martels**, southwest of Gaillac, near Giroussens (open May–Aug daily; Apr, Sept and Oct afternoons only;` Accessible by tourist train from Saint-Lieux; tel: 05 63 41 61 42), a floral park with 2,500 varieties of plants, greenhouses of exotic and aquatic plants and a farm of rare animals.

"The traveller who looks at the summer night from the terrace at Cordes knows that he need go no further and that if he wishes it, the beauty of this place, day after day, will banish solitude."
– ALBERT CAMUS

Cordes-sur-Ciel: architecture in the air

Driving north from Albi towards the valley of the Aveyron, one of France's most spectacularly sited towns appears before you on the summit of a rocky hill. The position of **Cordes-sur-Ciel ⓭** (Cordes-in-the-Sky) is its first attraction; the other is that it is a near-perfect medieval town. Although it was the first *bastide* to be built (in 1222, during the Albigensian Crusade) it does not have the trademark grid-pattern of streets of later *bastides* built on flatter sites. During the 14th century, great wealth was created here by leather- and cloth-working and linen-weaving but the town's prosperity came to an end in the 15th century. Away from the main routes of communication, Cordes survived intact into the 20th century and in the 1920s measures were taken to preserve it. It is now a well-to-do town of cobbled streets lined with Gothic houses, tastefully run as a harmonious unit by a population of artists and craftspeople, shopkeepers and restaurateurs.

Cars are not allowed in the old town: park at the bottom of the hill and walk up (the parking fee, which includes entrance to a museum, increases further up the hill). The main street is the **Grand Rue Raymond VII**, closed off at either end by a gateway, **Porte des Ormeaux** (west) and **Portail Peint** (east), beyond which is a staggered gateway, **Porte de la Jane** and **Porte du Vainqueur** (or du Planol) respectively.

Approximately halfway along the Grand Rue is the **Maison Fonpeyrouse d'Alayrac**, housing the tourist

BELOW: a medieval-style fête in Cordes-sur-Ciel.

Decorated door on a back street of Cordes-sur-Ciel.

BELOW: the carved faces on the Maison de l'Amour in St-Antonin-Noble-Val.

information office (tel: 05 03 56 29 77) and, above it, the premises of La Talavera, an association promoting Occitan culture. Across the street, almost opposite the tourist information office, is the **Maison du Grand Veneur** (now a restaurant), which has a sculpted hunting scene and gargoyles on its façade, but the street is so narrow you have to crane your neck to take it all in. Further down the same side of the street is the **Maison du Grand Écuyer** (now a hotel-restaurant), which has another ornate façade.

Back up the street, the handsome **Maison du Grand Fauconnier** is now the town hall. It is just off the **Place de la Halle**, where the covered market now shelters restaurant tables. One corner gives on to the shaded **Place de la Bride**, a viewpoint over the surrounding countryside.

Gorges de l'Aveyron

The grandly titled **St-Antonin-Noble-Val** , on the north bank of the river Aveyron, makes an interesting comparison with Cordes. This is another charming old medieval town but largely unrestored and somewhat unkempt. With no disrespect to Cordes, St-Antonin is still lived in rather than managed; which makes it a place to look for details rather than immaculate buildings.

Originally a Gallo-Roman settlement, St-Antonin was developed by wealthy merchants in the 13–15th century. The Ancien Hôtel de Ville beside the covered market predates this era of prosperity. It was built in 1125, making it one of the oldest civic buildings surviving in France. Restored by Viollet-le-Duc in the 19th century (when the belfry was added) it now houses a **museum** (open July–Aug Wed–Mon; Apr–June and Sept by arrangement; entrance fee; tel: 03 63 68 23 52). Adam and Eve are carved in bas relief on the façade. Along rue

Droite is the so-called **Maison de l'Amour**. The house itself is in bad repair but the medieval carving of a man and a woman kissing is still clear to see. The short rue Rive-Valat next door has a trickling canal alongside it.

St-Antonin is a centre for canoeing trips down the River Aveyron, which here flows through a wooded gorge. The drive (or cycle ride) downstream is also worthwhile, passing two picturesequely sited villages, **Penne ⑮** and **Bruniquel ⑯**.

Map on page 184

Montauban and Moissac

The *bastide* of **Montauban ⑰**, *préfecture* of Tarn-et-Garonne, was founded by the Count of Toulouse in 1144 and most of its old buildings are made of the brick typical of Lower Quercy and the area around Toulouse. In the 16th and 17th centuries it was one of the leading Protestant centres of France. As such it was (unsuccessfully) besieged by the king in 1621. It was the last Huguenot town to surrender to Louis XIII's army in 1628.

The main square is the **Place Nationale**, rebuilt in the 17th century after fires, which has brick houses and arches around it. In one of the arcades, on the corner of rue Malcousinat, a draper's metre-measure can be seen on a pillar. Such standard measures were often provided in the main square of a *bastide*.

The painter Jean-Auguste-Dominique Ingres (1780–1867) was born in Montauban and left much of his work to the town. It is housed in the **Musée Ingres** (rue de l'Hotel de Ville; open Tues–Sun; entrance fee; tel: 05 63 22 12 91), the former bishop's palace, which stands on the banks of the Tarn. Beside it is the 14th-century **Pont Vieux**. A famous Ingres painting, *The Vow of Louis XIII,* can be seen in the transept of the **Cathédrale Notre-Dame**, a classical building on the edge of the old town and noticeably out of character with it.

"However did women bring up babies on this platform suspended in mid-air? They must have tethered the toddlers like goats; and the children must have grown up with heads like steeplejacks."

– FREDA WHITE
on Penne in
Three Rivers of France

BELOW:
the Musée Ingres
in Montauban.

Map
on page
184

A game of hide and seek in the portal of Moissac Abbey.

Moissac , 25 km (15 miles) northwest of Montauban, on the north bank of the Tarn (close to its confluence with the Garonne), is not much to look at as you drive through its outskirts. And the abbey for which it is famous stands inauspiciously next to a railway line (the building of which, in 1856, entailed the demolition of the Abbey's refectory). A saving grace is that the hills around the town are covered with vineyards producing white Chasselas grapes.

The abbey was probably founded in the 7th century (although legend ascribes it to the 5th century), but it became most successful when it was affiliated to the abbey of Cluny in 1048. In 1793 it was damaged during the Revolution.

The tympanum over the south portal of the abbey church, the **Église St-Pierre**, was carved around 1130 and is one of France's finest pieces of Romanesque sculpture. Its subject is the Vision of the Apocalypse according to the evangelist St John (*Book of Revelation*, chapter IV). Christ is the central figure and all the other figures are looking at him. Closest to him are the four Evangelists in symbolic form: St Mark (represented by a lion), Luke (a bull), John (an eagle) and St Matthew (human face). Two tall seraphim frame this central group. Below and around them are the "twenty-four elders, robed in white and wearing crowns of gold". The central pillar supporting the tympanum is carved with six lions crossing over each other. Beside the door are elongated figures of St Peter (patron of the abbey) on the left and Isaiah on the right.

Just beside the church are the famous **cloisters** (entrance via the tourist office; open daily; entrance fee; tel: 05 63 04 01 85), built shortly before the church at the turn of the 11th–12th century, during Moissac's association with Cluny. There are 76 carved capitals, all different, most depicting Biblical scenes or the lives of saints. The corner pillars have marble plaques with bas reliefs. ❑

Bastides

Many towns in the Southwest are *bastides* – towns founded in the 13th and 14th centuries in lands under French and English dominion. Before the *bastides* were built most of the settled rural population of the Southwest lived in small farm groups or hamlets called *écarts,* although some communities were organised as a *sauveté* (around a religious foundation) or a *castelnau* (under the control and protection of a château). Such scattered communities were fragmented and difficult to administer. It was in a landowner's interest to have the minions living in close proximity to one another where they could be taxed and managed more efficiently.

The first *bastide* to be built was Cordes, in 1222. Around 300 more were built over the next 150 years, the last of them being Labastide-d'Anjou in 1373.

Medieval town planning

Allowing for the terrain, and with exceptions, *bastides* were generally built to a grid layout, their straight streets connecting at right angles. At the centre of the grid there would always be a square. Surveyors laid out the building plots meticulously to maximise revenue from the space available. Montauban and Villefranche-de-Rouergue are good examples of this regularity. Each inhabitant was also granted a plot or two of land outside the town, sufficient to "light a fire" – that is, to support a family.

This mathematical system of town planning was an accountant's dream. According to writer Gilles Bernard, "the grid was a precise fiscal 'reading' of the land, the tax-collector's way of enclosing the entire life and energy of an economic unit within a rigid fiscal framework... The founding of *bastides* was a way for the principal seigneurs to get a better financial return from their forests and farmland."

Once founded, the *bastide* had to be filled with people and a *bayle* was employed to recruit citizens, shunning the high-born (who might refuse to pay their taxes) and serfs who were already working a seigneur's lands. In a few cases, people had to be coerced to settle in a *bastide* or to build houses within a given time on the plots they had bought.

Evolution of the Bastides

Although all *bastides* were founded according to a similar rationale, each subsequently developed into something unique according to the needs of its inhabitants, their prosperity and the conditions of the outside world. The regular plans and property divisions were gradually broken down as the well-to-do replaced cheaply built houses, bought up adjacent plots or built themselves passageways over the streets. Shopkeepers, meanwhile, put up arcades around the squares to keep their customers dry and protected from the summer sun. And invariably a church would be built close to the main square.

In the late 14th century, during the Hundred Years' War, the town councillors of many *bastides* felt it necessary to build ramparts pierced by gateways, all of which interfered further with the original town plan. ❑

RIGHT: houses on the Grande Rue of Cordes-sur-Ciel, the first *bastide* town.

TOULOUSE

*The historic capital of the Languedoc, on the River Garonne and
Canal du Midi, has long been famed for its redbrick architecture,
churches, monasteries and distinctly southern way of life*

Map
on page
198

The only building materials in abundance on the plains of the River Garonne
around Toulouse were clay and sand – the raw ingredients of brick – and
an accumulation of brick-built churches and mansions in the historic city
centre has earned Toulouse the epithet of *La ville rose*, "the rose-coloured city".
This description is particularly apt at sunset when the architecture of the old city
takes on a variety of reddish hues.

Under the Raymond dynasty of counts, Toulouse was, from the 9th to the
13th century, the capital of a loose southern empire stretching from the borders of English Aquitaine to Provence – the capital, in fact, of the *langues d'oc*
– the lands where Occitan was spoken. Until the Albigensian Crusade eclipsed
their fortunes, the counts of Toulouse had prestige almost to rival the King of
France and a court famed throughout Europe. In the 15th and 16th centuries
Toulouse prospered again, this time from the short-lived woad industry. Many
of the 30 private mansions whose towers dominate the city centre were built by
wealthy merchants who cornered the market in the blue dye.

The city's fortunes are on the up again now, this time based on high technology. Beside the airport is the assembly plant for the Airbus, a highly successful
series of European-built passenger aircraft. This and a space research centre
have created work in a great number of specialist
ancillary companies.

Toulouse is considered by its inhabitants to be one
of the most pleasant places in France to live and work.
Midway between the Atlantic and the Mediterranean,
it leans unmistakably towards the latter with an outdoor lifestyle spurred on by the second-largest student population in France after Paris. The city is still
recovering, however, from the terrible explosion at
the chemical factory on the outskirts of Toulouse in
2001, when 29 people were killed, over 2,000 injured
and millions of euros worth of damage caused.
Although terrorism was briskly ruled out the real cause
of the accident is still a matter of great controversy.

The Place du Capitole

The best place to begin a tour of Toulouse is the **Place
du Capitole**, the vast central square formed on three
sides by three-storey red-brick buildings. In the middle of the square is an inlaid Croix Occitane, the 12-
pointed cross symbolising the Languedoc and now
used as a symbol of the Midi-Pyrénées region. The
artist, Raymond Moretti, placed the signs of the
zodiac on the points to extract a little extra symbolism
from the figure.

The fourth side of the square is formed by the 1760
neoclassical facade of the city hall, the **Capitole ❶**.
The name derives from the *capitouls* (consuls) who

PRECEDING PAGES:
brick house on
rue des Arts.
LEFT: rooftops
of Toulouse.
BELOW: café life
in Toulouse.

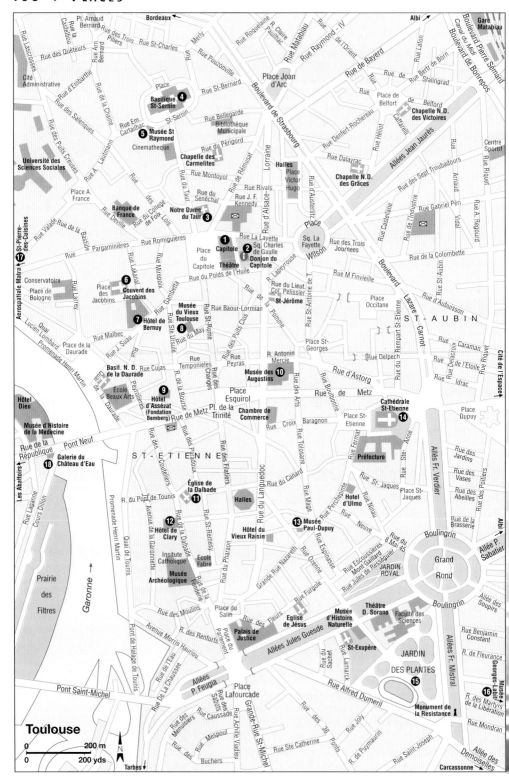

Toulouse

0 _____ 200 m

0 _____ 200 yds

administered the city under the counts of Toulouse. From the square, go through the Capitole's great double doors to enter the 17th-century courtyard, the Cour Henri IV. Facing you is a Renaissance gateway surmounted by the arms of Toulouse and a marble statue of Henri IV.

Beyond this gateway, turn left into the part of the building that can be visited by the public (open daily). The staircase and three salons on the first floor are decorated with a series of large murals. Over the stairs is a massive painting of the *Jeux Floraux* by Jean-Paul Laurens. This shows the origin, in 1324, of the oldest literary society in Europe, the Compagnie du Gai-Savoir, later renamed the Académie des Jeux Floraux, which was, it is said, set up by seven troubadours of Toulouse to preserve the Occitan language. Each year in May, gold and silver flowers are still awarded to nominated poets.

The first room you come to upstairs was intended as a place to celebrate marriages and is decorated with pictures on the theme of love by Paul Gervais. You then pass through a room with large Impressionist-like paintings to reach the main room upstairs, the **Salle des Illustres**, which overlooks the square. Created in 1892 to replace an earlier 17th-century room, it is an almost excessive celebration of events in Toulouse's history, along with flourishes of imaginary architecture and mythological figures. One end of the room is dominated by Jean-Paul Laurens' portrayal of the defence of Toulouse against Simon de Montfort during the Albigensian Crusade *(see page 29)*.

Square Charles de Gaulle

If you leave the city hall building on the opposite side from place du Capitole you emerge into leafy square Charles de Gaulle, on which stands the **Donjon**

INFO

Tourist information office, Toulouse: Donjon du Capitole; tel; 05 61 11 02 22; www.mairie-toulouse.fr

BELOW: waiter in a Toulouse café.

DYEING TO MAKE A FORTUNE

For a short period between the 15th and 16th centuries Toulouse enjoyed a golden age based on the lucrative export of woad (*pastel* in French), a deep-blue dye much sought after in Europe at the time.

The woad plant *(Isatis tinctoria)* cultivated in the Mediterranean region was intensively farmed in the Lauragais (the triangular area bounded by Albi, Toulouse and Castelnaudary), which became known as the Pays de Cocagne, after the *cocques* – balls of concentrated dye.

Speculators from Toulouse, dubbed *"les princes de pastel"*, capitalised on the city's location between the woad producers and the Atlantic ports to control first the local and then the European-wide trade. The personal fortunes that were made are attested to by the many private *hôtels* that still stand in the centre of Toulouse.

The boom did not last long, however. The Wars of Religion, a financial crisis and the arrival of indigo finished Toulouse's monopoly on blue dye towards the end of the 16th century.

La Fleurée de Pastel, a shop located in the 15th-century Hôtel Pierre Delfau (20 rue de la Bourse, close to the Hôtel d'Assézat), sells products dyed with woad and books about the history of Toulouse's brief-lived *pastel* industry.

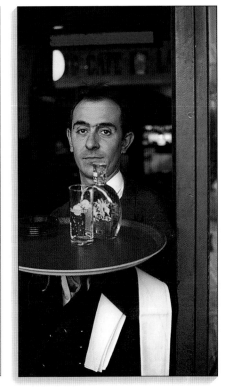

Gilded figure of a saint in the ambulatory of St-Sernin.

BELOW: wedding in Salle des Illustres, Hôtel de Ville.

du Capitole ②. Now housing the tourist information office, the building was erected in the 16th century to store the city council's archives but was restored by Viollet-le-Duc in the 19th century, according to his own notions of how it should be.

One of the best views of the red-brick spires of the city is to be had from the top-floor terrace of the café-restaurant in **Nouvelles Galeries** department store on rue Lapeyrouse (open Mon–Sat; tel: 05 34 45 98 98), a street that leads to the lively, oval-shaped **place Wilson**.

From the Capitole to St-Sernin

Returning to place du Capitole take rue de Taur past the handsome pink-brick façade of **Notre-Dame du Taur ③** (open daily). The name of the street and of this church allude to the story of St Saturninus (Sernin), first bishop of Toulouse (died *circa* 257), who was tied to a bull *(taur)* that he had refused to sacrifice to a pagan god and dragged to his death by the beast. The martyrdom is depicted in a mural inside the church.

At the end of the street is the **Basilique St-Sernin ④** (open daily), the most famous Romanesque pilgrimage church in southern France and the largest Romanesque church in the West. There was a church on the site as early as the 4th century but the building that can be seen today, built of brick and stone, was begun around 1080 and finished in the 14th century. From the outside its most striking features are the octagonal five-tiered bell tower and the Porte Miégevill, which is adorned by 12th-century Romanesque sculpture. It is worth walking a few steps to see the oldest part of the building, the 11th-century apse (the assembly of chapels at the east end, facing rue St-Bernard).

Step inside and you will be struck by the size of the place: it was clearly built to accommodate large numbers of pilgrim worshippers en route to Santiago de Compostela. The highlight of the interior is the ambulatory, where there are carved wooden altars and reliquaries, and the crypt (combined entrance fee). On the outside wall of the crypt are seven late 11th-century marble bas-relief carvings of God sitting in state, a seraph, a cherub, two angels and two apostles. The crypt is in two parts: the upper level contains the 13th-century reliquary of St Saturninus while the lower level has 14th-century statues of the apostles.

Adjacent to St-Sernin stands the city's archaeological museum, **Musée St-Raymond ❺** (place St-Sernin; open daily; entrance fee; tel: 05 61 22 31 44). Begin at the top and work your way downwards. The second floor covers Toulouse's history from the first settlers on the site, the Volques Tectosages (thought to be Celts from Germania), to the Roman town of Tolosa (finds from which include carved columns, mosaic fragments and gold torques). The first floor has a collection of cold marble busts from the period of the Roman Empire. In the basement are paleo-Christian sarcophagi sculpted with human figures and plant motifs. One shows Biblical scenes (Adam and Eve, Daniel in the Lion's Den). Another, the best-known, depicts the hunting of a wild boar.

Couvent des Jacobins

West of place du Capitole is another great Toulouse church, the red-brick **Couvent des Jacobins ❻** (open daily; free admission), considered a masterpiece of southern French Gothic style. Part of the first Dominican monastery, it was founded by St Dominic de Guzman in 1216 as a response to what he saw as the threat to Christianity posed by Albigensian heresy. In the middle of the church,

Map on page 198

Roman imperial bust on display in the Musée St-Raymond.

LEFT: marble relief of God in the crypt of St-Sernin.
BELOW: palm-shaped columns in Les Jacobins.

Sign advertising an organic food market in place du Capitole.

BELOW: paintings in the Musée des Augustins.

the altar stands above the remains of St Thomas Aquinas, who died in Italy in 1274. The church is best known for the "Palmier des Jacobins", a slender column which fans out into a vault of 22 ribs. The striking modern stained-glass windows (1951–64) are by Max Ingrand. A doorway in a corner of the church gives access to the restored cloister (entrance fee).

Round the corner from the Jacobins church is the 16th-century mansion of **Hôtel de Bernuy** ❼ (not open to the public but parts are visible from the street), built by Jean de Bernuy, a Spaniard who made his fortune in woad and who was rich enough to pay the ransom of the French King François I, who had been taken prisoner by Holy Roman Emperor Charles V. The oldest parts of the building (1504) are the façade and second courtyard, which have Gothic details. The very high tower, and the use of stone in the first courtyard (in an area where brick is the cheapest material), are signs of Bernuy's status and wealth.

The pedestrian streets

A string of pedestrianised streets, beginning with **rue St-Rome** and continuing with **rue des Changes**, leads south from place du Capitole. These are good places to stroll and shop, with here and there architectural details worth noting. On an inconspicuous side street off rue St-Rome is the 17th-century red-brick mansion of Hôtel Dumay which now houses the **Musée du Vieux Toulouse** ❽ (7 rue du May; open Mon–Sat afternoon only; entrance fee; tel: 05 62 27 11 50), its collections explaining the history of the city.

Another of the city's mansions, the **Hôtel d'Assézat** ❾, has been turned into the **Bemberg Foundation** (place d'Assézat, rue de Metz; open Tues–Sun; entrance fee; tel: 05 61 12 06 89; www.fondation-bemberg.fr). The 16th-century

Renaissance mansion was built for Pierre d'Assézat, a Protestant woad merchant, by Nicholas Bachelier. The collection inside is mostly made up of paintings and includes works by 18th-century Venetian artists, Impressionists, Pointillists and Fauves. Room 7 is dedicated to just one artist, Pierre Bonnard (1867–1947). There are also some Renaissance bronzes and rare books on display.

Follow rue de Metz from here across busy place Esquirol and you come to the **Musée des Augustins** (21 rue de Metz; open Wed–Mon; entrance fee; tel: 05 61 22 21 82; www.augustins.org). This former monastery, built in the 14th and 15th centuries, and converted into a museum in the 19th century, is chiefly visited for its outstanding collection of Romanesque capitals salvaged from Toulouse's churches. Around the larger courtyard Gothic sculpture is on display and upstairs are 17–19th-century paintings.

South of rue de Metz

South of place Esquirol and rue de Metz is a warren of narrow streets without a proper name. They are dotted with half-timbered houses and old mansions, which have all but fallen into decay. Still following the line of pedestrianised streets from place du Capitole, rue des Changes skirts **Place Esquirol** and continues for a short way to reach what is arguably the prettiest square in the city, **Place de la Trinité**, a delightful place to stop for an outdoor drink.

The 15–16th-century **Église de la Dalbade** ⓫ (rue de la Dalbade; open daily; free admission) looks so austere from the outside that it could be mistaken for a fortress. Over the doorway is a gaudy ceramic copy of Fra Angelico's *The Coronation of the Virgin*. Further down the street, on the opposite side from

"The Hôtel de Pierre has all the effulgent, restless energy of the south, enobled with trophies of arms and fruit. Deeply channelled pilasters flower into Corinthian capitals...Nothing stands still for a minute."

– ANDREW SHIRLEY,
South from Toulouse

BELOW: portal of the Église de la Dalbade.

the church, is the **Hôtel de Clary** , also known as the Hôtel de Pierre. It was built in 1538 but the overwhelming façade was added in the 17th century by a later owner, François de Clary. As president of the Toulouse parliament, Clary was in charge of the building of the Pont Neuf and unkind tongues of his time were wont to remark, "*Il y a plus de pierres du pont à l'hôtel de Pierre que de pierres au pont*": "There are more stones from the bridge in the Hôtel de Pierre than there are stones in the bridge."

No 15 rue Croix-Baragon, a lovely brick building with carvings around its first-floor windows and modern shops beneath, is thought to be the city's oldest house.

On a side street off rue Ozenne is the **Musée Paul-Dupuy** (13 rue de la Pleau; open Wed–Mon; entrance fee; tel: 05 61 14 65 50), the eclectic collection of an early 20th-century amateur art connoisseur laid out in a 17th-century mansion. The museum is particularly strong on the applied arts – glass, ivory, metalwork, clocks (one of the best collections in Europe), musical instruments, etc – from the Middle Ages to recent times. It also has works of art by Ingres, Delacroix, Toulouse-Lautrec and Dufy, as well as a large number of engravings, photographs, postcards and other graphic material.

The streets between rue du Languedoc and place St-Étienne comprise an area known as the **Quartier des Antiquaires**, although antiques dealers are not as plentiful as is suggested by the name and their premises are separated nowadays by many other types of shop.

BELOW: stained glass in Cathédrale St-Étienne.
RIGHT: bay window on place de la Trinité.

After seeing St-Sernin, Toulouse's Cathedral, **Cathédrale St-Étienne** (place St-Étienne; open daily), can be a disappointment. The nave (sometimes called Isarn's nave) was built in 1210, in Southern Gothic style. In 1272 Bishop Bertrand de L'Isle began work on a new choir which was out of alignment with the nave because it was planned to replace the latter altogether. The bishop's death, together with a shortage of funds, left the Cathedral in the unhappy state it is today. It does, however, have some 14th- and 15th-century stained glass, including a window in the ambulatory showing Charles VII, in crown and blue cape, and the dauphin Louis (later Louis XI), dressed as a knight and kneeling. At the base of the large pillar in between the nave and the choir (added in the 16th century), Pierre-Paul Riquet, creator of the Canal du Midi, is buried.

South of the Cathedral you can catch your breath in three gardens connected by footbridges dripping with foliage which cross the busy roads between the greenery: the **Jardin Royal**, the green traffic island of the **Grand Rond** or Boulingrin (the French transcription of the English Bowling Green); and the 18th-century **Jardin des Plantes** ⑮, on the south side of Allées Jules Guesde.

It's still a fair walk to one of Toulouse's most singular museums, the **Musée Georges-Labit** ⑯ (17 rue du Japon; open Wed–Mon; tel: 05 61 14 65 50) but worth the effort. This museum of Ancient Egyptian and Far Eastern art is housed in a mock-Moorish villa not far from the bank of the Canal du Midi. It was founded by Georges Labit (1862–99), an intrepid traveller and Orientalist from Toulouse, and is now owned by the city.

On the waterfront

Stroll away from the city centre east or west and you get the impression that old Toulouse is surrounded by water. The north and eastern sides of the centre are defined by the **Canal du Midi** *(see page 83)*, which joins the canal that runs beside the River Garonne towards Bordeaux at the port de l'Embouchure (now, sadly, a traffic island). The short **Canal de Brienne** also begins here. There are quiet, shaded paths along both banks suitable for strolling, jogging or cycling.

Near the junction of the Canal de Brienne and the River Garonne stands one

Map on page 198

TIP

For somewhere slightly different to eat try L'Occitania, a floating restaurant moored at 4 boulevard Bonrepos (opposite the railway station), which cruises along the Canal du Midi while you eat.

BELOW: relaxing by the Pont Neuf over the River Garonne.

"Incredible filth and vulgarity of the common people in Toulouse... everything I saw was ugly and coarse."

– STENDHAL,
Travels in the South of France

of the oldest buildings in Southwest France, the church of **St-Pierre-des-Cuisines**  (place St-Pierre; open daily, Sept–June mornings only; July–Aug afternoons only). It has recently been converted for use as a small, atmospheric concert hall but beneath the bank of seats a path leads through the ruins and stone sarcophagi of the 5th-century crypt.

The Promenade Henri Martin, lined by plane trees, leads along the river bank to **place de la Daurade**, a sunken riverside garden. A map of old Toulouse is set into the grass. *Bateaux-mouches* (barge) trips up the River Garonne depart from the quay here (Toulouse-Croisières tel: 05 61 25 72 57; departures daily July–Oct; Nov–June Tues–Sun; trip takes 90 minutes; fare payable), certainly a good way to get a view of Toulouse. An unlikely looking doorway on the south side of the square leads into the gloom of the Basilique Notre-Dame-de-la-Daurade, where a black Madonna is venerated.

The oldest of the bridges crossing the Garonne is the **Pont Neuf**, built of brick and stone between 1544 and 1632. At the end of it stands the distinctive silhouette of the **Galerie du Château d'Eau** (1 place Laganne; open Wed–Mon afternoons only; tel: 05 61 77 09 40), a 19th-century water tower transformed into a photographic gallery with changing exhibitions.

The opposite bank of the river from the city centre is rapidly taking on a cultural life of its own. A new gallery for modern and contemporary art, **Les Abattoirs** (76 allée Charles-de-Fitte; open Tues–Sun; entrance fee; tel: 05 62 48 58 00; www.lesabattoirs.org), is, as its name suggests, a stylishly converted 19th-century slaughterhouse. The permanent collection consists of 2,000 works from the second half of the 20th century, and regular exhibitions present modern art from an original perspective.

BELOW: courtyard of Les Abattoirs.
RIGHT: looking at art inside Les Abattoirs.

Air and space

You may have exhausted the city centre but you are not finished with Toulouse yet. Two of the most unusual sights – both contemporary rather than historical – are on the outskirts.

Toulouse airport at Blagnac may not look much as you arrive or depart, but beside it is one of Europe's largest aircraft factories, named after pioneer French aviator Clément Ader. It is not an obvious tourist sight but visits to the Airbus plant are very popular and they give an insight into the life of the city. Book in advance to visit **Airbus** (visits by prior arrangement; entrance fee; Taxiway tel: 05 61 18 06 01; www.taxifly.com) and be prepared to leave your passport at reception. A coach takes you for a short tour around the complex – passing a Caravelle and the first Concorde – before you are guided to a special viewing balcony overlooking the assembly lines.

Of more obvious appeal – especially for children – is the pride of Toulouse, the **Cité de l'Espace** (avenue Jean-Gonord; to get there take the road to Castres from the centre of Toulouse or turn off the orbital motorway round the east of the city at exit 17; open Tues–Sun; entrance fee; tel: 05 62 71 64 80; www.espace-cite.com), identifiable from afar by the Ariane rocket standing outside it. Science and fun are combined in this highly interactive celebration of the (mainly European) space industry. All the displays are scientifically accurate and most of the things you see are either authentic cast-off space equipment, prototypes or replicas. The kids will certainly take in something useful as they learn how to launch a missile, experience weightlessness for a split second or use a simulator to steer. The museum is divided into a building and an outdoor area, "the park", in which stands the Ariane rocket and a Mir space station. ❑

Map on page 198

In the 30 years from its creation in 1970 to the turn of the millennium, the European consortium Airbus Industrie won about 55 percent of the world's aircraft market.

BELOW: Mir space station in the Cité de l'Espace.

THE AEROSPACE INDUSTRY OF TOULOUSE

Toulouse can claim to be the air and space capital of France, if not of Europe, with its Airbus assembly plant and its "City of Space"

Clément Ader from Muret, near Toulouse, made the world's first motorised flight on 9 October 1890. If Ader's steam-powered plane (a later version of which is shown above) is less well remembered than the Wright brothers' aircraft (which was launched 13 years later) it may be because it rose a mere 11 cm (5 inches) off the ground and flew just 50 metres (55 yards).

As the French aircraft industry developed in the early years of the 20th century, Toulouse became its capital. It had all the right conditions: there was space for factories and runways to spare; clear skies could be relied upon because of the Mediterranean climate; and southwest France was safely removed from the battles of World War I.

Latécoère airlines began a commercial mail service between Toulouse and Rabat (Morocco) in 1919. In 1927 this developed into the historic Aéropostale service, for which pioneer airmen such as Jean Mermoz and Antoine de Saint-Exupéry flew record-breaking flights.

AIRBUS

Toulouse has one of the largest aircraft factories in Europe, the Usine Clément Ader, beside the airport at Blagnac. Here, the assembly line of the successful Airbus series of planes can be visited on a guided tour (see page 207). Airbus Industrie, rival to the US company Boeing, is a consortium of French, German, British and Spanish firms with its head-quarters at Toulouse.

▷ **AIRBUS ASSEMBLY LINE**
Components for Airbus planes are made in factories around Europe and brought to Toulouse for final assembly in the immense Usine Clément Ader, beside Blagnac airport.

△ **AIRBORNE POSTMAN**
The airman and author, Antoine de Saint-Exupéry, flew mail deliveries out of Toulouse in Aéropostale's early days. He disappeared while flying a mission in World War II.

◁ **CLÉMENT ADER**
A sculpted monument to the French aviator Clément Ader (1841–1926) stands in his hometown of Muret, south of Toulouse.

▷ **FLYING GIANT**
The next generation jumbo jet, a "flying hotel" for over 550 passengers, will be assembled in Airbus's Toulouse factory.

TOULOUSE GOES INTO SPACE

Toulouse was chosen as the site for France's showcase space museum, the Cité de l'Espace *(see page 207)*, for good reason. An estimated 10,000 people in the city work in space research and development, and related industries, for which Toulouse has been called the "European Space Capital". At the heart of all this astronautical activity is the Centre Spatiale de Toulouse (CST: Toulouse Space Centre), part of the National Centre for Space Research, which was set up in 1968 and employs nearly 2,500 people in its laboratories and offices near the Université Paul Sabatier. Its presence has stimulated many private companies to establish themselves in Toulouse – on streets with space-age names such as avenue des Cosmonautes and rue des Satellites – to supply the space industry with satellites, rocket parts and software systems, or market the products of space flight, notably satellite images.

◁ **ILL-FATED CONCORDE**
The Anglo-French supersonic airliner was a legend from its test flight in Toulouse in 1969 until a crash in Paris in July 2000, when 113 people were killed; it was taken out of service in October 2003.

▷ **THE BELUGA**
Large aircraft components are ferried between the different Airbus plants in this front-loading transporter plane.

◁ **SATELLITE CITY**
Astrium (Matra Marconi Space) and Alcatel Space are the two largest companies that build satellites and other space equipment in factories in Toulouse.

▷ **THE CARAVELLE**
The much loved Caravelle airliner, which was built in Toulouse, made its maiden flight to Istanbul in 1959.

GASCONY

From the Atlantic beaches and forests of the Landes to the lush farmlands of the Gers stretches the heartland of a people renowned in France for their geniality and good living

Map on page 214

n France, the people of Gascony are said to exemplify geniality, verve and courage. Their fertile province, green and beautiful, is today administered not under its 1,000-year-old title, Gascony, but under two newer departmental names: Gers and Landes. The rolling hills and valleys, wooded slopes, well-tended farms and vineyards of the Gers ease, in the west, to the Landes' vast forest of pines and its Côte d'Argent, a 100-km (60-mile) "silver coast" that is all glorious sandy beach. Rippling streams and rivers, small towns and villages rooted in history, isolated farmhouses and châteaux, grace a peaceable landscape that benefits from warm summers, a long sunny autumn, and a comparatively mild winter.

The good life

It is a region endowed with the good, simple things of life: clear, unpolluted skies, commendable wines and a prodigious variety of fresh country produce. Its cuisine is admired throughout France. Armagnac is produced here, along with that gastronomic delicacy, foie gras. Statistics record that Gascons live to a greater age than anyone in France. That their traditional cooking incorporates generous quantities of duck fat has fascinated medical science for years.

The Gers (pronounced *jairs* – Gascons sound the "s") is the most rural *département* in France. Nowhere else has so high a proportion of inhabitants engaged in agriculture – or almost as low a population density, 28 to the square kilometre (under 80 per square mile). Seasons provide a palette of colours – sunflowers, oceans of green corn, the pale gold of wheat. Trees are as eye-catching – mimosa, vividly blossoming fruit trees, sturdy oaks, chestnut and walnut. Driving on well-maintained roads – many in the Gers run along hilltop ridges following the original *routes royales* built centuries ago – you will see large flocks of geese and ducks but few people and relatively little traffic. This pleasant driving is also true of the Landes except in the height of summer, July and August, when the region becomes a sort of lake district in a forest by the sea and draws holidaymakers in crowds.

Gascony's architecture has evolved from old stone, oak and natural clay – a solid *maison gasconne* is softened by gentle ochre hues. Buildings in the Landaise style are low-pitched and impressively half-timbered. You will see a striking array of churches, cathedrals and chapels dating from the 13th century or even earlier. Some churches have elaborate belfries, tall steeples and slender spires, others flat-topped octagonal towers. In a 13th-century rush for "new", secure villages there came the *bastides (see page 193)*. Several (including Bassoues, Gimont and Mauvezin)

PRECEDING PAGES: surfer in action on the Atlantic coast. **LEFT:** farmland view in the Gers. **BELOW:** rearing geese for foie gras.

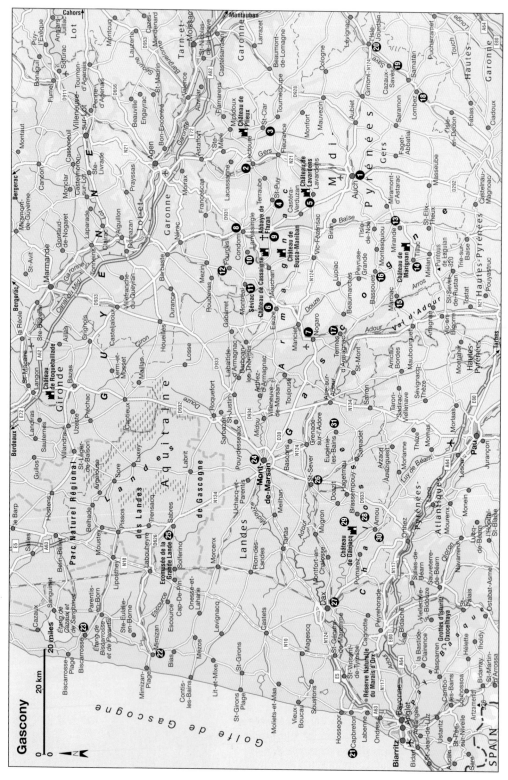

Gascony

retain their covered *halles* – markets with a pronounced medieval aura. These apart, you will also see countless plain country churches, the occasional raised gables adding graceful notes to the Gascon landscape.

Map on page 214

Musketeer Country

Auch ❶ (pronounced *osh*), capital of the Gers, is in what Gersois call the *pays des mousquetaires* – Musketeer Country. Less than an hour by road from Toulouse's Blagnac airport, it is a practical starting point for exploring the region. A silhouette on the skyline, the **Cathédrale Ste-Marie** (open daily) dates to 1489. Mainly Gothic, it has a Renaissance façade framed by two "wedding cake" towers. The finest features are inside – 113 carved oak choir stalls portraying more than 1,500 figures and scenes; in the chapels 18 stained-glass windows, completed in 1513, are by the master painter Arnaud de Moles.

Across the square from the cathedral is the **tourist information office** (tel: 05 62 05 22 89), in a 15th-century *colombage* (half-timbered) house, itself an architectural gem. Close by are shops, ancient alleyways and, a few steps down in a former monastery, the **Musée des Jacobins** (open daily; entrance fee; tel: 05 62 05 74 79), founded in 1793. Its collection is eclectic – the archaeology and art includes pre-Columbian objects from Latin America and a surreal 1539 Mexican mosaic in feathers. Standing 40-metres (130-ft) tall beside the cathedral is the 14th-century **Tour d'Armagnac** (not open to the public), a handy prison across the centuries. From here you can walk down the 370 steps of a broad stairway, the **Escalier Monumental**, on which, in plumed hat, boots and cloak, stands in bronze the most celebrated Gascon of all, D'Artagnan, captain of Musketeers to King Louis XIV *(see panel below)*.

"Musketeers" on horseback in a Gascon village fête.

BELOW: statue of D'Artagnan in Auch.

D'ARTAGNAN

Old soldiers, they say, never die. Dashing D'Artagnan and the Three Musketeers don't even fade away. Alexandre Dumas's famous adventure novel, *The Three Musketeers*, has been filmed in at least 25 versions. The epitome of Gascon passion and chivalry, D'Artagnan was more than a legendary hero of fiction. He really existed.

He was born Charles de Batz around 1613 in the château of Castelmore near Lupiac. The name D'Artagnan came from his mother's Montesquiou family. A younger son, he was sent away to be a soldier and soon became a *mousquetaire*, or king's guard, to France's Louis XIV. Promoted to *capitaine*, he served the king devotedly, handling such delicate missions as the arrest of his financier, Nicolas Fouquet. He married a high-class widow and fathered two sons – both named Louis. Appointed governor of Lille, he was called upon to take up arms against the Dutch. He died in the siege of Maastricht in 1673 from a musket shot in the throat. The king, it was reported, wept at the news.

The compelling story of the Gascon hero in life and in fiction is to be found in Lupiac in the **Centre D'Artagnan** (open July–Aug Tues–Sun; Sept–June afternoons only; entrance fee; tel: 05 62 09 24 09).

TIP

Look out for night markets which are held in Fleurance, Nogaro, Vic Fezensac and several other Gers towns in July and August. These are lively events at which you can not only shop for fresh produce but also have a drink or enjoy a meal at a pavement table.

BELOW:
beekeeper at work.

North of Auch

From Auch a 24-km (15-mile) drive north leads to **Fleurance**, a *bastide* and prominent market town, and 11 km (7 miles) further north to **Lectoure ❷**, eye-catchingly sited on a hill. Lectoure was prominent in the major events marking French history. It was an important city in Gallo-Roman times, and the main residence of the counts of Armagnac. Later it was involved in royal intrigues, religious wars and the Revolution. Walk along rue Nationale today and you will see 17th- and 18th-century houses. At the street's eastern end is the **Cathédrale St-Gervais**, originally built to the order of a bishop among whose guests, in 1273, was the English King, Edward I. It was, however, rebuilt in the 15th century. Inside, the vault rises 21 metres (68 ft) above a Gothic nave.

The neighbouring **Hôtel de Ville** was the bishop's palace; the tourist office is to one side. The bishop's basement kitchens are now the **Musée Archéologique** (open Wed–Mon; entrance fee; tel: 05 62 68 70 22), whose displays include sculpted sarcophagi, stone statues and a collection of tauroboles – stone altars used in the 2nd- and 3rd-century cult of bull worship. In some contrast, at 5 rue Ste-Claire, a few steps away, is the **Centre de Photographie** (open daily; entrance fee) with frequently changing shows. Northeast of Lectoure is the 14th-century **Château de Plieux**, restored by its owner, the writer, Renaud Camus, and used for contemporary art exhibitions (open Wed–Mon in summer; weekends only in winter; tel: 05 62 28 60 86).

St-Clar ❸, southeast of Lectoure, is the garlic capital of France. With a broad covered *halle,* it's a quiet town most days but becomes animated on Thursday, market day. The liveliest time of all is during the summer garlic fair when local contestants fashion amazing creations entirely from garlic heads.

Southwest of Lectoure, in **St-Puy ❹**, is **Château de Monluc** (open May–Oct Tues–Sun; Nov–Apr Tues–Sat; entrance fee; tel: 05 62 28 94 00), dating from the 10th century. A stalwart Gascon château fought over by kings across the centuries, it's best known for its Monluc wines, most especially a liqueur, *Pousse Rapière*, meaning "rapier thrust".

To the south, a broad-shouldered hillside giant dramatically looms over village houses in the style of a true *castelnau* (a settlement under the protection of a castle). The **Château de Lavardens ❺** (open July–Aug daily; entrance fee; tel: 05 62 64 51 20) was built in the 17th century and rescued from ruin by local people who conserve it lovingly to this day.

Eauze

To the west, captivating and composed among the vineyards of Armagnac country, is **Eauze ❻**, the Romans' Elusa. Its **Cathedral**, dating from the 15th century, is a blend of styles – the walls and rough interior surfaces using stone from the much earlier Gallo-Roman city. In the central place d'Armagnac is the half-timbered **Maison de Jeanne d'Albret** the facade of which has been classified a historic monument. Next to the Hôtel de Ville is a **museum** (open Wed–Mon; entrance fee; tel: 05 62 09 71 38) containing the **Trésor d'Eauze**: 28,003 Roman coins – denarii and sesterces – from the 3rd-century rule of emperor

Caracalla. Along with a few jewels, the coins were discovered in an archaeological dig on the outskirts of Eauze in 1985. Hammered patterns show Roman gods, animals and architecture – and what's labelled as imperial propaganda. On another floor, wall paintings illustrate bull worship and the use of sacrificial tauroboles. One stomach-churning scene depicts a woman's baptism in blood.

Near Eauze is the small town of **Nogaro ❼**, its **Formula 3** track and regular events an attraction for motor-racing fans.

Map
on page
214

Condom and Armagnac

Condom ❽, on the Baïse River, is a bright and prosperous cathedral town and a major Armagnac centre. Its name, bizarre to English speakers, is thought to derive from *condominium,* land ruled by 1st-century Vascons (later Gascons), or possibly from Roman terms: *condate,* meaning confluence, and *dum,* a hill. However, the town has accepted the inevitable, if accidental, association with birth-control and greets tourists in summer with an exhibition of contraceptives. Otherwise, its most important sight remains the **Cathédrale St-Pierre**, which was rebuilt in the 16th century on the ruins of an 11th-century abbey. Particularly esteemed are its vaulted cloisters.

An Armagnac producer shows off a glass of eau-de-vie.

A **Musée de l'Armagnac** (open Mon–Sat; entrance fee; tel: 05 62 28 47 17) in rue Jules Ferry retraces the history of the renowned *eau-de-vie*. The tourist information office will provide you with a list of local producers who welcome visitors. At both the **Château de Busca-Maniban** (open Easter–mid-Nov Tues–Sun; tel: 05 62 28 40 38), Mansencome, and the **Château de Cassaigne** (open daily; tel: 05 62 28 04 02) near Flaran, you can visit the *chais* (cellars), taste their products and tour centuries-old classic Gascon residences.

BELOW: still for producing Armagnac.

ARMAGNAC

France's oldest *eau-de-vie* is produced in a region covering about 130 sq km (50 sq miles) and broken down into three areas, each of which claims its product to be the finest: Bas-Armagnac to the west around Eauze and Nogaro; Haut-Armagnac to the east; and Ténarèze in between, with Condom as its "capital". Far from being a factory product, the spirit is made by some 5,000 *vignerons* (small producers).

Armagnac is produced by distilling white grapes. From the still – quite often an old copper alambic – it emerges colourless but time turns it golden. A quality Armagnac matures in an oak cask for 10 to 20 years. Once bottled, this ageing process stops. Armagnac must be a year old before it is sold. VO, VSOP or *Réserve* on the label mean it is at least four years old. *Hors d'Age* indicates a blend of spirits, none younger than 10 years. True distinction depends on factors that include soils, vinification and blending skills.

To see the distillation process for yourself, ask any tourist information office in the Armagnac region about producers open to the public, or visit the **Ecomusée de l'Armagnac** (tel: 05 58 44 88 38; open daily; Nov–Apr closed weekends; entrance fee), 3 km (2 miles) from the village of La Bastide d'Armagnac.

Shopping for clothes during Marciac jazz festival.

Graceful restoration

You are close here to the outstanding Cistercian **Abbaye de Flaran** ❾ (closed Tues; entrance fee; tel: 05 62 28 50 19), on the outskirts of Valence-sur-Baïse. Dating from 1151, the abbey, its cloister and newer buildings have been grace-fully restored. Exhibitions, concerts and other cultural events are regularly held at the abbey. In **La Romieu** (open daily except Jan and Sun morning; entrance fee), northeast of Condom, an imposing 14th-century collegiate church with Gothic paintings, also has a very fine cloister.

High walls and stout ramparts still guard **Larressingle** ❿, a singular example of a 13th-century fortified village. Inside is a church, a ruined château, tiny vil-lage houses (some now bijou boutiques), a small museum, and medieval mili-tary machines. For all the tranquil mood today, Larressingle's ancient stones evoke centuries of discord and war.

You will find a quite different and infinitely happier spirit, as well as glorious mosaic art, at the Gallo-Roman villas of **Séviac** ⓫ (open Mar–mid-Nov daily; entrance fee; tel: 05 62 29 48 57), which was discovered near the *bastide* town of **Montréal**. Séviac shows all the evidence of a luxurious lifestyle: hot-water systems; a swimming pool complete with mosaic waves; and great mosaic floors patterned with lush grapes and multi-coloured designs. The site includes a small museum.

Séviac is extraordinary, and so – in another way – is **Fourcès** ⓬, 6 km (4 miles) north of Montréal, or l2 km (7 miles) from Condom. A tiny 14th-century *bastide*, it's as pretty as a picture. It has a castle (now a hotel), an intriguing clocktower, medieval houses and bridge and a central square that is a perfect circle. In spring an annual flower show is held in Fourcès.

BELOW:
annual flower
show in Fourcès.

Mirande, Marciac and foie gras country

South of Auch, **Mirande** is a strikingly harmonious example of a classic 13th-century *bastide*, its streets around the central place d'Astarac as tidily planned as a chess board. A surprise note is struck in the bizarre – even Disneyesque – towers of its 1409 Gothic cathedral, explained in part by flying buttresses. Today the cathedral, demoted, is the **Église de Ste-Marie**. Beside it is the tourist information office and the **Musée des Beaux-Arts Décoratifs** (open Mon–Sat; entrance fee; tel: 05 62 66 68 10) with a significant collection of Italian, Flemish and French paintings from the 15th century. Displayed too are French ceramics from the 17th to the 19th century.

To the south is the medieval village of **Tillac** , a *bastide* with a clocktower. The little main street is all stout beams and tiny houses, and there is a half-timbered house bright with flowering window-boxes. If you're there on a sparkling day, it's worth going a little further south to **Puntous de Laguian**, a hill beside the N21 highway, for a spectacular view of the Pyrenees.

Known for its August jazz festival, **Marciac** , beside a lake, is otherwise a quiet *bastide* with a modest year-round jazz museum, **Les Territoires du Jazz** (open daily, closed Sat and Sun am; entrance fee; tel: 05 62 08 26 60).

Heading north, aim for **Bassoues** 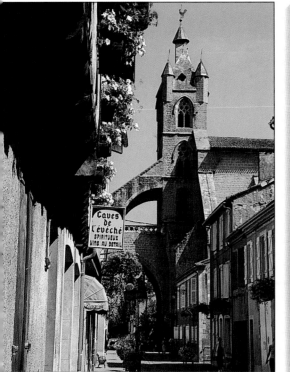, a 13th-century *bastide* with a tall, eye-catching **donjon**. Constructed by a nephew of Pope Innocent VI, the towering dungeon is at one end of the street, a covered *halle* – you drive right through it – at the other. It's a friendly village, and a good place to pause for a drink or meal.

Here you are close to the very heart of D'Artagnan country. Northward lies the snug *castelnau* (a community under the protectorate of a chateau) of **Lupiac** where the great Gascon was born. To the west, in a high stone tower at **Termes**

Map on page 214

TIP

For 10 days around 15 August, Marciac puts on one of Europe's best-known jazz festivals. Every day there's live jazz for free in the central square.

LEFT: the Église de St-Marie in Mirande.
BELOW: performer at Marciac jazz festival.

Promoting the local vintage during a village fête.

BELOW: a sign advertising foie gras.

d'Armagnac , Gascon history (including Henri of Navarre and, of course, D'Artagnan and the Musketeers) is evoked on five levels of the **Musée du Panache Gascon** (open Wed–Mon: winter closed am and Tues; entrance fee; tel: 05 62 69 25 12).

East of Auch, **Gimont**, **Samatan** and **Saramon** are important locally for their weekly winter markets for *gras* (fat), from which *foie gras* is made *(see box below)*. In nearby **Lombez** ⓲, the 14th-century former cathedral with its late-Gothic tower is set among old townhouses. **Mauvezin**, with a handsome *halle,* is also rich in history. At **Cazaux-Savès** ⓳ you can visit the 16th-century **Château de Caumont** (open July and Aug daily, afternoons only; closed Nov–Feb; Sept, Oct and Mar–June weekends only; entrance fee; tel: 05 62 07 94 20) a defensive Renaissance structure in glowing stone.

From the Toulouse-Auch highway it's worth the short detour to **l'Isle Jourdain** ⓴ to see, in the splendidly renovated *halle,* a fascinating bell and clock collection, the **Musée d'Art Campanaire** (closed Tues; entrance fee; tel: 05 62 07 30 01) which includes a celebrated carillon rescued from revolutionaries attacking the Bastille.

The Landes forest

In the Landes *département,* the prime attractions are the open-air pleasures of beach, lakes and forest. The forest, covering a million hectares (2½ million acres) of mainly maritime pines – a tree natural to the landscape – was planted in the 19th century to the order of Napoleon III. Even the dunes protecting forest from ocean are largely man-made. The forest today is the basis of an industry producing more than 9 million cubic metres (320 million cubic ft) of wood a year.

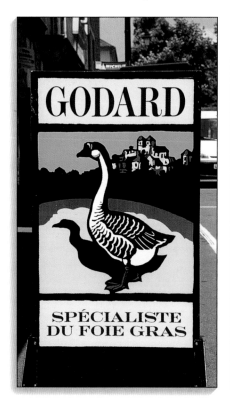

FOIE GRAS

Curnonsky, a famous gastronome, once declared foie gras to be "a pure marvel of the culinary art, a masterpiece that has assured the glory of our country". This light and luxurious pâté, whose name literally means "fat liver", is made from the enlarged livers of force-fed ducks (foie gras de canard) and geese (foie gras d'oie).

Gavage – the method of force feeding the animal with maize – was originally a cottage industry in which farmers' wives fed their free-range birds one by one. There are still some 4,000 small-scale home producers but production is fast shifting to mechanised manufacturers, operating under European Union controls, who buy fattened ducks from local breeders.

When the bird is slaughtered, its large, cream-coloured liver is carefully cleaned of blood vessels, seasoned, poached, pressed and then chilled. The result is one of the most fragrant of all flavours, a soft paste which is spread thickly on lightly toasted bread or served in a variety of other ways.

The Gers and Landes are the prime producing *départements* in France, together turning out 13,000 tonnes of foie gras a year from corn-fed ducks. A smaller quantity comes from geese.

Map
on page
214

Within its immensity is the **Parc Naturel Régional des Landes de Gascogne**, extending over nearly 3,000 sq km (1,160 sq miles), in which are 40 *communes* (villages) containing almost 50,000 inhabitants. The forest contains numerous *étangs,* or lakes: several near the coast are ideal for sailing and boating; others are small, quiet worlds of wildlife. The forest provides endless scope for horse-riding, fishing, cycling and rambling along marked paths. Tourist information offices can provide a *Plan Guide de la Randonnée* which includes main walking routes, cycling tracks and botanical areas to explore.

Along the Atlantic coast

Near the southern end of the Landes coast are two resorts: **Capbreton ㉑**, a long-established and now popular fishing port, and its chicer neighbour, **Hossegor**. Inland to the south is an 800-hectare (1,980-acre) protected marsh-land with abundant birdlife, the **Réserve Naturelle du Marais d'Orx** (Maison du Marais; open daily; guided tour on reservation; entrance fee; tel: 05 59 45 42 46).

Mimizan ㉒, a long way to the north, benefits from an exquisite lake (on the shore of which a former Duke of Westminster built a lodge, Woolsack, often visited by Winston Churchill) and the immense beach of **Mimizan-Plage**.

Further north still is **Biscarrosse ㉓**, with wonderful *étangs* (lakes) north and south, and the lively **Biscarrosse-Plage** a 15-minute drive away. Biscarrosse was the northern Landes base for France's pioneer aviators. Motors, propellers and amphibian aircraft, including a handsome 1912 Donnet-Lévèque, are on view in the town's **Musée Historique de l'Hydraviation** (open daily July–Aug, Sept–June Wed–Mon; entrance fee; tel: 05 58 78 00 65). Next door is the **Musée des Traditions** (open Tues–Sun; entrance fee; tel: 05 58 78 77 37) showing

France's west coast is a favourite choice of world-class surfers. Contests including Rip Curl Pro, Surf Pro-Junior, BodyBoard and BodySurfing, and Long Board Master, are held in August and September in Hossegor and Capbreton.

BELOW: the Réserve Naturelle du Marais d'Orx.

Well-read Gascon scarecrow.

Landes' life the way it was – farm tools and furniture, old photographs and newspapers, and a cunning cockroach trap.

The Landes inland

The prosperous administrative capital of the Landes *département*, **Mont-de-Marsan** ㉔, grew where the Douze and Midou rivers meet to become the Midouze. Combining culture with architectural history, the **Musée Despiau-Wlérick** (open Wed–Mon; closed public holidays; entrance fee), housed in a battlemented keep, displays a collection of modern figurative sculpture.

The **Ecomusée de la Grande Lande** ㉕ (open daily early April–early Nov; entrance fee; tel: 05 58 08 31 31) at Marquèze can only be reached by train – a six-minute journey from Sabres. The trip is especially worth doing if you are travelling with children. Classic Landaise farm buildings are faithfully conserved in a broad forest glade within the *parc naturel régional*. This is the backdrop for demonstrations of traditional aspects of rural life. You can see oxcarts at work, flocks of sheep being herded (and sheared in season), resin being extracted from pine trees (once a commercially important activity in the Landes), and a baker making bread which you can eat straight from the old oven.

There is marvellous sculpture in the capitals of pillars within the Benedictine abbey church in **St-Sever** ㉖, a town founded in 965 a little south and high above the Adour River. Nearby **Dax** ㉗ has been known since Roman times for its thermal spas – 18 at the last count, as well as the Romans' own hot springs in the **Fontaine Chaude**. The **Musée de Borda** (open Tues–Sat; entrance fee; tel: 05 58 74 12 91), close to the cathedral and rue St-Vincent, is named after a distinguished native son. Its exhibits cover art, archaeology and

BELOW: train to the Ecomusée de la Grande Lande.

Map on page 214

folklore. If a "flying banana" means anything to you, then you'll enjoy Dax's **Musée de l'Aviation Légère** (avenue de l'Aérodrome; open Mon–Sat; closed public holidays; entrance fee; tel: 05 58 74 66 19), which displays some 25 aircraft, including helicopters, flown since 1942 by the French Army Air Corps.

Exploring further south in the farmlands of the Chalosse and Amou, turn west off the D933 for St-Cricq and then south to **Brassempouy** ㉘. In the village **museum** (open daily; closed Mon Oct–June; entrance fee; tel: 05 58 89 21 73), down the street from the flamboyant 15th-century **St Saturninus** church, is the world's oldest carved human head. Carbon dating of the minuscule woman's head, sculpted from an ivory mammoth tooth discovered in archaeological digs in 1894 and soon dubbed the Dame de Brassempouy *(see page 21)*, revealed the astonishing date of 23,000 BC.

Just 6 km (4 miles) west of Brassempouy is the **Château de Gaujacq** ㉙ (open July–Aug daily; Sept–June Thur–Tues; guided visits only; entrance fee; tel: 05 58 89 24 61), a beautifully proportioned 17th-century country house with an arched gallery framing an inner garden. Here too is a plantarium: gardens containing some 3,000 species of flowers, trees and shrubs.

In **Amou** ㉚, a pretty riverside town 6 km (4 miles) south, the 17th-century **Château d'Amou** (open daily; guided visits July–Sept; by appointment May–Oct; entrance fee; tel: 05 58 89 00 08) sits grandly at the end of a tree-lined drive.

Over to the east, in a calm valley, is the spa town of **Eugénie-les-Bains** ㉛, named by Napoleon III in honour of his wife. More thrilling still, perhaps, is that today it is also the gastronomic realm of Michel Guérard, one of France's greatest chefs whose hotel-restaurant, Les Près d'Eugénie, and less costly *auberge*, **La Ferme aux Grives** (tel: 05 58 05 06 07), are located here. ❏

TIP

Shepherds in the Landes used to walk on stilts to watch over their flocks. This tradition can still be seen at village fêtes. Ask for details in the region's tourist information offices.

BELOW: Landes stilt walkers.

THE BASQUE COUNTRY

The French Basque Country is a tiny enclave whose attractions include superb Atlantic beaches, great Pyrenean mountain scenery and the unique culture of the people themselves

Map on page 228

The Basque Country (Pays Basque) nestles at the western end of the Pyrenees, cradled by thickly forested hills and flanked by the pounding surf of the Atlantic Ocean. It is an idiosyncratic enclave sheltering one of France's most distinct regional groups, an ancient nation which has clung stoically to its own language and cultural traditions. The French Basque Country covers three unofficial districts, all enclosed in the *département* of Pyrénées-Atlantiques. As soon as you see the language on the road signs there is no doubt you are in a country within a country; but the French Basques' assertion of their identity is far less strident than that of their compatriots across the border in Spain.

The rural interior, poorer, more agricultural and less dependent on tourism than the coast, is the bastion of the Basque culture. Here the people still speak Basque and paint their houses with red shutters (the colour originally came from ox blood). Sometimes, to the visitor, it can seem that the effort to maintain identity has stifled any independent creativity.

The coast, by contrast, has more foreigners (including French, of course) than Basques. The glorious melange of seaside architecture reflects the many different nationalities that have embraced this area, most recently the surfers who have made it the European capital of their sport. The beaches were severely damaged at the beginning of 2003 after the *Prestige* oil spill off the coast of Spain, but massive clean-up efforts have been successful, and sun and sea holidays here are as popular as ever.

PRECEDING PAGES: landscape in the Basque Pyrenees. **LEFT:** St-Jean-Pied de-Port. **BELOW:** Basque youngster.

Bayonne

Bayonne ❶, the capital of the Basque country, is a strategically located port at the confluence of two rivers and close to the border with Spain. It has been constantly besieged and was controlled by the English for almost 300 years, only being returned to France in 1451. Then the River Adour changed its course and the port silted up, until major engineering work in the 16th century created a new harbour and revived Bayonne as a major port and ship-building centre. The military architect, Vauban, reinforced it with a citadel.

The old centre, south of the River Adour across **Pont St-Esprit**, is divided into Grand Bayonne and Petit Bayonne by the River Nive. It is a remarkably intact ensemble of tall, timbered mansions, and is a pleasure to stroll around. The **Cathédrale Ste-Marie** was begun by the English and, unusually for this part of France, is northern Gothic in style. Despite damage during the Revolution it retains its delicate twin spires, some fine 15th- and 16th-century stained glass, 13th-century sculptures and beautiful Gothic cloisters. Next to the cathedral is the 14th-century **Château-Vieux**, with four towers and pepper-pot roofs.

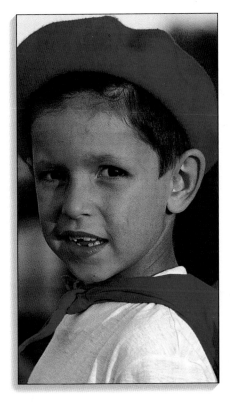

The writer Ernest Hemingway, visiting Bayonne in 1959.

Petit Bayonne, on the right bank of the river, is a regular grid of streets, built on reclaimed marshland in the 12th century; it has a lively, authentic, lived-in feeling about it with plenty of bars and restaurants. At its heart is the **Musée Basque**, on Quai des Corsaires (open Tues–Sun; tel: 05 59 59 08 98), a unique collection of Basque artefacts, imaginatively displayed after extensive renovation.

Bayonne also has a fine arts musuem, the **Musée Bonnat** (5 rue J. Laffite; open Wed–Mon; entrance fee; tel: 05 59 59 08 52), housing a collection that includes works by Rubens, Poussin, El Greco, a Goya self-portrait and 10 Ingres' paintings, including a superb *Woman Bathing*.

Bayonne is good for shopping, too, especially for Basque specialities such as the famous berets, espadrilles, linen and woollen blankets. Head for rue Port-Neuf where under its shady arcades you will find all manner of cafés, and shops selling seductive displays of Bayonne chocolate.

Biarritz and the Côte Basque

Biarritz ❷ is the biggest resort on the French Atlantic seaboard, a great swath of wide sandy beaches interspersed with rocky headlands which are planted with exotic plants, waving pink tamarisk and purple, blue and white hydrangeas. It is thoughtfully threaded with footbridges and promenades for strolling and viewing the thundering Atlantic surf. The best view is from the top of the **lighthouse** to the north (avenue de l'Impératrice; open July–Aug daily, Apr–June weekends only, Sept–Mar closed; entrance fee; tel: 05 59 22 37 00), though you'll have to climb 248 steps to appreciate it fully. You can see the great sweep of the bay, the deep green Atlantic water and the façades of the grand hotels, in particular the imposing red-brick façade of the legendary **Hôtel du Palais**.

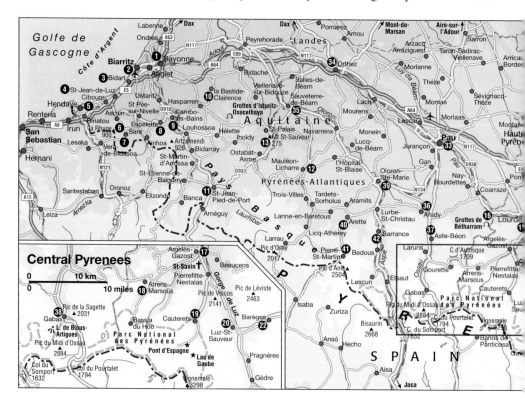

Map on page 228

Its perfect situation between the Pyrenees and the sea makes for a mild climate, though it can be rainy in winter and occasionally stormy in summer. Latterly it has attracted a large surfing community, and an influx of Australian and North American settlers have spiced up the genteel mix of retired Parisian ladies and their maids and poodles who still form a significant part of the population. Property is particularly sought after by rich Spaniards from over the border. There are plenty of good hotels (most within walking distance of the beaches) and excellent restaurants and shopping – a combination which makes Biarritz perhaps the best all-round seaside resort in France. It is good for children, too, with supervised beaches and sports facilities. For any architectural devotee it is a treat; many of its finest buildings, spanning Belle Époque, Art Déco and Art Nouveau styles, have been restored over the past 10 years.

The main beach is the **Grande Plage**, fringed with a colourful string of traditional striped canvas beach huts, rented out by the city authorities. Behind it is the exquisitely restored Art Déco **Municipal Casino**, with an elegant colonnaded café right next to the beach. Nearby is the newly renovated Belle Époque **Bellevue Casino**, now a superb exhibition space and conference centre with a luminous rotunda overlooking the sea.

Beyond the Grand Plage is the **Port des Pêcheurs**, which Napoleon III started to build and abandoned, and the metal footbridge, built by the Eiffel workshops in 1887, linking the promenade with the craggy islet of the **Rocher de la Vierge** with its statue on top. Below, when the tide goes out, are rock pools perfect for shrimping. On the promenade above is the neo-Gothic **Église de St-Eugénie**.

Round the headland is a small, more gentle, family beach at the **Vieux Port**, once the original whaling port. Bars and restaurants now occupy the old fishing

Vintage car in Biarritz.

BELOW: enjoying the waves at Biarritz.

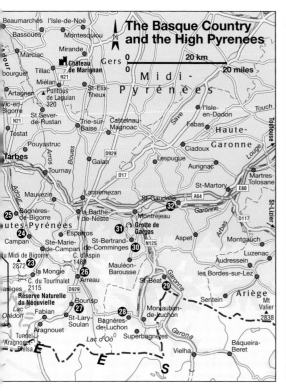

The Basque Country and the High Pyrenees

A Beach Fit for Kings

Until the 19th century Biarritz was nothing but a small whaling village at the end of a rocky cove. When sea bathing became fashionable during that century it began to develop as a seaside resort. From the early 1800s people would travel up from Bayonne by *cacolet,* a wicker chair strapped on the back of a mule.

Early cognoscenti – including Victor Hugo ("Biarritz is a lovely place," he wrote in 1843. "I have only one fear, that it may become fashionable.") and Wellington's officers on R&R from the siege of Bayonne – also discovered its charms. But the fortunes of Biarritz were really made when the wife of Napoleon III, the Empress Eugénie, arrived in 1854. She had visited the resort as a child on trips from Spain with her mother, and she persuaded her husband to build her a palace there. This he duly did: a superb villa, built in

the shape of an E on a plateau overlooking the Grande Plage.

By 1855 the railway had reached Bayonne and Biarritz was only 12 hours from Paris. The royal couple and all their court made it their summer capital, enjoying boat trips, horse racing along the beach, regattas, fireworks and musical soirées.

The Bellevue Casino was built in 1857, and soon Biarritz became the watering hole for the Beau Monde of Europe: Russian, German, Spanish and British as well as French. Star visitors of the time included Bismarck (who nearly drowned) and the notorious King Leopold of Belgium. After Sedan and the Fall of France in 1870, the Villa Eugénie became a hotel and casino, and was demolished after a fire in 1903. It was replaced by what is now the Hôtel du Palais.

Queen Victoria came for a month in 1889, along with an entire regiment of Hussars to protect her. Her son, the Prince of Wales and future King Edward VII, arrived from Calais in an 11-carriage train with his mistress. He came annually for several years, donating an ambulance to the town in gratitude. There was so much assorted European royalty that Biarritz rapidly became known as "the beach of kings".

In 1893 the first Sea Baths were built adding health spa attractions to the lure of the resort. Throughout the Belle Époque Biarritz continued to be the height of fashion and many grand hotels and villas were built. Fashion designers such as Coco Chanel, Patou, Jean Poiret, Lanvin and Hermes vied with each other in building idiosyncratic villas in outlandish styles.

After World War I Biarritz was less popular as the jet-set moved to the Riviera. But its fortunes revived during the 1950s when it attracted American film stars such as Gary Cooper, Bing Crosby, Frank Sinatra and Rita Hayworth, as well as the Duke and Duchess of Windsor. (There was even a classic Cadillac named "Biarritz".) In 1957 the future of Biarritz was sealed with the arrival of the American film star Deborah Kerr and her husband, the screenwriter Peter Viertel, who discovered the joys of surfing here. ❏

LEFT: portrait of Empress Eugénie, wife of Napoleon III.

Map on page 228

cottages. The biggest and most dramatic beach of all is the **Plage de la Côte des Basques**, where Basques would come on an annual pilgrimage to swim together. Most recently the surfers have taken over. The eroding cliff above the beach has been reinforced with a spectacular series of vertical terraces. The beaches continue to **Ilbarritz**, where there is a vast golf course, riding centre and secluded cafés right next to the shore.

There are not many "must-see" sights in Biarritz, but there are several museums worth a visit. The **Musée de la Mer** (89 esplanade du Rocher de la Vierge; tel: 05 59 22 75 40; open daily; afternoons only Christmas–mid-Jan; entrance fee), an ice cream-coloured 1930s Art Déco building, has underwater views of seals being fed, and of sharks. There is a good exhibition of whale skeletons along with whaling equipment, harpoons and the like. For those inclined there is a **Musée du Chocolat** (14–16 avenue Beau Rivage; open Mon–Sat; entrance fee; tel: 05 59 41 54 64), not to mention several enticing chocolate shops including that of master chocolatier Serge Couzigou who founded the museum. The **Musée de l'Art Oriental** (1 rue Guy Petit; open Tues–Sun; entrance fee; tel: 05 59 22 78 78) has a collection which includes jades, bronzes and porcelain from China, Nepal and India, and many Tibetan *thangkas* (paintings on silk). Anglophiles may enjoy the **Musée Historique de Biarritz** (rue Broquedis; open Tues–Sat; entrance fee; tel: 05 59 24 86 28), a collection of documents, costumes and furniture tracing the history of the town, housed in the former Anglican church of St Andrew.

You can also visit the Russian church of **St Alexandre-Nevsky**, with its blue onion domes, and the sumptuous Byzantine **Imperial Chapel**, built for Empress Eugénie by a student of Gothic revivalist, Viollet-le-Duc. Both stage concerts.

"When you find yourself hesitating between two beaches one of them is always Biarritz."
– SACHA GUITRY

BELOW: the beach at Biarritz.

Côte Basque

In 1902 the luckless English novelist George Gissing (1857–1903) settled in Ciboure with his French girlfriend, Gabrielle Fleury. The following year they moved to St-Jean-Pied-de-Port, where Gissing died after contracting pneumonia on 28 December.

South of Biarritz are two small, erstwhile whaling ports, **Bidart**  and **Guéthary**, now pleasant little resorts with good beaches. Bidart has a particularly interesting church with wooden arcading on three levels and the fronton court, common to all Basque villages, next to the Mairie. On the cliffs above is the little **Chapelle St-Madeleine** with a wonderful view out to sea. Guéthary, with its steep street leading down to the little harbour and beach, is verging on the fashionable, with several art galleries open to the public.

Just north of the Spanish border is **St-Jean-de-Luz** ❹, a chic little fishing port. The fishing today has dwindled but the fleet still supplies tuna, sardines, anchovies and a variety of other fish to the many excellent restaurants, which feature Basque specialities like stuffed pimentoes, squid cooked in its own ink and *ttoro*, a robust fish soup. There are plenty of *tapas*, too, this close to Spain.

There is a long sandy beach, sheltered within substantial jetties (built after the Empress Eugénie nearly came a cropper in her steam-powered paddle boat) and a high sea wall, which has bridges to the houses behind.

The town is most famous as the wedding location of Louis XIV and the Spanish Infanta María Teresa, which took place after the 1659 Treaty of the Pyrenees ended warfare between Spain and France. The door through which the royal pair left the church has been walled up ever since. The **Église St-Jean Baptiste**, where they were married, is one of the biggest Basque churches in France and the main sight to see. Burnt down and rebuilt several times since the first 12th-century church on the site, the present building dates from the 17th century and is a wonderful example of the simplicity and strength of the Basque archictecutural style, with a huge wooden nave shaped like a ship's hull, as much a

BELOW: festival on the beach in St-Jean-de-Luz.

nautical reference as the little boat dangling from it. Three wooden galleries surround the nave. Traditionally, Basque men would sit upstairs and the women below the nave. There is also an exuberantly gilded baroque altarpiece and a delicately chiselled 17th-century organ case. (You can hear the organ at Monday evening concerts during the summer.)

As you wander the old street of the port, you can see many fine houses, both half-timbered and of stone, a few of which, on rue de la République, date from the 16th century, having survived several fires and the tidal wave of 1680 that put paid to the rest. Distinguished 17th-century mansions include the houses on each side of the main square, where Louis XIV and the Infanta stayed separately before their marriage. The former house has four pepper-pot towers, the latter huge windows flooding it with light; overlooking the port, it is now used for exhibitions. The other side of the port is **Ciboure**, the birthplace of Maurice Ravel (1875–1937), although his family moved to Paris when he was only a year old. It has a sweet little old town and a 16th-century fortified church.

Beyond St-Jean-de-Luz is **Hendaye** ❺, another popular surfing beach with huge breakers and fine sand. The eccentric naval officer turned novelist, Pierre Loti, spent the last part of his life in a house on rue des Pêcheurs (closed to the public). Offshore is the **Île des Faisans**, where the Treaty of the Pyrenees was signed and which still remains under joint Spanish and French administration.

Inland Basque country

Inland the Basque Country is a world of sheep, cows and gentle rolling green hills: a "round shouldered land", as one 19th-century guidebook has it, dotted with little whitewashed houses and their inevitable red and green shutters. Here

Map
on page
228

Portrait of the novelist Pierre Loti (1850–1923), by Henri Rousseau. Loti died in Hendaye.

BELOW: *pottock* horses grazing on La Rhune.

Basque man dressed up for a traditional festival.

each village has its fronton court for playing *pelota,* and fathers and sons continue to play the sport of their ancestors. The sleepy appearance of these hills belies their frontier role, which has made smuggling an essential aspect of life. In peaceful times this has meant animals and goods, but in war time the skills of the mountain folk helped refugees from Franco's Spain across the border one way, and during World War II Allied pilots and Jewish refugees the other.

The summit of **La Rhune** ❻ (900 metres/3,000 ft) is the most western peak of the Pyrenees, a mountain wreathed in legend, once thought to be inhabited by witches and still scattered with ancient dolmens and tumuli. These can be discovered by hiking, but an easy way to see the view is by rack railway from Sare, a 35-minute journey on the **Petit Train de la Rhune** that ascends to the top. From here you can see the ocean, the forest of the Landes and the peaks of the Pyrenees. You can even go up by train at night and see the stars, dine at the summit and listen to Basque singing.

The village of **Sare** ❼, to the south of La Rhune, has a fine arcaded Basque church and typical Basque houses with the family name carved over the door lintel. You can visit the **Maison Basque de Sare** (Azaldegia; open Easter–Sept daily; entrance fee; tel: 05 59 85 91 92), an example of a Basque farmhouse with oak beams and stone walls. A few miles south of the village are the **Grotte de Sare** caves (open daily; afternoons only on weekdays in spring; entrance fee; tel: 05 59 54 21 88), long a place of refuge, and visitable today with son et lumière accompaniment.

Below La Rhune lies the little river port of **Ascain**, with its medieval bridge and 16th-century church with a huge square bell tower. Ascain was famous in the 17th century for its witchcraft trials and is known today for the ferocity of its

BELOW: the summit of La Rhune.

Map on page 228

pelota players. **Ainhoa** to the east is a *bastide* town with town walls and a grid-like formation of streets, still with many handsome old whitewashed houses and carved lintels. Down the road is the village of **Espelette ❽**, the market centre for *pottocks* – a race of small sturdy Basque ponies. It is also the source of the hot red pimento peppers which are an essential part of Basque cuisine. The October pepper fête is a good time to visit, when colourful red strings of peppers are hung from all the houses. There is a typical Basque church surrounded by a cemetery full of gravestones; the disc-shaped stellae which mark Basque graves are in odd contrast to the Art Déco grave of the first Miss World. Nearby is **Ixtassou**, source of the black cherries which are made into a jam traditionally eaten with the *brebis* (sheep's cheese) made hereabouts.

Cambo-les-Bains ❾ is a spa town, with a beautiful terrace overlooking the Nive valley. Well worth visiting is **Villa Arnaga** (open Apr–Sept daily, Mar weekends, Oct afternoons, closed in winter; entrance fee; tel: 05 59 29 70 57), the house of Edmund Rostand, author of *Cyrano de Bergerac*, with its 18th-century formal gardens and extravagantly decorated interior. Nearby is the village of **La Bastide-Clairence ❿**, an island of Gascons in the Basque Country and these days a thriving artistic centre. Close by are the **Grottes d'Isturitz et d'Oxocelhaya** (open daily; closed Mon–Tues mornings mid-Mar–mid-Nov; entrance fee; tel: 05 59 47 07 06), which enclose an underground river, impressive stalactites, and cave drawings of deer from 13,000 BC. Some of these can be seen but the most recently discovered have been left undisturbed and preserved in darkness.

In the hills to the south is the Irouléguy wine region; and at its heart the little village of **St-Étienne-de-Baigorry** with its medieval bridge and château.

"A people who sing and dance on top of the Pyrenees."

– VOLTAIRE
ON THE BASQUES

BELOW:
musicians at a
festival in Espelette.

Map
on page
228

Sign for a refuge on the road to Santiago de Compostela.

BELOW: St-Jean-Pied-de-Port.

The road to Santiago through the Basque Country

Wine, cherries and smuggling aside, what has most marked this part of the Basque Country is the pilgrim route to Santiago de Compostela *(see page 75)*. For centuries pilgrims have trudged towards **St-Jean-Pied-de-Port ⓫** to assemble for the passage through the Puerto de Ibañeta – once one of the main crossing points over the Pyrenees into Spain – to reach Roncesvalles. Pilgrims or tourists still come and St-Jean is packed with bars, restaurants and souvenir shops. Despite the little white tourist train that heaves its way up the narrow winding main street, there is still an authentic air about the town. There are plenty of simple rooms available for travellers, and pilgrim sanctuaries only open to bona fide pilgrims (you need to prove you have walked there or – modern concession – come by bike). All enter St-Jean the same way: across the old bridge flanked by prettily restored houses with balconies overhanging the river, through the porch with its stone benches, and past the **Église de Notre-Dame**, a much-restored Gothic structure. The walled citadel offers good views and an orientation table from which you can plot the direction of Roncesvalles and imagine setting forth with scallop shell and staff.

East of St-Jean-Pied-de-Port is the Soule region, remote and unspoilt, its forests and gorges best explored on foot. (The GR10 hiking trail runs through the area.) Such towns as there are include **Mauléon-Licharre ⓬**, which is still the main local centre of espadrille production, and **St-Palais**, an agricutural market centre. A short way to the south of St-Palais is **Gibraltar**, on **Mont St-Sauveur ⓭**. Here a disc-shaped stela marks the place where, traditionally, the various routes of the Santiago de Compostela pilgrimage across France joined up before crossing the Pyrenees. ❑

The Basques

Mystery surrounds the origin of the Basque people. The Basque language, Euskara or Euskera, is unrelated to any other language and is probably the most ancient tongue in Europe. Archaeological and anthropological evidence suggests that the Basques may be the last remaining enclave of Europe's indigenous population, possibly the descendants of Cro-Magnon man. Their folklore has no migration myth and it is likely that they have occupied the same homeland for the past 4,000 years.

Somewhat on the margin of history, and only briefly united under the kingdom of Navarre, the Basques managed to retain a sense of independence and of their own distinct identity through the centuries, more than any other ethnic group in Europe.

Until comparatively recently (considering their long, unbroken history), they were predominantly a rural rather than an urban people. The Basques have a strong family tradition, symbolised in particular by their houses, which are proudly kept in the family for many generations, the family name emblazoned on the door. Traditionally, the entire extended family lived in the house and its symbolic power was such that a man might even adopt the name of the house he entered, thus taking his wife's name.

Physically, the Basques tend to be big and strong people, and it is little wonder that their favourite sports involve trials of strength deriving from country chores. Log chopping, shouldering boulders weighing hundreds of pounds, cart-lifting, tugs of war and so on can be seen at traditional festivals throughout the Basque Country. Another distinctly Basque sport is *pelota*, for which every village has a court. This curious game is a bit like squash, being played incredibly fast against a wall, either with bare hands or with curved wicker gloves.

During festivals other Basque traditions can be seen, especially high-stepping dances performed by men to the sound of flute and drum or tambourine. The Basques are also renowned for their culinary skills.

RIGHT: Basque man in Ainhoa.

The independence movement

Basque nationalism was formalised at the end of the 19th century by Sabino de Arana Goiro (1865–1903). The Basque homeland, Euskadi, is made up of four Spanish provinces and three districts of France: Soule (Zuberoa), Labourd (Laburdi) and Basse-Navarre (Benavarra). As any Basque will tell you, Basque mathematics consist of one unusual sum: four plus three equals one – one Basque nation.

In the early 1960s, dedicated nationalists formed the terrorist movement ETA (Euskadi Ta Askatasuna – Euskadi and Freedom) which operates on both sides of the border but mostly in Spain. Most French Basques do not support full-blown nationalism, and certainly not terrorism, but they would like to see the government making concessions towards their national identity. In particular, they want their language to be given equal status with French and they want their own *département* to be carved out of Pyrénées-Atlantiques so that, at least at a local level, they can enjoy some measure of political autonomy. ❏

THE HIGH PYRENEES

Dramatic natural scenery, winter sport resorts and interesting wildlife make the great barrier of mountains across the south of France an irresistible place to explore at any time of year

Map on page 228

A great, jagged, snow-capped line of mountains, the Pyrenees forms a geographical and political barrier between France and Spain. From before the time of the Romans until after World War II (when tunnels were drilled under the summits and passes), there were few ways over them, except for those known to refugees, smugglers and others who needed to cross them in secrecy. However, neither the intimidating presence of these mountains nor the national frontier that runs along them deterred Basques in the west and Catalans in the east from maintaining their distinctive, trans-Pyrenean cultures in two countries. The slopes of these mountains are covered in a rich flora, which in turn supports many species of wild animal. Humanity has made what use it can of the Pyrenees, mining them for iron and other metals and grazing sheep in the richly watered pastures to produce milk from which superb cheeses are made. Tourism, a major source of income for the mountains' inhabitants, is nothing new and many famous writers and artists have left eloquent testimonies to the awesome beauty they discovered on their visits.

It is the peaks, valleys, towns and villages of the central part of the range that are covered here; the landscapes and settlements not of the Basque Country *(see previous chapter)* or the Ariège *(see page 259)* and Catalonia *(see page 287)* but rather those of Béarn, a society and culture of ancient origin that once formed an independent state but which now has no specific boundaries. Loosely, Béarn occupies two-thirds of the Pyrénées-Atlantiques *département*, with Pau as its capital.

Whether you want to ski on crisp snow, ramble among wildflowers in green forests, follow paths for serious mountain walkers or trace the road to Santiago de Compostela, linger beside lakes in peaceable valleys, or visit abbeys and churches, or the sanctuary of Lourdes, the choice of what to do and see is wide.

Routes in this section lead south into the mountains from the cities of Tarbes and Pau, reaching east to St-Gaudens and west to Orthez. The terrain usually dictates human movement, with pastoral valleys below the peaks often funnelling communications. All roads, however, share one huge thrill: when you look up you have before you the beauty of the Pyrenees.

PRECEDING PAGES: view of Pyrenean summits from the Pic du Midi. **LEFT:** skiing above St-Lary. **BELOW:** sledge-pulling dogs.

Tarbes

At first sight, **Tarbes ⓮**, fringed by industry, is unappealing. Yet the centre of this administrative capital of the Hautes-Pyrénées has a congenial personality, with cheerful squares, fountains, pavement cafés and markets. A flea market, **Marché aux puces**, is held every Thursday morning at the Halle Marcadieu. Southwest of the central place de Verdun, **Le Haras**, a national stud farm, maintains 70 classy stallions. The emperor

Lured by Lourdes

Five million visitors descend on Lourdes (pop.16,000) every year – more than visit any other shrine in Europe. In France, it is second only to Paris in the number of visitor beds. Such is the consequence of 14-year-old Bernadette Soubirous's vision of the Virgin on 11 February 1858, at the mouth of the Grotte de Massabielle, a riverside cave. The "Lady in White" appeared a further 17 times to this illiterate girl from a humble miller's family.

Bernadette's mystical experiences set off an immediate furore. The spring discovered after the ninth apparition and the first miraculous cures spurred families to bring their sick and their lame to Lourdes. Pilgrims and the merely curious flooded into the town in such numbers that the mayor blocked access to the cave.

The Church was sceptical, its officials alarmed. But with considerable foresight, the Bishop of Tarbes, Monsignor Laurence, soon arranged to purchase not only the cave and its immediate environs but an extensive area including what is today the great esplanade in front of the Basilique du Rosaire.

In 1864 the statue of the Madonna of Lourdes was inaugurated, with the words incised as Bernadette heard them: "Que soy era Immaculada Concepciou" ("I am she who was conceived without sin").

Bernadette remained in Lourdes for eight years after the apparitions. In July 1866, when she was 22 years old, she joined the Sisters of Charity in Nevers. Always asthmatic, she died there, aged 35, on 16 April 1879. On 8 December 1933, she was canonised by Pope Pius X.

During Bernadette's lifetime, a first church (the **Basilique Supérieure**) was consecrated in 1874 to meet the needs of pilgrims. Later, in 1883, work began on the vast **Basilique du Rosaire**, with 18 chapels, from which an exterior ramp was built leading to the Basilique Supérieure. Yet pilgrim numbers still grew, and by 1950 a greater space became imperative – a situation resolved by the **Basilique Souterraine de St-Pie X**, a modern concrete ellipse with capacity for 20,000 people.

Lourdes has changed and matured over the years. From chaotic beginnings, reception and medical centres have grown into orderly and well-managed organisations. Countless volunteers help tend and transport the handicapped in a refined show of logistics. The Masses in the sanctuaries (local and international), daily blessings of the sick, the sacramental and candle-lit processions all operate to an efficient schedule.

The temporal and the spiritual have gone hand in hand. Tourism and commerce have expanded. Shops, as well as hotels and a wide range of eating places, cater eagerly to the pilgrim crowds. A good deal of what's displayed is shoddy and vulgar.

For a visiting non-believer, Lourdes can be crowded and its appeal hard to fathom. Yet the intensity of the faithful who sit quietly in front of the Grotte, some in wheelchairs, or who walk through the small cave, touching the grey rock-face as they pass, can leave no one indifferent. ❑

LEFT: pilgrims assembled in front of the shrine of Lourdes.

Napoleon created the stud in 1806 and its architecture is appropriately Empire in style. As well as stables, a saddle room and smithy, there's a **Maison du Cheval** (open Mon–Fri; guided tours; entrance fee; tel: 05 62 56 30 80) with an educational display. North of place de Verdun is the **Jardin Massey**, in the English style of the 19th century, and beyond it a fine-arts museum, the **Musée Massey** (open Wed–Sun; entrance fee; tel: 05 62 36 12 83). You'll find aspects of modern history in the **Maison Natale du Maréchal Foch** (open Thur–Mon; entrance fee; tel: 05 62 93 19 02), an unassuming townhouse at 2 rue de la Victoire where the World War I military leader was born; and various objects, documents and photos in the **Musée de la Déportation et de la Résistance** (63 rue Georges Lassalle; open Mon–Sat; entrance fee; tel: 05 62 51 11 60).

Map on page 228

South of Tarbes

Since the visions of Bernadette Soubirous in 1858, the destiny of **Lourdes** ⑮ (tourist office, tel: 05 62 42 77 00) has been guided by the popularity of its shrine *(see facing page)*. But there is a little more to Lourdes than its religious significance. A far older history is underscored by the 11th-century **Château-Fort**, a hilltop castle perched above the town. Inside, the **Musée Pyrénéen** (access 1 rue du Bourg or 2 rue Le Bondidier; open Wed–Mon; entrance fee; tel: 05 62 42 37 37) displays an impressive collection on regional life. A funicular railway and short walk take you up the **Pic du Jer** (948 metres/3,110 ft) for a view of the Pyrenees.

The **Grottes de Bétharram** ⑯ (open late-Mar–late-Oct daily; Jan–mid-Mar Mon–Fri; entrance fee; tel: 05 62 41 80 04), west of Lourdes, are dramatic underground caverns containing weirdly shaped rocks and a lake. You can see them by way of a short walk, and trips on a barge and a mini-train.

TIP

Trie-sur-Baïse, north-east of Tarbes, holds regular piglet markets. The highlight is La Pourcailhade, a fête on 13 August with a competition in which contestants have to imitate a pig's squeal.

BELOW: nurses in Lourdes.

"You are nothing, palaces, domes, temples, tombs, in the presence of this incredible colisseum of Chaos."

— VICTOR HUGO ON THE CIRQUE DE GAVARNIE

The small town of **Argelès-Gazost** ⓱, 13 km (8 miles) south, has lively Tuesday and Saturday morning markets and is close to **Hautacam** and other ski stations. From a terrace by the tourist information office you have a view, weather permitting, of the Pyrenees in majestic close up – according to a map on the spot you can see seven valleys.

Southwest, through the winding Val d'Azun, and past a village with the memorable name of Bun, are two exaltingly lovely villages with Romanesque churches, **Aucun** and **Arrens-Marsous** ⓲ – good bases to take off for the **Col de Soulor** (1,474 metres/4,836 ft), immediately above, which is overlooked in turn from the west by the **Col d'Aubisque** (1,709 metres/5,607 ft). In Aucun, look out for the small, private **Musée Montagnard du Lavedan** (reservations only – check by phone before visiting: tel: 05 62 97 12 03). A Pyrenees National Park office is in Arrens. The GR10 walking route passes close by.

From Argelès, heading south, it's worth the short detour to see the village and superb Romanesque **Abbaye de St-Savin** (open daily), built in 1160. Inside are the saint's gilded tomb and 15th-century paintings on his life. The abbey possesses remarkable treasure, including wooden sculptures, among them a 12th-century Virgin of the Long Thumb. From the nearby St-Piétat chapel the Argelès valley below is a vast green bowl.

Cauterets ⓳, a lively all-seasons resort, has a Pyrenees National Park office, a thermal spa and a skating rink. Evoking a stylish era, the **Musée 1900** (closed Sun morning; entrance fee; tel: 05 62 92 02 02) displays glamorous18th- and 19th-century costumes in the elegance of the **Résidence d'Angleterre**, a former grand hotel. Sweeping mountain sights and walks are all around. Seeing the **Pont d'Espagne** and the waterfalls on the way up to it is a stunning experience,

BELOW:
Pont d'Espagne after spring rains.

HENRY RUSSELL AND VIGNEMALE

Before the 18th century the Pyrenees were fearsome peaks to be avoided, and it was not until the Romantic era that the idea of mountains as places of aesthetic inspiration took hold. Poets and painters then descended in droves to sketch and versify their beauty. Spa towns like Bagnères de Bigorre and Cauterets became favourites with Romantic poets and writers, including George Sand, Tennyson, Flaubert and Victor Hugo.

But no one celebrated the Pyrenees with as much determined passion as Henry Russell (1834–1909), of Irish-English antecedents and with a French mother. Russell's goatee beard and lean outline can be seen in a bronze sculpture as you enter Gavarnie.

"Comte" Henry Russell will forever be associated with Vignemale, which he climbed 33 times between 1861 and 1904. Wanting to winter in its heights, he gouged out seven tiny caves, with the help of a Gèdre mason, at altitudes up to 3,248 metres (10,657 ft), the last known as the Grotte du Paradis. As recompense for his outlay, he obtained in 1889 a 99-year-lease on the Vignemale summit, including 200 hectares (495 acres) above 2,300 metres (7,546 ft). On his death, aged 75, in Biarritz, his two brothers passed the concession to the Club Alpin Français.

especially after spring rains. From Pont d'Espagne it's a minimum one hour's walk up to the glacial **Lac de Gaube** (at 1,725 metres/5,660 ft) and a view of **Vignemale**, which at 3,300 metres (10,820 ft) is the highest peak in the French Pyrenees. Alternatively, you can take a cable car, then an open ski-lift, and walk the last 20-minute stretch.

Map on page 228

Gorge de Luz and Gorge de St-Sauveur

Returning 17 km (10½ miles) along the Gave de Cauterets, and turning southeast at Pierrefitte-Nestalas, you enter the 18-km (11-km) **Gorge de Luz**, its steep sides dense with deciduous trees. The gorge is within the Pays Toy, which has not always been as easy-going as it sounds: in 1406 tough Toy warriors chased the English out of Lourdes. **Luz-St-Sauveur** ❷⓿ sits at the gorge's end, a town tucked neatly in a valley among the mountains. This cosy setting gives Luz agreeable possibilities in all seasons: summer walking and excursions and an ever-expanding range of winter sports. In the town centre is the **Église des Templiers**, a Templar church that dates from the 11th century. Gravestones (not all of them old) form a semi-circle within the outer wall. The porch ceiling is intriguingly painted, the church's wooden pulpit strangely small.

On the outskirts of Luz, heading south, you cross the **Pont Napoléon**, a bridge built in 1859 by order of Napoleon III to provide his empress, Eugénie, easier access to the local thermal spa. Her zeal in "taking the waters" began a national vogue that still continues. The road leads into the **Gorge de St-Sauveur** and to the village of **Gèdre**, an animated ski resort. A further 9 km (5½ miles) south is the village of **Gavarnie** ❷⓵, its renowned and splendid sight the snow-patched **Cirque de Gavarnie**, a massive rock amphitheatre of spectacular beauty and

Victor Hugo (1802–85), who visited the Pyrenees.

BELOW: the dramatic Cirque de Gavarnie.

TIP

The most gruelling sections of the Tour de France are the *cols* of Tourmalet, d'Aspin and Soulor. Fit cyclists ride these and others for fun and can get a certificate to prove it (tel: 05 62 56 70 65 for information).

now a World Heritage Site. From the village you can walk beside a sparkling stream (or ride by donkey or horse) to the Cirque, a stunning semi-circular basin with peaks up to 3,000 metres (9,840 ft), carved out by rivers and glaciers, from which thunder gigantic waterfalls, most spectacularly the Grand Cascade de Gavarnie, the longest waterfall in Europe, plunging to 423 metres (1,388 ft).

For serious walkers it is a tougher hike up snowy slopes to the **Brèche de Roland** (2,804 metres/9,200 ft), a mighty breach in the rock, with Spain on the other side. From Gèdre, with time to explore and walk, you can also reach the **Cirque de Troumouse** and the **Cirque d'Estaubé**.

The Col du Tourmalet and Pic du Midi

East of Luz St-Sauveur, **Barèges** ㉒ is a little mountain town buzzing with activity. It has an elegant spa which operates between May and October for thermal treatment of bone and muscular problems, respiratory ailments and rheumatology, and in winter switches to après-ski fitness and relaxation sessions. On the slopes all around are summer-time rambling routes. With the spectacular **Massif de Néouvielle** to the south, Barèges is also a popular ski resort with access, including via an in-town funicular, to several pistes. At Pont de la Gaubie, further up the route du Tourmalet, is the **Jardin Botanique du Tourmalet** (open mid-May–mid-Sept daily; entrance fee; tel: 05 62 92 18 06), a garden displaying the wildflowers of the Pyrenees in recreated settings from rock to forest.

The high-altitude, virtually treeless road up the **Col du Tourmalet** can be greenly beautiful or bleak and windswept. Even in June snow can briefly close the route. At the summit (2,115 metres/6,939 ft) a silvery cyclist, *Le Géant de Tourmalet,* sculpted by Jean-Bernard Métais, honours cyclists; a note records

BELOW: Le Géant de Tourmalet.

that Tour de France cyclists first rode by in 1910 – though not, for sure, on tarmac. From the peak it's a short descent to **La Mongie**, a popular ski resort. More than that, it's the point of departure, by two cable cars, for the **Observatory and Museum** (open Wed–Mon; entrance fee; tel: 05 62 56 70 65 – access dependent on weather so call ahead) at the very pinnacle of the **Pic du Midi de Bigorre** ㉓ (2,872 metres/9,423 ft). Lunch alfresco overlooking spectacular snow-capped mountains – and one-tenth of all France – is a true thrill.

The superb new museum topping the Pic du Midi, with views up to the skies and across the snowy Pyrenees, is stunning. Astronomers saw the possibilities of the peak long ago and, in 1878, began building an observatory, an initiative that nearly ruined the scientific Société Ramond. Yet the observatory was completed and performed brilliantly in solar and lunar observations for more than a century, notably providing NASA with moon maps for Apollo missions. As techniques of space study advanced, its usefulness faded. Adapted and transformed, the Pic du Midi, its museum and its views, are an astonishing experience.

Down from La Mongie and a little north is the lovely Campan valley, the headwaters of the Adour River, the little town of **Ste-Marie-de-Campan** and the captivating village of **Campan** ㉔ itself. In its small cosmos are half-timbered houses, a fountain ornamented by strange faces, the *halle* dating from 1571, and an imposing church with a rococo altarpiece. Just 6 km (4 miles) north, bustling **Bagnères-de-Bigorre** ㉕, the area's leading town, has a thermal spa which existed before Roman times and was favoured by Henri IV and a host of personalities from Montaigne to Madame de Maintenon. Time marches on; the spa has long since been modernised. This was, though, the "Athens of the Pyrenees" in the 19th century and two museums are worth visiting: **Musée Salies**

A young skier being kitted out for a Pyrenean piste.

BELOW:
the observatory
on Pic du Midi.

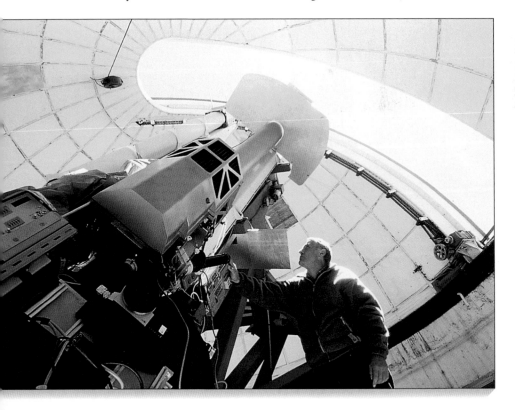

(open May–Nov Wed–Sun; entrance fee; tel: 05 62 91 07 26) and the **Musée du Vieux Moulin** (open Tues–Fri; entrance fee; tel: 05 62 91 07 33), an ethnographic collection in a former mill on the banks of the Adour River.

Vallée d'Aure

Southeast of Ste-Marie-de-Campan, the road leads up to **Payolle** (which stands near a lake), on through forests and up to the summit of the **Col d'Aspin** (1,489 metres/4,885 ft). The panoramic view encompasses a broad valley far below, the **Vallée d'Aure**. From the summit it's a winding 13 km (8 miles) to **Arreau** ㉖, a doughty little town of picture-perfect houses with wooden balconies enhanced by a setting at the confluence of two rivers, the Neste d'Aure and Neste du Louron. Notable buildings include the **St-Exupère** church, dating from the 11th century and with a glorious portal, and the simple, two-storey **Château des Nestes** (open Tues–Sat; tel: 05 62 98 63 15), which contains a tourist information office and, upstairs, the **Musée des Cagots**, telling the story of a fascinating but downtrodden minority group *(see panel below)*.

In the valley is a string of diminutive villages, beginning with **Cadéac**. The 15th–16th-century church in **Bourisp** ㉗ contains astonishing, recently restored frescoes on such themes as the Seven Deadly Sins, The Last Judgement, and a Tree of Jesse. There are modest museums: one at **Ancizan** on rural traditions and at **Vielle Aure** on the old manganese mines. **Sarrancolin** has, as well as a Romanesque church and ancient narrow streets, a working marble quarry. In summer, activities in the valley include fishing and caving (with local guides). In winter skiing rules – **St-Lary-Soulan** is a leading ski station where there is also a spa. Spain, via the Aragnouet/Bielsa tunnel, is not far away.

Two breeds of dog are kept by Pyrenean shepherds. While wolves and bears were still common the long-haired, white Patou was used to guard flocks. The much smaller Labrit is the traditional sheepdog being loyal, quick and hardworking.

BELOW: bells for tracking livestock.

THE FRENCH UNTOUCHABLES

Treated like lepers, the Cagots (sometimes called Capots, and also known as Crestianes or Crestias and, in the Basque Country and Navarre, Agots) were a people of uncertain origin in the southwest who were treated as a race apart and subjected to centuries of discrimination for no apparent reason other than for being who they were. Often of low stature, they were feared as "the little people" or even sorcerers.

By a 1550 order of Cardinal de Pelleté, they were forbidden to wash their hands in public fountains or to enter houses and taverns not their own; to touch any woman not their wife or any child not their own; and to eat and drink in any other company. Even in death, only a prelate of good will would attend to them and their graves were kept apart from other graves. Churches that tolerated them obliged them to enter by their own door, as in Campan, where their holy-water basin bears their supposed emblem, a goose foot.

Even after several major studies of them they remain a profound enigma. However, at least in the modern era the injustice of the treatment meted out to them and the cruelty of segregation has been belatedly recognised and shame for it is expressed.

Map on page 228

Dominating the valley to the south is the **Réserve Naturelle du Néouvielle**, a magnificent massif of snow-topped mountains approached from St-Lary-Soulan through forests and wildflower glades. From **Fabian**, west of St-Lary, a drive of 10 km (6 miles) up the winding **Route des Lacs**, edged by the fast-flowing Neste de Couplan, brings you to **Lac d'Orédon** (1,849 metres/6,066 ft), one of several high-altitude lakes. A little determined walking leads to others.

From Arreau, it is a relaxing 32 km (20 miles) through the verdant slopes of the Col de Peyresourde to **Bagnères-de-Luchon** ❷❽, a handsome town in the foothills. Its main street, Allées d'Étigny, is an avenue lined with linden trees. At its southern end is a large and splendid thermal **spa** (open Apr–Oct) which was built in 1848 over a Roman spa. It was Baron d'Étigny (1719–67), the Intendant of Gascony, Béarn and Navarre, who promoted Luchon and its thermal waters to the Maréchal de Richelieu and the Versailles court. Luchon took off and today, busily offering a wide range of mountain activities (a *bureau des guides* is next door to the tourist information office), hasn't looked back. Two agreeable summer side trips in the hills west of Luchon – into the Vallée d'Oueil and the more southerly Val d'Oô, where the **Lac d'Oô**, at 1,504 metres (4,935 ft) after an uphill hike, is a prize worth the effort.

St-Béat ❷❾, north of Luchon, on the Garonne River is known for its quality marble that has been quarried here since Gallo-Roman times.

Bearded angel, St-Bertrand-de-Comminges.

St-Bertrand-de-Comminges

Rising from a hilltop within a fortified village is the **Cathédrale Ste-Marie-de-Comminges** (guided visits to cloisters and choir, May–Sept daily; entrance fee; tel: 05 61 89 04 91) at **St-Bertrand-de-Comminges** ❸⓪, sometimes called the Mont St-Michel of the Pyrenees, although the comparison is misleading. St-Bertrand began as a Roman town, Lugdunum, probably founded by Pompey in 72 BC, the ruins of which are at the base of the hill. This had thermal baths, a theatre and a temple, to which a broad arcaded market place and a Christian basilica were added in the 5th century. After it was destroyed by northern invaders, the town lay in ruins until the 11th century, when the Bishop of Comminges, Bertrand de L'Isle (1083–1123), chose the site above it to build a cathedral. He was later canonised as St Bertrand and the town that grew up on the site adopted his name. The Cathedral, completed in 1348, is predominantly Gothic with some Romanesque features. The carving of the capitals in the cloisters is particularly exquisite. Within the church don't miss the accomplished 16th-century Renaissance wood-carving; the organ and the choir stalls richly embellished with detailed figures, animals and humorous animated scenes; and the 16th/17th-century tempera paintings of St Bertrand's tomb. Many of the stone and timber-framed houses of the town have been painstakingly restored.

Not far down the valley is another lovely Romanesque basilica, **St-Just-de-Valcabrère**, which was built in the 12th century and is particularly interesting for the amount and range of stone that was re-used in its construction, from Roman capitals to recycled marble sarcophagi.

BELOW: columns in St-Bertrand-de-Comminges.

Jeanne d'Albret, mother of Henri IV.

The nearby **Grottes de Gargas** ❸ (open daily; entrance fee; tel: 05 62 39 72 39), 6 km (4 miles) from St-Bertrand-de-Comminges, is famous for its 200-odd hand prints silhouetted in red, black, yellow and white *(see page 145)*, some of them dating from 33,000 BC. They were made by a variety of individuals, including women and children and some of the hands show signs of mutilation. Their significance is yet to be explained.

St-Gaudens ❷, 17 km (10 miles) east, vibrant capital of Haute-Garonne, stands on a plateau looking south across the Garonne River to the mountains. The **collegiate church**, dating from 1059, dominates the city centre. Its features include carved capitals and a 1829 organ, recently restored.

Pau, capital of Béarn

Pau ❸, to the west, is the capital of the Pyrénées-Atlantiques *département*, and has the extraordinary gift of pleasing almost everyone. In the 19th century, the British so took to Pau it was called *la ville anglaise (see panel below)*. The ancient capital of of Béarn, Pau was transformed in the late 15th century from modest *castelnau* (a settlement under the protection of a château) to royal city. When, in 1553, the future Henri IV was born in the château to Jeanne d'Albret, his cradle was a polished tortoise shell, which can be seen in the **Musée National du Château de Pau** (open daily; guided tours only; entrance fee; tel: 05 59 82 32 00). In an era of rabid religious violence, Henri grew up a Protestant, pragmatically turned Catholic to take the French throne, and promptly issued the Edict of Nantes legalising Protestant worship.

BELOW: Boulevard des Pyrénées, Pau.

The old town is full of charm (and restaurants), and a walk towards the **Palais Beaumont** and the **casino** (tel: 05 59 27 06 92) along the **Boulevard des**

A VERY BRITISH AFFAIR

If Pau seems more genteel than the average French town it may be because of its long-standing British connection. The attractions of its location and climate were first discovered by Wellington's troops in need of R&R during the Peninsular War in Spain. Later on, British doctors recommended its climate for rest cures. Between 1830 and 1914 Pau, dubbed *la ville anglaise,* was among the top visitor destinations in Europe, especially in winter.

Foreigners arrived from across the world, attracted by the grand boulevard des Pyrénées, the glamorous casino and the fine hotels. Much the largest contingent were the British. France's first golf course was opened in Pau in 1856. Horse racing began, and the Pau Hunt established as if this were just another British county.

Many Brits came to sketch and paint the mountains: Farnham Maxwell-Lyte, arriving with a lung ailment, recovered and took memorable photographs of the area. Mountain climbers included not only the redoubtable Henry Russell but also his friend Charles Packe. Both were preceded by an Englishwoman, Ann Lister, who on 7 August 1838, with Henri Cazaux of Gèdre as her guide, made the first attested ascent of Vignemale's Pique Longue (3,298 metres/10,820 ft).

Pyrénées is a revelation on a clear day when the mountains fill the horizon. Worth seeing, too, is the **Musée Bernadotte** (rue Tran; open Tues–Sun; entrance fee; tel: 05 59 27 48 42) honouring Jean-Baptiste Bernadotte, born in Pau in 1763, who became a *maréchal* (field marshal) for Napoleon, then King of Sweden, and founded there the dynasty that rules today. There is also a good **Musée des Beaux Arts** (open Wed–Mon; entrance fee; tel: 05 59 27 33 02) with works by Rubens, Degas and El Greco, as well as lots of Pyrenean landscapes.

West of Pau, two Béarn towns in particular, both historically strategic, retain medieval splendours and are worth exploring. In **Orthez ㉞**, drop into the tourist information office and you are in the 15th-century golden-stone house of Jeanne d'Albret, a Protestant museum reflecting her dedicated Calvinism. Even older is the 13th-century bridge, the **Vieux Pont**. A little southwest, in **Sauveterre-de-Béarn ㉟**, strikingly set above a bend in the Gave d'Oloron, the 12th-century **Église de St-André** and the **Tour Monréal** overlook another old bridge, a ruin rich in legends.

Vallée d'Ossau

Due south of Pau, and south of the wine region of Jurançon (its cooperative cellars at Gan), you enter the Vallée d'Ossau. Each village is a characterful place to stop. In **Arudy ㊱**, traditional items are displayed in the **Maison d'Ossau** (open Tues–Fri; Sept–June afternoons only; entrance fee; tel: 05 59 05 61 71). **Louvie-Juzon** has a Romanesque church and ancient houses.

At **Aste-Béon ㊲** you can see the results of a brilliantly imaginative ornithological experiment. **La Falaise aux Vautours** (open Apr–Sept daily; otherwise school holidays; advisable to phone before visiting; entrance fee; tel: 05 59 82

Map on page 228

Transhumance, the seasonal movement of livestock, is still practised in the Vallée d'Ossau. The flocks are taken up to their summer pastures in June and brought down again in October before the bad weather sets in.

BELOW: swimming near Sauveterre-de-Béarn.

Old woman in the mountains.

65 49) is an unusual, modern wildlife museum and observation centre. Its name means "Cliff of the Vultures". The novelty is that television cameras mounted on the limestone cliffs 1,000 metres (3,300 ft) above allow you to watch the behaviour of the nesting griffon vultures (recently joined by a pair of Egyptian vultures) on a giant screen, with only the minimum human intrusion.

Above **Laruns**, tiny **Aas** has the odd distinction of inventing a whistling "language". **Eaux-Bonnes** is a classical spa town with a seasonal casino. **Gourette** is a ski resort well known for its proximity to the Col d'Aubisque, an arduous test for cyclists. This is also the Route du Fromage (the Cheese Route).

Gabas ⓸, further south, on a Santiago de Compostela route and with a Pyrenees National Park office, sits prettily beneath the **Pic de la Sagette**. Southwest lies the **Lac de Bious-Artigues**; it's an easy walk from the lake (children do it) to the beautiful **Lacs d'Ayous**. Nearby **Artouste** leads to the **Lac de Fabrèges** from where cable cars rise to the starting point of a jaunty "Petit Train" (operates June–Sept; fare payable; tel: 05 59 05 36 99) which travels along 10 km (6 miles) of track to the **Lac d'Artouste**. South, with the forked bulk of the **Pic du Midi d'Ossau** (2,884 metres/9,462 ft) a forceful, jutting presence, is a green sweeping valley, the **Col du Pourtalet**, and the Spanish frontier.

Vallée d'Aspe

BELOW: the train to Lac d'Artouste.

A parallel north–south route is the scenically dramatic Vallée d'Aspe starting southwest of Pau at **Oloron-Ste-Marie** ⓸, an ancient town at the confluence of the *gaves* (rivers) d'Aspe and d'Ossau. A bishopric in AD 506, the first town, destroyed by the Normans, grew into the small town of Ste-Marie. The 12th-century **Église Ste-Marie**, formerly a cathedral, with its superbly sculpted portal, is the

town's finest feature; the hilltop **Quartier Ste-Croix**, set around a Romanesque church, comes a close second. Oloron has an active industry, including chocolate and woven textiles and berets, still vital headgear in the Southwest.

Southwest of Oloron, the mesmerising beauty of the hills of the **Vallée de Barétous** is inspiring – as it surely must have been for Alexandre Dumas. As with the Gascon-born D'Artagnan *(see page 215)*, true life inspired the characters of the Three Musketeers. In the village of **Aramits** was born Aramis; the loud Porthos (born in Pau) is thought to have owned a manor in **Lanne**; Athos came from further north, near Sauveterre.

From **Arette** ⓴, a road rises to **Pierre-Saint-Martin** ㉑ where an annual ceremony in July *(see right)* commemorates the 1375 Junte de Roncal, the oldest enduring peace treaty in Europe. A museum display in Arette's tourist office tells you more and shows costumes and traditions across the years. The point where the three realms of Aragón, Navarre and Béarn meet, just below the **Pic d'Anie** (2,504 metres/8,216 ft), is known as the Table de Trois Rois.

Along the Vallée d'Aspe graceful villages like **Sarrance** ㉒ and **Borce** sit snug below steep cliffs. To see what's above them, take the 4-km (2½-mile) side road to Lescun. There, **Pic Billare** (2,300 metres/7,550 ft) stands tall above the village church and, like a vision, the **Cirque de Lescun**, a great, glacial wall of rock and snow, unfolds (weather permitting) across the horizon.

For 11th-century crusaders, and for traders and weary pilgrims on the way to Santiago de Compostela, the pass of **Col du Somport** (1,632 metres/5,355 ft) was an unavoidable obstacle en route. Since 2003 it has finally been broached with a controversial 8-km (5-mile) road tunnel. The new traffic load presents a distinct threat to the peaceful existence of the Vallée d'Aspe. ❑

In a ritual held on 13 July at Pierre-Saint-Martin, high up on the frontier with Spain, Barétous valley mayors present three heifers to the people of the Roncal valley in Aragón (Spain). The annual tribute honours a 1375 agreement that resolved a dispute over pasturage.

BELOW: mowing the lawn in Borce, Vallée d'Aspe

THE WILDLIFE OF THE PYRENEES

The thick forests, Alpine meadows and steep rocky slopes of the Pyrenees are home to a diverse range of spectacular plants and animals

The vegetation that cloaks the Pyrenees varies by climate zone and altitude. The western part of the range is influenced by the Atlantic while the east is more Mediterranean in character. The Pyrenees are a plant-hunter's paradise. Botanists define distinct plant zones proceeding up the slope. There are oak forests on the foothills: common and white oak in the west and cork and evergreen oak in the east. True mountain forest begins around 800–900 metres (2,600–3,000 ft). From there up to 1,800 metres (5,900 ft) is the damp montane level with thick beech and fir forests. The next zone, to 2,400 metres (7,900 ft), is the sub-Alpine level where the main tree species are pine, birch and mountain ash. There is also grassland and moorland here.

Between the upper tree limit and the permanent snow line is the true Alpine level, at 2,400–2,900 metres (7,900–9,500 ft). Beyond this is the nival zone, rare in the Pyrenees, where the only plants that can grow are lichen and algae.

FAUNA

The mountains are also excellent for birdwatching. Rarer species include the golden eagle, the giant lammergeier (with a wingspan up to 3 metres/10 ft) and the Egyptian vulture. The rarest and most endangered of the 75 mammal species in the Pyrenees is the brown bear. The most unusual animal, however, is the web-footed desman *(Galemys pyrenaicus),* a kind of muskrat living near high mountain streams.

▷ **CAPERCAILLIE**
This turkey-like game bird with a singular mating call can be seen – or more likely heard – in coniferous forests.

▷ **FROM FOREST TO SNOW**
For every 200 metres (650 ft) of altitude, the average annual temperature drops by 1°C (1.8°F) and snow lingers that bit longer. The growing season shortens accordingly.

△ **ISARD**
Although sure of foot on rocky slopes, the Pyrenean chamois (known locally as the isard) lives lower down near the tree line and sometimes takes shelter in the forests.

△ **MARMOT**
This rodent, a large ground-dwelling squirrel, was reintroduced in 1950, having been absent from the Pyrenees for thousands of years.

▷ **GENTIANA BURSERII**
With its upward-tilted, yellow, bell-shaped flowers, this tall gentian is one of the more conspicuous species that can be found in Pyrenean Alpine meadows.

SAVING THE BROWN BEAR

One of the 10 most endangered animals in Europe, the brown bear *(Ursus arctos)* survives in a few remote places of the western Pyrenees, and in 1996 was reintroduced in the central Pyrenees. The numbers of this solitary omnivore were reduced during the 20th century by hunting and destruction of its forest habitat. The brown bear grows up to 2.5 metres (8 ft) long and lives on a diet of berries, nuts, insects, invertebrates, small mammals and fish. The bear is also an opportunistic hunter and will kill sheep if a flock is unprotected by a *patou*, the traditional Pyrenean sheep dog. Protests by farmers, especially in the Ariège, have threatened to halt a programme to reintroduce bears brought from Slovenia which aims to boost the number of individuals from under 10 (at present) to a population capable of sustaining itself (around 100). The most secure refuge of the bear up until now has been the Vallée d'Aspe in (but not confined to) the central area and the *zone périphérique* of the Parc National. The building of the new Somport tunnel will, environmentalists say, pose a further threat to the brown bear's survival.

◁ **LAMMERGEIER**
This enormous bird, also called the bearded vulture, drops animal bones on to the rocks below to crack them and extract the marrow.

△ **MIDWIFE TOAD**
The male of this unusual high-altitude species carries bundles of eggs wrapped around its legs until they are about to hatch.

◁ **GRIFFON VULTURE**
The commonest species of vulture in the Pyrenees is often to be seen soaring gregariously around high crags. It is identifiable by its short, square tail.

THE ARIÈGE

Although not the most lively part of the Southwest, the Ariège is nevertheless one of the most unspoilt, with caves, castles, mountains, forests and beautiful landscapes to tempt the traveller

Map on page 260

The Ariège has always been one of the most remote and independent regions of France, enfolded in quiet forested valleys, a lush land fed by abundant rivers. The protective massif of the Pyrenees makes a natural fortress of the Ariège, and communication across the mountain passes with Spain has often been more important than with the towns and villages of the plain below (though until very recently a living could be made carrying glacier ice down to the plain). Since 1994 communications between France and Spain have been enormously improved by the opening of the Puymorens tunnel between the Ariège and Spanish Catalonia, circumventing a particularly difficult mountain pass.

Depopulation is a major problem for the Ariège today, but an *escargot*-paced way of life and a natural self-reliance has kept rural traditions alive. The old ways are maintained by the Ariégeois peasants themselves and increasingly by the influx of "néo-paysans": the New Age generation seeking the same simple, ecologically balanced lives, weaving baskets on hilltops, growing their own vegetables, cheese making, living in teepees or building and repairing traditional wood and stone mountain dwellings.

The region is well preserved without being self-consciously rustic. For good or bad, the Ariège is more a side route than a major touristic thoroughfare. There are sights to see, but not too many. Ruined castles, small chapels and caves predominate over grand châteaux. In some ways it is what you can do here rather than where you can go that is the attraction. This is a place for simple pleasures: woodland and mountain walks, riding, fishing, swimming in rivers and cool mountain lakes, skiing, canoeing, cycling and the opportunity to see a wide variety of Pyrenean flora and fauna. Ariège is, above all, tranquil, and at times tranquillising.

Foix

Foix ❶, capital of the Ariège, is encircled by lofty hills and has a river rushing through it. Today it is a pleasant enough little town of winding old streets and half-timbered houses; but during the Middle Ages it was the seat of the counts of Foix and thus one of the great power bases of the Pyrenees. Evidence remains in the **Château** on the rock to the northwest of the town; châteaux, rather, since there are three different keeps, the earliest dating back to the 12th century, and well worth climbing for the strategic view it gives.

The **Musée de l'Ariège** (open Apr–Oct daily; Nov–Mar Wed–Sun; entrance fee; tel: 05 61 65 56 05), within the castle, has capitals from the old abbey of St Volusien, a collection of weapons and armour, prehistoric finds from nearby caves, and the interior of an *oustal*, a peasant mountain dwelling, complete with

PRECEDING PAGES: winter sports in the heights of the Pyrenees.
LEFT: café in Mirepoix.
BELOW: fresco in St-Lizier.

furniture, plates and fire irons. Plans are afoot to transform the château into a major tourist site by 2006, so opening hours may be affected.

The **Église de St-Volusien,** all that remains of the great Benedictine abbey around which the town grew up, was destroyed in the Wars of Religion, and virtually rebuilt in the 17th century. Still, it is worth visiting for its huge nave and capitals of painted bears – a recurring theme throughout the Ariège. Probably the best time to visit Foix is on its market days (Wednesday and Friday) when all the basket-weaving hippies come down from the hills.

Young musicians performing in Foix.

Around Foix

Just outside Foix, at Montgaillard, is **Les Forges de Pyrène ❷** (open daily; closed Jan; entrance fee; tel: 05 34 09 30 60), a museum and park constructed around one of the iron forges that once dominated the region. First you see a collection of tools required by a vast range of industries and crafts – vessels, scissors, hammers, saws and brushes needed to make combs, umbrellas, shoes, baskets, clogs, cakes, whips, yokes, barrels, carts and other everyday objects – along with early black and white photos of village life. Then you enter the forge itself, the water wheel turning and the huge hammer pounding red-hot metal bars to make these essential tools. A small gallery is devoted to the iron-ore industry and further displays show different craftspeople at work – bread-making, gold panning, rope-making and so on.

Northwest of Foix is the **Rivière Souterraine de Labouiche ❸** (open June–Sept daily; Apr–May afternoons only; Oct–Mar Sun only; entrance fee; tel: 05 61 65 04 11), the longest subterranean river in Europe, which you can follow on a guided tour by barge.

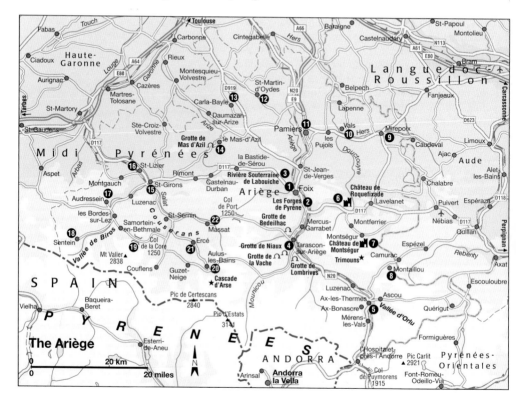
The Ariège

Tarascon-sur-Ariège and caves

Map on page 260

South of Foix is **Tarascon-sur-Ariège ❹**, a rather down-at-heel place, with an unsalubrious old town clustered rounds the remains of its château, perched on a little knoll. The major sights nearby, however, are the caves. The **Grotte de Bédeilhac** (open July–Aug daily; Sept–June afternoons only; guided tours; entrance fee; tel: 05 61 05 95 06) is a gigantic cave full of stalagmites with palaeolithic paintings of animals 15,000 years old on the walls. The **Grotte de Lombrives** (open June–Sept daily; Oct–May weekends only; guided tours; entrance fee; tel: 05 61 05 98 40) is also huge, one of the biggest caves in the world, with a 100-metre (330-ft) high main cave known as the Cathedral, where the persecuted Cathar heretics sought sanctuary. The troops of the Inquisition did not trouble to chase them, but simply walled up the entrance and left them to die. Here you can take a little train right through the caves, and get out again.

Best of all though is the **Grotte de Niaux** (open daily; entrance fee; tel: 05 61 05 88 37), which has some of the finest cave art in Europe: rough strong line drawings of bison, horses and deer. Unlike the caves at Lascaux in the Dordogne, where the paintings were at one point deteriorating from exposure, it is still possible to view the originals here, but entrance is strictly controlled and it is essential to book ahead, either by phone or in person at the caves. A long dim walk with hand-held lamps into the depths of the earth is rewarded by the deeply moving sight of wild animals seen in profile skilfully painted on the rock walls 12,000 years ago by our European ancestors. Niaux also has a lovingly assembled museum of local crafts, domestic objects, tools, traditional furniture and costumes; the kitchen even has authentic mouse droppings. Close to Niaux is the **Grotte de La Vache** (open July–Aug daily; Apr–Oct afternoons

"...the Roche Bédeilhac....stands upright in a valley among eminences. And round its head swirled a cloud dance of the seven veils, the shifting shafts of light illuminating now one face now another...Seldom have I seen a spectacle more exciting."

– ANDREW SHIRLEY, South from Toulouse

BELOW: illustration from the *Livre de la Chasse.*

GASTON FÉBUS

The most distinguished of the counts of Foix (also viscounts of Béarn) was Gaston III (1331–91), who has been described as "a 'Renaissance' man before his time". He is still thought of as something of a hero of the Pyrenees although in reality he was a complex, cruel and contradictory character.

A flamboyant and handsome man of action who loved hunting and fighting, he was also literate, attracting artists, writers and troubadours to his court. Out of his passion for hunting grew his influential treatise on the subject, the *Livre de la Chasse (Book of the Hunt).*

He proved himself skilled in leadership and diplomacy when, during the Hundred Years' War, he played off the English and French to make his own domain one of the most powerful in France.

Gaston was well aware of his own brilliance and beauty. Around 1360 he assumed the surname of Fébus (inspired by Phoebus, one of the epithets of the Greek god Apollo) as an allusion to his flowing blond hair. But as well as being vain, he was also an absolute ruler and capable of immense cruelty. He was responsible not only for the murder of his own brother but also of his only son, whom he suspected of a plot to poison him.

*Artigat in the Ariège
is the location of the
extraordinary story
of Martin Guerre
who disappeared in
1548. A man claim-
ing to be Martin
Guerre arrived in
Artigat in 1556.
He was for a time
accepted by Guerre's
wife and family –
though not without
contention – but
eventually exposed
as a clever impostor.*

only; guided tours; entrance fee; tel: 05 61 05 95 06), a small but rich archaeological site, with animal bones and artefacts such as fireplaces, flints and
weapons, some of which can be seen at an on-site exhibition.

If you can't get into Niaux then you can console yourself and amuse children
with a visit to the **Tarascon Parc de l'Art Préhistorique** (open Mar–mid-Nov
daily; entrance fee; tel: 05 61 05 10 10) where you can see facsimiles of the
Niaux paintings, including those no longer visible at Niaux, and play at being
cave-dwellers, try prehistoric hunting, tool-making and making fires in a sim-
ulated prehistoric park.

Ax-les-Thermes and Haute Ariège

Ax-les-Thermes ❺ has a natural reservoir of 61 springs which has made it a spa
town since Roman times. There is always a strong smell of sulphur in the air and
the locals like to sit with their feet soaking in the open-air public thermal bath
in the middle of town. Ax is a good base from which to explore the Haute
Ariège, which offers mountain walks in summer, and in winter, skiing at **Ax-
Bonascre** and **Ascou-Pailhères**.

A quarry at **Trimouns**, 1,800 metres (5,905 ft) above sea level, produces 10
percent of the world's talcum powder, or French chalk. The soft stone is transported by *téléférique* (cable car) to a factory at Luzenac. Visits to the works
are possible in summer (Ax-les-Thermes tourist office, tel: 05 61 64 60 60).

The **Vallée d'Orlu**, east of Ax, will bring you to the **Orlu Nature Reserve**,
a sanctuary for a range of increasingly rare animals and birds including isards,
marmots and golden eagles. There is also a **Maison des Loups**, a reserve with
observatories from which to see European and Canadian wolves.

RIGHT: talcum-
powder quarry
near Luzenac.

Montségur and the Pays d'Olmes

A few miles to the east of Foix you can pick up the Sentier Cathar (Cathar Route). Along the twisting D9 road look out for the craggy stone walls of the **Château de Roquefixade** ❻, perched so high it looks inaccessible.

The **Château de Montségur** ❼ (open daily; entrance fee; tel: 05 61 01 06 94) is the most arresting Cathar site of all. This ruined castle on the 1,216-metre (3,990-ft) summit of a great dome of rock (the "secure mountain") was the Cathars' last stronghold, attracting many sympathisers and pilgrims fleeing persecution. Around 500 people lived there from 1232, some in the keep of the castle itself, some in the village terraced around it.

In 1242 the Cathars gathered in the fortress sent out a band of soldiers to assassinate the Inquisitors in session at Avignonet, to the north. An avenging army of 10,000 men was despatched by the King of France, and it surrounded the mountain. The fate of the besieged Cathars was inevitable. Curiously, when the castle finally surrendered, the defenders were given 15 days before having to leave. Finally, those heretics who refused to recant (more than 200 of them) were brought down the mountain and burnt to death.

Today little remains but high defensive walls around an inner courtyard. Yet the place has a palpable spiritual atmosphere, and the steep ascent to the castle soon begins to feel like a pilgrimage. In the little village below is a **museum** (open Apr–Dec daily; Apr and Oct–Nov afternoons only; free admission) explaining more of the history of the Cathars and their lost treasure, which has been searched for throughout the region ever since.

Of more earthly interest is the nearby village of **Montaillou** ❽, which has yielded most of the known facts about the Cathars *(see panel below)*.

Map on page 260

"Even heresy can be packaged now. Everything begins in mysticism and ends in politics, said Charles Péguy. Not any more, it doesn't. In this part of the Midi, what starts in mysticism ends in tourism."
– CHRISTOPHER HOPE

BELOW: Château de Montségur.

THE BOOK OF THE VILLAGE

The international bestselling book *Montaillou* (1975), by the French historian, Emmanuel Le Roy Ladurie, is a detailed account of medieval peasant life. It is based on the records of the Inquisition in the village, which had become a centre for a Cathar revival after 1300.

When the Albigensian Crusade failed to destroy the heresy the Church sent in its shock troops – the Inquisition – whose investigations were to ravage Europe for the next three centuries. Jacques Fournier, the zealous Bishop of Pamiers, destined to become Pope at Avignon as Benedict XII, conducted the trials at Montaillou himself, and ensured the testimonies were carefully transcribed. The Inquisition's meticulous records preserve a remarkable picture of everyday life: family relationships, the way houses were constructed, how food was produced and what people ate as a daily diet. Even the lonely lives of the shepherds in the hills, who were particularly susceptible to the teachings of the ascetic independent Cathar preachers as they travelled round the countryside, were precisely described.

Because of the book, the small, unassuming little village of Montaillou – with barely the ruins of a castle remaining – has today become a centre for archaeological research and studies in Cathar history.

ATMOSPHER

*Bar sign on the main
square of Mirepoix.*

BELOW: craft
market in the
square at Mirepoix.

Mirepoix and the Basse Ariège

The *bastide* town of **Mirepoix** ❾ (tourist office, tel: 05 61 68 83 76) on the border of Ariège and the Aude, has a prosperous tone about it, the cafés full of English colonists indulging in an early snifter. The liveliest times to visit Mirepoix are on market days (Thursday and Saturday), or during the twice-monthly cattle market, one of the biggest in the region.

The main square is shaded by acacia trees and flanked by half-timbered arcades above shops and cafés, the wobbly façades painted in faded turquoise and pink. Note the ends of the protruding beams supporting the upper floor of the **Maison des Consuls** (also a stylish hotel) which have been carved with the likenesses of medieval faces and a variety of beasts.

The **Cathédrale**, southern Gothic in style, is worth a visit for its vast nave and lovely stained glass, and an excellent series of models which show its development from simple chapel to grand *église*.

To the north of the town of Pamiers is the sombre memorial at **Le Vernet**, the biggest of several concentration camps in the area, used first for Spanish Civil War refugees and then internees in World War II.

On the way to Pamiers, west of Mirepoix, it is worth making a special detour to **Vals** ❿ where there is a wonderful church carved from the rock, entered through a narrow cleft in the stone. First you reach a tiny vaulted chapel, 9th-century in origin, with 12th-century frescoes that have only recently been discovered. More rocky steps lead you into a larger church with a nave carved half out of the rock, and a lovely medieval wooden statue and crucifix. A door leads to an airy terrace which offers good views of the surrounding fragments of Roman walls, the village below and the Pyrenees beyond. A small **museum** (contact Camon tourist office: open July–Aug daily; tel: 05 61 68 88 26) in the village displays various archaeological finds from the site.

Pamiers ⓫ is a disconsolate kind of place, despite being the largest town in the *département,* and looks as if it has yet to recover from the Wars of Religion, which wrecked so many of its buildings. The **Cathédrale St-Antonin** has a Romanesque door and capitals and a fine brick bell tower, and the place del Camp has a few remaining half-timbered houses and a red-brick church with twin towers.

North-west of Pamiers gentle emerald valleys shelter exquisite small villages among flower-filled meadows. The village of **St-Martin-d'Oydes** ⓬ has half-timbered houses encircling a castellated red-brick church, and **Carla-Bayle** ⓭ is another treasure. It is perched on a hill – giving views of the lush hills and valleys surrounding it – and has a lovely artificial lake below, which is great for swimming. Its timbered houses and arcaded streets have been sensitively restored: their wattle-and-daub walls are still visible, and their big balconies, once used for drying wood, have been transformed into cute al-fresco bedrooms. A bastion of Protestantism in the Wars of Religion, the village is named after Protestant philosopher Pierre Bayle (born 1647) whose birthplace is now a **museum** (open Oct–May Wed, Thur and Sat–Mon; tel: 05 61 68 53 53).

Map on page 260

Le Mas-d'Azil ⑭ to the south is a one-cave town, but what a cave: so enormous you can actually drive through it, and so commodious it was sheltering Stone-Age Ariégeois long after the time other people were building houses. Wonderful finds have been made here, apart from the ones lost in the rubble that went to build roads in the 19th century. In the **cave** (open Apr–Sept Tues–Sun; Oct–Mar Sun pm only; tel: 05 61 69 97 71) and in the **Musée de la Préhistoire** (open Mar–Nov daily; Apr–May afternoons only except weekends; entrance fee; tel: 05 61 69 97 22) in the village can be seen exquisite tiny bone carvings, as well as bones and skulls of prehistoric animals. A diorama of people sitting round a fire shows the primitive if secure lives these cave-dwellers led. A large cavern in the centre with a convenient pulpit rock sheltered the Cathars, and later the Protestants, in the Wars of Religion, when 1,000 of them resisted a siege of five weeks by an army 14,000-strong.

St Girons

St-Girons ⑮ is a convenient place to stay, and a pleasant town with a good market (open Sat and Mon) under the plane trees by the river. The main reason to visit, however, is to see **St-Lizier** ⑯ up the road, once an important bishopric, now deserted for the town below and snoozing on its hill like an English cathedral town. It is a gem, perfectly restored with quiet streets and arcaded squares oozing bourgeois calm.

The town is dominated by the vast 17th-century **Palais des Évêques** (Bishops' Palace) and adjoining **Cathédrale de Notre-Dame de la Sède**. Inside, the **Musée Départemental de l'Ariège** (open July–Aug daily; Apr–June and Sept–Oct afternoons only) houses an ethnographical collection, focusing on

Pet duck in St-Lizier.

BELOW: carved capital, St-Lizier.

Wayside haystack sculpture.

the nearby valley of Bethmale, but the church is currently closed because 15th-century frescoes only discovered in 1992 are under restoration. The shady gardens of the Palace are surrounded by Gallo-Roman walls, making St-Lizier one of the most important Gallo-Roman sites in the Pyrenees.

But it is the **Cathédrale de St-Lizier** that is its greatest treasure. (Nobody seems to know quite why there are two cathedrals.) It is a fine example of the Pyrenean Romanesque style, started in the 12th century, incorporating Roman stones that were lying about. It also has frescoes discovered behind plaster that are believed to date from its 12th-century consecration. A painting of Christ in Majesty with two fingers raised in blessing bears the Latin inscription *Lex Mundi*: The Light of the World. There is also a superb two-storey cloister with marble columns and carved capitals, providing a haven of peace.

The Couserans

St-Girons is the main town of the **Couserans**, a series of sleepy valleys which have changed little since the stone age. The valleys are thickly forested but the trees are relatively young since the area was drastically deforested to make charcoal for the iron forges producing cannon balls for Napoleon's campaigns.

Head along the D618 from St-Girons towards **Audressein** ⓱ where, apart from a welcoming *auberge* (inn), there is a wonderful pilgrimage church by the river, **Notre-Dame de Tramezaygues** (the name means "between two waters") featuring some exquisite, if faded 13th-century murals of pilgrims and angels painted on the arches of the porch. The **Vallée de Biros**, with the peak of Mont Valier (2,839 metres/9,315 ft) in the background, is tranquil and green, and perfect for walking.

BELOW: clog maker in Audressein.

Sentein ⓭, the main town of the valley, has a church with an elaborate octagonal bell tower, abutted by later fortifications, three towers and a charming garden. It is a lovely village, with half-timbered houses and little bridges over the river.

The **Bethmale valley** is famous for its extraordinary high pointed clogs, its traditional costumes, and the unusual height of its inhabitants, said to derive from a Greek settler in the 17th century. They don't clog dance to order though and the best time to see them is on fête days (particularly 15 August). There are still clog makers, however, and you can watch them at work in the village of **Samortein-en-Bethmale**.

The road along the valley side offers wide views, and passes the **Lac de Bethmale**, where you can swim, picnic, fish, or even prepare a barbecue beside peaceful waters reflecting the mountains all around. Continue along the winding road on to the **Col de la Core** ⓲ where there are circling buzzards and panoramic views of snowy cloud-topped mountains in every direction. Note the sign for the Chemin de la Liberté dedicated to the local mountain guides – *passeurs* – who smuggled refugees through these mountain passes into Spain during World War II. Beyond is the Salat valley and **Seix**, a dull little town but good for canoeing and kayaking trips.

The Ustou and Garbet valleys

If you continue along the Valle d'Ustou you'll come to **Aulus-les-Bains** ⓴, one of the more eccentric places hereabouts. It became a thriving spa town after the original Roman spring was rediscovered in 1845. The diligence from Foix would arrive daily loaded with visitors wanting to take the therapeutic waters dispensed from marble fountains in a little grotto. They would stay in grand old hotels along the river and gamble in the casino. A brand new spa complex has recently given Aulus a new lease of life as the self-proclaimed cholesterol-treatment capital of France. The grotto has been fenced off, but the old hotels and overgrown gardens are still there in all their romantic faded grandeur, hinting at their former glory. Two have been bought by enterprising incomers who are attempting to restore them to their 1930s glamour.

Above Aulus a three-hour walk (considerately signposted in calorie-controlled distances) will bring you to the **Cascade d'Arse**, a magnificent waterfall with a funny name and splendid views.

From Aulus you can follow the Vallée du Garbet past lots of tumbledown houses (many with traditional gables of stepped granite) where tentative attempts at renovation are apparent. The village of **Ercé** ㉑ is famous for its bear training school, evidence of the time when every village hereabouts had its own dancing bear.

A stunningly beautiful drive, the D17 and then the D618, will bring you back to Tarascon-sur-Ariège via the town of **Massat** ㉒, where a few carved-stone doorways and the huge church are all that remain of its role as ancient capital of the Couserans. Massat also has an old watermill on the banks of the Arac River. On the D618, stop at the **Col de Port** (12 km/ 7 miles from Mossat) for more amazing views. ❑

Map on page 260

The pointed clogs of Bethmale feature in a legend from the time of Moorish invasions. A young man jilted by his fiancée in favour of an Arab prince took his revenge after the Christians recaptured the village by killing the girl and her lover and marching in the victory procession with their hearts skewered on the points of his clogs.

BELOW:
Ariège forest.

THE AUDE

Map on page 272

From the shore of the Mediterranean, a great sweep of plains and vine-clad hills dotted with remote Cathar castles converges on one of the greatest sights of all France: La Cité of Carcassonne

L anding by plane at Carcassonne is the best way to get an overview of the Aude: a patchwork of barley, maize and sunflowers to the west; to the east the vines of the Minervois and Corbières that are so critical to the region's economy (Aude is the second-biggest wine-producing *département* in France). To the north you can see the dark wooded slopes of the Montagne Noire; to the south the snow-capped Pyrenees. Further east lie the lagoons and beaches of the Mediterranean coast and the Roman city of Narbonne.

This plain between the Pyrenees and the Massif Central was always a key trade route between the Atlantic and Mediterranean, particularly once the Canal du Midi connected the two seas in 1682. It has also played an important role as a border region on the fluctuating Pyrenean frontier with Spain; and the hilltop fortresses which sheltered the Cathars were originally built as border defences.

Pepper-pot towers

The Romans never had such an aerial view but they knew a good geographical location when they saw one, and quickly colonised the ancient settlement of **Carcassonne ❶** (tourist office, tel: 04 68 10 24 30) on its strategic hill. It is easy to discern the distinctive citadel of pepper-pot towers rising above the plain. Today Carcassonne is one of France's most popular tourist sights, so visit **La Cité** out of season if you can.

Carcassonne's fortunes fluctuated over the centuries in the struggle for control of southern France. Evidence of settlement dates from the 6th century BC, and the Tectosage Gauls occupied the site in the 3rd century BC. After the Romans founded the colony of Narbonensis in 118 BC it rapidly became a busy town on the Narbonne–Toulouse road. Parts of the inner walls and towers date from the Roman period, including the Avar Postern Gate, the oldest gate in the town.

By the 12th century Carcassonne had become one of the great powers of the south, rivalling the Duchy of Toulouse. These were the golden years of the powerful Trencavels, invoked with T-shirts and plastic swords in the ubiquitous souvenir shops. Troubadours and poets entertained the nobility in the castle, frescoed and hung with tapestries, and construction started on the Basilique St-Nazaire.

But Carcassonne suffered cruelly during the ferocious 13th-century crusade against the Cathars; after a savage siege led by the notorious crusader, Simon de Montfort, Carcassonne eventually submitted in 1209. The French crown's newly acquired lands were close to what was then the Spanish frontier, so the citadel was massively reinforced with a second ring of ramparts and towers; fortifications so impressive it was not attacked during the Hundred Years' War.

PRECEDING PAGES: view of the walls and towers of Carcassonne. **LEFT:** a gateway into La Cité. **BELOW:** medieval fête, Carcassonne.

Filming Renoir's Le Tournoi dans la Cité *at Carcassonne.*

La Cité lost its role of frontier guard once the Treaty of the Pyrenees was signed in 1659 and the border moved to its present position. It declined into a ghetto of the poor. By the beginning of the 19th century local builders were eyeing the cut stone greedily, and the basilica's transept was being used as a blacksmith's forge. Just in time to save the Cité from total destruction, the newly created Commission des Monuments Historiques stepped in, and Viollet-le-Duc, the great Gothic revivalist and architectural historian, was commissioned to restore it.

Critics complain that Viollet-le-Duc's restoration is too perfect. The night-time illuminations do make it look a bit like Disneyland, especially during the summer festival depicting the burning of La Cité. But Viollet-le-Duc was not interested in preserving romantic ruins and, whatever its faults, his reconstruction is a rare opportunity to experience the atmosphere of a medieval town; it is satisfying to visit because you can see what these great citadels were like in use. Carcassonne has long been favoured by film makers as a medieval backdrop, from Renoir's first feature film, *Le Tournoi dans la Cité* (1928) to,

Map on page 272

more recently, *Robin Hood: Prince of Thieves* (1991). The Cité stands on a rocky spur overlooking a meander of the River Aude. The medieval town, about 10 hectares (25 acres) in total area, is completely encircled by a double wall of fortifications punctuated by massive towers. Only a little imagination is required to envisage it besieged by crusading armies.

The best approach is on foot over the bridge from the Lower Town (Bas Carcassonne) winding up to the ramparts of rough-hewn sandstone. Enter through the imposing twin towers of the **Porte Narbonnaise** gate with its portcullis and drawbridge (one of the more fanciful elements of the restoration). Between the ramparts are *les lices,* a further defensible space, once used for jousting and well worth walking round to get a good sense of the defences. Within is a warren of well-restored medieval houses and winding streets. Despite the souvenir shops and crowds of tourists this is still a real town with 200 permanent residents behind the lace curtains.

At the heart of the Cité is the **Château Comtal**, a castle within a castle, where every possible military defence tactic can be seen: watchtowers, posterns, covered wooden walkways and machicolations, the better for hurling boiling oil and stones on the attackers. You'll need to take a lengthy guided tour to see the Château Comtal, but this includes the **Musée Lapidaire** (open daily; entrance fee; tel: 04 68 11 70 77) and its collection of archaeological fragments and frescoes, old cannonballs and intriguing prints of the dilapidated citadel, before Viollet-le-Duc's enthusiastic restoration.

The **Basilique St-Nazaire** has some of the finest medieval stained glass in the Midi: seven exquisite windows making a wall of light in the east end of the church. Look out for the famous **Siege Stone**, which probably depicts the death of Simon de Montfort at Toulouse. If you have the stomach, you can also visit the **Musée de l'Inquisition** (open daily; entrance fee; tel: 04 68 47 00 09) featuring instruments of torture from all over Europe. **Imaginarium**, an interactive museum of the crusade against the Cathars (rue St Jean; open July–Aug daily 10.30am–7pm; Apr–June and Sept–Nov; tel: 04 68 47 78 78 for details), presents a multimedia history of the city.

It is a fairytale castle in a pop-up picture book, all crenellations, turrets, battlements. In summer you may see knights jousting below the massive walls...and a museum of medieval torture beside the little crêperie. First we take a close look at flaying, then we tuck into good jam crêpes.

– CHRISTOPHER HOPE

BELOW: well-dressed horses in Carcassonne.

The town below

Bas Carcassonne, across the Aude from the Cité, is an agreeable small town built around place Carnot (where a market is held) and two cathedrals. It retains more or less its original plan, with a grid pattern of streets typical of the many *bastides* established in the region during the 13th and 14th centuries, the better to control an increasing population. It was burnt down in 1355 by the Black Prince but subsequently prospered as one of the most important cloth manufacturing centres in the south.

The varied collections of the **Musée des Beaux Arts** (rue de Verdun; open June–Sept daily; Oct–May Tues–Sat; tel: 04 68 77 73 70), housed in a 17th-century building, and the **Maison des Mémoires** (Chemin des Anglais; open daily; entrance fee; tel: 04 68 71 08 65) – the house of the Surrealist poet Joe Bousquet – are worth browsing around.

The Lauragais, Montagne Noire and Minervois

Northwest of Carcassonne is the Lauragais, a fertile plain of wheat and maize studded with prosperous farms and turretted Renaissance châteaux. **Castelnaudary ❷** is a pretty, bustling town on the banks of the Canal du Midi, where there is a large marina, a good starting point for barge trips along the canal. The town is most famous as a contender for the *cassoulet* crown – Ford Madox Ford claimed the *cassoulet* (a casserole dish) he ate in Castelnaudary, "had sat on the fire for the last three hundred years".

Stone knight at Avignonet-Lauragais.

Midway between Castelnaudary and Carcassonne is the splendid town of **Bram ❸**, its red-roofed streets circling around a central church, making it easily visible from the air as you fly in.

North of Carcassonne the terrain changes. The Massif Central begins with the **Montagne Noire** *(see also page 188)*: the olives give way to chestnut trees, and the ochre plain fissures into deep black granite gorges flowing with the cold clear rivers that powered the textile, wool and paper industries that once flourished here. You can visit the paper mill at **Brousses-et-Villaret**, in the foothills of the range, which still produces fine-quality hand-made paper.

Appropriately nearby is **Montolieu ❹**, "Village du Livre": the book village of France, modelled on Hay-on-Wye in Britain and Redu in Belgium. Over a dozen small shops sell new and second-hand books. There is a recently opened English Bookshop, a shop selling hand-made paper and even a Café du Livre. The village spans two gorges on the edge of the Montagne Noire, its once crumbling houses now restored with pleasant terraces and gardens of palm trees clinging to the steep sides. It is becoming popular as a literary haven and residents include author Patrick Suskind.

BELOW: line-out in a southwest rugby match.

RUNNING WITH THE BALL

A museum in the service area of Port Lauragais, on the south side of the A61 motorway, beside a basin of the Canal du Midi, is dedicated to the Southwest's favourite sport, rugby. **L'Ovalie** (open daily; tel: 05 62 71 13 66) is an "evocation" of the game from its origins to its modern form. The museum's architecture of dome and staggered roofs is inspired by the two ways in which a rugby player can capture the ball – the scrum and the line-out. The sceptic may notice a passing similarity to a church. Inside, as the official leaflet disconcertingly puts it, "the architecture guides the visit, as if it were a rugby pitch: left, right, forward, backward, zigzagging".

If you can find your way around despite this you will learn how the sport was invented by William Webb Ellis during a game of football (soccer) at the English public school of Rugby, in 1823, when he momentarily grabbed the ball with his hands.

The exhibition also explains how rugby subsequently found mass appeal, inspired art, and seemingly betwitched the French – especially the descendants of the Occitans in the Southwest. Toulouse, 30 km (18 miles) up the A61, is considered France's rugby capital, the home of the top regional team, Le Stade Toulousain.

Map on page 272

In the Montagne Noire proper, tiny stone villages nestle into the sides of the gorges, tidy vegetable gardens cover the valley floor and here and there the forbidding ruins of castles peer from craggy perches. **Lastours** ❺ (open Feb–Dec daily; entrance fee; tel: 04 68 77 56 02) in the Orbiel valley, has ruins of four châteaux, as its name suggests, some of which undoubtedly sheltered the unfortunate Cathars. They make a fine excuse for climbing the gorge.

The **Clamoux valley** to the east has some magnificent gorges, as well. At **Cabrespine** ❻ there is a castle and a deep chasm, the **Gouffre de Cabrespine** (open Mar–Nov daily; entrance fee; tel: 04 68 26 14 22), which can be explored on an underground guided safari. To the east is the Minervois, serious wine country flanking the Canal du Midi. There is a particularly special church at **Rieux-Minervois** ❼, built with seven sides for unknown mystical reasons, though recent research suggests it might be located on a ley line linked to St-Guilhem-le-Désert. Look out for the superbly carved capitals inside.

The Aude Valley

Far to the south, in the Pyrenees, the River Aude plunges 1,200 metres (3,900 ft) from the valley of the Capcir and thunders northwards through deep fissured gorges past **Axat**. A spectacular side route from here takes you via the **Gorges de St-Georges** over the 1,506-metre (4,941-ft) **Col de Jau** and into Roussillon, crossing what was once the border between France and Spain.

The Aude continues past the river sports centre of **Quillan**. The **Musée des Dinosaures** (open daily; entrance fee; tel: 04 68 74 26 88) at **Espéraza** ❽ is recommended for anyone with small children. Parents might prefer the hat museum next door.

"It is said that Simon de Montfort, having taken Bram, put out the eyes, cut off the noses and top lips of one hundred of its garrison and told them to march to Cabaret [Lastours] in the hope that the mere sight of them would result in its surrender."

– JOY LAW,
The Midi

BELOW: Montolieu, the bibliophile's favourite village.

The Priest's Tale

Rennes-le-Château owes its arcane celebrity to the mysterious enrichment of the priest of the village, Abbot Bérenger Saunière, in the late 19th century, in circumstances which have never been satisfactorily explained.

According to legend, Saunière discovered a parchment, which the Lady Hautpool de Blanchfort, the last scion of an aristocratic family, had given to the then priest of Rennes-le-Château just before the French Revolution. To safeguard the secret in those troubled times the priest hid the parchment in a Visigothic pillar in the church of St Mary Magdalene. It was this document that Saunière supposedly discovered during repairs to the church in 1891. Around the same time he was spotted digging in the cemetery and defacing the cryptic inscription on the tomb of Lady Hautpool.

Saunière subsequently began spending extravagant quantities of money, lavishly embellishing the church, building himself a

villa and funding charitable works on a grand scale. When he died in 1917 he left everything, including the secret, to his housekeeper, Marie Denaraud, who had shared his riches, wearing the latest Paris fashions and expensive jewellery. She too took the secret to her grave when she died in 1953.

Since then the legend and what little evidence there is has fuelled endless speculation. Occultists and treasure hunters continue to arrive in Rennes-le-Château, equipped with maps of ley lines, charts of astrological orientations, and an eclectic range of theories to fit the few known facts.

But what was the secret? The mystery was popularised by a series of British television documentaries which led to the bestselling *The Holy Blood and the Holy Grail* by Michael Baigent, Richard Leigh and Henry Lincoln. They proposed the theory that Jesus did not die on the cross but escaped to Europe. Could Rennes-le-Château, they wondered, be the hiding place of the Holy Grail, or did Saunière discover Jesus' tomb? Jesus, their theory continues, was not merely a spiritual leader but the legitimate heir of King David. Furthermore, he was married to Mary Magdalene and they had children, thus creating a direct bloodline in France. Perhaps Bérenger Saunière was paid by the Church to suppress such dangerous knowledge?

Other theories suggest that the priest may have found the treasure of the Knights Templars, or the lost treasure of the Cathars, which was supposedly hidden in the locality after the fall of Montségur.

Vistors to Rennes-le-Château – mystics and sceptics alike – must make of this what they will. The first stop for all is the church, braving the devil which supports the holy water stoup placed at the entrance by Saunière. Next to the church is the **Bérenger Saunière Centre** (open daily; entrance fee; tel: 04 68 74 72 68), which comprises the presbytery where the priest lived (now a museum), the **Villa Bethania** (built by the priest to accommodate his guests) and, standing on the edge of the hilltop, the distinctive **Tour Magdala**, which Saunière had built as a private library. ❑

LEFT: devil guarding the entrance to Rennes-le-Château church.

Map
on page
272

Overlooking Espéraza is **Rennes-le-Château** ❾, a curiosity for those with a taste for the occult, since the tiny village at the top of a helter-skelter road lays claim to every myth going, from Cathar treasure to the Holy Grail of the Knights Templar (*see The Priest's Tale, opposite*).

The Aude skirts past **Alet-les-Bains** ❿, a spa town with beautifully preserved half-timbered houses, the romantic ruins of a once noble Benedictine abbey (now with much needed restoration planned) and, oddly, a casino.

A few kilometres to the south, the Aude flows through **Limoux** ⓫, a pleasant market town of medieval arcades and bridges. Limoux is famous for its sparkling wine, Blanquette de Limoux, good value and worth stocking up on. The town is also known for its carnival, which has taken place at weekends and fête days from January to March almost without interruption since the Middle Ages. Next to the tourist office on Promenade du Tivoli is the **Musée Petiet** (open July–Aug daily; Sept–June Mon–Sat; entrance fee; tel: 04 68 31 85 03), founded by Marie Petiet, a little-known artist who painted some beautiful pictures. Don't miss her *Blanchisseuses* (1882), a portrait of women ironing and gossiping.

TIP

You can continue mystery-hunting ad infinitum on the internet at: www.rennes-le-chateau.com and www.rennes-le-chateau. org – sites which cover every aspect of the Saunière case in detail.

Cathar country

The region around the old border between Languedoc and Roussillon (once the border of Spain and France), and now more prosaically the border between the *départements* of the Aude and Pyrénées-Orientales, is known as "Cathar country". The castles that sheltered the Cathars were originally built as frontier defences, constructed of crude stone at the top of the most inaccessible rocky pinnacles with wide-ranging views of the country around and of any approaching attackers.

LEFT: Tour Magdala, Rennes-le-Château.
BELOW: house in Alet-les-Bains.

The "Cathar Knights", a sculpture on the A61 motorway.

Following the "Cathar trail" provides an excuse to visit this glorious, wild country. To the west is **Puivert** (open daily; entrance fee; tel: 04 68 20 81 52), unusually built on the plain and easily accessible, and more of a palace than a castle despite its sturdy defences. Notable here are the Gothic vaulted rooms still extant, one with fine 14th-century carvings of musicians and their instruments. The **Musée de Quercorb** (open Apr–Sept daily; Oct, Nov and Mar weekends and school holidays; entrance fee; tel: 04 68 20 80 98) has a display of actual medieval instruments, local tools and a complete regional kitchen.

Puilaurens ⓭ (open Apr–Oct daily; Nov, Dec, Feb and Mar: weekends and school holidays; entrance fee; tel: 04 68 20 65 26) is perhaps the best example of just what remarkable refuges these fortresses were, whilst requiring only a modest 10-minute climb for today's pilgrims. Clambering up to the ramparts the full scale of the enterprise soon becomes apparent, as a single steep stone stairway zig-zags its precarious way to the top. No assailant could go unnoticed or unbombarded. The castle itself has been rebuilt and reinforced many times and is a graphic illustration of the complexities of medieval defence with its machicolations, slanted arrow slits and chutes down which stones and boiling oil could be tipped over encroaching enemies.

Pyrenean foothills

The Corbières are the Pyrenean foothills southeast of Carcassonne. Much of the land is untamed *garrigue* (scrubland), fragrant with honeysuckle and broom, though vines are planted on any promising slice of land. It is pretty wild and empty, though; the few roads there are snake deeply between great craggy limestone outcrops which create a curious enclosed feeling. Ensure you have a full

tank of fuel, or better still go by horse. In the valleys you can see evidence of the terrible floods of 1999 when bridges were washed away and villages flooded. Here and there you can see the ruins of castles on distant peaks; look out for **Aguilar** and **Durban-Corbières** along the D611. The villages are devoted entirely to wine and the buildings' ground floors have huge arched doorways to the *caves* (cellars). You can sample wines at the village cooperatives, or at the châteaux wine estates.

The main town of the Corbières, between Carcassonne and Narbonne, is **Lézignan-Corbières** ⓮, where the **Musée de la Vigne et du Vin** (open daily; entrance fee; tel: 04 68 27 37 02) will provide a good introduction to the area's main industry. The **Donjon d'Arques** ⓯ (open Mar–Nov daily; entrance fee; tel: 04 68 69 82 87) has a perfectly preserved 13th-century Gothic keep. The **Maison de Déodat Roche** on the same site (entrance fee; tel: 04 68 69 82 87), named after a historian born in Arques, contains an exhibition on Catharism.

Villerouge-Termenès ⓰ has grown up around its **castle** (open July and Aug daily; Sept–Nov and Mar–June weekends only; entrance fee; tel: 04 68 70 09 11), the great stone circular towers of which are pierced only by arrow slits. This castle is best known for harbouring the last Cathar "perfect" who was burnt at the stake in 1321, and the courtyard is used every year for an annual medieval banquet in his honour, complete with medieval menu and costumes. The castle also has a restaurant and medieval *rôtisserie*.

To the south, close to the border with Roussillon, is the highest castle of all, **Peyrepertuse** ⓱ (open Feb–Dec daily; entrance fee; tel: 04 68 45 03 26), which can only be reached by one long and winding road followed by a demanding climb. The site is so narrow that the castle itself is elongated to fit its dizzy

Map on page 272

The now ruined castles of Aguilar, Quéribus, Termes, Peyrepertuse and Puilaurens were known as the "five sons of Carcassonne" as they protected the city against attackers from the southwest.

BELOW: Corbières landscape.

Statue of Liberty lookalike on a roadside near Narbonne.

perch – only a few metres wide in parts. The walls grow out of bare limestone and are pierced by one narrow entrance. But it is still a massive fortress, with two towers at either end. In the old keep of St-Georges a simple Romanesque chapel remains, and a further flight of terrifyingly exposed steps leads up to the final refuge for the garrison. Here at the highest point, the wind takes your breath away, as does the view to the sea, to the gorge below and the peaks of the Pyrenees. No attacker ever took Peyrepertuse but it was eventually surrendered to the King of France and became another link in the French defences.

Visible from Peyrepertuse is **Quéribus** ⑱ (open Apr–Oct daily; Nov, Dec, Feb and Mar weekends only; entrance fee; tel: 04 68 45 03 69), which dominates the plain of Roussillon below, its solid keep like a jagged tooth on the ridge. Drive up the winding steep road to the second car park, from where there is a fairly easy walk up to the castle. This is one of the best-preserved castles in the Aude: a warren of steps carved out of rock, many tunnels, and stairs that surround the keep with its Gothic vaulted central hall. Quéribus is renowned as the final bastion of the Cathars, sheltering a few brave (or foolhardy) souls after the fall of Montségur, and only successfully besieged in 1255.

North east of the Corbières lies the 8th-century Benedictine **Abbaye de Lagrasse** ⑲, which though partly ruined is still home to a monastic community and can be visited (open April–Oct: daily except Sun morning; closed Nov–Mar; entrance fee; tel: 04 68 58 11 58).

Also well worth a detour is the **Abbaye de Fontfroide** ⑳ (open daily; guided tours only; entrance fee; tel: 04 68 45 11 08), beautifully restored with fine cloisters and chapter house, and a gorgeous rose garden. During the early 20th-century restoration visiting artists like Odilon Redon and Richard Burghstal contributed wall paintings and stained-glass windows. Once you have visited the abbey you can wander freely along marked paths in the hilly *garrigue* (scrubland) surrounding it, the natural flora of which is carefully protected.

BELOW: the Abbaye de Fontfroide.

Narbonne

In the 1st-century BC **Narbonne** ㉑ was a major port on the Via Domitia, the Roman road along the coast still followed by the *autoroute* today. It was the capital of the Narbonensis, the largest province of Roman Gaul. Today it is prosperous again thanks to the surrounding wine region, and is now the biggest city in the Aude *département,* though it has never regained its original importance.

North of the Canal de la Robine (another project of Paul Riquet, who built the Canal du Midi) is the restored **medieval quarter**, where Narbonne's tourist attractions bear witness to its glorious past. Roman fragments remain, most notably in the **Horreum**, the recently discovered underground storehouse with its granaries, grain chutes and warren of storerooms.

The town prospered throughout the Middle Ages until the harbour silted up and the River Aude was diverted at the end of the 14th century. Until then, Narbonne had been an important bishopric and the huge **Cathédrale St-Just**, modelled on the Gothic cathedrals of the north, was slowly being built. As

Narbonne declined, building stopped and only the chancel was constructed. This alone is vast – only Amiens and Beauvais are higher. It is beautifully decorated with 14th-century sculptures, carved tombs, frescoes and stained glass and a sensational 18th-century carved organ. Newly restored reliefs can be seen in the Chapelle de la Vierge, and gorgeous Aubusson and Gobelin tapestries adorn the walls of the side chapels. The Chapel of the Anonciade houses a treasure trove of manuscripts, jewelled reliquaries and tapestries. The unfinished transept is a courtyard. Between the cathedral and the adjacent **Palais des Archevêques** lie the cloisters, with four lovely galleries of 14th-century vaulting.

The Archbishops' palace

The **Place de l'Hôtel de Ville** is dominated by the huge complex of palace and cathedral which forms one side of it. Between two of the three massive 13th- and 14th-century towers of the palace is the **Hôtel de Ville**, with its 19th-century neo-Gothic façade by Viollet-le-Duc (the architect who restored Carcassonne and Notre-Dame in Paris). In the middle of the square is a recently discovered section of the Via Domitia.

Entering the palace complex through the low-slung medieval arches of the passage de l'Ancre, the **Palais Vieux** (Old Palace) is on the right. Here a sheltered courtyard has many pleasing details; note the Romanesque windows and the anchors hung high on the walls, reminders of Narbonne's nautical past.

On the left is the **Palais Neuf** (New Palace), housing Narbonne's most important museums. The collection displayed in the **Musée Archéologique** (open daily; closed Mon out of season; entrance fee; tel: 04 68 90 30 66) includes fragments of Narbonne's Roman heritage: reliefs, milestones, part of the original walls and a variety of humble domestic objects – coins, tools and glassware. The **Chapelle de la Madeleine**, with its 14th-century wall painting, houses a collection of Greek vases, sarcophagi and mosaics. The **Musée d'Art et d'Histoire** (open daily; entrance fee; tel: 04 68 90 30 54) is in the former apartments of the archbishop, richly furnished with painted ceilings and tiled floors; note the Roman mosaic in the Chambre du Roi (Louis XIV slept here in 1642). The art collection includes works by Canaletto, Brueghel, Boucher and Veronese, as well as a large selection of Montpellier faïence. You can visit the **Maison Natale de Charles Trenet** (avenue Charles Trenet; open Wed–Mon; tel: 04 68 65 15 60), birthplace of one of France's best-loved singers, near here.

South of the canal is the Bourg, an area of the city which has pleasant promenades and elegant mansions including the Renaissance **Maison des Trois Nourrices**, with its three carved caryatids – hence the name, "House of the Three Wet-Nurses". On the Boulevard du Dr Lacroix is the 13th-century Gothic **Basilique St-Paul** (open daily), built on the site of a much earlier church of which the crypt and a number of carved stone sarcophagi remain. The gastronomically inclined should not miss the splendid Art Nouveau *halle* (covered market hall) where a superb selection of local produce is on sale.

Map on page 272

INFO

Narbonne tourist information office: Place Roger Salengro; tel: 04 68 65 15 60.

BELOW: Palais des Archevêques, Narbonne.

Map
on page
272

In 1989 wine grower Jean-Louis Fabre found a whale on the beach at Port la Nouvelle. He has conserved the 200-metre (655-ft) skeleton in his cave where it has become a popular attraction. Tel: 04 68 48 00 39 for information.

BELOW:
the Aude coast near Port-la-Nouvelle.
RIGHT: flamingoes in a coastal *étang*.

The Aude coast

Between Narbonne and the sea is the **Montagne de la Clape**, a massif of black basalt covered in vineyards. At the top are a lovely windswept marine cemetery and the sailors' chapel of **Notre-Dame des Auzils** (open daily, afternoons only). **Narbonne-Plage** is a busy "city" beach. **Gruissan ㉒** to the south has a large resort and marina, but there are still remnants of the past in the old fishing village, built in a circle round the medieval Barbarossa tower. The windswept shore with its beach huts on stilts is where *37° 2* (*Betty Blue*, 1986) was filmed.

On the landward side of the **Étang de Bages et de Sigean** are other attractive fishing villages like **Bages** and **Peyriac-de-Mer ㉓**, which overlook the lagoon and its pink flamingoes. These are quiet, favoured retreats, with winding streets, waterside cottages, tiny art galleries and fish restaurants. To the south is the huge, drive-through animal park of **Sigean ㉔** (open daily; entrance fee; tel: 04 68 48 20 20) spread over an area of scrubland, woodland and lagoon. **Port-la-Nouvelle**, one of the Mediterranean's largest ports, also has a long sandy beach and there's a windfarm on the hillside above it.

The **Étang de Leucate**, to the south, is hugely popular for wind-surfing, land yachting, boat trips and sailing, and there are large marinas at Port Leucate and Port Barcares. But there are also several old-fashioned beach resorts around the lake, like **Leucate-Plage ㉕** and **La Franqui-Plage**, that date from the coming of the railway at the beginning of the 20th century. Beaches are sandy and safe, there are simple seafood restaurants and not much else.

Inland is the wine region of **Fitou**. The village of Fitou has a crumbling château, which has been under restoration for years by one determined family who have installed a delightful restaurant within its ancient walls. ❑

THE WINDY COAST

Several small towns in the Aude and neighbouring *départements* are benefiting from a tax which can only be described as a "windfall". The high winds that the inhabitants of these places have always been forced to endure have suddenly become something to celebrate. As France tries to boost its renewable energy sector, windfarms are being set up to harvest the free energy.

The technology to generate electricity for the national grid from the wind has been viable and economic for many years (as proven by countries such as Denmark) but it was only in the late 1990s that France – long dependent on nuclear power – took its first belated measures to encourage wind-power entrepreneurs.

Excruciating environmental vetting procedures are undertaken before the siting of a new windfarm is approved. But developers can invariably count on the co-operation of local mayors anxious to extract revenue from the few natural resources they have. As one mayor put it: "All we have here are vines, stones and wind."

The most prominent windfarms in the Aude are at Port-la-Nouvelle (easily seen from the coastal motorway), at Salleles-Limousis, in the hills north of Carcassonne, and most recently at Opoul, near Salses.

FRENCH CATALONIA

Map on page 272

*A lot is packed into this small corner of France with its distinct
Catalan national identity: Romanesque churches and modern art;
mountain landscapes; seaside resorts and fishing villages*

The Pyrénées-Orientales is the most southerly *département* of France, with
a climate to match; Perpignan, its capital, is very often the hottest place on
the weather map. The landscape is ravishing, from the wide beaches and
rocky coves of the coast to the awesome backdrop of the mountains. In between
are the vineyards and fruit orchards that provide much of the local income.

Considering its charms, the region is surprisingly little known, and sometimes
it seems the inhabitants prefer it that way. They are still trying to decide what
to call it, for a start. It is sometimes called Pyrénées-Roussillon, a traditional
geographic description which fails to tally with the government maps. Pyrénées-
Méditerranée is also offered – long-winded but more evocative.

Whatever it is actually called, this is French Catalonia and it has only been
part of France since it was signed over by Spain in 1659 as part of the Treaty of
the Pyrenees. It still guards its Catalan identity jealously, though showing little
inclination for true independence. The Catalan language is widely understood,
if not always spoken; many road signs are in both French and Catalan; and the
red and yellow striped flag is ubiquitous.

The coast includes long flat sandy beaches, rocky coves, busy resorts and
overdeveloped fishing villages like the celebrated Collioure. Only an hour
inland are the foothills of the Pyrenees, with magnif-
icent scenery and splendid walks. In summer this is a
favourite retreat from the sweltering heat of the plain,
but spring is lovely too: a feast of wild flowers and
blossoms. The locals prefer the *arrière-saison,* warm
autumn days of wine-making and mushroom-gathering.
In winter the ski resorts of the Cerdagne, some of the
biggest in France, come to life.

The cultural heritage includes some of the finest
Romanesque architecture in France, from important
abbeys to simple mountain chapels, many with
exquisitely sculpted carving. Today, many of these
buildings have been restored, and they are used as
atmospheric settings for concerts and exhibitions.

You can eat and drink well in Catalonia, too. The
local wine is increasingly celebrated for its quality,
and although gourmet restaurants are thin on the
ground you can eat heartily at rustic *auberges* (inns)
and feast on fish and seafood on the coast.

A southern hot spot

Perpignan ㉖ is one of the hottest towns in France,
with a strong southern ambience, its harsh sunlight,
palm trees, narrow shuttered streets and brightly
painted façades more redolent of Spain than France.
As capital of the Roussillon region, it is an important link in the developing Mediterranean sunbelt, a
major centre for wholesale freight, and surrounded

PRECEDING PAGES:
Collioure.
LEFT: in a café
in Perpignan.
BELOW: Catalan
crafts on sale.

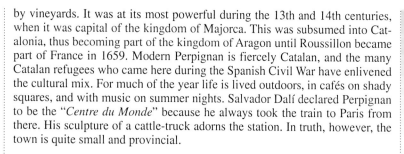

by vineyards. It was at its most powerful during the 13th and 14th centuries, when it was capital of the kingdom of Majorca. This was subsumed into Catalonia, thus becoming part of the kingdom of Aragon until Roussillon became part of France in 1659. Modern Perpignan is fiercely Catalan, and the many Catalan refugees who came here during the Spanish Civil War have enlivened the cultural mix. For much of the year life is lived outdoors, in cafés on shady squares, and with music on summer nights. Salvador Dalí declared Perpignan to be the *"Centre du Monde"* because he always took the train to Paris from there. His sculpture of a cattle-truck adorns the station. In truth, however, the town is quite small and provincial.

The old town

The most distinctive remnant of the past is the **Castillet**, a castellated red-brick tower and gateway which is all that remains of the town walls. It was once a prison and now houses the **Musée Casa Parail** (open Wed–Mon; entrance fee; tel: 04 68 35 42 05), which holds an excellent collection of rustic memorabilia, including agricultural implements, looms, craft tools, furniture and terracotta glazed pots.

In the middle of the old town is Perpignan's finest building, the 14th-century Gothic **Loge de Mer**, originally the shipping exchange. It is now a restaurant, where you can admire the Renaissance carved wooden ceilings and window frames. Next door is the **Hôtel-de-Ville** with arcades and latticed windows, at the centre of which is the masterpiece of Roussillon sculptor, Aristide Maillol, *The Mediterranée*. Nearby are several lively terrace cafés and restaurants.

The **Quartier St-Jean** around the Cathedral is the smartest part of town with some fine old red-brick mansions and winding atmospheric streets with antique shops, and second-hand bookstores. The **Cathédrale de St-Jean** is an imposing structure, built in the 14th and 15th centuries of river pebbles and thin red bricks in a local herringbone pattern, topped off with an elaborate wrought-iron belfry. The dim echoing interior has one vast nave glimmering with gilded altarpieces, frescoes and ornate wooden statues. On the left-hand side of the entrance you can see the carved Romanesque doorway of the original 11th-century church.

Adjoining the Cathedral is the **Chapelle du Dévot Christ** (open Tues–Sun), with a wrenchingly realistic carved 14th-century crucifix and modern stained-glass windows by Shirley Jaffe. Beside the chapel is the **Campo Santo**, the oldest cloistered cemetery in France, recently restored and used for concerts.

On rue de l'Ange is **Musée Hyacinthe Rigaud** (open Wed–Mon; entrance fee; tel: 04 68 35 43 40), a 17th-century mansion that has paintings by Rigaud himself (he was court painter to Louis XIV), several beautifully preserved medieval religious paintings and modern works by Maillol, Dufy and Picasso – in particular three 1954 Picasso portraits in crayon and chalk. There is also some wonderful reconstructed 13th-century Catalan pottery, decorated with simple artistry.

The vast **Palais des Rois de Majorque** (open daily; entrance fee; tel: 04 68 34 48 29) still occupies a substantial portion of the town to the south, its forbidding brick ramparts a challenge to the visitor. It dates from

Perpignan's La Sanch procession, on Good Friday, dates from the Middle Ages, when the Red Penitents Brotherhood accompanied condemned prisoners to the gallows. Today the townsfolk still trudge through the streets – some barefoot – garbed in sinister pointed black hoods and red robes, carrying crucifixes and reliquaries, and tolling bells.

BELOW:
Easter procession
in Perpignan.

the 13th century when it housed the court of James I of Majorca, and was further reinforced by Vauban; there is lavish accommodation and elegant gardens.

From the top of the Tour de l'Hommage is an excellent panorama of city, mountains and sea. The palace is built around a central arcaded courtyard, now used for concerts. This is flanked on one side by the Salle de Majorque, the great hall with its triple fireplace and great Gothic arched windows. Adjacent are two chapels, built one above the other, in the southern Gothic style with pointed arches, patterned frescoes and handsome Moorish tiling.

Just outside Perpignan is the Roman site of **Ruscino** (tel: 04 68 67 47 17), where a museum has been under construction for years; the site is finally open.

The Fenouillèdes

North of Perpignan is the fort at **Salses-le-Château** ㉗ (open daily; entrance fee; tel: 04 68 38 60 13), guarding the narrow gap between the wild Corbières hills and Mediterranean lagoons. Built by the Spanish between 1497 and 1506, it originally stood on the border between Spain and France, and is a superb example of Spanish military architecture with massive walls and rounded towers that look as if they have sprung organically from the ochre earth.

West of Perpignan and bordering the Aude *département* is the valley of the River Agly, the site of terrible flooding in 1999. The valley is flanked by the **Fenouillèdes**, a range of jagged rocky escarpments covered with vines. The name comes from *fenouil* (fennel), a locally abundant plant.

A brief detour from Estagel will bring you to **Tautavel** ㉘, one of the most important archaeological sites in Europe, where the earliest known European skull was discovered in 1971. There is a good museum, **Musée de la Pré-**

Map on page 272

INFO

Tourist information office, Perpignan: Palais des Congrès, place Armand-Lanoux; tel: 04 68 66 30 30.

BELOW: Fenouillèdes landscape.

Decorative fountain in St-Paul-de-Fenouillet.

BELOW:
St-Michel-de-Cuxa.

histoire (open daily; entrance fee; tel: 04 68 29 07 76), which combines thorough information with vivid reconstructions of Stone Age life. In summer you can visit the cave where Tautavel Man once lived, warmed by the rising sun across the ancient plain.

For wine tasting and shopping stop at **Maury, St-Paul-de-Fenouillet** ㉙, **Estagel** or **Château de Jau** (which also has an art museum and restaurant). Towers and castle ruins hereabouts are silhouetted against the sky and the hills are pierced by dizzily deep gorges. The best of the latter is the **Gorge de Galamus**, through which there is a narrow, one-car-wide road. The drama of the scenery is even better appreciated by clambering down to the tiny hermitage of St-Antoine clinging to the rock face, or by swimming or canyoning in the deep stoney pools and waterfalls.

The sacred mountain of the Catalans

Southwest of Perpignan looms **Canigou**, the "sacred mountain of the Catalans", its great, often snow-capped peak dominating the landscape. It is spectacular in spring with a foreground of peach and cherry blossoms. North of the mountain the Conflent valley winds up into the cooler foothills of the Pyrenees. Along the way **Ille-sur-Têt** ㉚ has a church and a museum, the **Centre d'Art Sacré** (open July–Aug daily; Sept–June closed Tues and weekend mornings; entrance fee; tel: 04 68 84 83 96) with sacred art from churches all over Roussillon pleasingly displayed in a 16th-century hospital. Nearby are the spectacular rock formations of **Les Orgues**, eroded into a fantasy world of towers and tunnels. Up in the vine-dotted hills to the north is another prehistoric site, **Bélesta**, which has a modern museum artfully accommodated in the medieval

château, where you can see an intriguing reconstruction of the neolithic tomb and its treasures, discovered here in 1983. At **Ansignan** a Roman aqueduct is still used for distributing water for agriculture.

A detour to the south and a winding road uphill will bring you to the **Prieuré de Serrabone** ③① (open daily; entrance fee; tel: 04 68 84 09 30), the first of several Romanesque abbeys tucked away in the lower flanks of the Canigou massif. The setting is sublime: utterly peaceful, the priory is surrounded by terraces of herbs and olives. The abbey itself is superb. It is built of the local pink marble, with a single cloister arcade overlooking the hills. Inside are marble flagged floors, a simple altar slab, columns with carved capitals, and a remarkable tribune embellished with carved flowers, animals and mischievous human faces.

The most important abbey, just outside Prades, is the 9th-century **St-Michel-de-Cuxa** ③② (open daily; closed Sun morning; entrance fee; tel: 04 68 96 15 35), which is best known today as the setting for an annual music festival, in honour of the cellist Pablo Casals who started it when he took refuge here from Franco's Spain. This festival, held in August, attracts classical music lovers from all over the world to the abbey church and dozens of smaller chapels around the Conflent valley, in search of the perfect combination of architecture, music and landscape.

The abbey was founded by the Benedictines in 878 and is a rare example of pre-Romanesque architecture in France, being built in the Mozarabic style by stonemasons using the Moorish keyhole arch introduced by the Muslims. St-Michel has undergone considerable restoration. It has one great square tower remaining. The interior of the church is a strong, austere space, with a huge stone barrel vault, flanked by two aisles. Below is an unusual palm-vaulted

Map on page 272

"...the mountain which many who have never heard the name have been looking for all their lives."

– HILAIRE BELLOC ON CANIGOU

BELOW: carved capitals in Prieuré de Serrabone.

*Catalans joining in
their national dance,
the* sardana.

BELOW:
Villefranche-
de-Conflent.

crypt. Best of all are the cloisters of pink marble columns and fine Romanesque capitals, carved by the legendary "Master of Cuxa" in the 12th century; observe closely the confident, strong carvings of mythical animals and local flora. Many of the capitals were looted after the Revolution and some were only rediscovered in 1909, holding up the bath-house in Prades. Half were eventually reinstated and the rest were shipped by a sculptor from the USA to the Metropolitan Museum in New York where they form the basis of the Cloisters Museum *(see page 72)*, a re-creation of a Romanesque monastery in the heart of Manhattan. The white marble altar stone was only discovered in 1969, supporting a balcony in the nearby town of Vinca.

Around Prades

Prades is a small market town which typifies the local style, with pink marble pavements. The church has a southern Gothic wrought-iron bell tower and the biggest baroque altarpiece in France, carved by Claude Sunyer, and recently restored so that it is even more dazzling than it was before. There is a small Pablo Casals museum inside the tourist office (rue Victor Hugo; tel: 04 68 05 41 02) with photos, faded news clippings and Casals' umbrellas. A plaque on a tiny red shuttered house on rue Pelieu commemorates the birthplace of Thomas Merton (1915–69), the North American poet-monk who was inspired ever after by his early years dominated by the sight of Canigou at the end of the street.

Above Prades is the Castellane valley, and the thermal spa of **Molitg-les-Bains** ㉝, where there is a huge, grand hotel – once a favourite of Casals – above a lake and romantic gardens. The road beyond continues through the village of **Mosset**, recently elected one of the "plus beaux villages de France", clinging to

the hillside, the last village before the old frontier with France. At the heart of the village is the Capelletta, a restored Romanesque chapel which often has exhibitions and concerts. Beyond Mosset, the road snakes up to the **Col de Jau** (1,506 metres/4,941 ft), giving magnificent views back down the valley on the way. On the other side of the pass you descend into the Aude.

Map on page 272

The upper Conflent valley

Continuing on the N116 up the main valley from Prades, after 6 km (4 miles) you come to **Villefranche-de-Conflent** ❸❹, sited at the narrowest point of the Têt valley, and at the confluence of three rivers. It was a fortress against Moorish invasion in medieval times, and until the 17th century was the administrative capital of the Conflent region. Fragments of the 11th-century walls remain, but in the 17th century Vauban added massive ramparts and gates.

Vauban also built **Fort Libéria** (open daily; tel: 04 68 96 22 96) high above the gorge, which you can visit by footpath or an underground passage of 1,000 steps, cut through the hillside. It was at one time a prison, accommodating among others two famous aristocratic women, accused of poisoning their relatives. A macabre tableau in a dingy cell shows their incarceration.

Villefranche today welcomes its visitors to marble streets quarried from the local pink stone, and beautifully restored dwellings and shop fronts. The 12th-century **Église de St-Jacques** has fine carved capitals and Catalan painted wooden statues as well as a 13th-century oak door embellished with intricate ironwork – indicating a once-important local industry. Wrought-iron signs are also seen on many of the shops which sell rustic local pottery, sheepskins and marble products. From Villefranche you can visit the nearby **Grottes des**

The "Fountain of the Cat" in the hill village of Mosset.

BELOW: Mosset on a winter's morning.

TIP

To climb Mount
Canigou, take the Jeep
from Prades
(tel: 06 09 71 91 62 or
04 68 05 24 24) or
Vernet-les-Bains (tel:
04 68 05 51 14) to
Chalet des Cortalets,
from where the
summit is a strenuous
two-hour hike.

BELOW:
the Little Yellow
Train in the snow.

Canalettes (open daily; entrance fee; tel: 04 68 96 23 11) where the caves of stalactites and stalagmites have recently become an unusual setting for concerts.
Villefranche is also the departure point for the **Train Jaune** *(see panel below)*
which will take you up to the mountain plain of the Cerdagne.

Vernet-les-Bains ③ is another spa town, once a great favourite with the
British. These days it's a little down-at-heel, though still favoured by a gentle
sheltered climate. Efforts are being made to restore its Belle Époque casino.

From the village of Casteil a few kilometres further up, you can walk to the
last of the great abbeys, **St-Martin-du-Canigou** (open Wed–Mon; guided visits only; entrance fee; tel: 04 68 05 50 03). This 9th-century early Romanesque
abbey is perched on a rock a third of the way up Mount Canigou and is only
accessible by Jeep or a 40-minute climb on foot. It is like a pilgrimage up
through the forest to the remote mountain site, and well worth the effort. Note
that only icons and canned drinks can be bought from the nuns and it is advisable to take a picnic.

The abbey was founded in the early 11th century by Guilfred, Count of
Cerdagne – you can still see the tiny tomb he carved for himself from the living rock. Most of the building was destroyed by an earthquake in 1433. It was
rebuilt but abandoned during the Revolution and only restored again in the
1930s. It is an irregularly shaped building, clinging to the rock, its ingenuity a
tribute to the early builders, with a newer church built right on top of an earlier
one (now the candle-lit crypt).

For the best view of the abbey on its rocky perch, continue on up the path until
you are above it. A leisurely walk back through the marked forest trail down the
other side is highly recommended.

THE LITTLE YELLOW TRAIN

The Train Jaune, the train affectionately known as the
"metro of the Pyrenees", runs along a 63-km (39-mile)
narrow-gauge track, through mountains and over bridges
and viaducts which span vertiginous gorges. It was an
extraordinary achievement when it was built in 1927, the
highest line in France.

Painted in the Catalan colours of red and yellow, the train
starts from Villefranche-de-Conflent (430 metres/1,400 ft)
and ends at Latour de Carol. On the way it passes through
Font-Romeu and Bolquère-Eyne, the highest railway station
in France at 1,593 metres (5,227 ft). The line runs through
19 tunnels and over two spectacular bridges – the granite
Séjourné viaduct spanning the Têt valley with 16 arches,
and the Gisclard suspension bridge. The views are best
from one of the open-air carriages – if you want to get a
seat in summer, it is advisable to arrive early.

You can get on and off the train on the same day with
the same ticket. One good walk is from Fontpedrouse
station to the baths at St Thomas les Bains.

Information is available from the stations at Villefranche-
de-Conflent, Mont-Louis, Font-Romeu, Bourg-Madame and
Latour de Carol; or tel 08 36 35 35 35 (premium line); or,
on the web, go to: ter.sncf.fr/train-jaune.

Cerdagne

From Villefranche a magnificent road, the main route to Andorra, climbs steeply up to the great plateau of the Cerdagne. On the way are the spectacular **Gorges de la Caranca**, the open-air thermal baths of **St Thomas-les-Bains** (open daily; tel: 04 68 97 15 44) – best when surrounded by winter snows – and, via a detour, the little village of **Planes**, which has a curious triangular 11th-century church.

Mont-Louis ㊱ is the gateway to the Cerdagne, a Vauban fortress which remains an outpost of the French military. The Cerdagne, once an independent state, and now divided between Spain and France, is today a chic retreat, popular with Barcelona residents as well as French. It is a major ski destination in winter, particuarly **Font-Romeu** ㊲, which along with Super-Bolquere and Pyrénées 2000 comprise one of the biggest ski resorts in France. The Cerdagne also provides sublime summer walking across high plateaux, with clear mountain lakes, pine and chestnut forests, wild horses and Pyrenean flora and fauna.

Apart from skiing, Font-Romeu also features the world's biggest **solar furnace** (open daily; entrance fee; tel: 04 68 30 77 86), established in 1969; with its giant convex mirrors it's an extraordinary sight, stepped across the valley.

Beyond is the curious phenomenon of **Llivia** ㊳, a Spanish enclave in French territory. When the Treaty of the Pyrenees was signed in 1659 all the villages in Roussillon were ceded to France. Llivia, however, was technically a town and so retained its Spanish nationality. It is quite surreal to visit the small town and suddenly find yourself in a tiny patch of Spain, with Spanish churches and *bodegas* (wine cellars). The French sniffily don't even signpost it.

There are many Romanesque churches to see in the Cerdagne, in particular at **Angoustrine**, where there are 13th-century frescoes; **Llo**, with its carved door-

Map on page 272

Vernet-les-Bains has two quite distinct literary associations. In the 1850s it was a fashionable spa and one visitor, Anthony Trollope, used is as a setting for a story, La Mère Bauche. *During World War II Arthur Koestler was interned at Vernet, as he describes in his 1941 book,* Scum of the Earth.

BELOW:
Vernet-les-Bains.

Pablo Picasso, who worked for a time in the town of Céret.

way; and **Dorres**, where there is an 11th-century church, Roman baths (tel: 04 68 04 66 87) in which you can still bathe, and a museum of stonemasonry. The tiny village of **St-Leocadie** has the highest vineyard in Europe and has a **Musée de Cerdagne** (open July–Aug daily; Sept–June Wed–Mon; groups by reservation; tel: 04 68 04 08 05) installed in a restored 17th-century farmhouse, devoted to exhibitions on rural life, architecture and history.

Capcir

Between the Cerdagne and the Ariège *départements* is the Capcir, a high mountain region of pine forests, glacial lakes and waterfalls, overlooked by the great peak of Pic Carlit (2,921 metres/9,584 ft), source of the Aude and the Têt rivers.

Until recently, the Capcir region was poor and abandoned, but through investment, the area has developed into a resort with several ski stations, dams and artificial lakes. And it is traversed by a spectacular road route from Mont-Louis down to the valley of the Aude River. The main ski resorts are Les Angles, Matemale and **Formiguères** ❹. Les Angles also has an animal park, **Parc Animalier des Angles** (open daily; tel: 04 68 04 17 20), where native species of the Pyrenees past and present – bears, reindeer, wolves and bison – can be seen. The **Grotte de Fontrabiouse** (open mid- Dec–mid-Nov daily; entrance fee; tel: 04 68 30 95 55) has an underground lake and galleries of bizarre rock formations.

Vallespir

South of Canigou is the Vallespir, the valley of the Tech River, famous for producing the first cherries of the year. It is enveloped in a cloud of pink blossom in the spring. The town of **Céret** ❹ has intimate little squares, painted Spanish

BELOW: snowboarding in Andorra.

THE HIGH-ALTITUDE COUNTRY

Andorra is both the great duty-free shop of Europe and, being 80 percent mountainous, the highest country in Europe. It is a beautiful place to walk in spring or summer, and to ski in winter.

Historically and politically, it has always been a curious phenomenon. From the 13th century it was ruled jointly by the bishops of Urgell in Spain and the counts of Foix, who ceded their sovereignty to the kings of France in the 16th century. Until the mid-1950s this tiny state of 468 sq km (181 sq miles) was a forgotten outpost wedged in the Pyrenees between France and Spain and blocked by snow for half the year. Then it woke up to its potential as a tourist attraction and tax haven, and now has a booming economy in which none of its 65,000 population has to pay tax. It finally entered the modern world in 1993 when it became a fully independent state.

Most of Andorra's 8 million visitors a year go shopping – for alcohol, cameras, hi-fi, leather goods, pharmaceuticals and particularly cigarettes.

However, there is another, more peaceful and timeless Andorra: a mountain wilderness of hiking routes (the GR7 and the GR11 both cross the country), ski resorts, thermal spas, and ancient villages and churches.

Map on page 272

tiles and colourful stucco buildings, giving it a very Spanish feel. Its Catalan roots are evident in regular bullfights and the August Sardana dance festival. The town was popular with Picasso, Braque and many other artists and it was here they first began experimenting with Cubist painting, one of the 20th-century's most important avant garde art movements *(see page 301)*.

A favourite subject for the artists was the 14th-century bridge across the Tech, the **Pont du Diable**, which can still be seen today. Céret is distinguished by the splendid modern building of the excellent **Musée d'Art Moderne** (open daily; closed Tues Oct–Apr; entrance fee; tel: 04 68 87 27 76). The collection includes works by the Catalan artists Tàpies and Capdeville, a Picasso series of bowls painted with bullfighting scenes and many paintings of Céret.

From Céret the D115 follows the Tech valley through the Vallespir to the spa town of **Amélie-les-Bains-Palalda** ❹ where fragments of Roman baths have been discovered. Most in evidence are the many spa hotels for those who like to spend their holidays focused on their ailments.

Municipal ornamentation on a public bench in Elne.

Beyond is **Arles-sur-Tech** ❷, whose 12th-century church, the **Église de Ste-Marie**, has pretty cloisters, 12th-century frescoes and a legendary sarcophagus beside the church door, which according to fervently believed local legend produces several drops of totally pure water every year. A short way further up the valley are the **Gorges de la Fou**, which lay claim to being the narrowest gorges in the world. An iron footbridge winds through a vertical slice of the earth, accessible only on foot; protective headgear is mandatory (open Apr–Nov daily; entrance fee; tel: 04 68 39 16 21).

Further into the Haut Vallespir, the town of **St-Laurent-de-Cerdans** ❸, right on the border with Spain, was in the past on a route taken by refugees. It has maintained production of traditional espadrilles and Catalan fabrics. A small museum demonstrates the production process and contains a fascinating collection of old photos and rustic footwear.

BELOW: making espadrilles.

The plain of Roussillon

Back down on the plain of Roussillon is a rich land of well-tended orchards and vineyards, baking hot in summer, though sometimes swept by the full force of the Tramontane wind, to which the windbreaks of cypresses and bamboo bear witness.

Thuir ❹ is a centre of production of byrrh (a sweet aperitif) and Dubonnet. The biggest oak barrel in the world can be seen in **Caves Byrrh** (open May–Sept daily; Apr Mon–Sat; Oct Mon–Fri; Nov–Mar by appointment; tel: 04 68 53 05 42).

At the heart of the plain is the old capital of Roussillon, **Elne** ❺, which was visited by Hannibal and his elephants on his way to Rome in 218 BC. Today it is best known for its 11th-century cathedral, and the music festival held there. The pride of Elne is the superb and well-preserved **cloisters** (open daily; entrance fee; tel: 04 68 22 70 90). The pale blue-veined marble has been vigorously sculpted into exquisite capitals, each embellished with a riot of flowers and arabesques. The south side of the cloister is the oldest (12th-century) and tells the story of the Creation, which is particularly worth seeking out.

Faces carved on the church at St-Genis-des-Fontaines.

Well worth a brief detour is **St-Genis-des-Fontaines**, where the medieval monastery has been restored. It has a superb 11th-century carved lintel and lovely cloisters – part reproduction, part made from original pieces determinedly tracked down after they were sold to an antique dealer in 1924.

The coast

Between Le Barcares and Argèles-sur-Mer the coast of Roussillon is a long straight expanse of flat sandy beaches, with several popular resorts. **Canet** is "Perpignan-on-Sea", with lots of amusements. **St-Cyprien** ㊻ has a substantial marina but is generally less frenetic. At its southern edge development has been limited and there is a nature reserve and beaches edged by pampas grass instead of hotels and cafés. **Argèles-sur-Mer** ㊼ is a huge resort with the biggest camp site in Europe, fortunately discreetly hidden.

The **Côte Vermeille** is by far the prettiest bit, a craggy coastline of rose-tinted rocks where the mountains meet the Mediterranean. Small coves and secluded beaches resist full-scale development, though the roads get very crowded in high season. The winding coastal corniche takes you right into Spain, with wild headlands like **Cap Béar** offering dazzling sea views.

Collioure ㊽ is the gem of the coast. It was first favoured by Matisse in 1904, who was inspired by the brilliant light; the fishing cottages painted turquoise, pink and yellow; the sapphire blue of the sea; and the exotic palms and cacti that flourish in the balmy climate. He was joined by artists like Derain, Dufy and Juan Gris, and a whole new art movement, Fauvism, resulted. Since then this perfect little fishing port has changed surprisingly little, bar the art galleries and souvenir shops that cram its tiny cobbled streets. You can follow a Chemin

BELOW:
vineyards near the coast at Collioure.

du Fauvisme around the town where empty frames focus on the views painted by the artists. Desirable purchases here include pottery, locally woven espadrilles, regional wine and anchovies – Collioure's main fishing crop.

There are four sheltered little beaches, mainly of pebbles, around the harbour, happily accommodating bathers and pleasure boats. The town is dominated by the **Château Royal** (open daily; entrance fee; tel: 04 68 82 06 43), a massive fortress, first established by the Templars and reinforced in 1669 by Vauban. He razed half the town in the process, the better to defend it.

The 17th-century church, **Notre-Dame-des-Anges**, was rebuilt on the quay next to the lighthouse, which now serves as a very nautical bell tower. The interior is stuffed with baroque altarpieces by Josep Sunyer and other Catalan masters. South of the town is the **Musée d'Art Moderne** (open Wed–Mon daily; entrance fee; tel: 04 68 82 10 19), housed in a charming old villa, featuring many good examples of works by lesser-known artists painting in the style of the Fauves; Henri Marre's rendering of Collioure's bright orange roof tops and blue sea says it all. There is also an excellent collection of 13–15th-century Moorish ceramics, a style that inspired Picasso.

Beyond Collioure is **Port-Vendres**, still an important fishing port, and **Banyuls-sur-Mer** ⑲, which produces a strong sweet wine from the terraced vines that cling to the hillsides. Banyuls is also famous as the birthplace of Aristide Maillol, the 19th-century French sculptor, and his house outside the town, **La Métairie**, can be visited to see several of his works, and a pleasing reconstruction of his kitchen (open daily; entrance fee; tel: 04 68 88 57 11). **Cerbère** is the most southerly point of the French coast, proudly flying the red and yellow Catalan flag. ❑

Map on page 272

The sculptor Aristide Maillol (1861–1944) making a sketch.

BELOW: fishing boats on the beach at Collioure.

The Art of the South

Two of the most important avant-garde art movements of the 20th century sprang into being in the little corner of Roussillon between the Pyrenees and the Mediterranean during the uncertain years just before the Great War. Within a few miles of each other and only a couple of years apart, Matisse and Picasso responded in different and revolutionary ways to the brilliant light and strong colours of the south. Fauvism and Cubism were the result.

Collioure *(see page 298)* is the birthplace of Fauvism. The colours and forms of the little Catalan fishing village first attracted Matisse in 1904: the stuccoed houses in shades of pistachio, rose and canary yellow, sheltered by dark green cypresses; the gaily painted fishing boats dragged up on the shore; and the great bulk of the château (which Picasso once tried to buy).

Matisse urged Derain to join him and the two artists expressed their emotional response to the colours that Derain described as "sticks of dynamite" with paint used straight from the tube applied in bright, primitive daubs. To the critics it was a scandalous new form of painting but to the artists it was merely a way of capturing what they saw. Matisse's *Landscape at Collioure* is a riot of colour, balanced with untouched white canvas conveying the intensity of the sunlight of the Mediterranean coast. These scandalous new paintings were dubbed Fauvism by the art critic Louis Fauxcelles. Regarding a classical sculpture in a room set aside for the new art at the Salon d'Automne in Paris, he exclaimed to Matisse, "Look! Donatello in a cage of wild beasts!" *(chez les fauves).*

Many other painters made the pilgrimage to Collioure, including Picasso, Dufy and Juan Gris. The little port still cherishes its artistic image. Today the château is used for exhibitions of modern art and there is a new Musée d'Art Moderne. Collioure's Hôtel Templiers, favoured by the Fauves (and also by

the Scottish architect, designer and artist, Charles Rennie Mackintosh, who came often to the region) is still in business.

A few miles inland is the little town of Céret. It isn't far from the border with Spain, and the tiled and painted façades and loggias of the buildings have a distinctly Spanish feel. The inhabitants speak Catalan, dance the *sardana*, and hold bullfights – so Picasso must have felt on familiar territory. The musical instruments of the *cobla*, the band that accompanies the *sardana*, became a frequent subject for Picasso.

Céret has been called the Vatican of Cubism and it was here in 1911 that Picasso and Braque worked furiously, exploring the possibilities of what would come to be called Cubism, trying to break reality down into its essential forms. Their efforts resulted in works like *Landscape at Céret* (Picasso, 1911) and Braque's *Rooftops, Céret* (1911). "A man like Picasso studies an object as a surgeon dissects a cadaver," Apollinaire wrote about this period.

In 1908, furious that Braque had deserted the Fauvist camp to be with Picasso, Matisse drew some small box-like shapes on a piece of paper to illustrate Braque's new work to Louis Fauxcelles – who immediately coined the term "Cubism".

Matisse was in Collioure at the same time but he and Picasso appear to have studiously avoided each other. According to Apollinaire, Matisse once saw an advertisement for a bouillon cube on a wall outside his house in Collioure and thought the Cubists were playing a joke on him.

Picasso and Braque would sometimes spend evenings together in Céret's Grand Café, and several of Picasso's drawings from Céret were done on the café notepaper. The Grand Café is still there, on the corner by the new museum: the marble-topped tables and the bottles of *eau de vie* and *marc* are recognisable from the drawings and collages of Picasso, Braque and Juan Gris. ❑

LEFT: Matisse's *Landscape at Collioure*.
CENTRE: *Femme à la Guitare* by Picasso.
BELOW: *Landscape at Céret* by Juan Gris.

HÉRAULT AND GARD

Two of France's most interesting cities, Montpellier and Nîmes, stand close to the beach resorts, nature reserves and historic ports that line the Mediterranean shore of the Lower Languedoc

The two *départements* of Hérault and the Gard cover what is geographically known as the Bas Languedoc, an area of vine-clad plains, scattered with a few hills, running beside the Mediterranean as far east as the Rhône, and inland nudging up to the Grands Causses.

Until the 1960s most of the coast here was mosquito-infested swamp, interspersed with tiny fishing villages. Massive government investment has since vanquished the mosquitoes and transformed wastelands into miles of golden beaches and purpose-built resorts perfect for the dedicated sea-and-sand holiday. There's lots of sunshine in this downmarket version of the South of France but also the threat of the dreaded Tramontane wind, which can drive even the most dedicated from the beaches.

Because development was so late, the tourism planners avoided the overbuilt excesses of the Spanish *costas* and the Riviera. Ecological considerations have been quite strictly observed, so that long stretches remain without buildings, there are lots of wildlife and nature reserves and the water has the reputation of being among the cleanest in the Mediterranean.

The food is good, too. The lagoons strung along the coast produce vast quantities of seafood, which is shipped all over France; but here you can eat it fresh from the sea, in unpretentious restaurants in small fishing villages or ports such as Sète or Agde. There are always *moules* (mussels), even on the children's menu, and you can also try a wide variety of different produce according to the day's catch: clams, sea snails, oysters, even sea urchins or sea crickets.

Wine is abundant since Languedoc-Roussillon is France's biggest wine-producing region – the Hérault is the biggest mass-producing wine region in the world – and its wines are increasingly respected for their quality. The local *vin de table, rosé* or red, is always acceptable, and very cheap. Inland is planted with huge areas of vines and even on the coast you can spot tiny pockets of vines tucked into any corner with suitable climate and soil conditions.

The region is a highly desirable place to live for foreigners and the French themselves. Since the 1960s the Montpellier conurbation, in particular, has become a hi-tech boom area, with IBM and many other technology companies moving in. The combination of employment and the sunny southern location with good beaches and accessible mountains close at hand is irresistible.

The biggest cities are Nîmes and Montpellier, the latter being the regional capital. Both have regular flights from London and Paris and are well worth visiting – either would make a suitable base for excursions into the hinterlands.

PRECEDING PAGES: jousting in boats, Sète. **LEFT:** view over Aigues Mortes. **BELOW:** participants in the *feria*, Nîmes.

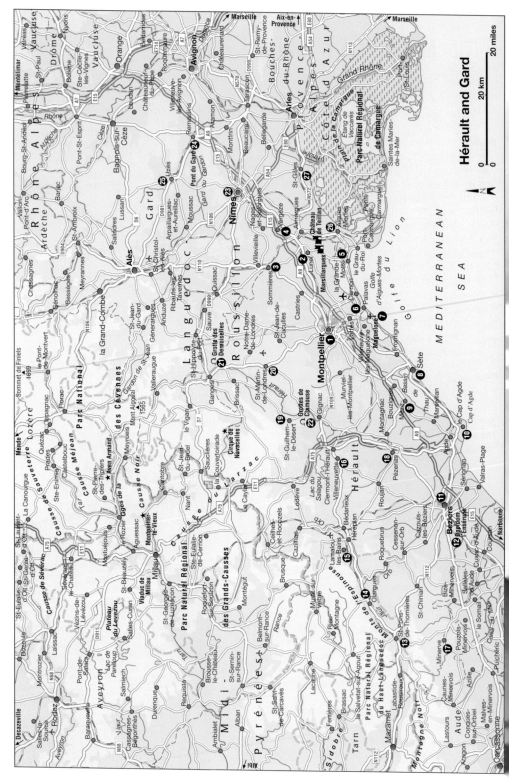

Hérault and Gard

Montpellier

In an area of ancient settlements and Roman colonisation, **Montpellier** is the relative newcomer, founded as recently as the 10th century. Viewed from the sea you can see its origins, with a lagoon of flamingoes in the foreground, the modern towers of the city beyond, and the hills of the Cévennes in the background. It developed from a simple farm on a low hill between lagoon and mountains, a meeting point for several transit routes, notably the pilgrim route to Santiago de Compostela, starting from Arles, and the critically important salt route, carrying precious salt from the lagoons.

It was connected to a small sea port by the River Lez, and by the 11th and 12th centuries was trading with the East, exporting wine, dyed cloth, leather, wool and jewellery. The **Église de Notre-Dame des Tables** became a famous sanctuary, so-called for the tables of the money changers spread out around it, exchanging currencies from France, Italy and Arab countries. The crypt is now a modern museum offering a multimedia version of the history of the city (place Jean-Jaurès; open Tues–Sat). Pilgrims, scholars, merchants and adventurers exchanged knowledge as well as goods. It became a cosmopolitan, tolerant city, a centre of art and learning, well known for its medical research, drawing on the knowledge of Jewish and Arab healers and philosophers. Montpellier still has the oldest medical school in the world, dating from 1220, adjacent to the cathedral.

The student city

Montpellier still has one of France's most venerable universities, and is very much a student city, with a quarter of its population under 25 years old. City life revolves around **Place de la Comédie** , popularly known as l'Oeuf after its original egg shape, where lively cafés, a 19th-century opera house and a bubbling fountain, the Fontaine des Trois Graces, combine with modern architectural shopping developments in a way typical of the city's style.

Around it are the intimate shaded squares and winding streets of the old town. They are car-free and never seem really crowded; it feels more like an overgrown village than a regional capital, with jazz music floating out of the upper storeys, and dogs, bicycles and pushchairs everywhere. Sadly the youthful population has embraced graffiti as a major form of expression, so many of the fine old doors are defaced.

Little remains of the medieval city since the devastation wreaked by the 16th-century Wars of Religion. All the churches were wrecked, apart from the cathedral, which still needed substantial rebuilding. It remains impressive, however, built like a fortress with two enormous towers flanking the porch. The town has grown around its ruined churches and the fragments can often be detected in the walls of the houses: here a row of carved arches, there the remains of an apse. Major 17th-century rebuilding resulted in many fine mansions built around courtyards with open stone staircases embellished by columns and carved balconies. If the doors are open wander in and take a peek, but the way to really see them properly is with

Maps:
Area 306
City 308

INFO

Tourist information office, Montpellier: 30 Allée Jean de Lattre de Tassigny; tel: 04 67 60 60 60; www.ot-montpellier.fr

BELOW: Promenade du Peyrou, Montpellier.

Flags of the French republic, a common sight in France.

the tourist office guided tour. A good example is the **Hôtel des Trésoriers de France**, originally the house of Jacques Coeur, Charles VII's famous treasurer. This now houses the **Musée Languedocien** 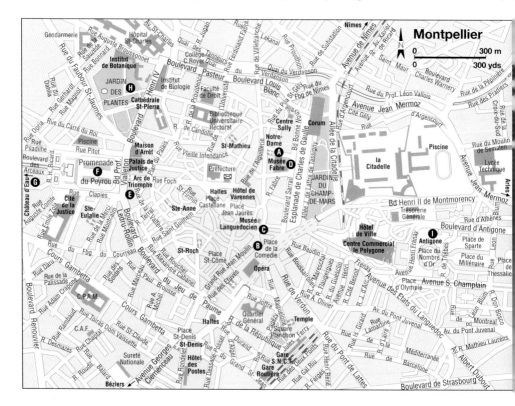 (7 rue Jacques Coeur; open Mon–Sat afternoons only; entrance fee; tel: 04 67 52 93 03) and its collection of Romanesque art and prehistoric artefacts.

One of Montpellier's finest buildings is the **Musée Fabre** ①. It is currently undergoing major renovation and is closed until 2006. Temporary exhibitions are held in the Pavillon Fabre (Esplanade; tel: 04 67 66 13 46).

To appreciate Montpellier's location between sea and mountains, head for the smart area around the cathedral and medical school, and stroll through the monumental **Arc de Triomphe** ② to the **Promenade du Peyrou** ③, a formal 18th-century square dominated by the **Château d'Eau** ④ and the **aqueduct** which used to bring water down to the city from the Cévennes. To the north is the **Jardin des Plantes** ⑤, one of the oldest botanical gardens in France, crammed with rare and wonderful plants – a tranquil retreat on a hot day. Montpellier is particularly proud of its modern architecture. The most highly praised example is the **Antigone housing estate** ⑥, designed by Catalan architect, Ricardo Bofill. While reflecting the 18th-century classicism of the city in monumental buildings with grand vistas, fountains and columns, it still works as sympathetic living accommodation, beautified with traditional promenades and shady arcades. Further new developments, pursued by Montpellier's long-entrenched Socialist mayor, Georges Frèche, include a magnificent modern swimming-pool complex and a modern tramway system.

A good way to get an insider look at the outskirts of Montpellier is to visit the *follies*, charming châteaux built by wealthy bourgeoisie as summer residences, surrounded by fine parks and vineyards. Several, including **Château de Flaugergues**, **Château de la Mogère**, **Château d'O** and **Château de Laverune** are open to visitors, and stage festivals, exhibitions and wine tastings.

East towards Nîmes is the town of **Lunel** ❷, once a famous educational centre, settled by the Jews in the 11th century, though today more famous for raising bulls and producing a very pleasant Muscat wine. Nearby **Sommières** ❸ is much prettier, with shady riverside walks, an ancient Roman bridge and a 12th-century market square. Due to frequent river flooding many of the houses are built on stone arcades so the water can run beneath. East of Montpellier is **Vergèze** ❹, the source of the famous Perrier water, which was discovered by the English. You can tour the factory and taste the natural fizz *in situ*.

The coast

Back on the coast the Languedoc-Roussillon tourism initiative really begins with the Modernist ziggurats (pyramidal towers) at **La Grande Motte** ❺, one of a number of hugely popular beach cities established in the 1960s. You either love 'em or hate 'em, but they accommodate vast numbers of sunseekers with remarkable ease. Purpose-built accommodation provides marinas, housing and every possible kind of sports facility from tennis and golf to water-sports, all flanked by golden beaches, ecologically planted sand dunes and pine-shaded walks perfumed by an aromatic melange of honeysuckle, orange blossom, lavender and tamarisk.

East of La Grande Motte are the resorts of **La Grau-du-Roi**, once a tiny fishing village, and **Port-Camargue**, its marina being the largest in Europe. Heading west you come to **Palavas** ❻ and **Carnon**, both the traditional resorts

Maps:
Area 306
City 308

The English novelist and poet, Lawrence Durrell, author of The Alexandria Quartet *and* The Avignon Quincunx, *lived in Sommières (in a villa he called "the Vampire house") until his death there in November 1990.*

BELOW: arcades in Sommières.

The singer Georges Brassens, who was born in Sète.

BELOW:
eating fish in Sète.

for Montpellier, with unpretentious low-rise villas and good beaches. On a peninsula between lagoon and sea are the remains of the monastery of **Maguelone** ❼ (access from Palavas; open daily), known for its care of the sick in the 12th and 13th centuries and now worth visiting for its calm atmosphere, the fine carvings around the doorway of the church and the view from the bell tower.

Sète and the Bassin de Thau

Further down the coast is the port of Sète, between the Bassin de Thau and the sea. **Sète** ❽ is one of the Mediterranean's biggest industrial and fishing ports, but at its heart is an old town built over a network of canals and bridges with shops selling ships' lamps and propellers. It is an ideal place for landlubbers fond of seafood and most of its restaurants can be found along the Grand Canal, with its funky Italianate houses painted in dusty shades of rose pink, pistachio and Camargue blue. Quayside restaurants serve huge platters of *fruits des mers* – mussels, oysters, sea snails – all delivered straight off the boat.

From Sète, cruise boats take passengers round the **Bassin de Thau** and its oyster beds, and promise fishing trips and al-fresco *sardines grillades* – "Attention, no tables, no chairs, no forks," proclaims the billboard.

Sète has the **Centre Régional d'Art Contemporain** (CRAC; 29 quai Aspirant Herber; open Wed–Mon afternoons only; tel: 04 67 74 94 37). Above the town is the **Cimetière Marin**, on Mont St-Clair, where Sète's most famous son, poet Paul Valéry, is buried. Nearby is a small museum, the **Museé Paul Valéry** (rue François Resnoyes; open Wed–Mon; entrance fee; tel: 04 67 46 20 98). Also up here is the open-air **Théâtre de la Mer**, or Théatre Jean-Vilar, in a citadel built by Vauban. From Mont St-Clair there are views over the oyster beds of the

Bassin de Thau, and to the south, a long stretch of undeveloped, sandy beach. Boisterous water-jousting tournaments, a medieval throwback, are a popular spectator sport in Sète and along the coast.

On the northern shore of the lagoon are the fishing villages of **Mèze** ❾ and **Bouzigues**, with their little harbours full of yachts and fishing boats, and their excellent seafood restaurants. Bouzigues has a museum dedicated to shellfish breeding, the **Musée de l'Étang de Thau** (open daily; entrance fee; tel: 04 67 78 33 57).

Just north of Mèze is the site of the biggest cache of dinosaur eggs discovered in Europe, in 1996, now the wonderful open-air dinosaur park, **La Plaine des Dinosaures** (RN113; open daily; entrance fee; tel: 04 67 43 02 80). Parents can stroll along walks shaded by pine trees while their children discover life-size models and skeletons peering out of the trees. There are also display cases of eggs and fossils, giant footprints, and an archaeological dig to watch. For hands-on experience, there is a sandpit with a dinosaur skeleton to dig up.

Either side of the lagoon will bring you to **Le Cap d'Agde** ❿, another vast modern seaside city. Built in vernacular style and pleasing colours of ochre and terracotta, with plenty of palm trees, it doesn't offend. It incorporates the port and, further inland, the old town itself, with its famous black basalt cathedral. Agde also has the largest nudist colony in Europe, complete with *naturiste* shopping mall and nightclubs. There are two museums of interest. The **Musée Agathois** (5 rue de la Franternité; open daily; closed Tues in winter; entrance fee; tel: 04 67 94 82 51) in the old town, is devoted to the history of Agde from its Greek foundation to the present day. The **Musée de l'Éphèbe** (open daily; entrance fee; tel: 04 67 94 69 60), in Le Cap d'Agde, presents an intriguing survey of underwater archaeology, including amphorae and boats discovered on the seabed and the famous statue of *Éphèbe,* a Greek bronze of a boy which was discovered in 1964 in the River Hérault.

Inland Hérault

Inland is wine country, with serried ranks of vines as far as the eye can see. **Béziers** ⓫ derives its livelihood from wine but is best known for its passion for rugby and bullfights, and historically for the appalling massacre of thousands of Cathars and citizens in 1209. "Kill them all. God will recognise his own!" ordered the presiding bishop. On the left bank of the River Orb, the steep streets rise to the vast 14th-century **Cathédrale St-Nazaire**, with its fine sculpture, stained glass and frescoes. Climb the tower for a good view. Neighbouring streets house the **Musée des Beaux Arts**, also known as **Musée Fabregat** (Hôtel Fabregat, place de la Révolution; closed Sun afternoon and Mon; entrance fee; tel: 04 67 28 38 78), with its mainly French and Italian collection, and the **Musée du Bitterrois** (open Tues–Sun; entrance fee; tel: 04 67 36 71 01), which has exhibitions on local history, wine and the Canal du Midi *(see page 83)* engineered in the 17th century by Pierre-Paul Riquet, Béziers' famous son. His statue stands in allée Pierre-Paul Riquet where rows of plane trees shade the restaurants and swallows fly down the middle.

Map on page 306

Mending nets in Sète.

BELOW: the Cathedral, Béziers.

Plaque beside the Canal du Midi, remembering Riquet.

BELOW: detail of a canal boat.
RIGHT: Fonserannes locks on the Canal du Midi, Béziers.

Outside Béziers is the pre-Roman site of **Oppidum l'Ensérune** , overlooking the Béziers plain. The original Roman settlement is poignantly revealed in the foundations of houses, terracotta storage jars, stone sarcophagi and Roman columns. The **Musée de l'Oppidum d'Ensérune** (open Tues–Sun; entrance fee; tel: 04 67 37 01 23) displays archaeological fragments, vases, jewellery and weapons of Celtic, Greek and Roman origin. From the hill you can see an extraordinary medieval crop formation, the **Étang de Montady**, a clever agricultural drainage system resembling the spokes of a wheel.

To the north is the **Parc Naturel Régional du Haut-Languedoc**, a different world of high limestone *causses*, rugged plateaux and wooded slopes where you will find remote sheep farms, bizarre rock formations and deep river gorges. The park covers over 1,300 sq km (500 sq miles) of forest and mountains, with plenty of good places for walking, cycling or horse riding, and where it is possible to glimpse the mouflons, eagles and wild boar which once were common in the Southwest. The offices of the park are in **St-Pons-de-Thomières** and this is one of the best places to enter it.

Following the D908 through the park you pass the little village of **Olargues**, with its 12th-century bridge over the River Jaur, then **Lamalou-les-Bains**, a small spa town with a restored Belle Époque spa building and theatre, palm trees and neat pink villas. **Villeneuvette** is an early new town, established by Louis XIV for workers in the silk trade, with purpose-built factories and workers' housing. Despite the sombre tone of the notice above the town gate, "Honneur au Travail" – Honour through work – it is today cheerfully revitalised, the abandoned houses reclaimed by a more fortunate generation of painters and artisans.

The Minervois

To the west are the parched, arid hills covered by vines – and little else – that constitute the Minervois. This region produces increasingly respected wine, and is a favourite retreat for wine writers. **Minerve** ⓱ itself is well worth a visit, perched on its rocky outcrop at the confluence of two rivers, defended by the Candela, the octagonal tower which is all that remains of the original château. The little village looks as defiant as it did in 1210 when it resisted the vengeful Simon de Montfort in a siege that culminated in the immolation of 140 Cathars who refused to renounce their faith. Today the village is easily breached by a bridge spanning the gorge; turn right into the town and follow the route of the Cathars past the Romanesque arch of the **Porte des Templiers**, to the 12th-century **Église St-Étienne**, within which is a 5th-century marble altar table. There is a lovely modern sculpture of a dove next to the church, the symbol of the holy spirit which was preferred by the Cathars to the traditional corporeal cross. A rocky path follows the river-bed below the town, where the water has cut natural caves and underground bridges from the soft limestone. Here the Cathars' funeral pyre was built.

Pézenas ⓲ is a well-preserved Renaissance town, a centre of government and culture in the 16th and 17th centuries. It is full of elegant townhouses with discreet inner courtyards, antique shops and second-hand book stores. At the tourist office in place Gambetta pick up a guide to follow a walking tour of the town which takes you to the best examples of architecture, such as the **Hôtel des Barons de Lacoste**, at 8 rue François Oustrin, with its carved stone staircase, and the **Maison des Pauvres**, at 12 rue Alfred Sabatier, a house with three galleries. Just inside the 14th-century Faugères gate are the streets of the **Jewish**

Map on page 306

The most powerful medieval siege engine was the trebuchet, used to great effect at Minerve. A hefty, counterpoised see-saw, the trebuchet was capable of hurling a boulder over 180 metres (200 yards) against the walls of a fortress.

BELOW: Hôtel de Lacoste in Pézenas.

The 17th-century playwright Molière in costume.

BELOW:
villager of St-Guilhem-le-Désert.

ghetto, which still have a sinister feeling of enclosure about them. Try the *pâtés de Pézenas*, little cakes which are the nearest the French get to mince pies *(see page 100)*. The actor and playwright Molière visited Pezenas and performed here several times between 1650 and 1656 during an itinerant phase of his life

All around Pézenas the vines are industriously cultivated, but in the distance rise the blue hills of the Cévennes, the beginnings of the Massif Central, which are now breached by the A75 *autoroute*. Hidden away in a gorge above the River Herault is the Romanesque monastery of **St-Guilhem-le-Désert** ⑲ (open daily; entrance fee; tel: 04 67 57 44 33), founded by Guillaume of Aquitaine (St William of Gellone) who retired here as a hermit in the 9th century after a lifetime of crusades. His piety, and a relic of the true cross awarded to him by Charlemagne, ensured a following and a monastery was established. Although the abbey itself has been badly restored and only sections of the original cloister remain (the rest is in the New York Cloisters Museum, *see page 72*) it is still a handsome sight. The museum contains St William's tomb, an early 7th-century sarcophagus, and other relics. The lovely curves of the apsidal chapels overlook a village honeycombed by streams tumbling through gardens and under bridges; here and there modest Romanesque palaces are lovingly preserved.

Continuing inland you come to **St-Martin-de-Londres** ⑳, with a superb medieval square, an 11th-century church and several good restaurants. Beyond is limestone country, riddled with caves. The most spectacular of them is the **Grotte des Demoiselles** ㉑ (open daily; entrance fee; tel: 04 67 73 70 02). A funicular train transports you to the weird calcified world of the **Cathédrale des Abysses**, with its extraordinary stalagmites and stalactites.

The **Grottes de Clamouse** ㉒ (near Gignac; open daily; entrance fee; tel: 04 67 57 71 05) is another extraordinary, if chilly, experience. There are stalactites shaped like dripping candles and stalagmites like soaring Gothic columns, and the waters of underground rivers and pools reflected on the cavern roofs.

Nîmes

Nîmes ㉓ competes with Arles for the title of the "Rome of France", and with Montpellier for the city with the most modern architecture in the Mediterranean sunbelt. It has a more workaday atmosphere than either of its competitors, however, taking its magnificent monuments for granted and living a casual, southern lifestyle in the big street cafés and shady medieval squares. The biggest events of the year are the *ferias,* bacchanalian bullfight festivals which attract thousands of visitors but remain essentially a Nîmois street party. The bullfights take place in the superb Roman amphitheatre, **Les Arènes** Ⓐ (boulevard des Arènes; open daily; entrance fee; tel: 04 66 76 72 77) which reverberates with the roar of the crowd as the bull meets its fate to the sound of a bugle call. The arena is an amazing piece of engineering, providing excellent vision for huge crowds, and is used for music and opera performances as well as bullfights. The best view is from the top tier of seats (traditionally reserved for slaves and women). Though smaller than the arena at Arles, it is better preserved, with two storeys of 60 stone arcades to a height of 21 metres (69 ft), surrounding the corridors and *vomitoria* (exits), and the greal oval arena. After the Romans left, the amphitheatre was built up into a fortress and by the Middle Ages was crammed with slum housing. Centuries of rubbish had added 6 metres (20 ft) to the original ground level by the time it was finally cleared in the early 19th century. The new **Musée des Cultures Taurines** (6 rue Alexandre Ducros; open Tues–Sun; tel: 04 66 36 83 77) will tell you all you need to know about bullfighting.

Other Roman sites include the recently discovered **Castellum ❸** on rue de Lampéze, a water tower which was the original distribution point for the water from the Pont du Gard. **Porte Augustus ❻**, on boulevard Gambetta, was one of the original Roman gates of the city with two large arches providing a dual carriageway for carts and chariots and two smaller arches for pedestrian traffic.

Most magnificent of all Nîmes' monuments is the 2,000-year-old **Maison Carrée ❹** (open daily; free admission; tel: 04 66 36 26 76), one of the best-preserved Roman temples in existence. A great flight of stone steps leads to finely fluted Corinthian columns adorned with a sculpted frieze of acanthus leaves. It has remained in almost constant use as legislative seat, tomb, church, stables and, briefly, an exhibition space for American artist, Julian Schnabel. Today it displays drawings and photos of current archaeological work, one splendid result of which is a fresco discovered in 1992. Sadly, the temple suffers from constant traffic pollution and, worst of all, the huge Roman terracotta jar that stood outside was recently smashed to smithereens by vandals.

Adjacent is the **Carrée d'Art ❺** (place de la Maison Carrée; open Tues–Sun; entrance fee; tel: 04 66 76 35 80), a vast glass and steel art gallery designed by Norman Foster as a tribute to the ancient temple. The collection focuses on

Maps:
Area 306
City 316

Tourist information
office, Nîmes:
6 rue Auguste;
tel: 04 66 58 38 00;
www.ot-nimes.fr

BELOW: Maison Carrée in Nîmes.

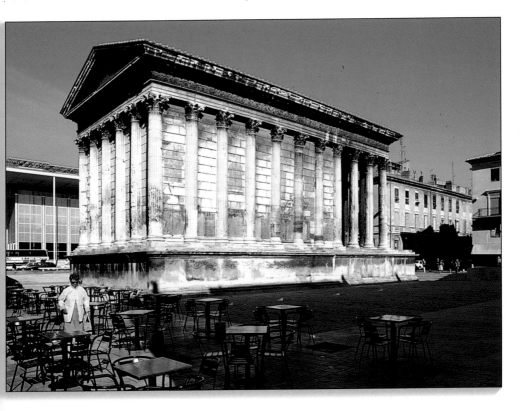

A tough local cotton of white warp and blue weft had been made in Nîmes for centuries before it achieved lasting fame as the material (de Nîmes) used by Levi-Strauss to make jeans (denim) for the gold diggers of California.

European modern art since 1960, with particular emphasis on avant-garde movements such as Arte Povera and New Realism, and work by Mediterranean painters. Artists include Martial Raysse, Christian Boltanski and Claude Viallet.

This mix of ancient history and modern development is typical of Nîmes. There are commissioned art works all over the city: a Philippe Starck bus stop; a fountain designed by Martial Raysse – a modern version of a crocodile tied to a palm tree – in **Place du Marché**, where the corn market used to be held.

The old town is a pleasing warren of narrow streets, shady squares and fountains. There are many 16th- and 17th-century houses, a legacy of the prosperous days of textile manufacturing, when the Protestant population processed the wool and silk of the region.

Museums and views

Nîmes has several good museums. The **Musée du Vieux Nîmes** ❻ (place aux Herbes; open Tues–Sun; entrance fee; tel: 04 66 36 00 64) in the old town, pre-

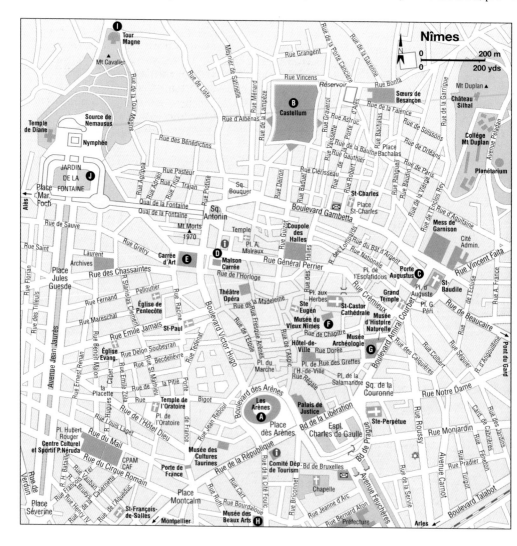

serves the tools of local industries and artefacts of regional life, giving an intriguing glimpse into humdrum history. There is furniture, pottery, shoes and fabrics (including some early "denim", shawls and silks), and lots of tools, including hammers for every conceivable occupation.

The **Musée Archéologique** (13 bis boulevard Amiral Courbet; open Tues–Sun; entrance fee; tel: 04 66 76 74 80), housed in the old Jesuit college building, has a fine collection of Roman statues, sarcophagi, entablature, coins, mosaics and Roman glass, and a rare pre-Roman statue, the *Warrior of Grézan*. The **Musée d'Histoire Naturelle** (open Tues–Sun; entrance fee; tel: 04 66 76 74 80), in the same building as the Archaeological Museum, has some important Iron Age menhir statues.

The **Musée des Beaux Arts** (rue Cité-Foulc; open Tues–Sun; entrance fee; tel: 04 66 67 38 21) has been elegantly restored by architect Jean-Michel Wilmotte. The collection includes French, Italian, Flemish and Dutch works, most notably Jacopo Bassano's *Susanna and the Elders*, Rubens' *Portrait of a Monk*, and the *Mystic Matrimony of St Catherine* by Michele Giambono. The *Marriage of Admetus*, a mosaic only discovered in 1882, takes pride of place in the centre of the main floor.

For the best overview of Nîmes climb up to the **Tour Magne**, once part of the Roman city walls. From here you can see the red roofs of the city and the surrounding *garrigue* (limestone plateau) landscape. The tower is reached from the **Jardin de la Fontaine**, the beautiful formal gardens constructed in the 18th century around the spring that was used to improve the quality of the city's water supply after the Pont du Gard aqueduct was abandoned. Among shady chestnut trees you will find the ruined "Temple of Diana", a mysterious Roman

The pre-Roman settlement of Nîmes was colonised in 31 BC by a legion of Roman veterans from the Egyptian campaign. Their emblem, a crocodile chained to a palm tree, became the symbol of the city. The local football team is known as "Les Crocos".

BELOW: leaping bullfighter in the Course Landaise.

FRENCH BULLFIGHTING

Bullfighting is still enormously popular in southern France, both in the flesh and on TV. The *corrida* is considered an art form; the nobility of the bulls and performance of the *toreadors* passionately debated. If you can stomach it, watching a bullfight in the ancient Roman arena of Nîmes is a dramatic experience.

In the Spanish-style *corrida* the bull is killed: the *matador* in his elegant costume plays out a stylised performance with his cloak and finally pierces the bull with his sword.

The Course Camarguaise is more sport than ritual; the bulls are not killed but spend only 15 minutes in the arena, to be chased by the *raseteurs*, who gesture and run to attract the bull and then try to snatch the *cocarde* and *ficelles* (rosette and tassels) attached to its head, using a *crochet*, or metal comb. The bull chases the *raseteur* who leaps the barrier to escape, often just in time.

The Course Landaisee, in Gascony, is also bloodless. It involves fast and frisky cows, not bulls, loosely tethered by a long cord. Its stars are *écarteurs*, agile young men in embroidered bolero jackets who face the charging cow and twist away with split-second timing from its capped horns; and *sauteurs*, wearing a sash and tie, who dive, leap or somersault over the charging animal.

fragment, and a network of deep green pools and stone terraces which provides a cool retreat on a hot day.

The eastern Gard

The **Pont du Gard** ㉔ is one of the southwest's unmissable sights, a massive Roman aqueduct still proudly spanning the Gardon River after 2,000 years. At 48 metres (157 ft) it was the highest bridge the Romans ever built, and originally carried water from the springs at Uzès to Nîmes, along a channel 50 km (30 miles) long, often through underground channels dug out of solid rock. Three great storeys of golden limestone arches have resisted the erosion of time and the tampering of previous generations. In the floods that devastated Nîmes and the surrounding region in 1988 and 2002, the Pont du Gard stood firm when several other bridges collapsed. It is most stunning seen early in the morning or at dusk, best viewed from the 18th-century road bridge which runs alongside. Sadly it is no longer possible to walk across the top tier of the aqueduct.

Recent renovation work on the Pont du Gard has created a visitors centre, **Le Portal** (open June–Aug daily; entrance fee; tel: 04 66 37 50 99), an auditorium in the former quarry, a pedestrian promenade and restaurants.

Nîmes is surrounded by vineyards producing **Costières de Nîmes**. To the north are the *garrigues*, wild rough scrubland of exposed limestone outcrops covered with aromatic herbs and silvery olive trees. These are the foothills of the Cévennes, threaded by deep river gorges and scattered with the fragments of the bridges and the water channels of the aqueduct.

Uzès ㉕ is a sweet little town, beautifully restored, with more estate agents and architects per inhabitant than anywhere else in France. At its centre is a medieval

"As I humbled myself, suddenly something lifted up my spirits, and I cried out: 'Why am I not a Roman!'"

– JEAN-JACQUES ROUSSEAU ON THE PONT DU GARD

BELOW: the scientist Louis Pasteur.

PASTEUR AND THE SILKWORMS

In the mid-19th century silk production in southern France, particularly the Cévennes *(see page 174)*, was blighted by a disease called pebrine. The great chemist, microbiologist and medical scientist Louis Pasteur (1822–95) was called in to investigate in 1865 and he based himself in Alès.

The four years that Pasteur spent in Alès resulted in triumph for the scientific methods he pioneered but they were also marred by personal tragedy. No sooner had Pasteur arrived in Alès than he received news of his father's death. In the next 12 months two of his daughters also died.

Nevertheless, Pasteur applied himself to the task in hand, first collecting as much information as he was able about the nature of the disease and about remedies already tried. By January 1867 he was able to identify a microscopic organism, *nosema*, as the agent responsible for the epidemic. He proposed that farmers examine their silkworm eggs under a microscope and destroy those infected with the spores of the parasite.

Despite suffering a stroke which left him partially paralysed, Pasteur remained in Alès overseeing the work until he was sure that the disease had been eradicated.

arcaded square of soft ochre stone, the **Place aux Herbes**, with shady vaulted cafés and an excellent market for buying baskets, Provençal fabric and pots. The **Tour Fenestrelle** is Uzès' most distinctive sight, a 12th-century arcaded bell tower reminiscent of Pisa, which is all that remains from the Romanesque cathedral smashed during the 16th-century Wars of Religion, when Uzès was a centre of Protestantism. Many mansions remain, along with a splendid, privately owned palace, **Le Duché d'Uzès** (guided tours daily; entrance fee; tel: 04 66 22 18 96), which combines a 12th-century central tower, a Burgundian tiled chapel, and an ornate Renaissance façade. You can see the dungeons and hologram ghost and the view from the battlements. The 17th-century **Cathédrale St-Theodorit** has a superb 18th-century organ with painted shutters, and is the main location of the Uzès music festival in July.

South of Nîmes, on the salt flats and sun-bleached blue lagoons of the **Petite Camargue**, stands the perfectly preserved walled town of **Aigues-Mortes** ㉖ (tourist office, tel: 04 66 53 73 00), the "place of dead waters" (referring to the surrounding saline marshes). Once an important port but now marooned 5 km (3 miles) from the sea, it was built by Louis XI in the 13th century as the embarkation point for the Seventh Crusade. Its strict grid pattern can be appreciated by visiting the museum, which includes access to part of the walls and a visit to the **Tour de Constance**.

Across the salt lagoons to the northeast is **St-Gilles** ㉗, also once an important medieval port, but abandoned by the sea even earlier than Aigues-Mortes. Today it is worth visiting for the 12th-century façade of its abbey church, originally established by the monks of Cluny Abbey as a shrine to St Gilles and a resting place on the pilgrimage route to Santiago de Compostela. ❑

Map on page 306

On 13 January 1208, the Papal legate, Peter of Castelnau, left St-Gilles Abbey and headed northeast. The next morning he was murdered by an unknown horseman on the banks of the Rhône. This incident sparked the Albigensian Crusade (see page 27).

BELOW: the Pont du Gard. **OVERLEAF:** shepherd in the Pyrenees.

Insight Guides

Travel Tips

✵ INSIGHT GUIDES Phonecard

One global card to keep travellers in touch.
Easy. Convenient. Saves you time and money.

It's a global phonecard

Save up to 70%* on international calls from over 55 countries

Free 24 hour global customer service

Recharge your card at any time via customer service or online

It's a message service

Family and friends can send you voice messages for free.

Listen to these messages using the phone* or online

Free email service - you can even listen to your email over the phone*

It's a travel assistance service

24 hour emergency travel assistance – if and when you need it.

Store important travel documents online in your own secure vault

For more information, call rates, and all Access Numbers in over 55 countries, (check your destination is covered) go to **www.insightguides.ekit.com** or call Customer Service.

JOIN now and receive US$ 5 bonus when you join for US$ 20 or more.

Join today at

www.insightguides.ekit.com

When requested use ref code: **INSAD0103**

OR SIMPLY FREE CALL
24 HOUR CUSTOMER SERVICE

UK	0800 376 1705
USA	1800 706 1333
Canada	1800 808 5773
Australia	1800 11 44 78
South Africa	0800 997 285

THEN PRESS ⓪

For all other countries please go to "Access Numbers" at **www.insightguides.ekit.com**

* Retrieval rates apply for listening to messages. Savings based on using a hotel or payphone and calling to a landline. Correc at time of printing 01.03

(INS001)

powered by ✵ *ekit*

"The easiest way to make calls and receive messages around the world"

CONTENTS

Getting Acquainted

The Place

Situation: Southwest France covers the area between the Atlantic and the Mediterranean, bordered by the Pyrenees to the south and the Massif Central to the north.
Area: About 114,000 sq. km (44,000 sq. miles) – a fifth of the land area of France.
Population: 7.3 million. Aquitaine region: 2.8 million. Languedoc-Roussillon: 2. 1 million. Midi-Pyrenees: 2.4 million.
Language: French is the official language but Catalan, Basque and Occitan are also spoken, and sometimes used in signposting.
Religion: Predominantly Catholic, with a small percentage of Protestants, Muslims and Jews.
International dialling code: +33.
Time zone: France is one hour ahead of Greenwich Mean Time.

Telling the Time

The 24-hour clock is frequently used in France when giving times: 8am is *huit heures*, noon (*midi*) is *douze heures*, 8pm is *vingt heures*, and midnight (*minuit*) is *zéro heure*.

Climate

Most of the Southwest has hot and dry summers with temperatures often rising above 30°C (86°F). Winters are mild and often wet, and spring too often has heavy rainfall.

Early autumn can be the best time to visit with warm days up to late October. November can be blustery, cold and wet.

The Mediterranean coast has hot

Temperatures

Temperatures in France are always given in celsius (centigrade). Here are some fahrenheit equivalents:
0°C = 32°F; 10°C = 50°F;
15°C = 59°F; 20°C = 68°F;
25°C = 77°F; 30°C = 86°F;
35°C = 95°F.

summers and mild winters, with daytime temperatures rarely lower than 10°C (50°F) degrees. The Atlantic Coast can be as warm as the Med, but is wetter in winter. Strong winds can blow for several days, and particularly affect the Mediterranean coastal plain.

The High Pyrenees have snow between November and March, which can make access difficult, but skiing does not usually begin in earnest before January.

The area has seen dramatic storms in recent years, causing major floods and damage.
Weather information: (in English) Tel: 08 36 70 12 34. For local forecasts dial 08 36 68 02 followed by the *département* number. On Minitel, go to 3615 METEO. On the web go to: www.meteo.fr.

Government

This book covers the regions of Aquitaine (capital Bordeaux), Midi-Pyrenees (capital Toulouse) and Languedoc-Roussillon (capital Montpellier).

Each region is divided into several *départements*, each of which is further divided into disparately sized *communes* with a district council controlling a town, village or group of villages under the direction of the local mayor.

Until recently, France was ruled largely by central government, but the Paris-appointed *préfets* lost much of their power in the 1980s when the individual *départements* gained their own directly elected assemblies, giving them far more financial and administrative autonomy. The role of the *préfet* is now more advisory than executive and the *préfecture* is based in the

principal town of each *département*.

Communes are responsible for most local planning and environmental matters; tourism and culture are mostly dealt with at regional level, while the state controls education, the health service and security.

French *départements* are identified by an individual number, which is used as a convenient reference for administrative purposes, for example it forms the first two digits of the postcode in any address and the last two figures on vehicle licence plates.

The Economy

The area is largely agricultural, raising cattle, ducks and geese, and producing cereals, fruit and vegetables. Wine production is increasingly important, and the wine itself improving in quality. Tourism, especially in the Atlantic and Mediterranean coastal regions, plays a major part in the economy. Around Toulouse, Bordeaux and Montpellier there is considerable industrial development, with Montpellier an important centre of high-tech industry, and aerospace, centred on Toulouse.

Currency

Since 1 January 2002 the euro has replaced the French franc.

The euro (abbreviated €) is available in 500, 200, 100, 50, 20, 10 and 5 euro notes, and 2 and 1 euro, 50, 20, 10, 5, 2 and 1 cent coins. There are 100 cents to one euro. It is possible that the 1 and 2 cent coins will be eliminated.

Weights and Measures

The metric system is used in France for all weights and measures, although you may encounter old-fashioned terms such as *livre* (about 1 pound weight – 500 grammes) still used in smaller shops and markets. As a kilometre is five-eighths of a mile, a handy

Conversions

Weight:
3.5 oz = 100 g
1.1 lb = 500 g
2.2 lb = 1 kg
Length/height:
0.39 inches = 1 cm
1.094 yds = 1 m
0.62 mile = 1 km
Volume:
2.113 pints = 1 litre
0.22 Imp gallons = 1 litre
0.26 US gallons = 1 litre
2.2 Imp gallons = 10 litre
2.6 US gallons = 10 litre

reckoning while travelling is to remember that 80 kilometres = 50 miles.

Electricity

Electric current is generally 220/230 volts. It alternates at 50 cycles,
not 60 as in the United States, so North Americans will need a transformer for shavers, travel irons, hairdryers, etc. Gas and electricity are supplied by the state-owned EDF-GDF (Electricité de France-Gaz de France). Contact them about supply, bills, or in case of power failures.

Remember that in rural areas electricity sometimes flickers or cuts out altogether, and you will need a good supply of candles and torches. You also need computer back-up and ideally some form of surge control.

Fuel

Butane gas is widely used for cooking (and sometimes water and heating) in small towns and villages without mains gas supply. If you stay in rented accommodation you may need to change the bottle and buy new ones from a garage or local shop. Contact EDF-GDF (see above) if you have a gas leak.

Planning the Trip

Visas and Passports

To visit France, you need a valid passport, and all visitors to France require a visa except for citizens of EU countries.

Citizens of the USA, Canada, Australia or New Zealand do not need a visa for stays of up to three months. If in doubt check with the French consulate in your country, as the situation may change. If you intend to stay in France for more than 90 days, then you should apply for a *carte de séjour*.

Embassies and Consulates

Before going to an embassy or consulate, phone and check opening hours. You may need to make an appointment. Otherwise, the answerphone will usually give an emergency contact number. You'll find a list of embassies and consulates in the *Pages Jaunes* (Yellow Pages; pagesjaunes.fr) under the heading *Ambassades et Consulats*.

Paris Embassies and Consulates

Australia
4 rue Jean Rey, tel: 01 40 59 33 00. Metro: Bir-Hakeim. Open: 9am–6pm Mon–Fri; Visas: 9.15am–12.15pm Mon–Fri.
UK
35 rue du Fbg-St-Honoré, tel: 01 44 51 34 56. Metro: Concorde. Open: 9am–noon, 1.30–5.30pm Mon–Fri.
Consulate: 18 bis rue d'Anjou, tel: 01 44 51 33 01. Open: 2.30–5.30pm Mon–Fri.

Canada
35 avenue Montaigne, tel: 01 44 43 29 00. Metro: Franklin D Roosevelt. Open: 9am–noon, 2–5pm Mon–Fri. **Visas:** 37 avenue Montaigne, tel: 01 44 43 29 16. Open 8.30–11am Mon–Fri.
Ireland
12 avenue Foch. **Consulate** 4 rue Rude, tel: 01 44 17 67 67. Metro: Charles de Gaulle-Etoile. Open: 9.30am–noon Mon–Fri; by phone 9.30am–1pm, 2.30–5.30pm Mon–Fri.

New Zealand
7 ter rue Léonard de Vinci, tel: 01 45 00 24 11. Metro: Victor-Hugo. Open: 9am–1pm Mon–Fri.
South Africa
59 quai d'Orsay, tel: 01 53 59 23 23. Metro: Invalides. Open: 8.30am–5.15pm, by appointment Mon–Fri. **Consulate:** 8.30am–noon.
US
2 avenue Gabriel, tel: 01 43 12 22 22. Metro: Concorde. Open: 9am–6pm Mon–Fri, by appointment. **Consulate** (for visas): 2 rue St-Florentin, tel: 01 43 12 22 22. Metro: Concorde. Open: 8.45–11am Mon–Fri. **Passport service:** 9am–3pm Mon–Fri.

Consulates in the Southwest
UK
353 blvd de President Wilson, Bordeaux, tel: 05 57 22 21 10.

Customs

If you buy goods in France for which you pay tax, there are no longer any restrictions on the amounts you may take home with you. However, EU law has set "guidance levels" which are as follows:
● up to 800 cigarettes, 400 small cigars, 200 cigars or 1kg loose tobacco.
● 10 litres of spirits (over 22 percent alcohol), 90 litres of wine (under 22 percent alcohol) or 110 litres of beer.
From outside the EU:
● 200 cigarettes or 100 small cigars, 50 cigars or 250g loose tobacco
● 1 litre of spirits (over 22 percent alcohol) and 2 litres of wine and

beer (under 22 percent alcohol)
● 50g perfume

Visitors can carry up to €7,600 in currency.

Andorra is not part of the European Union, so although a wide range of goods, from cigarettes to cameras, can be purchased there at duty-free prices, you are liable to pay duty on returning to France. You can also be subject to stiff fines for not declaring purchases. Pick up a brochure from the customs post (douaniers) as you enter Andorra to ensure you know the current spending limits on all items.

Tax Refunds

Non-EU residents can claim a refund (average 13 percent) on Value Added Tax (TVA) if they spend over €175 in any one shop. At the shop ask for a detaxe form and when you leave France have it stamped by customs. Send a stamped copy back to the shop, which will then refund the tax you paid, either by bank transfer or by crediting your credit card. Detaxe does not cover food, drink, antiques or works of art.

Health and Insurance

Southwest France has no out-of-the-ordinary health hazards but it is still advisable to be prepared for the unforeseen. EU nationals staying in France are entitled to use the French Social Security system, which refunds up to 70 percent of medical expenses (but sometimes less, e.g. for dental treatment).

To get a refund, British nationals should obtain form E111, available from post offices, before leaving the UK (or E112 for those already in treatment). This form is open-ended; you don't need a new one every time you travel.

If you undergo treatment while in France the doctor will give you a prescription and a feuille de soins (statement of treatment). The medication will carry vignettes (little stickers) which you must stick onto your feuille de soins. Send this, the

prescription and form E111, to the local Caisse Primaire d'Assurance Maladie (in the phone book under Sécurité Sociale). Refunds can take over a month to come through.

Nationals of non-EU countries should take out insurance before leaving home. Consultations and prescriptions have to be paid for in full, and are reimbursed, in part, on receipt of a completed fiche.

Money Matters

French banks usually open 9am–5pm Mon–Fri (some close for lunch 12.30–2.30pm); some banks also open on Saturday. All are closed on public holidays, and sometimes from noon on the previous day. All banks have foreign exchange counters. Commission rates vary between banks. Most banks accept travellers' cheques, but Eurocheques are no longer accepted, due to widespread fraud.

CREDIT CARDS AND CASH MACHINES

Major international credit cards are widely used in France. Visa is the most readily accepted, American Express less so.

French-issued credit cards have a special security microchip (puce) in each card. The card is slotted into a card reader, and the holder keys in a PIN number to authorise the transaction. Occasionally, UK/US cards with magnetic strips cannot be read by French machines. Most retailers understand the problem; if you come across one that doesn't, explain that the card is valid, and that you would be grateful if the transaction could be confirmed by phone, by saying: Les cartes internationales ne sont pas des cartes à puce, mais à bande magnétique. Ma carte est valable et je vous serais reconnaisant d'en demander la confirmation auprès de votre banque ou de votre centre de traitement.

If your cash withdrawal card carries the European Cirrus symbol, withdrawals in Euro can be made

Credit Card Loss

In case of credit card loss or theft, call the following 24-hour services which have English-speaking staff:
AmEx: 01 47 77 72 00
Diners Club: 01 49 06 17 17
MasterCard: 01 45 67 84 84
Visa: 08 36 69 08 80.

from bank and post office automatic cash machines bearing the same symbol by using your card's PIN number. The specific cards accepted are marked on each machine, and most give instructions in English.

What to Bring

France is a civilised country and you should be able to buy anything you need. There will be plenty of things to buy so leave space in your suitcase or pack another fold-up bag.

Pharmacies offer a wide range of drugs, medical supplies and toiletries, along with expert advice, but you should bring any prescription drugs you might need. A second pair of glasses or contact lenses is recommended (and a legal requirement if driving).

Sunscreen and anti-mosquito products are advisable in summer. If you bring electrical equipment you will need adaptors.

You will only need to really dress up for big city restaurants or casinos. Don't be too casual, however; be prepared to dress for dinner after a day at the beach. Dress appropriately for visiting churches; a scarf or shirt is always useful as a cover-up.

Most sports equipment can be hired but you should bring personal equipment such as walking boots.

In big cities you'll find English-language newspapers and magazines, and English bookshops. Ensure you have up-to-date local guides, phrase books and maps, though the latter are increasingly available in supermarkets. Don't forget essentials like passport, driving licence and insurance papers.

Getting There

BY AIR

There is a variety of low-cost flights to the region. However bear in mind that it is a volatile market and there are bound to be changes, so do your homework first.

Air France flies from Gatwick to Toulouse, from Birmingham to Toulouse, and from Dublin to Bordeaux. UK tel: 0845 0845 111; France tel: 08 02 80 28 02; www.airfrance.com

British Airways flies from Gatwick to Bordeaux, Montpellier and Toulouse, and from Birmingham to Bordeaux and Toulouse. UK tel: 0845 77 333 77; www.britishairways.com

GB Airways flies from Gatwick to Montpellier. Tel: 0845 773 3377; www.gbairways.com

Bmibaby flies from East Midlands to Toulouse, and Cardiff to Toulouse. 0870 264 2229; www.bmibaby.com

Bmi flies from Manchester to Toulouse. Tel: 0870 607 0555; www.flybmi.com

Easyjet flies from Gatwick to Toulouse. Tel: 0870 600 0000; www.easyjet.com

Ryanair flies from Stansted to Bergerac, Biarritz, Carcassonne, Montpellier, Nîmes, Pau, Perpignan and Rodez. Tel: 0871 246 0000; www.ryanair.com

Flybe flies from Birmingham to Toulouse, and from Southampton to Toulouse and Bergerac. Tel: 08705 676 676; www.flybe.com

Aer Lingus flies from Dublin to Toulouse. Tel: 0845 084 4444; www.aerlingus.com

Pre-trip Websites

www.yahoo.fr
(portal and search engine for finding French websites)
www.franceguide.com
(official tourist information site)
www.holidayfrance.org.uk
www.tourisme.fr
www.francetourism.com
(official tourist information site for the US)

BY FERRY

Which ferry you take depends on your starting point in the UK and how much driving you want to do in France. Since the Channel Tunnel (see "By Car", page 326) opened, ferry services have become increasingly competitive. It's worth shopping around for discounts and special offers.

The following companies operate across the English Channel to various ports. All carry cars as well as foot passengers.

Brittany Ferries offers sailings from Portsmouth to Caen, and Poole to Cherbourg (summer only), and St Malo. The Brittany Centre, Wharf Road, Portsmouth PO2 8RU; tel: 08705 360 360; www.brittany-ferries.com.

P&O sails from Portsmouth to Cherbourg, St Malo and Le Havre, and also operate the short sea route from Dover to Calais. Channel House, Channel View Road, DoverCT17 9TJ; tel: 08705 202 020; www.poferries.com.

Hoverspeed Fast Ferries operates a Superseacat service from Newhaven to Dieppe crossing in 2 hours. International Hoverport, Dover CT17 9TG; tel: 08705 240 241; www.hoverspeed.co.uk.

You could also consider travelling by ferry to Northern Spain. Brittany Ferries go to Santander from Plymouth and P&O Ferries go from Portsmouth to Bilbao; tel: 08405 20 20 20.

Transmanche sails from Newhaven to Dieppe. Tel: 0800 917 1201; www.transmancheferries.com

SeaFrance sails from Dover to Calais. Tel: 08705 711 711; www.seafrance.com

BY TRAIN

Eurostar services from London Waterloo to Paris offer a quick connection onto the French rail network, although this generally involves changing stations in Paris.

TGV trains (*trains à grande vitesse* – or high-speed trains) to Bordeaux, Toulouse and Biarritz

Ticket Validation

Any rail ticket bought in France must be validated before travel by inserting it in the orange automatic date-stamping machine at the entrance to the platform. Failure to do so may incur a surcharge.

leave from Gare Montparnasse. TGV trains to Montpellier, Nîmes and Perpignan go via Avignon, from the Gare de Lyon. For bookings and information, tel: 08705 848 848 or visit **Rail Europe's Travel Shop**, 179 Piccadilly, London W1; www.raileurope.co.uk. Rail Europe can arrange ferry bookings, discounted tickets for young people and the *Carte Vermeil* for senior citizens, which gives a generous discount on tickets, and *Eurodomino* rail passes *(see below)*. Tickets can be booked for through journeys from outside France.

SNCF (Société Nationale des Chemins de Fer de France) is the French national rail company. For reservations and information, tel: 08 36 35 35 35; www.sncf.fr. Prior reservation is essential for travel on TGVs. French railway stations will accept Visa, MasterCard and most credit cards.

Rail Passes

A variety of passes and discounts are available within France. A *Eurodomino* pass allows unlimited travel on France's rail network for 3 to 8 days' duration within one month, but must be bought before travelling to France. Discounted rates are available to children 4–11, young people 12–25 and over 60s.

Visitors from North America also have a wide choice of passes, including *Eurailpass*, *Flexipass* and *Saver Pass*, which can be purchased in the US. Tel: 212 308 3103 (for information) and 1 800 223 636 (reservations).

Bicycles

For long-distance train travel bicycles need to be transported separately, and must be registered

Rail Websites

www.eurostar.co.uk
(cross-channel trains)
www.raileurope.com
(travel agent specialising in
European rail travel)
www.sncf.fr
(French state railway company)
www.eurotunnel.com
(Le Shuttle)

and insured. They can be delivered
to your destination, though this may
take several days. On Eurostar you
need to check in your bike at least
24 hours before you travel or wait
24 hours at the other end.

Sleepers

For long-distance journeys you can
travel overnight by *couchette* (a
sleeping car shared with up to six
other people) or *voiture-lit* (a more
comfortable sleeping car for up to
three people). Both these services
are available in 1st and 2nd class,
and must be reserved in advance.

BY BUS

Long-distance buses are the
cheapest way to get to the
Southwest. **Eurolines** (tel in UK:
01582 404 511; tel in France: 08
36 69 52 52) has regular services
from London to Bordeaux, the
Basque Country and Toulouse. The
journey takes about 22 hours.

BY CAR

If driving your own car from the UK,
remember that most of France
heads south in the summer. The
school holidays last through July
and August, and the roads are at
their worst around 15 August, a
major national holiday. An ingenious
scheme exists to reduce summer
traffic by directing drivers on to
alternative scenic diversions away
from the congested main routes –
look out for the small green BIS
(Bison Futé) signs.

All *autoroutes* have *péage* toll-

booths, where payment can be
made by cash or credit card. For
information on French motorways
see www.autoroutes.fr. To plan a
route go to www.iti.fr.

Channel Tunnel

Le Shuttle carries cars and their
passengers from Folkestone to
Calais on a simple drive-on-drive-off
system (journey time 35 minutes).
Payment is made at toll booths
(which accept cash, cheques or
credit cards). Prepaid tickets and
booked spaces are available, but
no booking is necessary as you can
just turn up and take the next
available service.

Le Shuttle runs 24 hours a day,
all year round, with a service at
least once an hour through the
night. The toll-free motorway link
between Rouen and Abbéville
makes this a reasonable alternative
for motorists to the longer ferry
crossings. Information and
bookings from **Le Shuttle Customer
Services Centre**, PO Box 300,
Folkestone, Kent CT19 4QW;
tel: 0990 353 535. In France
tel: 08 01 63 03 04.

Motorail

A comfortable though pricey option
is the Motorail. You put your car on
the train in Calais or Paris and
travel overnight to Bordeaux, Brives,
Toulouse or Narbonne. *Couchettes
(see* sleepers *above)* are obligatory,
however, and the total price for car
and family can be steep, depending
on the season. For UK bookings,
contact **Rail Europe**, tel: 08702
415 415; www.frenchmotorail.com.

Hitch-hiking

People do hitch-hike *(faire de
l'autostop)* in France, but it's
safer and more reliable to arrange
lifts with a hitch-hiking agency
such as **Allô-Stop**, 8 rue
Rochambeau, Paris; tel: 01 53 20
42 42 (open 9am–6.30pm
Mon–Fri; 9am–1pm, 2–6pm Sat;
credit cards accepted). Call several
days ahead to be put in touch with
drivers. There's a flat agency fee,
which varies depending on
travelling distance.

Tour Operators

The many UK operators running
holidays to France include:
Ace Study Tours
Tel: 01223 835 055
www.study-tours.org
Cultural tours.
Allez France
Tel: 0800 731 2929
Gastronomic holidays.
Alternative Travel Group
Tel: 020 7241 2687
www.alternative-travel.co.uk
Visits to wine estates.
Arblaster and Clarke
Tel: 01730 893 344
www.winetours.co.uk
Bike and Sun Tours
Tel: 01287 639 739,
www.bikeandsuntours.co.uk
Motorcycling in the Pyrenees.
Cox and Kings
Tel: 020 7873 5006
Botanical tours of the Pyrenees.
Erna Low Consultants
Tel: 020 7584 2841
www.ernalow.co.uk
Spa holidays.
Exodus Travel
Tel: 020 8675 5550
www.exodustravels.co.uk
Trekking in the Pyrenees.
French Life
Tel: 08704 448 877
www.frenchlife.co.uk
For gîtes, cottages, hotels and
campsites.
Headwater Holidays
Tel: 01606 720 199
www.headwater-holidays.co.uk
Walking trips.
Limosa Holidays
Tel: 01263 578 143
Birdwatching.
LSG Theme Holidays
Tel: 01509 231 713
Language, painting and walking.
Prospect Music and Art Tours
Tel: 020 7486 5705
St Peter's Pilgrims
Tel: 020 8244 8844
www.stpeter.co.uk
Lourdes pilgrimages.
VFB Holidays
Tel: 01242 240 339
www.vfbholidays.co.uk
Skiing and walking.

Practical Tips

Tourist Information

Every town and city, and almost every small village will have its own *office de tourisme*, sometimes also referred to as the *maison* or *bureau de tourisme*, or the *syndicat d'initiative*. Usually on or near the main square, this can invariably be relied upon to supply the best available map of the locality as well as information about restaurants, accommodation, sights and events. Staff will pass on a variety of free leaflets about local accommodation, restaurants and places of special interest to visit. Especially in small places, these offices often close at midday, and some may not open again in the afternoon.

For more in-depth information you may need to buy a book in a local shop. If there is no tourist office in a town you can get a wide range of help and information from the local *mairie* (town hall).

Newspapers and Magazines

Most of the major British and a few North American papers can be picked up from newsagents *(maisons de la presse)* in the centre of major towns, at train stations and airports, and along most of the coast in summer. The Paris or Toulouse edition of the *International Herald Tribune* is widely available.

The French themselves read local papers. In Bordeaux they read *Sud-Ouest*, in Toulouse *Dépêche du Midi*, in the South, *Midi Libre* or *L'Indépendant*.

The ex-pat English-language paper of the Dordogne, *The News*, is a good source of information and

opinion. It is available on subscription from The News, 3 Chemin de la Monzie, 24000 Périgueux (www.frenchnews.com).

Postal Services

Post offices or PTTs are generally open 9am–noon and 2–6pm Mon–Fri, 9am–noon Sat, though main post offices in large towns don't usually close for lunch. In small villages, they generally only open in the morning.

Inside major post offices, individual counters are marked according to the services they provide; if you just need stamps, go to the window marked "Timbres".

If you need to send an urgent letter overseas, ask for it to be sent *par express*, or through the Chronopost system which is faster but much more expensive. Chronopost is also the fastest way to send letters and parcels inside France; packages up to 25g in weight are guaranteed delivery within 24 hours.

For a small fee, you can arrange for mail to be kept *poste restante* at any post office, addressed to Poste Restante, Poste Centrale (for main post offices), then the town post code and name. A passport must be presented when collecting *poste restante* mail.

Stamps are also available at tobacconists *(bureaux de tabacs)* and other shops selling postcards and greetings cards. For standard-weight letters within France and most of the EU, a €0.46 stamp is needed.

Telegrams can be sent during post-office hours or by telephone (24-hours); to send a telegram abroad, tel: 08 00 33 44 11.

Fax and photocopying facilities are often available at major post offices and *maisons de la presse* (newsagents). Many supermarkets now have coin-operated photocopiers. Minitel *(see page 328)* is being replaced by the internet and is not always available in post offices.

Tourist Information Offices at Home/Abroad

National Tourist Offices
France maintains information offices in many capital cities abroad, including:
London
178 Piccadilly, London W1V 0AL
Tel: 0891 244 123
Fax: 020 7493 6594
www.franceguide.com
New York
Maison de la France,
44 Madison Ave, NY 10020
Tel: 212 838 7800
Sydney
12 Castlereagh St, Sydney
NSW 2000
Tel: 61 2 9231 52 44

Regional Tourist Offices
Each region of France has its own tourist information office. This will put you in touch with the tourist information office of a particular town you wish to visit.
Aquitaine (for Bordeaux and the Gironde, Dordogne, the Landes,

the Basque Country and the western Pyrenees)
23 Parvis de Chartrons
33074 Bordeaux
Tel: 05 56 01 70 00
Fax: 05 56 01 70 07
www.crt.cr-aquitaine.fr
Languedoc-Roussillon (for the Cévennes, Hérault and Gard, the Aude, French Catalonia and the eastern Pyrenees)
20 rue de la République
34000 Montpellier
Tel: 04 67 22 81 00
Fax: 04 67 58 06 10
www.sunfrance.com
Midi-Pyrénées (for the Lot, Aveyron, the Tarn, Toulouse, the Gers, Ariège and the central Pyrenees)
54 Boulevard de l'Embouchure
BP 2166
31022 Toulouse
Tel: 05 61 13 55 55
Fax: 05 61 47 17 16
www.tourisme-midi-pyrenees.com

Telephones

The French telephone system is now very efficient, and you can usually find operational telephone boxes *(cabines publiques)* in every sizeable village.

Telephone numbers have been rationalised to 10 figures, always written – and spoken – in sets of two, e.g. 01 23 45 67 89. Regional telephone numbers are prefixed as follows: Paris, Ile de France region 01; Northwest 02; Northeast 03; Southeast and Corsica 04, and Southwest 05. When dialling from outside the country omit the zero. If you want numbers to be given singly rather than in pairs, ask for them *chiffre par chiffre.*

PUBLIC PHONES

Coin-operated phones take most coins but card phones are now very common and simple to use. It is worth purchasing a phone card *(une télécarte)* if you are likely to need to use a public call box, as most have been converted to take cards. Cards are available from post offices, stationers, railway stations, some cafés and *bureaux de tabac.*

Calls from metred cabins in cafés, shop or restaurants are generally more expensive than those made from public phone boxes. If you need to make a phone call in a small village with no public phone, look out for a blue *téléphone publique* plaque on a house. This means the owner is officially appointed to allow you to use the phone and charge the normal amount for the call.

MAKING A PHONE CALL

To make a call from a public phone box, lift the receiver, insert card or coin, then dial the number. When you replace the receiver, any unused coins will be returned to you. If you wish to make a follow-on call and have coin credit left, do not replace the receiver but press the *Appel Suivant* button and dial the new number. The cheapest times to telephone are weekdays 7pm to 8am and at weekends.

Phone Directories

Phone directories *(annuaires)* are found in all post offices and in most cafés. The *Pages Blanches (White Pages)* lists names of people and businesses alphabetically. The *Pages Jaunes (Yellow Pages)* lists businesses and services by category. They are also available on the internet at www.pagesjaunes.fr.

International Calls

To make an international call dial 00 followed by the country's international call number. This can be found in the front of the *Pages Jaunes (Yellow Pages)* section of the phone directory *(annuaire)* or on the information panel in a telephone box.

Reverse-Charge Calls

To make a reverse-charges call (call collect) within France, call 3006 and ask to make a PCV *(pay-say-vay)* call. Telephone calls can only be received at call boxes displaying the blue bell sign.

Free Calls

When dialling free numbers *(numéros verts,* which generally begin with 08) from a public phone you must insert card or money first in order to make the connection. The coins used will be returned immediately after the call. The card wll not be debited for the amount.

International Dialling Codes

Australia 00 61	**South Africa** 00 27
Canada 00 1	**UK** 00 44
Ireland 00 353	**US** 00 1
New Zealand 00 64	**Monaco** 00 377

Useful Numbers

French directory enquiries *(Renseignements)* 12
International directory enquiries 3212
Telephone engineer 13
International news (French recorded message, France Inter) 08 36 10 33
To send a telegram (all languages): international 08 00 33 44 11, within France 36 55
Speaking clock 36 99

MINITEL

Minitel is the computer-based videotext information system linked to the telephone, pioneered by the French long before the internet. Most homes and hotels have a terminal and most post offices offer use of the Minitel as a telephone directory (on 3611) and information resource. It is rapidly being superseded, however, by the internet.

TV and Radio

TELEVISION

France has six terrestial TV channels. **TF1** is the biggest, privatised since 1987, featuring movies, game shows, dubbed soaps, audience debates and the main news at 8pm.

France 2 is a state-owned station mixing game shows, documentaries and cultural chat shows.

France 3 has local news, sports, excellent wildlife documentaries and a late-night Sunday Cinema, *Minuit*, with classic films in the original language (VO for *version originale*). It also has a news and documentary programme, *Continentales*, broadcast five days a week with news broadcasts from around Europe in the original language with French subtitles.

Canal+ offers satellite and cable subscription channels with recent movies (sometimes original language), exclusive sport and late-night porn.

Arte is a Franco-German hybrid specialising in intelligent arts coverage and films in the original language. From 5.45am–7pm its wavelength is shared with the educational channel, *La Cinquième*.

M6 is a youth-oriented channel with a base of music videos supplemented by magazine programmes such as *Culture Pub*.

Any suitably connected television can supplement these channels with a range of internationally broadcast satellite stations.

Videos

Due to the difference in transmission standards, French and American TVs and video recorders won't work in France, so you won't be able to watch videos on the PAL system unless you have a multi-standard TV and VCR (which most of the French now do). If you want to bring videos to watch in your rented villa check if the TV is suitable – parents take note as a supply of videos can make or break a holiday with kids.

RADIO

All wavelengths are given here in MHz.

87.8 France Inter. State-run, MOR music and international news.

90.9 Chante France. 100 percent French *chanson*.

91.7–92.1 France Musique. State classical music channel with concerts and jazz.

93.5–93.9 France Culture. High-brow state culture station concentrating on literature, poetry, history, cinema and music.

96.4 BFM. Business and economics. Wall Street information in English every evening.

98.2 Radio FG Gay station. As well as music it has an explicit lonely-hearts section.

101.5 Radio Nova. Hip hop, trip hop, world music and jazz.

104.3 RTL. The most popular French station which mixes music and talk programmes.

104.7 Europe 1. News, press reviews, sports, business and good weekday breakfast news.

105.5 France Info. 24-hour news, economic updates and sports. Repeated every 15 minutes so good for learning French.

BBC World Service broadcasts can be received in France on shortwave between 6.195 and 12.095 MHz.

Travelling with Children

Sightseeing with children is only likely to be difficult in steep, hilly villages which can be very difficult to negotiate with a pushchair. Many conventional museums may not be of interest to kids but there are a wide range of educational attractions which will appeal to them, such as specialised zoos.

A wide range of activities can be found to suit children of all ages from cycling to river bathing, rambling through the countryside and exploring castles. Most towns and villages have swimming pools, tennis courts and playgrounds.

French Public Holidays

On public holidays, banks, post offices and public offices are closed. Food shops – in particular *boulangeries* (bakeries) – will, as a rule, still open, even on Christmas Day.

It is common practice, if a public holiday falls on a Thursday or Tuesday, for French businesses to *faire le pont* (literally, bridge the gap) and have the Friday or Monday as a holiday too. Details of closures should be posted outside banks, etc. a few days before the event but it is easy to be caught out, especially on days like 15 August (Feast of the Assumption), which is the climax of the summer and the biggest holiday of the year.

Foreign embassies and consulates observe French public holidays as well as their own.

The following public holidays are celebrated annually nationwide:

The beach and the sea are the easiest ways to amuse children, and private beach concessions with sun-loungers and parasols are the easiest of all; just book your parasol on the shore and watch the kids make sandcastles. Inflatables are often provided and there are sometimes bouncy castles, too.

Many seaside resorts have children's clubs on the beach, where for a fee children can be left for a few hours to take part in organised sports and fun events.

When hiring a car, be sure to book any baby seats in advance – though larger hire companies usually have a few ready to go.

Hotels and Restaurants

Most hotels have family rooms so children do not have to be separated from parents and a cot (*lit bébé*) can often be provided for a small supplement, although it is a good idea to check in advance.

Eating out is easy, especially during the day. All but the poshest restaurants welcome young

- **1 January** New Year's Day (*Nouvel An*)
- **Easter Monday** (*Lundi de Pâques*)
- **1 May** Labour Day (*Fête du Travail*)
- **May** Ascension Day (*Ascension*), on a Thursday 40 days after Easter
- **8 May** Victory Day (*Fête de la Libération*) to commemorate the end of World War II
- **May/June** Pentecost (*Pentecôte*), 10 days after Ascension.
- **14 July** Bastille Day (*Quatorze Juillet*)
- **15 August** Assumption Day: (*Fête de la Assomption*)
- **1 November** All Saints' Day (*Toussaint*)
- **11 November** Armistice Day: (*Fête de l'Armistice*)
- **25 December** Christmas Day (*Noël*)

Youth Organisations

CIDJ, Centre d'Information et de Documentation de la Jeunesse
101, quai Branly, 75740 Paris
Cedex 15
Tel: 01 44 49 12 25
Fax: 01 40 65 02 61

Loisirs de France Jeunes
(For information on holiday centres for children and teenagers)
30 rue Godot-de-Mauroy
75009 Paris
Tel: 01 47 42 51 81
Fax: 01 42 66 19 74

children: just choose one with a terrace and they can run around while you have another glass of wine. Many restaurants offer a children's menu or will split a *prix-fixe* menu between two children or even give you an extra plate to share your own meal.

French shops are well provided with all child necessities. Disposable nappies *(couches jetables)* are easy to find, and French baby food is often of gourmet standard, especially the puréed artichoke.

Holiday Centres

It is quite common in France, as in the USA, for children to spend at least part of their summer holiday at a holiday centre. For information, contact the tourist office or the "Loisirs Accueil" service in individual *départements*. (head office tel: 01 44 11 10 44; www.loisirsacceuilfrance.com)

Business Travellers

The most important thing to know about doing business in France, and especially the south, is that people always prefer to meet in person. You will often be expected to go and see someone, even to discuss something that could easily be dealt with over the phone.

Most major banks can refer you to lawyers, accountants and tax consultants; several US and British

banks provide expatriate services, in Paris and locally. Chambres de Commerce et d'Industrie can provide local information, and a calendar of trade fairs is available from the **Chambre de Commerce et d'Industrie de Paris**, 27 av de Friedland; tel: 01 53 40 48 48.

BUSINESS INFORMATION

BFM on 96.4 FM is an all-news business radio. **Les Echos** gives stock quotes on the website www.lesechos.com. Business directories *Kompass France* and *Kompass Régional* also give company details and detailed French market profiles on 3617 KOMPASS.

The standard English-language reference is *The French Company Handbook*, a list of all companies in the 120 Index of the Paris Bourse, published by the International Herald Tribune (tel: 01 41 43 93 00).

Travellers with Disabilities

TRAVEL

Le Shuttle (tel in UK: 0990 353 353) – the channel tunnel car-on-a-train service – is a good option for disabled passengers as they are allowed to stay in their vehicle. **Eurostar** trains (UK special requests, tel: 020 7928 0660) give passengers with wheelchairs first-

class travel for second-class fares. Getting on and off ferries may not be the most attractive option but most ferry companies will offer facilities if contacted beforehand. Vehicles fitted to accommodate people with disabilities pay reduced tolls on autoroutes.

Autoroute *Guide*

An *autoroute* guide for disabled travellers *(Guides des Autoroutes à l'usage des Personnes à Mobilité Réduite)* is available free from **Ministère des Transports**, Direction des Routes, Service du Contrôle des Autoroutes, La Défense, 92055 Cedex, Paris; tel: 01 40 81 21 22.

Taxis

If you have a disability, a French taxi driver cannot refuse to take you. Moreover, he or she must help you into the vehicle and is obliged to transport a guide dog for a blind passenger.

ACCESS

In many places, such as small hill villages with cobbled streets and inaccessible cliff-top castles, wheelchair-use is simply not feasible. In bigger cities there is usually reasonably good provision for wheelchair users – especially in newer museums.

In small towns and cities parking for the disabled is almost invariably provided and indicated by a blue

Contacts for People with Disabilities

CNRH (Comité National de Liaison pour la Réadaptation des Handicapés), 236 bis rue de Tolbiac, Paris 75013; tel: 01 53 80 66 85; www.handitel.org. Publishes an all-purpose tourist guide for those with disabilities.

RADAR (Royal Association for Disability and Rehabilitation)
Unit 12, City Forum, 250 City Rd, London EC1V 8AF; tel: 020 7250 3222; www.radar.org.uk. RADAR has an information department

(open 10am–4pm Mon–Fri) which gives specialist advice and sells *Getting There*, a guide to special facilities in airports.

Mobility International USA
PO Box 10767,
Eugene, Oregon USA 97440.
Tel: 541 343 1284
Fax: 541 343 6812.
www.miusa.org.
Offers international exchanges, information and technical aid for those with disabilities.

wheelchair sign. The international orange disabled parking disc scheme is also recognised in France.

Even when a place claims to have access for disabled people, it's always wise to check first.

If you need to hire a wheelchair or other equipment, enquire at the local pharmacy.

ACCOMMODATION

Gîtes Accessible à Tous lists *gîte* accommodation equipped for those with disabilities. It is available from: **Maison des Gîtes de France**, 59 rue St-Lazare, 75009 Paris; tel: 01 49 70 75 85; fax: 01 42 81 28 53.

The French Federation of Camping and Caravanning (Fédération de Camping-Caravanning) guide indicates which camp sites have facilities for disabled campers. It is obtainable from Deneway Guides, Chesil Lodge, West Bexington, Dorchester DT2 9DG; tel: 01308 898 132. Price £12.

The Michelin **Green Guide – Camping/Caravanning France** lists sites with facilities for the disabled. The **Association des Paralysés** publishes *Où Ferons-nous Étape?* which lists accommodation suitable for travellers with disabilities. Contact: 22 rue du Père Guérin, Paris 75013; tel: 01 44 16 83 83.

Medical Treatment

The standard of medical treatment in France is high. A complete list of doctors can be found in the *Pages Jaunes* under *Médecins Qualifiés*. To get a Social Security refund, choose a doctor or dentist registered with the state system; look for "Médecin Conventionné" after the name.

A consultation will cost at least €20, of which a proportion can be claimed back *(see under Health & Insurance, page 324, for procedure)*.

For a list of hospitals consult the *Pages Blanches* under *Hôpital Assistance Publique*.

Emergency Numbers

In cases of medical emergency, either dial 15 for an ambulance or call the Service d'Aide Médicale d'Urgence (SAMU), which exists in most large towns and cities – numbers are given at the front of telephone directories.
Ambulance 15
Police *(Police)* 17
Fire brigade *(Pompiers)* 18
Ambulance (SAMU) 15

PHARMACIES

Pharmacies sport a green neon cross which you cannot miss. They have a monopoly on issuing medication, and also sell tampons and a wide range of homeopathic medicines. Most open from 9am or 10am to 7pm or 8pm. Staff can provide basic medical services like disinfecting and bandaging wounds, attending to snake or insect bites (for a small fee) and will indicate the nearest doctor on duty.

French pharmacists are highly trained; you can often avoid visiting a doctor by describing your symptoms and seeing what they suggest. They are also qualified to identify mushrooms, so you can take in anything you've collected which you aren't sure about.

Towns have a rota system of *pharmacies de garde* at night and on Sunday. A closed pharmacy will have a sign indicating the nearest open pharmacy. Otherwise you can enquire from the *Gendarmerie* (police station). Toiletries and cosmetics are usually cheaper in supermarkets.

OPTICIANS

Any optician will be able to supply new glasses, but remember to bring your prescription. Also remember that drivers are required by law to carry a spare pair of glasses or contact lenses.

Security and Crime

Sensible precautions regarding personal possessions is all that should be necessary. Be aware of pickpockets in cities, and be careful on trains, especially when travelling at night, that doors are securely locked.

Police are fairly visible on the main roads of France during the summer months.

In the case of a serious accident or medical emergency, phone either the Police (17) or the Sapeurs-Pompiers (18). Though primarily a fire brigade, the latter are trained paramedics, and both they and the police have medical back up and work in close contact with SAMU. In rural areas the local taxi service often doubles as an ambulance, so it is worth finding out the number, from the tourist office or *mairie* (town hall).

LOST PROPERTY

To report a crime or loss of belongings, visit the local *gendarmerie* or *commissariat de police*. Telephone numbers are given at the front of local directories, or in an emergency, dial 17. If you lose a passport, report first to the police, then to the nearest consulate. If you have the misfortune to be detained by the police for any reason, ask to telephone the nearest consulate for a member of the staff to come to your assistance.

Tipping

Service of 10 percent is usually included in restaurants as part of the bill; leave an extra tip if you are particularly pleased. *Service compris* is generally indicated at the foot of the *carte* (bill). If in doubt, ask: *Est-ce que le service est compris?*

Service is also usually included in taxi fares, though an extra 1–1.50 euro tip will be appreciated. The same amount is also appropriate for doormen, porters, guides and hairdressers. In bars and cafés you will be charged more for service at a table, and less at the bar. It is usual just to leave small change as a tip.

Toilets

Anyone may use the toilet in a bar or café whether they are a customer or not, unless it is specified. (Ask for *les toilettes* or *les WC* – pronounced V-C). Public toilets vary considerably and many are still old-fashioned squat toilets. Men and women sometimes use the same facilities.

Student Cards

Students will find a valid student identity card is useful in obtaining discounts on all sorts of activities, including admission to museums and galleries, cinemas, theatres, etc. Reductions may sometimes be allowed by backing up your card with your passport.

Opening Hours

The sacred lunch hour is still largely observed in the south, which means that most shops and offices will close at midday and may not re-open till 2pm or 2.30pm. Big hypermarkets *(grandes surfaces)* usually stay open through lunch and till 7pm or 8pm at night. Many shops may also close in the morning or all day on Monday or Wednesday. Opening hours for food shops, hardware stores and other useful shops are generally 8.30am to 1pm and 2.30pm to 7pm. Most shops close on Sunday though *bureaux de tabac* (cigarettes and stamps) and *maisons de la presse* (newspapers and magazines) will usually open Sunday mornings.

Banks are usually open 9am–noon and 1.30–5pm Mon–Fri, though these times can vary.

Boulangeries are open daily (but Sunday mornings only), though some small villages may have a closing day. Usual hours are 9am to 7pm

(with a break for lunch noon–2 or 3pm), though some may open earlier.

Petrol stations usually open at 8.30am, close for lunch noon–2pm or 2.30pm and close around 9pm except on motorways; those attached to supermarkets may stay open for credit-card sales only.

Except during the months of July and August most museums close for lunch from noon to 2pm. They also close on certain public holidays, notably 1 January, 1 May and 25 December. Most monuments and museums in France charge a modest entrance fee. This is indicated with the opening times (in brackets) in the Places section of the book. Where nothing is said to the contrary, admission is free.

Public offices usually open 8.30am–noon and 2–6pm. Most will close for lunch. *Mairies* (town halls) will also close for lunch and in smaller places may only open in the morning 9am–noon.

Museum opening

Municipal museums are usually closed on Monday, national museums on Tuesday.

Religious Services

The presence of so many English people in Southwest France means there are some English churches and they will welcome visitors. For more information on churches and chaplains in France, contact the **Intercontinental Church Society**, 1 Athena Drive, Tachbrook Park, Warwick, CV34 6NL; tel: 01926 430 347; fax: 01926 330 238; www.ics-uk.org.

Travelling with Pets

Animal quarantine laws have been revised and it is possible to re-enter Britain with your pet without quarantine. Conditions are stringent, however, with tough health requirements and restricted points of entry. For further information you are advised to contact the Ministry of Agriculture,

World Heritage Sites

Several places in Southwest France have been denominated World Heritage Sites by UNESCO (see www.unesco.org). They are as follows (with the dates of their nomination):

● 1979 The prehistoric paintings in the caves of the Vézère Valley, in the Dordogne, especially the paintings at Lascaux.
● 1985 The Roman aqueduct of the Pont du Gard near Nîmes.
● 1996 The Canal du Midi, between Toulouse and the Mediterranean coast.
● 1997 The fortified Cité of Carcassonne.
● 1997 Pyrenees (both French and Spanish)
● 1998 The various routes towards Santiago de Compostela (in Spain) that cross Southwest France, converging on the Pyrenees.
● 1999 The historic wine town of St-Émilion in the Gironde.

The Cévennes were classed as a biosphere reserve by UNESCO in 1985.

or the French consulate if you are abroad. Once in Europe, travelling between countries other than Britain and the continent requires only a valid vaccination certificate.

Getting Around

Travelling in France

It is possible to get around by train and bus, though a car (or bicycle) is essential if you want to explore more inaccessible places independently. Bus and train services are adequate between towns and cities but small villages may only get one bus a day, or none at all.

Maps

A first essential for touring is a good map. The large-format Michelin atlases or sheet maps are good for driving. For walking or cycling, IGN (Institut Géographique National) maps are invaluable. The Top 100 (1:100,000, 1cm to 1km) and Top 50 (1:50,000, 2cm to 1km) maps have all roads and most footpaths marked. For even greater detail, go for the IGN blue series 1:25,000 maps.

Town plans are often given away free at local tourist offices. Most good bookshops should have a range of maps, but they may cost less in hypermarkets or service stations.

Stockists of French maps in the UK include:

Stanfords International Map Centre, 12–14 Long Acre, Covent Garden, London WC2E 9LP; tel: 020 7836 1321.

The Travel Bookshop, 13 Blenheim Crescent, London W11 2EE; tel: 020 7229 5260; www.thetravelbookshop.co.uk

By Bus

Details of routes and timetables are generally available free of charge either from bus stations (gare routière), which are often situated close to rail stations, or from tourist offices. They will also give details of coach (long-distance bus) tours and sightseeing excursions which are widely available.

By Train

Information on services is available from stations (gare SNCF). If you intend to travel extensively by train it may be worth obtaining a rail pass before leaving home (see Getting There, pages 325–6). Before buying a ticket in France, check on any discounts available. Children under 4 travel free, from 4 to 12 at half-fare. People travelling in groups of six or more can also obtain discounts (20–40 percent depending on numbers). All tickets purchased at French railway stations have to be put through the orange machines at the stations to validate them before boarding the train. These are marked compostez votre billet.

Driving

British, US, Canadian and Australian licences are all valid in France and you should always carry your vehicle's registration document and valid insurance (third party is the absolute minimum, and a green card – available from your insurance company – is strongly recommended). Additional insurance cover, which can include a get-you-home service, is offered by a number of organisations including the British and American Automobile Associations and **Europ-Assistance**, Sussex House, Perrymount Road, Haywards Heath, West Sussex RH16 1DN; tel: 01444 411 999 fax: 01444 459 292 www.europ-assistance.co.uk Another useful address is: **FFAC** (Fédération Française des Automobiles Club et des Usagers de la Route), 8 place de la Concorde, 75008 Paris; tel: 01 56 89 20 70; fax: 01 53 30 89 29, which co-ordinates with automobile

Busy Periods

French roads are busy from the end of July when the school holidays begin and for the following 2–3 weeks, and at their worst around 15 August, a national holiday. Special routes attempt to reduce summer traffic; look out for the small green BIS (Bison Futé) signs. A brochure on the Bison Futé is available in English; enquire at your nearest French Government Tourist Office.

clubs from other countries, mainly assisting with breakdowns.

RULES OF THE ROAD

Drivers should follow the rules of the road and always drive sensibly. Heavy on-the-spot fines are given for traffic offences such as speeding and drink-driving offences (if you do not have enough cash you will be required to pay a deposit).

Britons must remember to drive on the right: it doesn't take long to get used to, but extra care should be taken when crossing the carriageway, for instance, to use a service station. It is very easy to come out and automatically drive on the left – especially if there is no other traffic around. Put a sticker on the dashboard as a reminder.

The minimum age for driving in France is 18; foreigners are not permitted to drive on a provisional licence.

Full or dipped headlights must be used in poor visibility and at night; sidelights are not sufficient unless the car is stationary. Beams must be adjusted for right-hand drive vehicles, but yellow tints are not compulsory.

The use of seat belts (front and rear if fitted) and crash helmets for motorcyclists is compulsory. Children under 10 are not permitted to ride in the front seat unless fitted with a rear-facing safety seat, or if the car has no rear seat.

Nearly all autoroutes (motorways)

are toll roads. *Autoroutes* are designated A roads and national highways N roads. D roads are usually well maintained, while C or local roads, may not always be so.

Carry a red warning triangle to place 50 metres (55 yards) behind the car in case of a breakdown or accident (strongly advised, and compulsory if towing a caravan). In an accident or emergency, call the police (dial 17) or use the free emergency telephones (every 2 km/1 mile) on motorways. If another driver is involved, lock your car and go together to call the police. It is useful to carry an European Accident Statement Form (obtainable from your insurance company) which will simplify matters in the case of an accident.

Speed Limits

Speed limits are as follows, unless otherwise indicated: 130 kph (80 mph) on motorways; 110 kph (68 mph) on dual carriageways; 90 kph (56 mph) on other roads except in towns where the limit is 50 kph (30 mph). There is also a minimum speed limit of 80 kph (50 mph) on the outside lane of motorways during daylight with good visibility and on level ground. Speed limits are reduced by 20 kph (12 mph) on motorways) in wet weather.

On-the-spot fines can be levied for speeding; on toll roads, the time is printed on the ticket you take at your entry point and can thus be checked and a fine imposed on exit.

Fuel

Unleaded petrol *(essence sans plomb)* is now widely available in France. Leaded petrol is no longer available, and has been replaced by a substitute unleaded petrol for leaded-fuel vehicles. A map showing the location of most filling stations is available from main tourist offices. Petrol is cheapest at hypermarkets and most expensive on motorways.

CAR HIRE

Hiring a car is expensive in France, partly because of the high VAT (TVA) rate – 33 percent on luxury items. It can be much cheaper to arrange car hire before leaving home, especially if it is for a short visit. Most airlines offer preferential car-hire rates for fly-drive packages, although this can have an unexpected disadvantage. At a small airport such as Carcassonne you can find that everyone on an incoming flight besieges the same car-hire desk. SNCF, the national rail company, offers a train/car rental scheme.

There are often good weekend

Priorité à Droite

Traditionally, priority on French roads was always given to vehicles approaching from the right, except where otherwise indicated. Nowadays, on main roads, the major road will normally have priority, with traffic being halted on minor approach roads with one of the following signs:
• **Cédez le passage** – give way
• **Vous n'avez pas la priorité** – you do not have right of way
• **Passage protégé** – no right of way.

A yellow diamond sign indicates that you have priority, the diamond sign with a diagonal black line indicates that you do not have

priority. Take care in small towns and rural areas without road markings where you might be expected to give way to traffic coming from the right, especially farm vehicles. Note that if an oncoming driver flashes their headlights it is to indicate that he or she has priority, not the other way round. Priority is always given to emergency and public utility services.

In theory drivers already on a roundabout now have priority over those entering it, but beware; some drivers still insist that priority belongs to the driver entering the roundabout.

Car Hire Companies

Ada
Tel: 04 91 79 37 19
Avis
Tel: 08 02 05 05 05
Budget
Tel: 04 91 64 08 08
Europcar
Tel: 08 25 35 23 52
Hertz
Tel: 01 39 38 38 38
Rent-a-Car
Tel: 08 36 69 46 95

offers (Fri evening to Mon morning). Week-long deals are better at the bigger hire companies – with Avis or Budget, for example, it's around €245 a week for a small car with insurance and 1,700km (1,056 miles) included. Most of the international hire companies will allow the return of a car to other cities in France and abroad. Be warned that low-cost operators may have an extremely high excess charge for dents or damage.

The minimum age to hire a car is 18, but most companies will not hire to anyone under 25, or 21 if paying by credit card. Some hire companies charge a daily supplement of around €20 for younger drivers. The hirer must have held a full licence for at least a year. Most companies have an upper age limit of 60–65.

Take your licence and passport with you to collect your car. And ensure that you are given all the relevant information about what to do in case of an accident or a breakdown; telephone numbers in case of emergencies, etc. and what procedure to follow. Any reputable company will take the time to explain all this to you.

MOTORCYCLES & MOPEDS

Rules of the road are largely the same as for car drivers. The minimum age for driving machines over 80cc is 18. GB plates must be shown and crash helmets are compulsory. Dipped headlights must be used at all times. Children under 14 years are not permitted to be carried as passengers.

Cycling

Bicycles (*vélos*) are usually available for hire, often from cycle shops. Local tourist offices keep information on hire facilities. French Railways have them for hire at several stations in the region and they do not necessarily have to be returned to the same station. Bikes can be carried free of charge on buses and some trains (*Autotrains*); on other, faster services you will have to pay.

On Foot

France has a network of waymarked footpaths, called *Grandes Randonnées*, which are well signposted and offer good facilities for walkers en route.

The paths are classified with a GR number and there are countless opportunities for exploring on foot, either following a long route, or on one of the shorter circular tours. The IGN Blue Series maps at a scale of 1:25,000 are ideal for walkers.

Contact regional tourist offices for information about local clubs and events.

Various walking holidays with accommodation either in hotels or under canvas are available from private tour operators

Walking by the Book

A good basic guidebook for serious walkers is Rob Hunter's book **Walking in France**, while **Classic Walks in France**, by Hunter and Wickers, suggests 20 tours in the most beautiful areas of the country. Both are published by Oxford University Press. A series of regional walking guides based on the French Topoguides include **Walks in the Dordogne**. They are published by Robertson McCarta.

Independent travellers can take advantage of low-priced accommodation offered in *gîtes d'étapes*, hostels offering basic facilities which are to be found on many of the GR routes and in mountain regions. For more information contact the Gîtes de France organisation (*see Where to Stay, page 336*).

City Transport

The centres of interest of all the cities in this book are small enough to be negotiated on foot, and a car is a liability with busy traffic and parking problems. For longer journeys Toulouse has a metro system, and Montpellier has launched the first stage of its tram project. For the latest information log on to: www.railway-technology.com/projects/montpellier.

Taxis

Taxis are normally readily available at railway stations and at official taxi ranks in city centres. Outside the cities check telephone directories or local notice boards for taxi companies.

Where to Stay

Choosing Accommodation

Accommodation in Southwest France varies from grand city hotels or seafront palaces to rudimentary mountain refuges. In between you can rent villas or *gîtes*, camp, or stay in a wide range of small-town hotels, country *auberges* and *chambres d'hôtes*. During the summer it is advisable to book, especially in the coastal regions, but outside the peak holiday period (between mid-July and mid-August, when the French head south en masse) you should find accommodation easily. Some hotels, especially in the Pyrenees and more remote areas, will close between November and February, and most camp sites will be closed during the winter months.

Hotels

All hotels in France conform to national standards and carry star ratings, set down by the Ministry of Tourism, according to their degree of comfort and amenities. Prices (which are charged per room, rather than per person) range from as little as €30 for a double room in an unclassified hotel (i.e. its standards are not sufficient to warrant a single star, but it is likely to be clean, cheap and cheerful), to around €100 for the cheapest double room in a 4-star luxury hotel.

Hotels are required to display their menus outside, and details of room prices should be visible either outside or in reception, as well as on the back of bedroom doors. It is possible for a hotel to have a 1-star rating, with a 2-star restaurant.

When booking a room you should

Accommodation Websites

Hotels

www.relaischateaux.fr
(Relais & Chateaux hotels)
www.chateauxhotels.com
(Chateaux & Hotels de France)
www.logis-de-france.fr
(Logis hotel network)
www.hotelformule1.com
(information on cheap, main road
hotels)

Other Places to Stay

www.fuaj.org
(youth hostels)
www.gites-de-france.fr
(the official site for *gîtes ruraux*,
gîtes d'étape, bed-and-breakfasts
and farm camping)
www.campingfrance.com
(multilingual guide to all the camp
sites of France)

---

normally be shown it before
agreeing to take it; don't hesitate to
ask. Supplements may be charged
for an additional bed or a cot *(lit
bébé)*. You may be asked when
booking if you wish to dine,
particularly if the hotel is busy –
and you should confirm that the
hotel's restaurant is open (many
are closed out of season on Sunday
or Monday evenings).

Lists of hotels can be obtained
from the French Government Tourist
office in your country or from
regional or local tourist offices in
France. If you just want an overnight
stop to break a journey, you may
find clean, modern, basic chains
like Formule 1 handy.

Logis de France

Logis de France is France's biggest
hotel network. It acts as a sort of
quality-control stamp for over 5,000
private hotels in small towns and
the French countryside. Most of
these hotels are one- or two-star
and they vary greatly in facilities,
atmosphere and level of service.
Contact the **Fédération Nationale
des Logis et Auberges de France**,
83 ave d'Italie, 75013 Paris; tel: 01
45 84 70 00, or the French
Government Tourist office for a
Logis de France handbook.

Bed & Breakfast

Bed and breakfast *(chambre d'hôte)*
accommodation is fairly widely
available in private houses, often
on working farms, whose owners
are members of the Fédération
Nationale des Gîtes Ruraux de
France. Bookings can be made for

an overnight stop or a longer stay.
Breakfast is included in the price
and evening meals – usually made
with local produce and extremely
good value – are often available.

Hotels Abroad offer a straightforward hotel and bed and breakfast
booking service which can include
ferry bookings if desired. They will
book accommodation at either a
single destination or various stops
around the region. Contact 5
World's End Lane, Green St Green,
Orpington, Kent BR6 6AA; tel:
01689 857 838; fax: 01689 850
931. www.hotelsabroad.co.uk

If you do not wish to book
anything in advance, just look out
for signs along the road (usually in
the countryside) offering *chambres
d'hôtes*. You will be taking pot luck,
but you will be fairly safe for a bed
off-season and may be delighted by
the good value of the simple farm
food and accommodation on offer.

Gîtes

The Fédération des Gîtes Ruraux de
France was set up around 40 years
ago with the aim of offering grants
to owners to restore rural
properties and let them out as
holiday homes. These *gîtes*
(literally: places to lay one's head)
ruraux are an inexpensive way of
enjoying a rural holiday in regional
France. The properties range from
very simple farm cottages to grand
manor houses and even the odd
château. They are all inspected by
the Relais Départemental (the
county office of the national
federation) and given an "*épi*" (ear
of corn) classification according to

level of comfort. Prices average
€185–275 per week in August for a
2–4 person *gîte*.

Gîtes are always completely self-
catering (in some cases you will be
expected to supply your own bed
linen), but most have owners living
nearby who will tell you where to
buy local produce (or even provide it
themselves). Note that some of
these properties will be off the
beaten track – which is often what
makes them so appealing in the
first place – and a car, or at the
very least a bicycle, is usually
essential. Bicycles can often be
hired locally or even from *gîte*
owners.

Brittany Ferries are UK agents
for Gîtes de France; bookings can
be made through The Brittany
Centre, Wharf Rd, Portsmouth PO2
8RU; tel: 08705 360 360. The list
of *gîtes* in the Brittany Ferries
brochure is only a selection of
those available.

In France, contact the **Maison de
Gîtes de France**, 59 rue St Lazare,
75009 Paris; tel: 01 49 70 75 85;
fax: 33 142 81 28 53. The Gîtes de
France brochure *Gîtes Accessibles à
Tous* lists *gîte* accommodation with
access and services for the
disabled. You can also investigate
gîtes at www.gites-de-france.com.

THE GÎTE D'ÉTAPE

Gîte d'Étape accommodation –
which is often found in mountain
areas, or along long-distance
footpaths – is intended for overnight
stays by hikers, cyclists, skiers or
horse-riders. These *gîtes* are often
run by the local village, and tend to
be spartan, with bunk beds, and
basic kitchen and washing facilities.
Reservations are recommended,
especially in busy periods. *Gîte de
neige*, *gîte de pêche* and *gîte
équestre* are all variations on the
standard *gîte d'étape*, lending
themselves to skiing, fishing and
horse-riding respectively.

Mountain refuges *(refuges)* range
from large and solid stone houses
to very basic huts. All have bunk-
bed accommodation, and many also

offer food – some of it of surprisingly high quality. Many are open only June–September; they should always be booked in advance. Prices vary between €6 and €15 per person. Lists of refuges are available from local tourist offices.

Camping

Camping is a very popular option in France: camp sites *(les campings)* can be surprisingly luxurious, and many are run by local councils. Prices range from €6 to around €15 per night for a family of four, with car, caravan or tent. Note that in summer camp sites can get crowded, especially on the coast. Camping rough *(camping sauvage)* is discouraged but you may be given permission if you ask. Be very careful camping anywhere there is a fire risk.

Camp sites are graded from one-star (minimal comfort, water points, showers and sinks) to four-star luxury sites which allow more space for each pitch, and offer above-average facilities. The majority of sites are two-star. To get back to nature look out for camp sites designated *Aire naturelle de camping* where facilities will be absolutely minimal, with prices to match. Some farms offer camping pitches under the auspices of the Fédération Nationale des Gîtes Ruraux – these are designated *Camping à la ferme*, and again facilities are usually limited.

The *Guide Officiel* of the French Federation of Camping and Caravanning (FFCC), available from French Government Tourist Offices,

lists 11,600 sites nationwide, and indicates those which have facilities for disabled campers. The Michelin *Green Guide – Camping/Caravanning France* is very informative, and also lists sites with facilities for the disabled.

Hotel Listings

Hotels are grouped according to the chapters of the book. Hotel locations are listed in alphabetical order below the area name. The prices of the hotels are indicated as follows:
€ = Budget: under €55
€€ = Moderate: €55–115
€€€ = Expensive: €115+
All prices given are per double room. Breakfast is not normally included. Credit cards are accepted unless otherwise indicated.

BORDEAUX AND THE GIRONDE

Arcachon
Hôtel Marinette
15 Allée José-María-de-Heredia
Arcachon
Tel: 05 56 83 06 67
Fax: 05 56 83 09 59
www.hotel-marinette.com
Arcachon's Ville d'Hiver (a luxury winter resort built in the 1860s) has some beautiful Belle Époque villas, and this is one of them. The rooms are comfortable, there is an attractive leafy garden and the hotel is good value for money. The Marinette's restaurant also offers excellent value, though be aware that it is only open in high season. **€**

Bordeaux
Le Bayonne Etche-Ona
15 Cours de l'Intendance
33000 Bordeaux
Tel: 05 56 48 00 88
Fax: 05 56 48 41 60
www.bordeaux-hotel.com
A grand, central hotel in the Triangle d'Or district, with an 18th-century façade and a modern interior. No restaurant. **€€**
Grand Hôtel Français
12 rue du Temple
33000 Bordeaux
Tel: 05 56 48 10 35
Fax: 05 56 81 76 18
www.grand-hotel-francais.com
All modern comforts in this gracefully elegant 18th-century mansion in the centre of town; close to the cathedral, museums, wine centre and theatre. No restaurant. **€€**
Hôtel de l'Opéra
35 rue Esprit-des-Lois
33000 Bordeaux
Tel: 05 56 81 41 27
Fax: 05 56 51 78 80
Adjacent to the Grand Théâtre, though much of the contemporaneous 18th-century decor has been modernised. Given its central location, try and get a room at the back of the hotel to minimise traffic noise. The management is friendly and helpful; excellent value. **€**
Hôtel de la Presse
6 rue Porte-Dijeaux
33000 Bordeaux
Tel: 05 56 48 53 88
Fax: 05 56 01 05 82
www.hoteldelapresse.com
Off the main shopping area, rue Ste-Catherine, the Hôtel de la Presse still manages to remain quiet and restful. Comfortable bedrooms are all air conditioned with double glazing, and there is a charming courtyard. **€**

Cap-Ferret
Hôtel des Pins
rue de Fauvettes
33950 Cap-Ferret
Tel: 05 56 60 60 11
Fax: 05 56 60 67 41
A small hotel built at the beginning of the 20th century in a quiet part

Youth Hostels *(Auberges de Jeunesse)*

To stay in most hostels you need to be a member of the International Youth Hostel Federation, or join the Fédération Unie des Auberges de Jeunesse.
Fédération Unie des Auberges de Jeunesse (FUAJ), 27 rue Pajol, 75018 Paris; tel: 01 44 89 87 27; fax: 01 44 89 87 10. The federation is affiliated to the

International Federation.
Youth Hostels Association, Trevelyan House, 8 St Stephen's Hill, St Albans, Herts AL1 2DY; tel: 01629 592 600.
In the US, contact: **American Youth Hostelling International**, PO Box 37613, Dept USA, Washington DC 20013/7613; tel: 0202 783 6161.

of town, surrounded by gardens. Close to the sea and the Bassin d'Arcachon. Dining on the shady terrace. €

Castelnau-du-Médoc
Château du Foulon
33480 Castelnau-du-Médoc
Tel: 05 56 58 20 18
Fax: 05 56 58 23 43
Splendid château in its own parkland outside the village. No restaurant but breakfast *en famille* at the magnificent *grand table*. No credit cards. €€

Lacanau-Océan
L'Auberge du Marin
4 rue du Lion
33680 Lacanau-Océan
Tel: 05 56 03 26 87
Basic, but with clean and comfortable rooms, close to the beach, and with first-class family cooking at a surpringly reasonable price. €

Margaux
Le Pavillon de Margaux
33460 Margaux
Tel: 05 57 88 77 54
Fax: 05 57 88 77 73
www.le-pavillon-margaux.com
Typical 19th-century local architecture, with terrace where you can dine beneath the trees surrounded by vineyards. €€
Relais de Margaux
Chemin de l'Ile Vincent
33460 Margaux
Tel: 05 57 88 38 30
Fax: 05 57 88 31 73
www.relais-margaux.fr
In a large park in the heart of the Médoc, this former wine cellar belonging to the chateau has been transformed into a luxury hotel with comfortably individualised rooms. There are a number of conference and seminar areas. €€

Martillac
Les Sources de Caudalie
Château Smith Haut Lafitte
33650 Martillac
Tel: 05 57 83 83 83
www.sources.caudalie.com
A spa hotel offering guests a chance to try vinotherapy. €€€

Wallowing in Wine

Les Sources de Caudalie in Martillac is the world's first wine spa, offering "vinotherapy" – skin treatments using the by-products of the Bordeaux wine industry.

Pauillac
Château Cordeillan-Bages
Route des Châteaux
33250 Pauillac
Tel: 05 56 59 24 24
Fax: 05 59 59 01 89
www.cordeillanbages.com
A 17th-century Bordeaux-style château, with a terrace overloooking the vineyards. Now housing the Bordeaux school of wine. €€€
Château Guges
29 rue de la Croix-des-Gunes
Cissac-Médoc 33250 Pauillac
Tel: 05 56 59 58 04
Fax: 05 56 59 59 46
A five-minute drive from Pauillac on the D104, this is a family-run wine château. The decor is luxurious and impressive, the welcome friendly and informal. Despite breakfast being an optional extra, the rooms here are outstanding value. No credit cards. €€

St-Émilion
Logis de La Cadène
3 place du Marché-au-Bois
33330 St-Émilion
Tel: 05 57 24 71 40
Fax: 05 57 74 42 23
Situated in the heart of this ancient small town, the *chambres d'hôte* here are a perfect base for exploring all that St-Émilion has to offer. Book in advance, as there are only three double rooms available. Closed January. €

St-Macaire
L'Abricotier
33490 St-Macaire
Tel: 05 56 76 83 63
Fax: 05 56 76 28 51
This small hotel-restaurant is a real find, a short drive from the village just off the RN113 towards La Réole. The rooms are unpretentious and comfortable, and the restaurant (complete with terrace)

offers imaginative and high-quality cooking. €

DORDOGNE

Brantôme
Le Chatenet
24310 Brantôme
Tel: 05 53 05 81 08
Fax: 05 53 05 85 52
A 17th-century country manor house standing in its own grounds. Spacious, elegantly furnished bedrooms and a warm, family ambience. €€
Domaine de la Roseraie
Route d'Angoulême
24310 Brantôme
Tel: 05 53 05 84 74
Fax: 05 53 05 77 94
www.domaine-la-roseraie.com
Renovated 17th-century hotel just outside Brantôme. Quietly situated in 4 hectares (10 acres) of parkland and much loved by artists. Breakfast in the rose garden in summer, sit by the open fire in winter. €€

Le Buisson de Cadouin
Manoir de Bellerive
Route de Siorac
24480 Le Buisson de Cadouin
Tel: 05 53 22 16 16
Fax: 05 53 22 09 05
www.bellerivehotel.com
Magnificent manor house in its own mature parkland. Breakfast on the balustraded terrace overlooking the river. Most rooms have views of the river or formal gardens. €€

Champagnac de Belair
Le Moulin de Roc
24530 Champagnac-de-Belair
Tel: 05 53 02 86 00
Fax: 05 53 54 21 31
www.moulinduroc.com
A 17th-century former watermill with great character. Bedrooms are pretty and cosy and there are lovely waterside gardens. The cuisine is well recommended. €€

Coly
Manoir d'Hautegente
24120 Coly
Tel: 05 53 51 68 03
Fax: 05 53 50 38 52

www.manoir-hautegente.com
A lovely 13th-century manor house beside a little lane in wooded grounds. Originally a forge, and later a mill, the house has been in the same family for 300 years. Spacious, comfortable bedrooms are furnished with antiques and there is a vaulted dining room serving excellent cuisine. €€

Domme
L'Esplanade
24250 Domme
Tel: 05 53 28 31 41
Fax: 05 53 28 49 92
Wonderful views of the Dordogne from this hotel perched above Domme. Excellent restaurant serves trout, salmon or rack of lamb and truffle specialities. €€
La Daille
Florimont-Gaumiers
24250 Domme
Tel: 05 53 28 40 71
Small, English-run, farmhouse-hotel surrounded by gardens in beautiful, open countryside. The comfortable rooms are in a separate modern building; the dining room is in the main farmhouse and serves a light cuisine based on local produce. Minimum three nights stay. No credit cards. €€

Les Eyzies-de-Tayac
Le Centenaire
Rocher de la Penne
24620, Les-Eyzies-de-Tayac
Tel: 05 53 06 68 68
Fax: 05 53 06 92 41
www.hotelducentenaire.fr
Situated at the foot of Les Eyzies, the hotel incorporates sophisticated amenities into a country style. There is a four-star restaurant, a heated outdoor pool, a sauna, an exercise room, and flowery dining areas and gardens. €

Gramat
Château de Roumégouse
Route de Brive
46500 Gramat
Tel: 05 65 33 63 81
Fax: 05 65 33 71 18
www.chateauderoumegouse.com
A Relais et Châteaux 19th-century chateau in wooded parkland. On fine

evenings you can dine on the terrace with views out over the river. €€

Puymirol
Les Loges de l'Aubergade
52 rue Royale
47270 Puymirol
Tel: 05 53 95 31 46
Fax: 05 53 95 33 80
www.aubergade.com
Situated in the centre of a small fortified town this 13th-century residence was once the home of the counts of Toulouse. The owner-chef, M. Trama, not only serves excellent cuisine but provides a huge selection of cigars besides. There is a terraced garden and the rooms have jacuzzis or massage showers. €€

Hotel Price Guide

€ = **Budget** under €55
€€ = **Moderate** €55–115
€€€ = **Expensive** €115+
Prices are per double room.

La Roque-Gageac
La Belle Étoile
24250 La Roque-Gageac
Tel: 05 53 29 51 44
Fax: 05 53 29 45 63
In the main street, a hotel and restaurant of great charm, with wood fire, Périgord cooking and rooms overlooking the river. €€

St-Cyprien-en-Périgord
Hôtel l'Abbaye
rue de L'Abbaye
24220 St-Cyprien-en-Périgord
Tel: 05 53 29 20 48
Fax: 05 53 29 15 85
www.abbaye-dordogne.com
An 18th-century manor with views of hills and forests and the old town. Meals served in the original stone-walled kitchen with fireplace or in the garden. €€

Trémolat
Le Vieux Logis
24510 Trémolat
Tel: 05 53 22 80 06
Fax: 05 53 22 84 89
www.vieux-logis.com
Village hotel run by the same family

for 400 years. Some of the rooms have four-poster beds and the galleried dining room looks out onto the garden. Excellent restaurant. €€€

LOT

Cahors
À l'Escargot
5 Boulevard Gambetta
46000 Cahors
Tel: 05 65 35 07 66
Fax: 05 65 53 92 38
Hotel-restaurant in medieval building with tastefully furnished rooms in annexe, and two dining rooms serving generous meals – with snails, of course. €
Le Terminus
5 avenue Charles-de-Freycinet
46000 Cahors
Tel: 05 65 53 32 00
Fax: 05 65 53 32 26
www.balandre.com
A small, grand-hôtel from the turn of the 20th century, offering warm hospitality and graciously decorated rooms. Gastronomic restaurant, Le Balandre. €€

Gourdon
Bissonier
51 boulevard des Martyrs
46300 Gourdon
Tel: 05 65 41 02 48
Fax: 05 65 41 44 67
www.hotelbissonier.com
An attractive hotel-restaurant near the medieval centre of town. There are good views from the terrace and a pretty courtyard. Modern bedrooms. €

Rocamadour
Ste-Marie
place des Senhals
46500 Rocamadour
Tel: 05 65 33 63 07
Fax: 05 65 33 69 08
www.hotelsaintemarie.fr
Built on a ledge on the rocks with a splendid view out over the countryside and medieval town, particularly from the terrace-café. Modern bedrooms and rustic decor in the public rooms. €

Domaine de la Rhue
46500 Rocamadour
Tel: 05 65 33 71 50
Fax: 05 65 33 72 48
www.domainedelarhue.com
Charming converted stable block
next to 19th-century château outside
Rocamadour, with a pool. €€

Hôtel Les Vieilles Tours
Route de Payrac
46500 Rocamadour
Tel: 05 65 33 68 01
Fax: 05 65 33 68 59
www.chateauxhotels.com
Partly 13th-century building,
peacefully situated in 2 hectares
(5 acres) of land, 3 km (2 miles)
outside Rocamadour. €€

Le Troubadour
Route de Padirac
46500 Rocamadour
Tel: 05 65 33 70 27
Fax: 05 65 33 71 99
www.rocamadour.com
Discreetly distanced from
Rocamadour, this modern hotel has
all its rooms on the ground floor.
A relaxing place with countryside all
around. €

St-Céré
Villa Ric
Route de Leyme
46400 St-Céré
Tel: 05 65 38 04 08
Fax: 05 65 38 00 14
A small restaurant-hotel with a
summer terrace, set among trees
and with a magnificent view across
the hills of St-Céré. €€

St-Cirq-Lapopie
La Pélissaria
46330 St-Cirq-Lapopie
Tel: 05 65 31 25 14
Fax: 05 65 30 25 52

Hotel Breakfasts

Breakfast is not normally
included in the price of a hotel,
and it is often expensive – it can
be as much as €6 or €7.50. If
you are staying in a town or city
you are generally better off going
out to a bar or café for coffee
and croissants – which is all
you'll get from the hotel anyway.

A 13th-century house built on the
hillside with lovely views out over
the valley. There is a little terraced
garden and the rooms are carefully
and comfortably furnished. €€

Souillac
Château de la Treyne
La Treyne
46200 Souillac
Tel: 05 65 27 60 60
Fax: 05 65 27 60 70
www.chateaudelatreyne.com
Secluded château surrounded by
trees and parkland overlooking the
Dordogne River. Tennis and
canoeing are available. €€€

AVEYRON AND THE CÉVENNES

Conques
Sainte-Foy
rue Principale
12320 Conques
Tel: 05 65 69 84 03
Fax: 05 65 72 81 04
www.hotelsaintefoy.fr
Restored village hotel of stone and
timber, furnished with antiques and
with spacious bedrooms. Courtyard
for warm-weather dining. It stands
adjacent to the famous abbey of
Conques. €€

La Malène
Manoir de Montesquiou
48210 La Malène
Tel: 04 66 48 51 12
Fax: 04 66 48 50 47
www.manoir-montesquiou.com
This beautiful 15th-century manor
house in the spectacular Gorges du
Tarn has wonderful views, an inner
court, rooms in the turret and four-
poster beds. €€

Meyrueis
Château d'Ayres
48150 Meyrueis
Tel: 04 66 45 60 10
Fax: 04 66 45 62 26
www.chateaud'ayres.com
Château in the middle of the
Cévennes National Park, on the site
of a former monastery, secluded in
its own wooded grounds. Inside are
wood panelling, vaulted ceilings and

intriguing bedrooms. Traditional
Languedoc cuisine is served. €€

Hôtel du Mont Aigoual
rue de la Barrière
48150 Meyrueis
Tel: 04 66 45 65 61
Fax: 04 66 45 64 25
www.hotel-mont-aigoual.com
A modern hotel in the Gorges
de la Jonte. It has a nice pool
and a large grassy garden.
The popular restaurant on the
ground floor enjoys some local
renown. €€

Millau
Hôtel Château de Creissels
Route de St-Affrique
12100 Millau
Tel: 05 65 60 16 59
Fax: 05 65 61 24 63
www.chateau-de-creissels.com
Converted 13th-century castle
with good views. Regional food is
served in the vaulted dining room.
€€

Peyreleau
**Grand Hôtel de la Muse et du
Rozier**
La Muse
12270 Peyreleau
Tel: 05 65 62 60 01
Fax: 05 65 62 63 88
This is a roomy and comfortable
modern hotel with a garden for
dining. €€

St-Jean-de-Bruel
Hôtel du Midi
12230 St-Jean-du-Bruel
Tel: 05 65 62 26 04
Fax: 05 65 62 12 97
An informal, welcoming hotel
in a quiet town, with a dining
room overlooking the River
Dourbie and a diminutive
swimming pool a step or two
away from the front door.
Four family rooms in the annexe.
€

Ste-Énimie
Château de la Caze
48210 Ste-Énimie
Tel: 04 66 48 51 01
Fax: 04 66 48 55 75
This preserved castle standing
beneath cliffs and beside the river

is one of the landmarks of the
Gorges du Tarn. (Closed Nov–Apr.)
€€€

ALBI AND THE TARN

Albi
Hostellerie St-Antoine
17 rue Saint-Antoine
81000 Albi
Tel: 05 63 54 04 04
Fax: 05 63 47 10 47
www.saint-antoine-albi.com
Charming 18th-century *auberge* (inn)
which has been in the same family
for five generations. Most rooms
look out onto the garden. €€
Grand Hôtel d'Orléans
Place Stalingrad
81000 Albi
Tel: 05 63 54 16 56
Fax: 05 63 54 43 41
Traditional family hotel in a 19th-
century building. €€

Castres
Hôtel Renaissance
17 rue Victor Hugo
Tel: 05 63 59 30 42
Fax: 05 63 72 11 57
Converted 17th-century building, all
old tapestries and antique furniture,
and with restaurant. €€

Cordes-sur-Ciel
Hostellerie du Vieux Cordes
rue St-Michel
81170 Cordes-sur-Ciel
Tel: 05 63 53 79 20
Fax: 05 63 56 02 47
www.thuries.fr
Hotel in an old monastery, with
shady terrace overlooking the valley.
The restaurant serves authentic
cassoulet and delicious fish dishes.
€€

Cuq-Toulza
Cuq-en-terasses
81470 Cuq-Toulza
Tel: 05 63 82 54 00
Fax: 05 63 82 54 11
www.cuqenterasses.com
Beautifully decorated former
presbytery with several terraces in
a tiny hamlet on a hill just outside
Cuq-Toulqa. Meals by reservation.
€€

Hotel Price Guide

€ = Budget under €55
€€ = Moderate €55–115
€€€ = Expensive €115+
Prices are per double room.

TOULOUSE

Hôtel des Capitouls
22 Descente de la Halle aux
Poissons, 31000, Toulouse
Tel: 05 34 32 61 63
www.hotelsdecharmetoulouse.com
Small hotel with Japanese-style
elegant decor; close to the river and
with its own chic restaurant (Le 19)
opposite for sushi and steak
tartare. €€€
Grand Hôtel de l'Opéra
1 place du Capitole
31000 Toulouse
Tel: 05 61 21 82 66
Fax: 05 61 23 41 04
www.grand-hotel-opera.com
Centrally located off the main
square, the hotel is in a courtyard
hidden behind its two well-known
restaurants, Les Jardins de l'Opéra
(see page 350) and the Grand Café
de l'Opéra. €€€
Hôtel des Beaux Arts
1 place du Pont Neuf
31000 Toulouse
Tel: 05 34 45 42 42
Fax: 05 34 45 42 43
An 18th-century building beside
the river which has been a hotel for
100 years. It doesn't have a
restaurant but beneath the hotel is
the lively Brasserie des Beaux Arts.
€€
Hotel de Grand Balcon
8 rue Romiguières
Tel: 05 61 21 48 08
Very convenient for centre of town
and very cheap, though in need of
its planned renovation so select
your room with care. €
Grand Hôtel Capoul
13 place Wilson
Tel: 05 61 10 70 70
Fax: 05 61 21 96 70
www.capoul.com
An Art Déco hotel on a square in
the centre of the city, with original
furnishings and a popular brasserie
attached. €€

GASCONY

Auch
Hôtel de France
place de la Libération
32000 Auch, Gers
Tel: 05 62 61 71 84
Fax: 05 62 61 71 81
A splendid hotel on the main square
of Auch with accomplished chef
Roland Garreau presiding over the
kitchens. €€

Capbreton
L'Océan
85 avenue G. Pompidou
40130 Capbreton
Tel: 05 58 72 10 22
Fax: 05 58 72 08 43
www.hotel-capbreton.com
Grand white hotel near the port and
beach. Big balconied bedrooms.
Restaurant and tea room. €€

Condom
Hôtel des Trois Lys
32100 Condom, Gers
Tel: 05 62 28 33 33
Fax: 05 62 28 41 85
www.lestroislys.com
Formerly a private mansion, this
charming hotel with its 18th-century
façade and light, airy rooms offers
stylish comfort. There is a bar, a
swimming pool and a restaurant, Le
Dauphin. €€

Eugénie-les-Bains
Les Prés d'Eugénie
40320 Eugénie-les-Bains
Tel: 05 58 05 06 07
Fax: 05 58 51 10 10
www.relaischateaux.com
Michel Guérard, inventor of *cuisine
minceur* and among France's most
eminent chefs, runs an empire here
with an immensely luxurious spa
hotel and stylishly rustic *auberge*.
Two restaurants offer healthy eating
with great style. *(See page 350.)* A
treat for any gourmet. €€–€€€

Fourcès
Château de Fourcès
32250 Fourcès
Tel: 05 62 29 49 53
Fax: 05 62 29 50 59
www.chateauforces.com
Superbly restored château in a

ravishing setting on the edge of a *bastide* village. It has fine, spacious rooms and a swimming pool edged with tall trees. The food is also a treat – professional and inventive – and the service friendly. €€

Gimont
Château de Larroque
32200 Gimont
Tel: 05 62 67 77 44
Fax: 05 62 67 88 90
www.chateaularroque.com
An exquisitely proportioned mansion, long and low, set on the brow of rolling Gers parkland. With 16 elegant rooms, scented gardens, a pool and tennis court, it is both peaceful and seductively romantic. You can dine well here, too. €€€

Hossegor
Les Hortensias du Lac
1578 avenue du Tour du Lac
40150 Hossegor
Tel: 05 58 43 99 00
Fax: 05 58 43 42 81
www.hortensia-du-lac.com
A pretty cluster of balconied rooms and cottages beside a lake on the Landes coast, with the stunning length of Atlantic beach only a short distance away. The hotel also has a good restaurant. €€

Sabres
Auberge des Pins
rue de la Piscine
40630 Sabres
Tel: 05 58 08 30 00
Fax: 05 58 07 56 74
www.aubergedespins.fr
Deep in the forest of the Landes, near the fascinating Ecomusée de Marquèze, is this *auberge* built in the Landaise style. It has comfortable rooms, some with jacuzzis. The traditional restaurant is well known for its regional cooking. €€

THE BASQUE COUNTRY

Ainhoa
Hôtel Ohantzea
64250 Ainhoa
Tel: 05 59 29 90 50
Fax: 05 59 29 89 70

A 17th-century half-timbered farmhouse in the green countryside of the inland Basque Country. It has been in the same family for three centuries. The large bedrooms have rustic furniture. No restaurant. €

Biarritz
Hôtel du Palais
1 avenue de l'Impératrice
64200 Biarritz
Tel: 05 59 41 64 00
Fax: 05 59 41 33 67 99
www.hotel-du-palais.com
A splendid hotel overlooking Biarritz's famous Grande Plage which was originally built for the Empress Eugénie. It has excellent facilities including a thalassotherapy spa and a seawater swimming pool. €€€€
Maison Garnier
29 rue Gambetta
64200 Biarritz
Tel: 05 59 01 60 70
Fax: 05 59 01 60 80
www.hotel-biarritz.com
A 19th-century Basque house with seven exquisitely restored rooms, all with antique furniture. €€

Hotel Price Guide

€ = **Budget** under €55
€€ = **Moderate** €55–115
€€€ = **Expensive** €115+
Prices are per double room.

Louisiane
rue Guy Petit
64200 Biarritz
Tel: 05 59 22 20 20
Fax: 05 59 24 95 77
www.louisiane-biarritz.com
Despite its unprepossessing modern exterior this is a conveniently located chain hotel with its own swimming pool. €€
Château du Clair de Lune
48 avenue Alan-Seeger
64200 Biarritz
Tel: 05 59 41 53 20
Fax: 05 05 59 41 53 29
Elegant late 19th century family house set in a quiet park just outside town. Breakfast at the *grande table*. No restaurant. €€

St-Étienne-de-Baigorry
Arcé
64430 St-Étienne-de-Baigorry
Tel: 05 59 37 40 14
Fax: 05 59 37 40 27
www.hotel-arce.com
Beside a river in a little Basque village with a beautiful, overhanging dining terrace. A very popular hotel with its airy public rooms, beamed dining room and charming bedrooms. €€

St-Jean-de-Luz
Hôtel Parc Victoria
5 rue Cépé
64500 St-Jean-de-Luz
Tel: 05 59 26 78 78
Fax: 05 59 26 78 08
www.parcvictoria.com
A 19th-century villa with a formal park, gardens and lawns. Luxurious rooms with marble bathrooms, some with balconies. Lunch by the pool, dine on the terrace. €€€
Chantaco
Golf de Chantaco
64500 St-Jean-de-Luz
Tel: 05 59 26 14 76
Fax: 05 59 26 35 97
www.hotelchantaco.com
Luxurious amenities in a beautiful Spanish-style building with huge fireplaces and French windows on to the garden and pool. Good restaurant. €€€

St-Jean-Pied-de-Port
Hôtel Central
place Charles de Gaulle
64220 St-Jean-Pied-de-Port
Tel: 05 59 37 00 22
Fax: 05 59 37 27 79
Old family hotel with views over the River Nive, and a restaurant specialising in eels from the river. €€
Maison Ramcèsamy
Quartier Rey 64290 Lasseube
Tel: 05 59 04 26 37
Bed and breakfast accommodation owned by Anglo-French couple, Isabelle and Simon Brown. Exquisite meals and tranquil views of rolling hills from the garden and swimming pool. Good base for exploring the Béarn region, Pau and the neighbouring Pyrenean valleys. €

HIGH PYRENEES

Arreau
Hôtel d'Angleterre
Route de Luchon
65240 Arreau
Tel: 05 62 98 63 30
Fax: 05 62 98 69 66
www.hotel-angleterre-arreau.com
In one of the prettiest of the
Pyrenees villages this is a well-run,
comfortable hotel in a valley below
the Col d'Aspin. Excellent
restaurant and swimming pool. €€
Le Miramont,
44 avenue des Pyrénées
65400 Argelès-Gazost
Tel: 05 62 97 01 26
Fax: 05 62 97 56 67
A most attractive hotel with Art
Déco touches, with 25 very
comfortable rooms – 19 with
balconies – a small garden and
excellent restaurant, Le Casaou.
Handy for the mountains, and a
short drive from Lourdes. €€

Bagnères-de-Luchon
Hôtel d'Étigny
31110 Luchon
Tel: 05 61 79 01 42
Fax: 05 61 79 80 64
Right opposite the impressive
thermal spa of this attractive town,
this classic hotel, with 61 rooms
and suites, could be a good base to
explore the mountains. €€

Cauterets
Hôtel du Lion d'Or
12 rue Richelieu
65110 Cauterets
Tel: 05 62 92 52 87
Fax: 05 62 92 03 67
www.hotel-lion-dor.net
In a popular resort town with
numerous hotels, this has to be
one of the nicest. A 19th-century
townhouse adorned with pretty
flowering window boxes, it is
centrally located and charmingly
furnished. You'll get friendly and
helpful service, too. €€

Gavarnie
Hotel Compostelle
rue de l'Eglise
Tel: 05 62 92 49 43
Sweet little hotel on the edge of the

Relais et Châteaux

Relais et Châteaux is a group of
prestigious, independently owned
hotels and restaurants in historic
buildings. A guide to them is
available from: **Relais et
Châteaux**, 35–37 Grosvenor
Gardens, London SW1W OBS;
tel: 020 7630 7667.

village of Gavarnie with fine views of
the Cirque, and its own parking.
Proprietor Yvan is also a mountain
guide and can organise walks. €

Gèdre
La Brèche de Roland
65120 Gèdre
Tel: 05 62 92 48 54
Fax: 05 62 92 46 05
A famous old mansion in the
mountains. There is a garden and
you can dine on the terrace. The
owner will help you arrange sporting
and helicopter trips. €

Lourdes
Grand Hôtel de la Grotte
66 rue Grotte
65100 Lourdes
Tel: 05 62 94 58 87
Fax: 05 62 94 20 50
www.hotel-grotte.com
Traditional grand hotel just below
the château with ring-side rooms
overlooking the basilica. €€
Hôtel Majestic
9 avenue Maransin
65100 Lourdes
Tel: 05 62 94 27 23
Fax: 05 62 94 64 91
Moderate option near the shrines
with good comfortable rooms, a
terrace and simple restaurant. €

Luz St-Sauveur
Hôtel Le Montagu
65120 Luz St-Sauveur
Tel: 05 62 92 81 71
Fax: 05 62 92 94 11
www.hotelmontagu.com
An attractive 55-room hotel. It is
located in a spectacular ski area in
winter and close to walks and
streams and the high Col du
Tourmalet. The hotel also has a
good restaurant. €€

Oloron Sainte-Marie
Alysson Hotel
boulevard des Pyrénées
64400 Oloron Sainte-Marie
Tel: 05 59 39 70 70
Fax: 05 59 39 24 47
www.alysson-hotel.fr
On the outskirts of town, this is a
pleasant modern hotel, with
gardens and a pool, and interesting
cuisine. A good base to explore the
beauties of Béarn. €€

Orthez
Hôtel-Restaurant La Reine Jeanne
44 rue Bourg-Vieux,
64300 Orthez
Tel: 05 59 67 00 76
Fax: 05 59 69 09 63
An imaginative and stylish
restoration of an old townhouse
provides this appealing hotel with
an elegant atrium. The 20 rooms
are well-equipped, and the
restaurant is first class. €€

Pau
Continental
2 rue du Maréchal-Foch
64000 Pau
Tel: 05 59 27 69 31
Fax: 05 59 27 99 84
Prestigious, comfortable hotel in a
wonderfully dated style. Near the
centre of town. €€
Grand Hôtel du Commerce
9 rue Maréchal Joffre
64000 Pau
Tel: 05 59 27 24 40
Fax: 05 59 83 81 74
A traditional and comfortable hotel
centrally located close to the
château. Its most appealing feature
is its lovely patio restaurant. €

St-Bertrand-de-Comminges
L'Oppidum
Ville Haute
31510 St-Bertrand-de-Comminges
Tel: 05 61 88 33 50
Fax: 05 61 95 94 04
www.hotel-oppidum.com
Next to the cathedral. Its 15 rooms
are comfortable and there is a
restaurant. €€

Sauveterre-de-Béarn
Hôtel de la Reine Sencié
rue du Pont de la Légende

64390 Sauveterre-de-Béarn
Tel: 05 59 38 95 11
Fax: 05 59 38 99 10
Sauveterre doesn't have much of a
selection of hotels but this at least
is a picturesque place with
medieval arches above the river
beside the ruined bridge. Behind
are the remains of the château and
old town. Access is by a fairly steep
and narrow road. There is a terrace
overlooking the river. **€**

Sauveterre-de-Comminges
Hostellerie des 7 Molles
31510 Sauveterre-de-Comminges
Tel: 05 61 88 30 87
Fax: 05 61 88 36 42
www.hotel7molles.com
Spacious hotel surrounded by
meadows and trees. The home farm
supplies sausages, foie gras and
trout and other home-made
products. **€€**

Tarbes
Hôtel Henri IV
7 avenue Bertrand Barère
65000 Tarbes
Tel: 05 62 34 01 68
Fax: 05 62 93 71 32
A pleasant, centrally located hotel
in the classic style. All its 24 rooms
are soundproofed, and with modern
comforts and facilities. **€€**

ARIÈGE

Aulus-les-Bains
Les Oussaillès
09140 Aulus-les-Bains
Tel: 05 61 96 03 68
Fax: 05 61 96 03 70
Mock Gothic turrets adorn this little
hotel with balconied rooms. You can
feast on delicious salads, trout or
veal or ask for a picnic basket to
take away; even vegetarians are
catered for. **€**

Ax-les-Thermes
Le Grillon
rue St-Udaut
09110 Ax-les-Thermes
Tel: 05 61 64 31 64
Fax: 05 61 64 67 76
www.hotel-le-grillon.com
Mountain hotel and restaurant with

magnificent views from the terrace.
Good local fare including duck
cutlet with honey. **€€**

Foix
Lons
6 place Georges Duthil
09000 Foix
Tel: 05 61 65 52 44
Fax: 05 61 02 68 18
www.hotel-lons-foix.com
Situated next to the river, this
friendly hotel has a terrace and a
pleasant restaurant. **€**

Mirepoix
La Maison des Consuls
6 place Couverte
09500 Mirepoix
Tel: 05 61 68 81 81
Fax: 05 61 68 81 15
www.maisondesconsuls.com
A 13th-century building in a lovely
arcaded square, with rooms
overlooking medieval streets. No
restaurant. **€€**

St-Girons
Eychenne
8 avenue Paul Laffont
09200 St Girons
Tel: 05 61 04 04 50
Fax: 05 61 96 07 20
A beautiful old family-run hostelry
with a friendly atmosphere, elegant
rooms, swimming pool and
secluded courtyard. **€€**
La Clairière
avenue de la Résistance
09200 St Girons
Tel: 05 61 66 66 66
Fax: 05 34 14 30 30
Modern wood-shingled hotel and
restaurant just outside St Girons,
with garden and swimming pool.
Restaurant offers such delights as
trout *en papillote*, duck cutlet, or
veal with *mousserons*, tiny local
mushrooms. **€**

THE AUDE

Carcassonne
Hôtel de la Cité
place de l'Église
11000 Carcassonne
Tel: 04 68 71 98 71
Fax: 04 68 71 50 15

Hotel Price Guide
€ = **Budget** under €55
€€ = **Moderate** €55–115
€€€ = **Expensive** €115+
Prices are per double room.

www.hoteldelacité.orientexpress.com
Luxury hotel with all the trimmings,
plush velvet and marble bathrooms,
all within the walls of Carcassonne's
atmospheric Cité. It also has a good
restaurant, La Barbacane. **€€**
The Bristol
7 avenue Foch
11000 Carcassonnne
Tel: 04 68 25 07 24
Fax: 04 68 25 71 89
Traditional grand 19th-century hotel
near the station, with rooms
overlooking the Canal du Midi. **€€**
Trois Couronnes
2 rue des Trois Couronnes
11000 Carcassonne
Tel: 04 68 25 36 10
Fax: 04 68 25 92 92
A modern hotel by the river in
the lower town, which makes up
for its unprepossessing appearance
with a stupendous view of La
Cité, and a very good restaurant.
€€

Limoux
Grand Hôtel Moderne et Pigeon
place Général Leclerc
11300 Limoux
Tel: 04 68 31 00 25
Fax: 04 68 31 12 43
www.grandhotelmoderneetpigeon.fr
Former convent with beautiful
stained-glass lobby, comfortable
rooms and popular restaurant. **€€**

Narbonne
Hôtel France
6 rue Rossini
11100 Narbonne
Tel: 04 68 32 09 75
Fax: 04 68 65 50 30
Small old-fashioned hotel in quiet
street near the covered food
market. No restaurant. **€**
Chateau l'Hospitalet
Route de Narbonne Plage
11100 Narbonne
Tel: 04 68 45 34 47
Fax: 04 68 45 27 17

Wine domaine on the Clape Massif in an idyllic setting of vineyards overlooking the sea. Rooms in the *auberge* plus a restaurant, and a few small museums thrown in. €€

Ornaisons
Relais du Val d'Orbieu
11200 Ornaisons (on D24)
Tel: 04 68 27 10 27
Fax: 04 68 27 52 44
Comfortable renovated farmhouse outside the village, with pool, tennis court and restaurant. €€

Villesque-des-Corbières
Domaine Haut Gléon
11360 Villesque-des-Corbières
Tel: 04 68 48 85 95
Fax: 04 68 48 46 20
Wine estate with comfortable rustically stylish accommodation in renovated stable wing. No restaurant, but excellent wine to taste. €€

FRENCH CATALONIA

Banyuls-sur-Mer
Les Elmes
Plages des Elmes
66650 Banyuls-sur-Mer
Tel: 04 68 88 03 12
Fax: 04 68 88 53 03
Excellent little seaside hotel with its own beach and a good restaurant. €€

Céret
La Terrasse au Soleil
Route Fontfrède
66400 Ceret
Tel: 04 68 87 01 94
Fax: 04 6887 39 24
www.laterrasse-au-soleil.com
Gorgeous restored farmhouse overlooking the artists' town of Céret, with terrace gardens, pool, and a celebrated restaurant. €€€
Hotel des Arcades
1 place Picasso
66400 Ceret
Tel: 04 68 87 12 30
Fax: 04 68 87 49 44
Small hotel artistically decorated with balconies overlooking the market square. €

Collioure
Casa Pairal
Impasse des Palmiers
66190 Collioure
Tel: 04 68 82 05 81
Fax: 04 68 82 52 10
www.roussillonhotel.com
Luxurious 19th-century Catalan villa in palm tree-shaded garden with fountains and pool. No restaurant. €€
Les Templiers
quai de l'Amirauté
66190 Collioure
Tel: 04 68 98 31 10
Fax: 04 68 98 01 24
www.hotel-templiers.com
Right on the quayside of this attractive resort, with a funky old-fashioned bar full of donated art, pleasantly decorated rooms and a good restaurant. €€

Molitg-les-Bains
Château de Riell
66500 Molitg-les-Bains
Tel: 04 68 05 04 40
Fax: 04 68 05 04 37
www.relaischateaux.com
Neo-Gothic folly of a hotel full of Art Nouveau decor, with exotic gardens, pool and superb restaurant, which uses local ingredients, especially herbs, with great originality. (Closed Nov–Mar.) €€€
The Grand Hôtel Thermal
66500 Molitg-les-Bains
Tel: 04 68 05 00 50
Fax: 04 68 05 02 91
Part of the same complex as Château de Riell, above; not as pricey but almost as splendid, with marble spa rooms, swimming pool and marble terrace. (Closed Nov–Mar.) €€

Mosset
Mas Lluganas
66500 Mosset
Tel: 04 68 05 00 37
Fax: 04 68 05 04 08
www.maslluganas.com
A simple *ferme auberge* in a quiet valley, offering meals based entirely on the farm produce, ducks, foie gras, beef, garden vegetables, peaches and cherries. Further accommodation available at La Forge, beside the river. €

Olette
La Fontaine
3 rue de la Fusterie.
Tel: 04 68 97 03 67
Fax: 04 68 97 03 67
Village hotel on the route to Font Romeu, with pleasant rooms and hearty meals of rabbit or lamb. €

Perpignan
Hôtel de la Loge
1 rue Fabrique d'en Nabot
66000 Perpignan
Tel: 04 68 34 41 02
Fax: 04 68 34 25 13
www.hoteldelaloge.fr
Charming little hotel in 16th-century building in the middle of the old town, with secluded courtyard. €€
La Poste et Perdrix
6 rue Fabrique d'en Nabot
66000 Perpignan
Tel: 04 68 34 42 53
Fax: 04 68 34 58 20
Run by the same family since 1832 and the decor looks pretty much unchanged since then. But it is friendly and cheap. €
Hotel de France
quai Sadi Carnot
Tel: 04 68 34 92 81
Centrally located on quai Vauban, next to the river and the Castillet, is this traditional 19th-century hotel with antique furniture and original lift. $
Villa Duflot
Rondpoint Albert Dunnezan
66000 Perpignan
Tel: 04 68 56 67 67
Fax: 04 68 56 54 05
www.villa-duflot.com
Comfortable modern luxury hotel with swimming pool and highly regarded restaurant. Oddly located in the middle of the commercial zone, but convenient for motorway stopover (Perpignan Sud exit). €€€

Valcebollère
Les Écureuils
66340 Valcebollère
Tel: 04 68 04 52 03
Fax: 04 68 04 52 34
Mountain inn in the Cerdagne, with attractive rooms and serving local cuisine. Proprietor Étienne Lafitte will take you on guided mountain walks following smugglers' paths €€

HÉRAULT AND GARD

Collias

Hostellerie le Castellas
30210 Collias (take D3 from D981)
Tel: 04 66 22 88 88
Fax: 04 66 22 8428
www.lecastellas.com
Charming hotel, converted from
several village houses, with elegant
restaurant, sheltered garden, tiny
pool and pretty rooms. €€

Ganges

Château des Madières
34190 Ganges
Tel: 04 67 73 84 03
Fax: 04 67 73 55 71
A 14th-century fortress with
spectacular views over the Vis River
gorge. Renaissance fireplace and
medieval arches combine with
modern comfort. €€

Hotel Price Guide

€ = **Budget** under €55
€€ = **Moderate** €55–115
€€€ = **Expensive** €115+
Prices are per double room.

Montpellier

Hôtel du Palais
3 rue du Palais
34000 Montpellier
Tel: 04 67 60 47 38
Fax: 04 67 60 40 23
Close to the Jardin des Plantes, off
a quiet, shady square in a smart
part of town; old mansion with
balconied rooms. €€

Demeure des Brousses
538 rue du Mas des Brousses
Route de Vauguières
34000 Montpellier
Tel: 04 67 65 77 66
Fax: 04 67 22 22 17
www.demeure-des-brousses.fr
An 18th-century farmhouse
surrounded by a park, with good
restaurant. €€

Nîmes

Le Royal Hôtel
3 boulevard Alphonse Daudet
30000 Nîmes
Tel: 04 66 58 28 27
Fax: 04 66 58 28 28

Artistic little hotel next to the
new art museum, with palm-fronded
lobby, and popular *tapas* bar. €€

New Hôtel la Baume
21 rue Nationale
30000 Nîmes
Tel: 04 66 76 28 42
Fax: 04 66 66 76 28 45
www.new-hotel.com
A 17th-century mansion with
elegant modern interior, chic,
spacious rooms and bathrooms.
Restaurant and room service. €€

Hotel La Maison de Sophie
31 avenue Carnot, Nîmes
Tel: 04 66 70 96 10
www.hotel-lamaisondesophie.com
Discreet and elegant hotel in
mansion with pool and flower-filled
garden. Very popular with stars
during the *Feria*. $$$

L'Hacienda
Chemin du Mas de Brignon
30320 Marguerittes (near Nîmes)
Tel: 04 66 75 02 25
Fax: 04 66 75 45 58
www.hotel-hacienda-nimes.com
A large farmhouse hotel north of
Nîmes, with swimming pool,
terraces and restaurant. €€

St-Saturnin-de-Lucian

Ostalaria Cardabela
10 place de la Fontaine
34800 St-Saturnin-de-Lucian
Tel: 04 67 88 62 62
Fax: 04 67 88 62 82
Tastefully restored small hotel, with
stone walls, tiled floors and modern
furniture. Stylish bedrooms. €€

Sète

Grand Hotel
17 quai Maréchal de Lattre-de-
Tassigny
34200 Sète
Tel: 04 67 74 71 77
Fax: 04 67 74 29 27
www.sete-hotel.com
Splendid Belle Époque hotel with
enclosed glass atrium overlooking
Sète's Grand Canal. €€

Uzès

Hôtel d'Entraigues
place de l'Evêché
30700 Uzès
Tel: 04 66 22 32 68
Fax: 04 66 22 56 10

A 17th-century townhouse hotel
with antique-furnished rooms and a
pool curiously suspended over the
dining room. Also a restaurant,
Jardins de Castille. €€

Vergèze

La Passiflore
1 rue Neuve
30310 Vergèze
Tel: 04 66 35 00 00
Fax: 04 66 35 09 21
English-run village hotel with
enclosed courtyard; attractively
decorated, very friendly and
excellent food, from French classics
to apple crumble. Well placed for
autoroute travellers or the
Camargue. €€

Pont du Gard

La Begude Saint-Pierre
RD981 (adjacent to Pont du Gard)
Tel: 04 66 63 63 63
www.hotel-saintpierre.fr
Newly renovated old post house,
with huge garden and swimming
pool, parking and restaurant. $$

Where to Eat

Eating Out

One of the great pleasures of visiting Southwest France is its glorious food, and wherever you go you will find a wide variety of different restaurants from simple *auberges* to the great classics.

Many hotels have their own restaurants, and many restaurants also have rooms to rent. This selection includes good regional restaurants with typical local dishes as well as some of the great stars of French cuisine.

In the regions it is always worth seeking out typical local restaurants and sampling the specialities of the region. Increasingly, the regional produce is itself the focus of the great chefs who compete in their stylish treatment of "peasant" food and traditional dishes. Sometimes the results can be sensational, but very often the simple classics, a perfect duck cutlet, a slow-cooked *cassoulet*, fresh goats' cheese, grilled sardines or a plateful of oysters still deliver the taste of the region best.

Dining Habits

It is essential to be aware of dining hours in the Southwest. Most people stop for *midi* (lunchtime), and often lunch will start as early as midday. By one o'clock it is almost too late, and they may not serve at all beyond 2pm. Evening meals are usually at 8pm and in smaller or country places you may not get dinner after 9pm.

At the height of the season, or if you have a particular place in mind, reservations are recommended. Restaurants often have outdoor tables for dining out in fine weather.

The French usually eat salad after the main course and sometimes with the cheese. Cheese comes before dessert. You will almost always be given bread with your meal, water will be supplied if asked for, and should be safe to drink. You will find wine lists often reflect the region so all the wine regions will have predominantly local wines on the list. The restaurateur will usually be delighted to advise you. All restaurants will offer a *vin de pays* by the carafe *(pichet)* or demi-carafe and this is almost always good value and perfectly drinkable.

Although some restaurants are divided into *fumeurs* and *non fumeurs* (smoking or non-smoking) smoking is still widely accepted in France and you may need to specify if you prefer a non-smoking section.

Cafés

Although there has sadly been a significant decline in the number of French cafés in recent years, they remain a French institution, good for morning coffee, reading the paper, drinks or snacks. In smaller towns and villages they are very much the centre of local life. Note that if you drink at the bar it is usually cheaper than sitting at a table. Apart from wine, there is a variety of aperitifs available, many of them locally produced; Byrrh or Banyuls for example, and sweet Muscat is often served chilled as an aperitif. Excellent brandy in the form of Cognac or Armagnac is also produced here.

Restaurant Listings

Restaurants are grouped according to the chapters of the book. Restaurant locations are listed in alphabetical order below the area

Lunchtime Specials

There are usually cheaper menus available at lunchtime, when most French people eat their biggest meal of the day.

name. The prices of the restaurants are indicated as follows:

€ = Budget: under €25
€€ = Moderate: €25–50
€€€ = Expensive: €50+

(average menu prices per person, not including wine or coffee. Note that menu prices at lunchtime are often half the price of the evening menu.) Credit cards are accepted unless otherwise indicated.

BORDEAUX AND THE GIRONDE

Arcachon
Chez Yvette
59 boulevard de Général-Leclerc
Tel: 05 56 83 05 11
Excellent fresh seafood combined with seasonal local vegetables in dishes like *fricassée* of octopus with Espelette peppers or *soupe de poisson d'Arcachon* (fish soup). €€

Arcins-en-Médoc
Le Lion d'Or
place de la République
Tel: 05 56 58 96 79
Not quite the usual village *auberge*, although well frequented at lunchtime by the local workers. Specialises in fish from the Gironde estuary and game in season. The cooking is Bordelais style at its purest, the ambience unpretentious yet comfortable, and the moderate menu prices include wine. €€

Bordeaux
Le Vieux Bordeaux
27 rue Buhan
Tel: 05 56 52 94 36
Charming restaurant with a secluded courtyard for summer dining, and classic cuisine. €€
Le Chapon Fin
5 rue de Montesquieu
Tel: 05 56 79 10 10
Bordeaux's finest restaurant decor (a turn-of-the-20th-century winter garden) is the setting for celebrated and delicious cooking, which combines traditional *cuisine bordelaise* (Bordeaux cuisine) with more personal and inventive touches. €€€

Menus

Menus must by law be displayed outside any establishment. Most places will offer a *prix-fixe* menu, a set meal at a particular price, sometimes (but not always) including wine. Otherwise you must order separate items from the menu. Eating from a fixed-price menu is nearly always the best value, unless you really only want just one or two particular dishes.

Le Pavillon des Boulevards
120 rue Croix de Seguey
Tel: 05 56 81 51 02
A meal at Denis Franc's restaurant, with its ultra-modern decor, is usually full of surprises: no one in the Southwest makes a more creative use of contrasting tastes and textures. €€
Le St-James
3 place Camille-Hostein
Tel: 05 57 97 06 00
Simple and often rustic ingredients are given Mediterranean-style treatment by master-chef Jean-Marie Amat in this old wine-grower's house, revamped by the celebrated architect, Jean Nouvel. Splendid view over the Garonne. €€€

Libourne
Les Démons de Bacchus
4 rue Fonneuve
Tel: 05 57 25 01 00
It would be hard to find better value than in this old-fashioned restaurant and wine bar just off the place Abel-Surchamp. Traditional cuisine includes an *omelette aux cèpes* (mushroom omelette) to die for, and some mouth-watering grills. The delicious bread here is all home-made. €

Margaux
Auberge de Savoie
1 place de la Ramoilles
Tel: 05 57 88 31 76
A good-value restaurant with tempting regional dishes on the menu such as duck liver quiche with truffles. €

Montalivet
Hôtel-Restaurant de la Plage
Tel: 05 56 09 31 13
15 km (11 miles) south of Soulac-sur-Mer, this excellent restaurant is right on the sea-front of a relatively quiet and charming old-fashioned resort. Fish features prominently on the menu, the cooking is outstanding and great value for money, and children are made especially welcome in this friendly and family-run business. €

Pauillac
Château Cordeillan-Bages
Tel: 05 56 59 24 24
The emphasis in this 17th-century former charterhouse is on unfussy but modern cuisine and top-quality produce, which chef Thierry Marx selects with great care. A staggering selection of Bordeaux. Closed Sat pm. €€€

St-Émilion
Hostellerie de Plaisance
place du Clocher
Tel: 05 57 55 07 55
Splendid views of the exquisite medieval town of St-Émilion and surrounding vineyards as you dine on local cuisine and, of course, local wine at the heart of wine country. €€
Les Epicuriens
27 rue Guadet
Tel: 05 57 24 70 49
The high quality of cooking and service in this temple to *la haute cuisine* is reflected in the prices, yet the value remains unbeatable. This is local *Bordelais* cuisine at its highest level: try the pastry-baked pigeon with baby turnips or tournedos of duck breast. The wine list, too, reflects the pride and care which Francis Goullée takes in this superb restaurant. €€

Sauternes
Le Saprien
14 rue Principale
Tel: 05 56 76 60 87
As well as carefully prepared local cuisine, there is an imaginative touch to several local dishes like duck cutlet or fish from the Gironde.

The restaurant is in a delightful, ancient village house, with a terrace overlooking the vineyards. €–€€

DORDOGNE

Bergerac
Le Cyrano
2 boulevard Montaigne
Tel: 05 53 57 07 30
Good-value restaurant for the classic cuisine of Périgord accompanied by delicious Bergerac wines. €€

Brantôme
Le Moulin de l'Abbaye
1 Route de Bourdeilles
Tel: 05 53 05 80 22
Sit on the terrace of the old mill that was once the house of the Abbé Pierre de Bourdeilles, watch the River Dronne roll by and sample the excellent cuisine; pigeon with *cèpes*, duck foie gras, *crème brûlée* with local Périgord strawberries. €€

Les Eyzies-de-Tayac
Le Centenaire
Tel: 05 53 06 68 68
Regional cuisine in an elegant setting. The keynotes of chef Roland Mazère's superb cooking are foie gras and *cèpe* mushrooms in every guise. A particularly wide-ranging wine list. €€

Limeuil
Hôtel Isabeau de Limeuil,
rue de Port
Tel: 05 53 63 39 19
Enjoy a meal down near the old harbour. Try their hot foie gras with apples. €€

Périgueux
Hercule Poirot
2 rue de la Nation
24000 Périgueux
Tel: 05 53 08 90 76
Renaissance building with fine

Restaurant Prices

€ = **Budget** under €25
€€ = **Moderate** €25–50
€€€ = **Expensive** €50 and over

vaulted ceilings serving the best of Périgord cuisine. €€

Sarlat-la-Canéda
La Madeleine
1 place de la Petite Rigaudie
Tel: 05 53 59 10 41
All forms of regional delicacies from foie gras to truffles on offer in this popular hotel/restaurant in Sarlat, centre of Périgord cuisine. €€€
Les Quatre Saisons
2 Côte de Toulouse
Tel: 05 53 29 48 59
Quiet, pretty restaurant offering good menus at all prices. In summer tables are set in an attractive flowered courtyard. €–€€
Saint-Romain-et-Saint-Clément
Le Moulin de Feuyas
Tel: 05 53 55 03 99
Charming *auberge* on the banks of the Dordogne, where you can dine simply on local delicacies, from duck and goose to peaches and raspberries. Reservation essential. $$

LOT

Cahors
Claude Marco
Lamagdelaine
Tel: 05 65 35 30 64
A creeper-covered old *bergerie* (barn) with vaulted ceilings and summer terrace. Specialities include the *pot au feu* with duck or *filet de bœuf* with morel mushrooms. €€

Figeac
La Dineé du Viguier
4 rue Boutaric
Tel: 05 65 50 08 08
Hotel-restaurant in medieval château serving such delights as gigot of monkfish with truffles and Quercy tart with morel mushrooms. €€

Poudenas
Le Moulin de la Belle Gasconne
Tel: 05 53 65 71 58
Mme García is author of a cookbook on Southwestern French food and cooks it to perfection in

Picnics

The French create superb ready-prepared fresh foods, and a visit to a *boulangerie* for bread, and a delicatessen for cheese, ham, salad and fruit can provide you with a perfect picnic. Cool the wine and water in the river.

her tranquil stone-built riverside mill. Dine on the terrace and try the *Grand Repas Gascon* (the house speciality large lunch). €€€

Puymirol
Les Loges de l'Aubergade
52 rue Royale
Tel: 05 53 95 31 46
Despite jokey names like *hamburger de foie gras chaud aux cèpes*, controversial Michel Trama's culinary creations can be as instantly appealing as the 13th-century building in which his restaurant is housed. €€€

Rocamadour
Sainte-Marie
place de Senhals
Tel: 05 65 33 63 07
Rustic restaurant with a terrace serving excellent local cuisine. €

St-Cirq-Lapopie
Auberge de Sombral
Tel: 05 65 31 26 08
Charming medieval village inn with a delightful terrace serving local dishes like Quercy lamb. (Lunch only.) €€

St-Médard
Le Gindreau
Tel: 05 65 36 22 27
Truffles, local lamb and foie gras are among the highlights of Alexis Pelissou's delicious, carefully spiced and seasonally oriented cuisine. A bewildering choice of top-class Southwest wines. €€

Souillac
La Vieille Auberge
1 rue de la Recège
Tel: 05 65 32 79 43
Grandly decorated old *auberge* with rooms overlooking the river, offering

local delicacies such as artichokes stuffed with foie gras and truffles. €€

AVEYRON AND THE CÉVENNES

Conques
Hôtel Ste-Foy
rue Principale
Tel: 05 65 69 84 03
One of Aveyron's best hotel-restaurants, a charming stone and timber building beautifully restored, with intimate but spacious dining room and flowery courtyard. Inventive cooking and menu changed daily. €€

Espalion
Le Méjane
8 rue Méjane
Tel: 05 65 48 22 37
In his tiny underrated restaurant, the inventive Philippe Caralp offers a delicate and refreshing version of regional cuisine. The excellent wine list and friendly service are an added bonus. €€

Lacave
Le Pont de l'Ouysse
Tel: 05 65 37 87 04
Talented chef Daniel Chambon champions local produce (crayfish, *cèpes*, truffles, foie gras) in his succinct but inventive range of dishes. The wine list has a good selection of Cahors. €€

Laguiole
Michel Bras
Tel: 05 65 51 18 20
The salad plants, herbs and mushrooms of the surrounding Aubrac plateau, as well as locally produced meat and cheese, form the backbone of Michel Bras's inspired cuisine, which has earned him a third Michelin star. €€€

ALBI AND TARN

Albi
Le Jardin des Quatre Saisons
19 boulevard de Strasbourg
Tel: 05 63 60 77 76

Popular local restaurant for high-quality peasant-style cooking, such as terrine of snails with pig's trotters and truffles. €€

Cordes-sur-Ciel
Grand Écuyer
Hant de la Cité
Tel: 05 63 53 79 50
Splendid Gothic building with wonderful views. Try duck *foie gras*, pigeon with rosemary and local Gaillac wines. €€

St-Félix-Lauragais
L'Auberge du Poids Public
Tel: 05 62 18 85 00
Glorious food at very good value prices are on offer from Claude Taffarello, who is a standard-bearer of the culinary traditions, products and wines of the Lauragais region. €€

Sidobre
Relais du Sidobre
8 Route de Vabre, Lacrouzette
Tel: 05 63 50 60 06
This minimally decorated restaurant concentrates on classic regional food, served in cosy surroundings in winter, on a terrace in summer. €

Cuisine Minceur

The light, low-calorie cooking of *cuisine minceur* was invented by chef Michel Guérard in the 1970s. It makes less use of fatty meats and dairy products than traditional French cooking and more use of vegetables.

TOULOUSE

Brasserie des Beaux-Arts
1 quai de la Daurade
Tel: 05 61 21 12 12
Lively popular *brasserie* on the corner of the quay by the river. The shellfish is displayed outside and the oysters are recommended. €
Brasserie Le Bibent
5 place du Capitole
Tel: 05 61 23 89 03
One of the best-known of the many old cafés around the the main square of the city, and one of the

most formal. Elegant Belle Époque plasterwork inside. €€
La Daurade
quai de la Daurade
Tel: 05 61 22 10 33
Permanently moored, floating restaurant serving regional specialities, including grilled meats and fish. Economical lunchtime menu. €
Frégate
1 rue d'Austerlitz
Tel: 05 61 21 62 45
Long-established restaurant overlooking place Wilson, serving classic dishes such as *cassoulet*, and duck in all its forms. €€
Les Jardins de l'Opéra
place du Capitole
Tel: 05 61 23 07 76
The top Toulouse restaurant, a grand Belle Époque extravaganza, serving luxurious classics like foie gras ravioli and truffles. €€€
Jonque du Yang Tsé
boulevard Griffoul-Dorval
Tel: 05 61 20 74 74
Excellent and original Szechwan Chinese cooking in a converted barge on the Canal du Midi. €€
Michel Sarran
21 boulevard A. Duportal
Tel: 05 61 12 32 32
Handsome 19th-century building houses a restaurant serving Sarran's individual specialities. Booking recommended. €€€
Le Pastel
237 Route de Saint-Simon
Tel: 05 62 87 84 30
Friendly restaurant with a delightful terrace giving on to an informal, English-style garden. Owner-chef Gérard Garrigues excels in his judicious use of spices and imaginative treatment of vegetables. €€
Le Sherpa
rue de Taur 46
Tel: 05 61 23 89 29
Crêperie between the place du Capitole and St-Sernin church. Young, informal atmosphere. A variety of teas and ice creams are available as well as savoury or sweet crêpes. €
La Cantine du Curé
2 rue des Couteliers
Tel: 05 61 25 83 42

Cosy little restaurant in the old quarter near the river offers hearty "peasant" dishes at very reasonable prices. $

GASCONY

Auch
Jardin des Saveurs
2 place de la Libération
Tel: 05 62 61 71 84
Restaurant of the celebrated Hôtel de France, where chef Roland Garreau has succeeded in producing regional cuisine with great style. €€€

Condom
Table des Cordeliers
rue Cordeliers
Tel: 05 62 28 03 68
Restaurant housed in a 14th-century chapel with a terrace in summer. Superb regional cuisine and *foie gras de la maison*. €€

Eugénie-les-Bains
Les Prés d'Eugénie
Tel: 05 58 05 06 07
Michel Guérard, inventor of *cuisine minceur*, runs two restaurants here along with an immensely luxurious spa hotel and rustic *auberge*.
Restaurant Michel Guérard offers food with the emphasis on healthy eating with great style (€€€); and the gorgeously rustic *auberge*, **La Ferme aux Grives** offers very reasonably priced *cuisine villageoise*: country-style lunches and dinners. (€€)

Lectoure
Hôtel-Restaurant de Bastard
Tel: 05 62 68 82 44
Tucked into this sturdy hotel, close to the cathedral, is the small, high-windowed restaurant long ruled over by the esteemed Jean-Luc Arnaud. Imaginative menus feature Gascony's most delicious specialities. Drinks overlooking the pool are a good start to a meal. €€

Magescq
Relais de la Poste
Tel: 05 58 47 70 25
It's worth going out of your way to

savour the superb cooking of Bernard Coussau and his son Jean in this handsome restaurant (it's a glamorous hotel, too). Varied menus include fresh salmon from the Adour River, and the desserts are delicious. €€€

Manciet
La Bonne Auberge
Tel: 05 62 08 50 04
Just off the main east–west N124, this excellent restaurant has a sunny interior terrace and an elegant dining room. The cuisine is classy, the menus following seasons and Gascon favourites. The restaurant also has a remarkable collection of Armagnacs. €€

Restaurant Prices

€ = **Budget** under €25
€€ = **Moderate** €25–50
€€€ = **Expensive** €50+

Mimizan
Au Bon Coin du Lac
Tel: 05 58 09 01 55
This is a family-run hotel situated on a freshwater lake a mile or so from the coast, with a fine restaurant specialising in the refined cooking of fish bought from the nearby bay of Arcachon. Try sole soufflé with langoustines, for example. €€

Montréal
Chez Simone
Opposite the church
Tel: 05 62 29 44 40
A fine old building attractively decorated with frescoes and housing a restaurant known for its duck and foie gras, truffle omelettes, and range of fine old Armagnacs. €

Uchacq
Didier Garbage
RN 134
Tel: 05 58 75 33 66
Didier Garbage is one of the regions's finest and most colourful chefs. His *cuisine du terroir* (country cuisine) – using the

freshest authentic local food – draws enthusiasts to his restaurant just north of Mont-de-Marsan. €€

THE BASQUE COUNTRY

Ainhoa
Ithurria
place du Fronton
Tel: 05 59 29 92 11
A family-run restaurant in a traditional Basque house, with peaceful gardens and an intimate atmosphere. Typical dishes include *foie gras des Landes*, roast pigeon with garlic or Basque *cassoulet* with red beans. €€

Barcus
Hotel Chilo
Tel: 05 59 28 90 79
Friendly hotel in a small village near the Spanish border serving exceptional food which draws visitors from far and wide; imaginative Basque specialities cooked by the Chilo family from the fresh game, fruit and vegetables they collect every day from the market. €

Biarritz
Café de la Grande Plage
1 avenue Edouard VII
Tel: 05 59 22 77 88
Overlooking the Grande Plage, good for people watching and ocean gazing, a fully restored 1930s-style brasserie cafe, with a wide range of drinks, snacks and meals. €
Café de Paris & Bistrot Bellevue
5 place Bellevue
Tel: 05 59 24 19 53
Stylish Art Déco restaurant close to the sea front, serving classic cuisine; the Bistrot Bellevue serves delicious fish dishes. (Chic rooms above have magnificent sea views, and some have huge terraces.) €€€
Campagne et Gourmandise
52 avenue Alan Seeger
Tel: 05 59 41 10 11
Restaurant a few kilometres south of Biarritz where you can dine on a terrace with splendid views of the Pyrenees. Regional cooking with a twist includes dishes like fricassée

of mushrooms with a herb topping or oxtail with foie gras. €€
Le Clos Basque
12 rue Louis Barthou
Tel: 05 59 24 24 96
Authentic little bistro with stone walls and Spanish tiles, and a pretty terrace. It serves local cuisine including Basque specialities, such as squid with peppers. €
Le Galion
17 boulevard du Gén. de Gaulle
Tel: 05 59 24 20 32
Terrace overlooking the beach and casino gardens. Well-prepared Basque seafood. Especially good are the stuffed squid in a sauce of their own ink. €€
Goulue
3 rue E. Ardouin
Tel: 05 59 24 90 90
Cosy Belle Époque-style restaurant with pictures of old Biarritz on the walls. For classic local dishes, try a plateful of baby squid or monkfish cooked with bacon. €€
La Villa Eugénie
Hôtel du Palais
1 avenue de l'Impératrice
Tel: 05 59 41 64 00
A very grand establishment (Empress Eugénie lived here) with a view over the sea, but the service is relaxed and the superb cuisine decidedly Basque. €€€

Bidarray
Auberge Iparla
Chemin de l'Eglise
05 59 37 77 21
This typical red-shuttered Basque house shelters another star in the Alain Ducasse empire, and gives stylish treatment to local classics; trout, pork and sausages, and tuna from St Jean de Luz. €€

Cambo-les-Bains
Chez Tante Ursule
Bas Cambo
Tel: 05 59 29 78 23
Small rustic restaurant serving Basque classics like pimentoes stuffed with salt cod or salads with foie gras or black pudding. €

Espelette
Euzkadi
Tel: 05 59 93 91 88

Basque restaurant in a house with a half-timbered façade hung with clusters of Espelette peppers. €€

St-Jean-de-Luz
Chez Mattin
63 rue E. Baignol
Tel: 05 59 47 19 52
A restaurant well known for its Basque specialities, with traditional decor and a warm family welcome. Sample the stuffed peppers or the Basque gâteau. €€

St-Jean-Pied-de-Port
Les Pyrénées
19 place du Général de Gaulle
Tel: 05 59 37 01 01
A very popular hotel-restaurant with a terrace, well known for the quality of its Basque/Gascon cuisine. Chef Firmin Arrambide has for decades proved unfailingly inventive dishes while remaining deeply rooted in the Basque culinary tradition. Rooms available. It gets a mention (not by name) in the last chapter of David Lodge's novel, *Therapy*. €€€

Tipping

A service charge is usually included in the final bill, so there is no need to add more, unless the service has been particularly good, in which case a couple of euros is always acceptable.

Urt
Auberge de la Galupe
place du Port
Tel: 05 59 56 21 84
This unspoilt 17th-century inn offers stunning, rustic yet highly sophisticated cuisine with a strong Basque streak, particularly inspired when cooking locally caught fish. €€

HIGH PYRENEES

Arudy
Hôtel de France
1 place de l'Hôtel de Ville
Tel: 05 59 05 60 16
In a small, ancient town is this friendly old hotel with a large dining

room offering unpretentious but very good *cuisine régionale*. Rooms are modest and comfortable. €

Bagnères-de-Luchon
Auberge de Castel-Vielh
Route de Superbagnères
Tel: 05 61 79 36 79
Country inn in typical Pyrenean style with garden and terrace, with a popular restaurant serving local delicacies. Rooms available. €€

Lannes
Hôtel-Restaurant Lacassie
Tel: 05 59 32 62 05
In the Barétous valley, this attractive little hotel southwest of Oloron is deep in Musketeer country. Unpretentious and pleasant, it offers good regional meals. Rooms are available. €

Pau
Restaurant La Brochetterie
16 rue Henri-IV
Tel: 05 59 27 40 33.
Restaurant near the château, popular for its grilled duck and spit-roasted pig and lamb. €
Chez Pierre
16 rue Louis-Barthou
Tel: 05 59 27 76 86
"Très British" in style with golf clubs over the bar, but the cooking definitely isn't; count on local foie gras and Béarnais *cassoulet*. €€

St-Bertand-de-Comminges
Lugdunum
Valcabrère
Tel: 05 61 95 88 22
Culinary history is celebrated here with recipes compiled by Apicius, the ancient Roman gastronome of the 1st century. For example, young boar or partridge served with wines seasoned with spices from the region. Reservations essential. €€

Tarbes
L'Ambroisie
48 rue Abbé Tornne
Tel: 05 62 93 09 34
Near the cathedral and the Maison du Maréchal Foch, this is probably the nicest restaurant in Tarbes. Specialities including *escalope de foie gras* and exquisite salads,

cooked with what the critics call an incontestable brio. €€

ARIÈGE

Aulus-les-Bains
Les Oussaillès
Tel: 05 61 96 03 68
Here you can feast on delicious salads, trout or veal or ask for a picnic basket to take away; vegetarians are also catered for. €

Carla-Bayle
Auberge Pierre Bayle
rue Principale
Tel: 05 61 60 63 95
Bar and restaurant with views of the Pyrenees for simple local cuisine such as warm *chèvre* (goat's cheese) salad with honey, and *confit de canard* with *cèpes*. €

Foix
Auberge des Myrtilles
D17 Route Verte west of Foix up to the Col de Marrous
Tel: 05 61 65 16 46
A sweet little half-timbered mountain *auberge*, tucked away in the forest, specialising in grills, local trout and duck sausage and, naturally, *tarte aux myrtilles*, mountain bilberry tart. €
Le Phoebus,
3 Cours Irénee-Cros
Tel: 05 61 65 10 42
Popular local restaurant with balcony facing the château, for local produce with a rich twist; try duck liver with caramelised apples or duck with Amagnac. Good wine list. €

Roquefixade
Le Relais des Trois Châteaux
Palot
Tel: 05 61 01 33 99
Pretty hotel and restaurant offering a changing menu according to season; try combinations like eel with shrimps, kidneys with *cèpes*, or frogs' legs with grapes. €

St-Girons
Eychenne
8 avenue Paul Laffont
Tel: 05 61 04 04 50

A beautiful old family-run hotel and restaurant with a friendly atmosphere and courtyard for summer dining. Try the monkfish with saffron or duck *confit* with *cèpes*. €€

THE AUDE

Bages
Portanel
passage du Portanel
Tel: 04 68 42 81 66
One of a number of excellent fish and seafood restaurants in this tiny *étang* village; this one in a fisherman's cottage with views of the lagoon specialises in serving eel in every imaginable way. The *menu de dégustation* (taster menu) offers 10 different eel dishes. €–€€

Carcassonne
La Barbacane
Hôtel de la Cité, place de l'Église
Tel: 06 68 71 98 71
A palatial neo-Gothic setting in tune with the film-set atmosphere of Carcassonne's Cité. Franck Putelat's excellent cuisine is highly catholic in its use of ingredients and cooking styles. Also has rooms.
Brasserie le Donjon
2 rue Comte Roger
Tel: 04 68 25 95 72
Within the walls of the Cité is this smart restaurant serving traditional dishes like *cassoulet* or foie gras with great style. €€
Jardins de la Tour
11 rue Porte d'Aude
Tel: 04 68 25 71 24
Pretty, idiosyncratic restaurant within the Cité with garden dining and authentic regional dishes and fish. Reserve in high season. €
Le Languedoc
32 allée d'Iéna
Tel: 04 68 25 22 17
After visiting the medieval Cité head for this local restaurant in the Basse Ville for an authentic *cassoulet*, the regional Languedoc dish of beans, pork, duck and sausages. €€

Fontfroide
Abbaye de Fontfroide
Tel: 04 68 45 11 08

Chef Florent Denaules dishes up delights like pig's trotters and oyster croquettes in the evening, but for lunch head for tuna steak-frites in the bistro version, at the **Cuisiniers Vignerons** (tel: 04 68 41 86 06), in an old abbey barn with a shady terrace. €–€€

Restaurant Prices

€ = **Budget** under €25
€€ = **Moderate** €25–50
€€€ = **Expensive** €50+

Fontjoncouse
Auberge du Vieux Puits
avenue Saint Victor
Tel: 04 68 44 07 37
Traditional bourgeois French restaurant in the wilds of the Corbières. Good wine list, obsequious service, and regional "peasant" dishes elaborately prepared; desserts are especially stylish. €€€

Limoux
Maison de la Blanquette
46 bis prom. du Tivoli
Tel: 04 68 31 01 63
A town restaurant with rustic decor and a very good wine selection, including, of course, the local sparkling wine, Limoux *champenoise*. €€
Relais de Pigasse
11590 Ouveillan
Tel: 04 67 89 40 98
Stylishly renovated 17th-century posting house on the Canal du Midi, brainchild of English *vigneron*, Bertie Eden. Sample his excellent Minervois wines and dine in the vaulted interior or beside the canal on authentic regional dishes served with appropriate wine. $$

Narbonne
Table St Crescent
ave Générale Le Clerc
Tel: 04 68 41 37 37
Just outside town, at the Palais du Vin, is one of Narbonne's top restaurants, a modern stylish establishment with a vine-covered terrace. It specialises in the best wines and dishes of the region. €€

FRENCH CATALONIA

Belesta
Chez Pierre
Tel: 04 68 84 52 70
Cosy little village restaurant with a glass roof, a verandah and splendid mountain views. Friendly owners serve robust local delicacies such as duck cutlet and foie gras, as well as a variety of wines from local vineyards and their own liqueurs. €

Castelnou
Le Vicomte
Château de Castelnou
Tel: 04 68 53 32 08
Medieval château in restored village serving traditional Catalan cuisine such as *boules de Picoulat* (Catalan meatballs in spicy sauce). €€

Céret
La Cerisaie
Route Fontfrède
Tel: 04 68 87 01 94
Charming restaurant with classy Paris-style cooking in a renovated farmhouse with great views in the foothills of the Pyrenees. Try the soufflé of foie gras with artichokes, baked red mullet, artistically stuffed courgette flowers and excellent Roussillon wines. €€€
Les Feuillants
1 boulevard Lafayette
Tel: 04 68 87 37 88
Pleasant restaurant with shady terrace serving stylish versions of traditional Catalan cuisine. €€

Collioure
Les Templiers
12 quai de l'Amirauté
Tel: 04 68 98 31 10
Restaurant and hotel famous for the many artists who stayed here, Matisse and Braque among them, and the canvases they donated. Dine on the terrace near the sea and sample Collioure's anchovies, platters of seafood and local wine. €–€€
Neptune
Route Port Vendres
Tel: 04 68 82 02 27
Right on the bay with wonderful canopied sea views, and full

nouvelle Catalan cuisine; *salade chemin des Fauves* made of eggs, artichokes, tapenade and tomato confit, or lobster ravioli with cardamom vinaigrette. €–€€

Perpignan
Casa Sansa
2 rue Fabrique Nadal
Tel: 04 68 34 21 84
Authentic Catalan restaurant in the narrow streets of the old town, very popular with locals and always lively. Try the rabbit with figs or beef *daube* with orange. €€
Le France
place de la Loge
04 68 51 61 71
Chic central restaurant in one of Perpignan's best Renaissance buildings, recently rescued from a ubiquitous burger chain, with alfresco dining on southern classics from *moules marinières* to *crème catalane*. €€
Les Trois Soeurs
2 rue Fontfroide
Tel: 04 68 51 22 33
Fashionable new restaurant with stylish modern bar and terrace tables on cathedral square. Catalan cooking with a delicious twist, like monkfish with *mousserons* (wild mushrooms), sea bass with sesame seeds, lamb with honey, and spiced pears. €

Port-Vendres
Ferme Auberge des Clos de Paulilles
Baie de Paulilles
6666 Port-Vendres
Tel: 04 68 98 07 58
On a small bay surrounded by vineyards, this restaurant showcases Paulilles wines. Dine on the patio overlooking the sea and sample each course with a different wine from rosé to rich reds and aged Banyuls. Open evenings and Sun lunch. €€

Prades
Jardin de L'Aymeric
3 avenue du Général de Gaulle
Tel: 04 68 96 53 38
The best bet for stylish regional cooking though the excess of neon detracts from the atmosphere. €

Tautavel
Le Petit Gris
Route d'Estagel
Tel: 04 68 29 42 42
Popular family restaurant with great views of the plain, serving excellent Catalan *cargolade* – snails, pork, sausages, etc. on your own personal grill. €

Villefranche-de-Conflent
Auberge St Paul
place de l'Église.
Tel: 04 68 96 30 95
Smart little restaurant in a restored Romanesque building. Service is gracious, the food elegant and imaginative – the bill will be reasonable if you stick to *prix-fixe* menus. €€

Restaurant Prices

€ = Budget under €25
€€ = Moderate €25–50
€€€ = Expensive €50+

HÉRAULT AND GARD

Bouzigues
Côte Bleue
avenue Louis-Tudesq
Tel: 04 67 78 30 87
This bustling family restaurant with views over the Bassin de Thau is one of the best places to sample a vast variety of shellfish, mussels, langoustines and the local Bouzigues oysters. €

Montpellier
Jardin des Sens
11 avenue St-Lazare
Tel: 04 99 58 38 38
One of the south's top restaurants and a newcomer to Michelin's three-star pantheon. It is run by local twins Jacques and Laurent Pourcel, and devoted to the cuisine of Languedoc and the Mediterranean. Ultra-modern, carefully calculated decor. Exemplary delights include squid stuffed with ratatouille and crayfish tails, *bourride*, the local fish soup and traditional pastries. Lovely garden. Rooms available. €€€

L'Olivier
12 rue Aristide Olivier
Tel: 04 67 92 86 28
Art Déco style, smooth service, classic cuisine, the best local wine, and right on the new tramway. €€
Maison de la Lozère
27 rue Aiguillerie
Tel: 04 67 66 46 36
Regional produce served in a 13th-century vaulted dining room (and sold in the adjoining shop). €
Le Petit Jardin
20 rue J. Rousseau
Tel: 04 67 60 78 78
Remarkably quiet restaurant in the centre of town, with a delightful large, shady garden with a view of the cathedral. Good local fish, salads and fresh pasta with vegetables. €€

Nîmes
L'Enclos de la Fontaine
quai de la Fontaine
Tel: 04 66 21 90 30
Restaurant of Hotel Imperator with interior garden, much favoured by bullfighters at *feria* time. Try local specialities like *brandade* (creamy salt cod), *escabèche* (marinated fish) or sea bass with fennel compote. €€€
L'Esclafidou
7 rue Xavier-Sigalon
Tel: 04 66 21 28 49
Charming little restaurant on a tiny hidden *place*, cosy in winter and shady terrace in summer; for Provencal cuisine with lots of olive oil, garlic and herbs; generous salads, fish and omelettes – try the *omelette aux cèpes* in season. €
Jardin d'Hadrien
11 rue de l'Enclos
Tel: 04 66 21 86 65
One of Nîmes most highly regarded restaurants, with wood-beamed dining room and shady garden; try the cod simply cooked with olive oil, red mullet with tapenade, or courgette flowers stuffed with *brandade* (salt cod). €€
Le 9
rue de l'Etoile
Tel: 04 66 21 80 77
Fashionable restaurant tucked away in the old town, with a

Food/Drink Websites

www.bottin-gourmand.com
Guide to the food, drink and
restaurants of France.
www.gourmetseeker.com
For all the finer things in life.
www.fromages.com
Guide to French cheeses.
www.frenchfoods.com and
www.winesoffrance.com
Official sites of French food and
drink producers.

theatrical atmosphere, serving
Mediterranean dishes like *moules
gratinées* and *poivrons à
l'anchoiade* (green peppers
stuffed with anchovies). Open till
late and a popular wine bar during
the *feria*. €€

St-Guiraud
Le Mimosa
Tel: 04 67 96 67 96
Beautifully decorated 18th-century
winegrower's house in tiny village,
with superb cuisine, long popular
with Montpellier cognoscenti. €€€

St-Saturnin de Lucian
Auberge Le Pressoir
17 place de la Fontaine
Tel: 04 67 88 67 89
Good regional cooking (fresh trout,
farmhouse chicken) in a friendly
artistic atmosphere; regular art and
photography exhibitions are held, as
well as jazz and theatre evenings. €

Nightlife

Out on the Town

The major cities in the region all
have substantial student
populations so there are plenty of
bars and nightclubs. For the latest
place to go pick up a copy of the
local listings magazine or
newspaper, either from the tourist
office or *maison de la presse*.

In smaller towns and villages
there will be little going on at night
unless there is a festival taking
place. Cafés and bars will stay open
all day, often until late. Bars are
always good for morning coffee,
and if they don't have croissants or
bread available will have no
objection to you eating your own
from the *boulangerie*.

BORDEAUX

Bars around place de la Victoire are
popular with students. **Le Boeuf sur
le Toit** (15 rue de Candale)
sometimes has rock concerts, and
clubbing is popular on quai de
Paludate. **The Cricketeers** (72 quai
de Paludate) has English-style
billiards and darts, and blues
evenings. Converted port
warehouses have been turned into
clubs like **Caesar's** (quai Louis
XVIII), with cabaret and disco, and
Le Nautilus (122 quai de Bacalan),
which plays house and techno.

TOULOUSE

Of all the Southwest cities Toulouse
has the liveliest nightlife but it
changes all the time; get the latest
details from the weekly *Flash*.
Most bar activity takes place
around place St Pierre and place

Arnaud-Bernard. Good bars include
Rag Time (14 place Arnaud-
Bernard) for jazz, **Casa Manolo**
(24 rue des Trois-Pilliers), for
flamenco and *tapas*, **Puerto
Habana** (12 Port St-Étienne), for
dancing and salsa; **Bikini** (Route de
Lacroix-Flagarde) has rock concerts.

MONTPELLIER

With the youngest population in
France, Montpellier has dozens of
bars and clubs, and a thriving gay
scene. See *La Gazette* for details.
Most of the action takes place
around place Jean-Jaurès.
Philosophy cafés are the latest
thing, with discussions on anything
from astrology to theology. Try the
Brasserie Le Dome, (2 avenue
Clémenceau), **Le Jam** (100 rue F.
de Lesseps), **Café des Arts** in the
Brasserie du Corum and **Café des
Femmes** in **Le César** (place du
Nombre d'Or).

For an internet connection, head
for the **Cybersurf Café** (22 place du
Millénaire) which serves food and
drink and has access to computers.

NÎMES

The **Trois Maures** (10 boulevard
des Arènes) is a large, old-
fashioned *brasserie*. **La Bodeguita**
(3 boulevard Alphonse-Daudet) is a
Spanish *tapas* bar with flamenco,
tango, jazz and poetry. **The
Haddock Café** (13 rue de l'Agau) is
a club and café with food served
late, and music and philosophy
evenings.

Culture

Culture is delivered in spades throughout the Southwest as part of its festival calendar which features high-class jazz and classical music festivals, theatre, opera and dance. There are also art and photography shows, folklore festivals and a host of other arts and crafts to enjoy. *(See festival listing for locations and schedules.)* Even small towns and villages stage events during the summer months, and for events in larger cities tourist offices provide complete listings.

BORDEAUX

Theatres

Theatres include the **Grand Théâtre**, in place de la Comédie; the **Théâtre Fémina**, at 8 rue de Grassi, and the **Espace Culturel du Pin Galant**, avenue de la Libération and avenue de l'Yser, at Merignac, west of Bordeaux.

Cinemas

Trianon Jean Vigo, in rue Franklin, shows films in the original language.

TOULOUSE

Theatres

The **Théâtre du Capitole**, in place du Capitole, for opera and dance, and the **Théâtre National de Toulouse Midi-Pyrénées** for plays.

Cinema

Cinémathèque, 69 rue du Taur, shows original-language movies. Also **Le Cratère**, 95 Grande Rue St-Michel.

Music

The Orchestre National du Capitole is one of France's top symphony orchestras and can be heard in **La Halle aux Grains**, place Dupuy.

MONTPELLIER

Music

Performances by L'Orchestre Philharmonique de Montpellier can be seen at **CORUM**, a conference centre, concert hall and performance space on esplanade Charles de Gaulle.

Comedy

Comedy can be seen at **Opéra Comédie**, place de la Comédie.

Cinemas

Several cinemas show original-language and English films. Check out *La Gazette* for listings.

NÎMES

Concerts

There are opera, dance and concerts in the **Arena** throughout the summer.

Cinema

Original-language films can be seen at **Le Sémaphore**, 25a rue Porte de France.

Festivals

Throughout the year there are festivals all over the region. Every village or town has its own fête day and also celebrates its particular harvest of apples, cherries or garlic. Carnival is celebrated with music, dancing and sometimes bullfights. Many towns and cities host major cultural festivals of music, both jazz and classical, opera, theatre, photography or art, and these often take place in historic buildings from Romanesque abbeys to Roman amphitheatres. There are fêtes for tuna and for donkeys, for snails, for puppets and for wine.

Festivals are a wonderful way to really get the flavour of a place; although many of the major festivals take place during the summer months, other events depend on the season; wine festivals, for example, take place in October after the *vendange* (grape picking). Religious festivals are often celebrated with great ceremony, and Easter and Christmas both offer the opportunity to see and participate in local events.

January

Espelette: Foire aux Pottocks – Basque Horse Fair
Gavarnie: Festival of the Pyrenees
Limoux: Carnival (weekends Jan to April)

February

Nîmes: Carnival Feria (Feb or March)
Périgueux: Mardi Gras (Feb or March)

March/April
Perpignan: Procession de la Sanch – Good Friday
Arles-sur-Tech: Bear-chasing Festival

April
Lourdes: Sacred Music Festival
Bayonne: Ham Fair

May
Bertric Burée (Dordogne): Snail Festival
Mimizan: Festival of the Sea
Vic-Fezensac (Gers): Pentecost bullfights.
Nîmes: Feria and bullfights at Pentecost
Ceret: Cherry Festival
Marmande: Strawberry Festival

June
Montpellier: Theatre Festival
Uzes: Music and Dance Festival
Bordeaux: Wine Festival
Capbreton: Festival of the Sea
Itxassou Cherry Festival
Auch: Music Festival
23 June, Fête de St-Jean (Feast of St John the Baptist/Midsummer's Night): bonfires and festivities all over the region

July
14 July, Bastille day: celebrations all over the region. The fireworks at Carcassonne are particularly spectacular
Carcassonne: Médiévales – jousting, costumes and crafts
Montpellier: Dance Festival and Radio Festival
Pau: Theatre, Dance and Music Festival
St-Bertrand-de-Comminges: Music Festival
Condom: International Folklore Festival
St-Jean-de-Luz: Tuna Festival
Vic Fezensac: Tempo Latino
Bayonne: Jazz Festival and Medieval Market
Cahors: Jazz
Foix: Medieval Days
Biarritz: Surfing Championships
Pamiers: Theatre Festival
Toulouse: Music Festival
Cordes-sur-Ciel: Medieval Festival
Mirande: Country Music Festival

Mont de Marsan: Flamenco Occitan Folk Festival. Held in a different town each year

August
St-Jean-Pied-de-Port: Sheepdog Competitions
Bayonne: Fêtes de Bayonne
Biarritz: Basque Sports Finals
Hossegor: World Surfing Championships
Prades: Pablo Casals Classical Music Festival with St-Michel-de-Cuxa as its main venue
Sète: Nautical Jousts
Ceret: Catalan Dance Festival
Lautrec: Rose Garlic Festival
Marciac: World-class Jazz Festival
15 Aug, Assumption Day: Holiday and fêtes all over region
Sarrant: Fête Médiévale
Roquelaure: Fête Médiévale

All that Jazz

For 10 days around 15 August, one of Europe's best-known jazz festivals takes place in Marciac in the Gers *département*. Top-ranking musicians draw crowds to evening concerts. During the day, every day, there's live music for free in the central square.

September
Toulouse: Piano Festival
Elne: Music Festival
Montpellier: Mediterranean Cinema
Nîmes: Grape-picking Festival and bullfights
Dax: Bullfights
Rocamadour: Pilgrimage
Journées du Patrimoine. Private historical monuments open their doors to the public throughout France
Eugénie-les-Bains: Fêtes Impériales *(see box)*
Lavardens: Scarecrow Competition

October
Wine harvest celebrations in all wine regions.
St-Émilion: Beginning of grape harvest (Proclamation du ban des Vendanges)
Espelette: Red Pepper Festival

Empire Days

On 8 May 1861, in his Tuileries palace, Napoleon III proclaimed the birth of Eugénie-les-Bains, named after his empress. In September the village holds its *fêtes impériales* when everyone dresses in Empire style.

Perpignan: Visa Pour Image – world photojournalism festival
Nontron: Chestnut Fair
Mirepoix: Apple Festival

November
Bordeaux: Theatre, Dance and Music

December
Marche de Gras. Foie gras, duck and geese fairs held all over region
Christmas. Celebrations in French Catalonia include the *pessebre* nativity plays
Nîmes. Midnight Mass in the Arènes

Sport

Spectator sports include the local passion of rugby, bullfights in Nîmes, Dax and several smaller places, Basque sports like *pelote*, or simply a gentle game of *pétanque* in a village square. Information from local tourist offices.

Participant Sports and Activities

Southwest France has a huge range of sports and activities to choose from. There is also lying on the beach of course, but even beach bums can indulge in surfing, wind-surfing and water-skiing.

The sea is usually warm enough for swimming from June to September, and almost every town will have a municipal pool, though it may only be open in school holidays. Even small villages often have a tennis court, though you may have to become a temporary member to use it – enquire at the local tourist office or *mairie* (town hall), which will also provide details of all other local sporting activities.

The mountains and river valleys offer walking, riding, cycling and climbing, river rafting and canoeing, and skiing in the winter months.

General information on sports and activities can be had from local tourist offices or national organisations. Many UK tour operators offer holidays tailored to specific activities. *(See list of tour operators on page 326.)*

Canal Boating

Many firms along the length of the Canal du Midi rent out boats for leisurely cruising. For information contact: **La Maison du Canal**, 8 rue des Péniches, 34500 Béziers; tel: 04 67 62 18 18.

Canoeing & Kayaking

Fédération Française de Canoë-Kayak et des Sports Associés en Eau-Vive, 87 quai de la Marne, 94340 Joinville-le-Pont; tel: 01 45 11 08 50; fax 01 48 86 13 25.

Caving and Pot-holing

Contact the **Fédération Française de Spéléologie**, 130 rue St-Maur, 75011 Paris; tel: 01 43 57 56 54 or the **Comité Régional Midi-Pyrénées de Spéléologie**, 7 rue André-Citroen, 31130 Balma; tel: 05 61 11 71 60.

Climbing

Dozens of climbing clubs provide beginners' courses and also guides and monitors for day outings.

For climbing information contact the **Club Alpin Français**, 14 avenue Mirabeau, Nice; tel 04 93 53 37 95 or 3 rue St-Michel, Avignon; tel: 04 90 82 34 82.

Cycling

Taking your own bike *(vélo)* to France is relatively easy *(see Getting There, page 325)*; once there, it can be carried free on most ferries and trains *(see Getting Around, page 333)*. Some youth hostels rent cycles and also arrange tours with accommodation in hostels or under canvas.

Package cycling holidays are offered by various organisations, with camp site or hotel accommodation; luggage is normally transported each day to your next destination.

It is advisable to take out insurance before you go. Obviously the normal rules of the road apply to cyclists *(see Getting Around, page 335)*. The IGN 906 *Cycling France* map gives details of routes, cycling clubs and places to stay *(see Maps section for stockists, page 333)*.

Advice and information can be obtained from The Touring Department, **Cyclists Touring Club**, Cotterell House, 69 Meadrow, Godalming, Surrey GU7 3HS; tel: 01483 417 217. Their service to members includes competitive cycle and travel insurance, free detailed touring itineraries and general information sheets about France, whilst their

Spas and Thalassotherapy

The Pyrenees is famous for its thermal spas. Places like Bagnères de Luchon, Cauterets, Alet-les-Bains, Ax-les-Thermes and Vernet-les-Bains have attracted health-seeking travellers for centuries, and although many of these spas are now slumbering in genteel decline you can still go and drink the waters and be treated with different forms of water baths and massage for a wide variery of ailments, from rheumatism to skin diseases or high cholesterol.

Around the Southwest there are many other spas, their names often suffixed "-les-Bains". Each has its own particular specialisation. The luxurious Eugénie-les-Bains treats obesity. Digestive, urinary, rheumatic and other maladies are treated in spas including Castéra-Verduzan and Lectoure in the Gers, and Prechacq and St-Paul les Dax in the Landes. For more information on spa treatments contact the **Féderation Thermale et Climatique Française**, 18 rue de l'Estrapade, 75005 Paris; tel: 01 43 25 11 85.

More popular than conventional spa treatment these days is thalassotherapy (treatment with seawater). Biarritz is a major centre of thalassotherapy; its two main institutions are the **Institut Louison Bobet**, 11 rue Louison Bobet, 64200 Biarritz; tel: 05 59 41 30 01, and **Les Thermes Marins**, 80 rue Madrid, 64200 Biarritz; tel: 05 59 23 01 22.

tours brochure lists trips to the region, organised by members.

The club's French counterpart, **Fédération Française de Cyclotourisme**, is at 8 rue Jean-Marie-Jégo, 75013 Paris; tel: 01 44 16 88 88.

Fishing

Here you have a choice of sea- or fresh-water fishing. The season opens around the second Saturday in March. For freshwater fishing you will need to be affiliated to an association. For general information and addresses of local fishing associations contact: **Maison de la France**, Paris; tel: 01 42 96 70 00.

Golf

The Southwest has many excellent golf courses, and the weather means golf can be played all year round. Most of the clubs provide lessons with resident experts. For information contact the **Fédération Française de Golf**, 68 rue Anatole France, Levallois Perret 92306; tel: 01 41 49 77 00; fax 01 41 49 77 01.

Horse Riding

Horse riding and pony trekking are popular activities, with Centres Équestres all over the region – in rural areas, the mountains and less inhabited parts of the coast. **Fédération des Randonneurs Équestres**, 169 rue Blanqui, 33300 Bordeaux; tel: 05 56 26 52 03.

Skiing

The Pyrenees has several major resorts, which provide downhill skiing and cross-country skiing. In the Eastern Pyrenees the biggest resort is Font Romeu, and there are others at Bonascre, Porte-Puymorens and Les Angles. In the Central Pyrenees the biggest is Barèges/La Mongie with others at Cauterets and Gavarnie.

For skiing and mountain climbing in the Pyrenees contact the **Centre d'Information Montagnes et Sentiers**, BP 88, 09200 St Girons; tel: 05 61 66 40 10. For more information, contact the **Fédération Française de Ski**, 50 avenue des Marquisats, 74000 Annecy; tel: 04 50 51 40 34; www.ffs.fr.

Water-sports

All along the Mediterranean coast you can water-ski, wind-surf or scuba dive; surfing is very popular on the Atlantic coast. **Fédération Française d'Études et de Sports Sous-Marins**, 24 quai Rive-Neuve, 13007 Marseille; tel: 04 91 33 99 31; fax 04 91 54 77 43.

Surfing

Surfing equipment may be rented in the various resorts. For general information, contact the **Fédération Française de Surf**, Plage Nord, boulevard du Front de Mer, BP 28, 40150 Hossegor; tel: 05 58 43 55 88; fax: 05 58 43 60 57.

The most popular area for surfing is Lacanau. Contact **Lacanau Surf Club**, tel: 05 56 26 38 84 and **Surf Sans Frontières**, tel: 05 56 02 27 60. Both these clubs have instructions in English.

Walking

Walking holidays are popular in France, and there is an extensive, well-signposted network of *sentiers de grande randonnée* (long-distance footpaths). For more detailed information *see Getting Around, page 335*. For information on maps, *see page 333*. Each *département* has its own ramblers' organisation which arranges guided walks of a day or more, as well as walks to see local flowers or wildlife. For local information, contact the relevant tourist office, or **Fédération Française de Randonnée Pédestre**, 14 rue Riquet, 75009 Paris; tel: 01 44 89 93 90; fax 01 40 35 85 48.

Shopping

Where to Shop

Shopping in Southwest France is usually both efficient and pleasurable, whether you're buying a fresh baguette or croissants from the village *boulangerie*, contemplating the quality and range of food in the supermarkets or strolling the elegant boulevards of the big cities.

Markets

Markets are one of the best places to shop, whether you simply want fresh fruit, vegetables, meat, fish or eggs, or are looking for locally made specialist products or handicrafts to take home. Most villages and towns have a market at least once a week, and in big cities they are usually daily. They start quite early and for the best produce, freshly picked mushrooms, wild strawberries, free-range eggs, go early. By noon it will all be over. Look out for local delicacies such as cheese, olives, honey, *charcuterie* and pâtés, foie gras, spices, herbs and special breads, all of which can easily be transported home if you have a car. There are also lots of flea markets *(marché aux puces* or *brocantes)* with antiques, second-hand goods, old tools, old linen and pottery, but you'll need to be early to find any real bargains.

Night Markets

Night markets during July and August are a summer highlight in several towns in the Gers, including Vic Fezensac, Fleurance and Nogaro. As well as shopping you can eat and drink at cafés or just enjoy the atmosphere.

Supermarkets

Most towns will have a large hypermarket outside the centre, excellent for grocery shopping and a wide range of other goods. The same complex may also have a petrol station and services such as dry-cleaning, photo shops, pharmacies, etc. But take the time to shop in town centres, where you will find excellent butchers, fishmongers and vegetable shops – they may be slightly more expensive than the supermarket but you will get invaluable service and shop-keepers will be happy to advise you about how to cook a certain food. You will also find specialist pâtisseries, chocolate shops, clothing or leather goods shops. Apart from food, regional products well worth buying include baskets, pottery, berets and walking sticks, linen, espadrilles, wine and Armagnac.

Specialist Outlets

Truffles, Foie Gras, Confits

Aux Armes du Périgord
1 rue de la Liberté, 24200 Sarlat-le-Caneda
Tel: 05 53 59 14 27
La Ferme de Turnac
24150 Domme
Tel: 05 53 28 10 84
Le Gers Gourmet
Gayarin, 32400 St-Germe
Tel: 05 62 69 61 07
Conserverie Godard
Gourdon
Tel: 05 65 41 03 97

Jambon de Bayonne

Pierre d'Ibaialde
41 rue des Cordeliers
Bayonne
Tel: 05 59 25 65 30

Maison Montauzer
17 rue de la Salie, Bayonne
Tel: 05 59 56 84 04

Olive Oil

F. Nadal
4 rue des Marchands, Nîmes.
Tel: 04 66 67 64 06
Tiny old-fashioned shop selling olive oil from huge vats, hand-made soaps, herbs, honey, coffee and spices.
L'Oulibo
Bize-Minervois (Aude)
Tel: 04 68 46 10 37
Olive oil mill, museum and co-op.

Oysters

Union de Bataliers d'Arcachon
Arcachon
Tel: 05 56 54 83 09
B. Pedemay
Impasse du Grand Coin, Petit Piquey, Lège-Cap-Ferret.
Tel: 05 56 60 58 18

Chocolate, Sweets and Cakes

Chocolaterie Cazenave
19 Arceaux, Port-Neuf, Bayonne
Tel: 05 59 59 03 16
Chocolaterie Henriet
place Clémenceau, Biarritz
Tel: 05 59 24 24 15
Paries
27 place Clémenceau, Biarritz
Basque sweets.
Villaret
13 rue de la Madeleine, Nîmes
Tel: 04 66 67 41 79
Boulangerie and pâtisserie: wide choice of bread, tarts and the Nîmois speciality, croquants.

Anchovies

Societé Roque
17 Route d'Argelès
Collioure
Tel: 04 68 82 22 30

How To Buy Wine

For wine to drink while you are in France, buy from cooperatives, markets or wine merchants en vrac (in bulk), in 5- or 10-litre plastic containers. Often good-quality wine is available like this at half the price of bottled wine. Drink it up quickly though – it won't travel well.

Wine Shops

Bordeaux

L'Intendant
2 allées de Tourny, Bordeaux
Tel: 05 56 48 01 29
La Vinothèque
8 Cours du 30 Juillet, Bordeaux
Tel: 05 56 52 32 05
Maison du Tourisme et du Vin
La Verrerie, Pauillac
Tel: 05 56 59 03 08
Maison du Vin de St-Éstephe
place de L'Église, St-Éstephe
Tel: 05 56 59 30 59
Maison des Vins de Graves
61 Cours Maréchal Foch, Podensac
Tel: 05 56 27 09 25
Maison du Sauternes
14 place de la Mairie, Sauternes
Tel: 05 56 76 69 83
Maison du Vin des Côtes de Blaye
11 Cours Vauban, Blaye
Tel: 05 57 42 91 19
Maison du Vin des Côtes de Bourg
place de l'Éperon, Bourg
Tel: 05 57 68 46 47

Bergerac and Cahors

Maison de Vin de Bergerac
2 place du Dr Cayla, Bergerac
Tel: 05 53 57 07 42
Syndicat Interprofessionel du Vin de Cahors
avenue Jean-Jaurès
Cahors
Tel: 05 65 23 22 21

Costières de Nîmes,

Maison des Costières
19 place Aristide-Briand
quai de la Fontaine, Nîmes
Tel: 04 66 36 96 20
For tastings and information on local wines, and as an added bonus a bodega (wine cellar) at feria time.

How to Claim Back the Value Added Tax

Most purchases include TVA (Value Added Tax) at a base rate of 20.6 percent but as high as 33 percent on some luxury items. Visitors from outside the EU can claim back TVA if they spend more than €300 in one place. Ask the shop for a completed bordereau (export sales invoice) to be shown, along with purchases, to customs when you depart. Then you have to send the form back to the shop, which will refund the TVA – although this will take some time.

Hérault

Caves Notre-Dame
1348 avenue de la Mer,
Montpellier,
Tel: 04 67 64 48 00
Maison Régionale des Vins et des Produits du Terroir
34 rue Saint-Guilhem,
Montpellier
Tel: 04 67 60 40 41

Minervois

La Tuilerie
La Livinière
Tel: 04 68 91 42 63
Old tile factory stylishly converted to offer sale and tastings of the produce of several local vineyards, including the first *cru* of Languedoc, La Livinière. Friendly, with English-speaking service.

How to Pay

Supermarkets will accept credit cards but smaller shops may not. Visa is the most commonly accepted, and American Express the least popular. For markets you'll need cash. Always keep receipts so you can exchange unsatisfactory purchases.

Aude and Roussillon

Palais du Vin
Route de Perpignan, Narbonne
Tel: 04 68 41 49 67
Wide selection of Languedoc wines.
Côtes du Roussillon
19 avenue de la Grande Bretagne,
66000 Perpignan
Tel: 04 68 51 31 81

Corbières

Maison des Terroirs en Corbières
11200 Château de Boutenac
Tel: 04 68 27 73 00
Showcase for Corbières wines.

Fitou

Cave des Producteurs de Fitou
11510 Fitou
Tel: 04 68 45 71 41

Collioure

Caves les Dominicains
place Orfila, Collioure.
Tel: 04 68 82 05 63

Cognac

Rémy Martin
20 rue de la Société Vinicole,
Cognac
Tel: 05 45 35 76 66
Cognac Otard
Château de Cognac,
127 boulevard Denfert-Rochereau,
1601 Cognac
Tel: 05 45 36 88 88

Armagnac

Janneau Fils SA
50 avenue de la Gare, 32100
Condom
Tel: 05 62 28 24 77
Domaine de Laubuchon
32370 Manciet
Tel: 05 62 08 50 29

Local Products

Makhila

Traditional Basque walking sticks of carved wood and silver.
Ainciart Bergara
Larressore
Tel: 05 59 93 03 05
Shop established in 1789.
M Leoncini
37 rue Vieille Boucherie, Bayonne
Tel: 05 59 59 18 20

Basque Linen

Boutiques Berrogain
Carrefour des Cinq-Cantons,
Bayonne
Tel: 05 59 59 16 18
Established in 1800.
Berrogain
boulevard de BAB, Anglet
Tel: 05 59 57 31 31

Basque Berets

Musée du Béret
place St-Roch, Nay
Tel: 05 59 61 91 70
A museum with a boutique attached.

Catalan Fabrics and Espadrilles

Les Toiles du Soleil
Le Village, St-Laurent-de-Cerdans
Tel: 04 68 39 50 02

Language

The *Lingua Franca*

Basque, Catalan and Occitan are spoken in parts of the Southwest but the *lingua franca* and official language everywhere is French.

French is the native language of more than 90 million people and the acquired language of 180 million. It is a Romance language descended from the Vulgar Latin spoken by the Roman conquerors of Gaul. It still carries the reputation for being the most cultured language in the world and, for what it's worth, the most beautiful. People often tell stories about the impatience of the French towards foreigners not blessed with fluency in their language. In general, however, if you attempt to communicate with them in French, they will be helpful.

Since much of the English vocabulary is related to French, thanks to the Norman Conquest of 1066, travellers will often recognise many helpful cognates: words such as *hôtel*, *café* and *bagages* hardly need to be translated.

Words & Phrases

How much is it? *C'est combien?*
What is your name? *Comment vous appelez-vous?*
My name is... *Je m'appelle...*
Do you speak English? *Parlez-vous anglais?*
I am English/American *Je suis anglais(e)/américain(e)*
I don't understand *Je ne comprends pas*
Please speak more slowly *Parlez plus lentement, s'il vous plaît*
Can you help me? *Pouvez-vous m'aider?*
I'm looking for... *Je cherche*

Where is...? *Où est...?*
I'm sorry *Excusez-moi/Pardon*
I don't know *Je ne sais pas*
No problem *Pas de problème*
Have a good day! *Bonne journée!*
That's it *C'est ça*
Here it is *Voici*
There it is *Voilà*
Let's go *On y va. Allons-y*
See you tomorrow *A demain*
See you soon *A bientôt*
Show me the word in the book
Montrez-moi le mot dans le livre
yes *oui*
no *non*
please *s'il vous plaît*
thank you *merci*
(very much) *(beaucoup)*
you're welcome *de rien*
excuse me *excusez-moi*
hello *bonjour*
OK *d'accord*
goodbye *au revoir*
good evening *bonsoir*
here *ici*
there *là*
today *aujourd'hui*
yesterday *hier*
tomorrow *demain*
now *maintenant*
later *plus tard*
this morning *ce matin*
this afternoon *cet après-midi*
this evening *ce soir*

On Arrival

I want to get off at...
Je voudrais descendre à...
Is there a bus to the Louvre?
Est-ce qu'il ya un bus pour le Louvre?
What street is this? *Dans quelle
rue sommes-nous?*
Which line do I take for...? *Quelle
ligne dois-je prendre pour...?*
How far is...?
A quelle distance se trouve...?
Validate your ticket
Compostez votre billet
airport *l'aéroport*
train station *la gare*
bus station *la gare routière*
Métro stop *la station de Métro*
bus *l'autobus, le car*
bus stop *l'arrêt*
platform *le quai*
ticket *le billet*
return ticket *aller-retour*
hitchhiking *l'autostop*

toilets *les toilettes*
This is the hotel address
C'est l'adresse de l'hôtel
I'd like a (single/double) room...
*Je voudrais une chambre (pour
une/deux personnes)* ...
....with shower *avec douche*
....with a bath *avec salle de bain*
....with a view *avec vue*
Does that include breakfast? *Le
prix comprend-il le petit déjeuner?*
May I see the room? *Je peux voir
la chambre?*
washbasin *le lavabo*
bed *le lit*
key *la clef*
lift/elevator *l'ascenseur*
air conditioned *climatisé*

On the Road

Where is the spare wheel? *Où est
la roue de secours?*
Where is the nearest garage? *Où
est le garage le plus proche?*
Our car has broken down *Notre
voiture est en panne*
I want to have my car repaired
Je veux faire réparer ma voiture
It's not your right of way *Vous
n'avez pas la priorité*
**I think I must have put diesel in the
car by mistake** *Je crois que j'ai mis
du gasoil dans la voiture par erreur*
the road to... *la route pour*...
left *gauche*
right *droite*
straight on *tout droit*
far *loin*
near *près d'ici*
opposite *en face*
beside *à côté de*
car park *parking*
over there *là-bas*
at the end *au bout*
on foot *à pied*
by car *en voiture*
town map *le plan*
road map *la carte*
street *la rue*
square *la place*
give way *céder le passage*
dead end *impasse*
no parking *stationnement interdit*
motorway *l'autoroute*
toll *le péage*
speed limit *la limitation de vitesse*
petrol *l'essence*
unleaded *sans plomb*

diesel *le gasoil*
water/oil *l'eau/l'huile*
puncture *un pneu crevé*
bulb *l'ampoule*
wipers *les essuies-glace*

Shopping

**Where is the nearest bank (post
office)?** *Où est la banque/Poste/
PTT la plus proche?*
I'd like to buy *Je voudrais acheter*
How much is it? *C'est combien?*
Do you take credit cards? *Est-ce
que vous acceptez les cartes de
crédit?*
I'm just looking *Je regarde
seulement*
Have you got...? *Avez-vous...?*
I'll take it *Je le prends*
I'll take this one/that one *Je
prends celui-ci/celui-là*
What size is it? *C'est de quelle
taille?*
Anything else? *Avec ça?*
size (clothes) *la taille*
size (shoes) *la pointure*
cheap *bon marché*
expensive *cher*
enough *assez*
too much *trop*
a piece *un morceau de*
each *la pièce (eg ananas, €2 la
pièce)*
bill *l'addition*
chemist *la pharmacie*
bakery *la boulangerie*
bookshop *la librairie*
library *la bibliothèque*
department store *le grand magasin*
delicatessen *la charcuterie*
fishmonger's *la poissonerie*
grocery *l'alimentation/l'épicerie*
tobacconist *tabac (can also sell
stamps and newspapers)*
market *le marché*
supermarket *le supermarché*
junk shop *la brocante*

Sightseeing

town *la ville*
old town *la vieille ville*
abbey *l'abbaye*
cathedral *la cathédrale*
church *l'église*
keep *le donjon*
mansion *l'hôtel*
hospital *l'hôpital*

town hall *l'hôtel de ville/la mairie*
nave *la nef*
stained glass *le vitrail*
staircase *l'escalier*
tower *la tour (La Tour Eiffel)*
walk *le tour*
country house/castle *le château*
Gothic *gothique*
Roman *romain*
Romanesque *roman*
museum *le musée*
art gallery *la galerie*
exhibition *l'exposition*
tourist information office
l'office de tourisme/le syndicat d'initiative
free *gratuit*
open *ouvert*
closed *fermé*
every day *tous les jours*
all year *toute l'année*
all day *toute la journée*
swimming pool *la piscine*
to book *réserver*

Dining Out

Table d'hôte (the "host's table") is one set menu served at a set price.
Prix fixe is a fixed price menu.
À la carte means dishes from the menu are charged separately.
breakfast *le petit déjeuner*
lunch *le déjeuner*
dinner *le dîner*
meal *le repas*
first course *l'entrée/les hors d'oeuvre*
main course *le plat principal*
made to order *sur commande*
drink included *boisson comprise*
wine list *la carte des vins*
the bill *l'addition*
fork *la fourchette*
knife *le couteau*
spoon *la cuillère*
plate *l'assiette*
glass *le verre*
napkin *la serviette*
ashtray *le cendrier*

Breakfast and Snacks

baguette **long thin loaf**
pain **bread**
petits pains **rolls**
beurre **butter**
poivre **pepper**
sel **salt**
sucre **sugar**

confiture **jam**
oeufs **eggs**
...à la coque **boiled eggs**
...au bacon **bacon and eggs**
...au jambon **ham and eggs**
...sur le plat **fried eggs**
...brouillés **scrambled eggs**
tartine **bread with butter**
yaourt **yoghurt**
crêpe **pancake**
croque-monsieur **ham and cheese toasted sandwich**
croque-madame **...with a fried egg on top**
galette **type of pancake**
pan bagna **bread roll stuffed with salad Niçoise**
quiche **tart of eggs and cream with various fillings**
quiche lorraine **quiche with bacon**

First course

An *amuse-bouche, amuse-gueule* or appetiser is something to "amuse the mouth", served before the first course.

anchoiade **sauce of olive oil, anchovies and garlic, served with raw vegetables**
assiette anglaise **cold meats**
potage **soup**
rillettes **rich fatty paste of shredded duck, rabbit or pork**
tapenade **spread of olives and anchovies**
pissaladière **Provençal pizza with onions, olives and anchovies**

La Viande – Meat

bleu **rare**
à point **medium**
bien cuit **well done**
grillé **grilled**
agneau **lamb**
andouille/andouillette **tripe sausage**
bifteck **steak**
boudin **sausage**
boudin noir **black pudding**
boudin blanc **white pudding (chicken or veal)**
blanquette **stew of veal, lamb or chicken with a creamy egg sauce**
boeuf à la mode **beef in red wine with carrots, mushroom and onions**
à la bordelaise **beef with red wine and shallots**

à la bourguignonne **cooked with red wine, onions and mushrooms**
brochette **kebab**
caille **quail**
canard **duck**
carbonnade **casserole of beef, beer and onions**
carré d'agneau cassoulet **rack of lamb stew with beans, sausages, pork and duck, from Southwest France**
cervelle **brains (food)**
confit **duck or goose preserved in its own fat**
contre-filet **cut of sirloin steak**
coq au vin **chicken in red wine**
côte d'agneau **lamb chop**
daube **beef stew with red wine, onions and tomatoes**
dinde **turkey**
entrecôte **beef rib steak**
escargot **snail**
faisan **pheasant**
farci **stuffed**
faux-filet **sirloin**
feuilleté **puff pastry**
foie **liver**
foie gras **goose or duck liver pâté**
cuisses de grenouille **frog's legs**
grillade **grilled meat**
hachis **minced meat**
jambon **ham**
lapin **rabbit**
lardon **small pieces of bacon, often added to salads**
magret de canard **breast of duck**
médaillon **round pieces of meat**
moelle **beef bone marrow**
mouton navarin **stew of lamb with onions, carrots and turnips**
oie **goose**
perdrix **partridge**
petit-gris **small snail**
pieds de cochon **pig's trotters**
pintade **guinea fowl**
Pipérade **Basque dish of eggs, ham, peppers, onion**
porc **pork**
pot-au-feu **casserole of beef and vegetables**
poulet **chicken**
poussin **young chicken**
rognons **kidneys**
rôti **roast**
sanglier **wild boar**
saucisse **fresh sausage**
saucisson **salami**
veau **veal**

Poissons – Fish

Armoricaine **made with white wine, tomatoes, butter and cognac**
anchois **anchovies**
anguille **eel**
bar (or *loup*) **sea bass**
barbue **brill**
belon **Brittany oyster**
bigorneau **sea snail**
Bercy **sauce of fish stock, butter, white wine and shallots**
bouillabaisse **fish soup, served with grated cheese, garlic croutons and *rouille*, a spicy sauce**
brandade **salt cod purée**
cabillaud **cod**
calamar **squid**
colin **hake**
coquillage **shellfish**
coquilles Saint-Jacques **scallops**
crevette **shrimp**
daurade **sea bream**
flétan **halibut**
fruits de mer **seafood**
hareng **herring**
homard **lobster**
huître **oyster**
langoustine **large prawn**
limande **lemon sole**
lotte **monkfish**
morue **salt cod**
moule **mussel**
moules marinières **mussels in white wine and onions**
oursin **sea urchin**
raie **skate**
saumon **salmon**
thon **tuna**
truite **trout**

Légumes – Vegetables

ail **garlic**
artichaut **artichoke**
asperge **asparagus**
aubergine **aubergine/eggplant**
avocat **avocado**
bolets **boletus mushrooms**
céleri **celeriac**
rémoulade **served with mayonnaise**
champignon **mushroom**
cèpes **cep mushroom**
chanterelle **wild mushroom**
cornichon **gherkin**
courgette **courgette/zucchini**
chips **potato crisps**
chou **cabbage**
chou-fleur **cauliflower**
concombre **cucumber**
cru **raw**

crudités **raw vegetables**
épinard **spinach**
frites **chips, French fries**
gratin dauphinois **sliced potatoes baked with cream**
haricot **dried bean**
haricots verts **green beans**
lentilles **lentils**
maïs **corn**
mange-tout **snow pea/mange-tout**
mesclun **mixed-leaf salad**
navet **turnip**
noix **nut, walnut**
noisette **hazelnut**
oignon **onion**
panais **parsnip**
persil **parsley**
pignon **pine nut**
poireau **leek**
pois **pea**
poivron **bell pepper**
pomme de terre **potato**
radis **radish**
roquette **arugula, rocket**
ratatouille **Provençal vegetable stew of aubergines, courgettes, tomatoes, peppers and olive oil**
riz **rice**
salade Niçoise **egg, tuna, olives, onions and tomato salad**
salade verte **green salad**
truffe **truffle**

Fruits – Fruit

ananas **pineapple**
cavaillon **fragrant sweet melon from Cavaillon in Provençe**
cerise **cherry**
citron **lemon**
citron vert **lime**
figue **fig**
fraise **strawberry**
framboise **raspberry**
groseille **redcurrant**
mangue **mango**
mirabelle **yellow plum**
pamplemousse **grapefruit**
pêche **peach**
poire **pear**
pomme **apple**
prune **plum**
pruneau **prune**
raisin **grape**
Reine claude **greengage**

Sauces – Sauces

aioli **garlic mayonnaise**
béarnaise **sauce of egg, butter, wine and herbs**

forestière **with mushrooms and bacon**
hollandaise **egg, butter and lemon sauce**
lyonnaise **with onions**
meunière **fried fish with butter, lemon and parsley sauce**
meurette **red-wine sauce**
Mornay **sauce of cream, egg and cheese**
Parmentier **served with potatoes**
paysan **rustic style, ingredients depend on the region**
pistou **Provençal sauce of basil, garlic and olive oil; vegetable soup with the sauce.**
provençale **sauce of tomatoes, garlic and olive oil**
papillotte **cooked in paper or foil**

Puddings – Dessert

Belle Hélène **fruit with ice cream and chocolate sauce**
clafoutis **baked pudding of batter and cherries**
coulis **purée of fruit or vegetables**
gâteau **cake**
île flottante **whisked egg whites in custard sauce**
crème anglaise **custard**
pêche melba **peaches with ice cream and raspberry sauce**
tarte tatin **upside down tart of caramelised apples**
crème caramel **caramelised egg custard**
crème Chantilly **whipped cream**
fromage **cheese**
chèvre **goat's cheese**

In the Café

drinks *les boissons*
coffee *café*
...with milk or cream *au lait or crème*
...decaffeinated *déca/décaféiné*
...black/espresso *noir/expresso*
...filtered coffee *filtre*
tea *thé*
...herb infusion *tisane*
...camomile *verveine*
hot chocolate *chocolat chaud*
milk *lait*
mineral water *eau minérale*
fizzy *gazeux*
non-fizzy *non-gazeux*
fizzy lemonade *limonade*
fresh lemon juice served with sugar *citron pressé*

fresh orange juice *orange pressée*
full (eg full-cream milk) *entier*
fresh or cold *frais, fraîche*
beer *bière*
...bottled *en bouteille*
...on tap *pression*
pre-dinner drink *apéritif*
white wine with cassis
(blackcurrant liqueur) *kir*
kir with champagne *kir royale*
with ice *avec des glaçons*
neat *sec*
red *rouge*
white *blanc*
rose *rosé*
dry *brut*
sweet *doux*
sparkling wine *crémant*
house wine *vin de maison*
local wine *vin de pays*
Where is this wine from? *De quelle région vient ce vin?*
pitcher *carafe/pichet*
...of water/wine *d'eau/de vin*
half litre *demi-carafe*
quarter litre *quart*
after-dinner drink *digestif*
brandy from Armagnac region of France *Armagnac*
Normandy apple brandy *calvados*
cheers! *santé!*
hangover *gueule de bois*

Language Courses

There are many study tours and language courses available. For information, contact the following:

Central Bureau for Educational Visits and Exchanges, 10 Spring Gardens, London SW1, tel: 020 7389 4004.

Language Course Abroad, 01509 211612; www.languagesabroad.co.uk

Centre des Échanges Internationaux, 1 rue Jolzen, Paris 75006; tel: 01 40 51 11 71. Sporting and cultural holidays and educational tours for 15–30 year-olds. Non-profit making organisation.

Alliance Française, 101 boulevard Raspail, Paris; tel: 01 45 44 38 28. Non-profit making, highly regarded French language school, with beginners' and specialist courses. Centres throughout France.

Further Reading

Books

Apart from the Dordogne, perhaps, surprisingly little has yet been written about the Southwest in English. But when you start to hunt around libraries and second-hand bookshops (not least in Montolieu – *see page 274*) you can turn up some interesting books on the region or on the whole of France but with a chapter or two on the Southwest.

History

The Hundred Years' War by Christopher Allmand (Cambridge University Press, 1988). An introduction to the medieval war which marked the Southwest.
The Identity of France by Fernand Braudel (Collins, London, 1988 and 1990). Un-put-downable historical analysis, weaving major events with everyday life, by one of France's most brilliant historians.
The Cambridge Illustrated History of France by Colin Jones (Cambridge University Press, 1999). An excellent overview of French history in general, in which the quality of the illustrations matches that of the text.
The Perfect Heresy. The Revolutionary Life and Death of the Medieval Cathars by Stephen O'Shea (Walker, 2000). Account of the Cathars.
The Albigensian Crusade by Jonathan Sumption (Faber & Faber, London 2000). Readable blow-by-blow account of the demise of the Cathars.
The Hundred Years' War Vol 1: Trial by Battle by Jonathan Sumption (Faber and Faber, London, 1999). First in a series of books documenting the war.
Eleanor of Aquitaine by Alison Weir (Pimlico, 2000). Readable biography of a fascinating figure.

The Return of Martin Guerre by Natalie Zemon Davis (Harvard University Press, 1984). Account of the Ariège mystery which was turned into a film.
France: A History in Art by Bradley Smith (Doubleday, New York, 1984). The history of France through the eyes of artists.

Fiction

Black Dogs by Ian McEwan (Jonathan Cape, 1992). Short novel set in the Grands Causses.
Firelight and Woodsmoke, Applewood and *Scent of Herbs* by Claude Michelet (Orion, 1993). Translation of three French novels (available as an omnibus edition) depicting turn-of-the-20th-century village life in the region.
Chocolat by Joanne Harris (Doubleday, 1999). Poignant and trenchant story of village life.
Signs of the Heart: Love and Death in the Languedoc by Christopher Hope (Macmillan, London, 1999). Contemporary novel set in the region.
The Sun Also Rises (*Fiesta* in the UK) by Ernest Hemingway (1926). A group of expatriates from Paris visit Bayonne en route to Pamplona.

Rural Life

Mourjou. The Life and Food of an Auvergne Village by Peter Graham (Viking Penguin, London, 1998). Dedicated food lover describes life of a village through its food.
The Generous Earth by Philip Oyler (Hodder & Stoughton, 1950). Pre- and post-World War II life in the rural Dordogne.
Life in a Postcard. Escape to the French Pyrenees by Rosemary Bailey (Bantam, 2002). Account of Insight editor's life in France.
The Ripening Sun. One Woman and the Creation of a Vineyard by Patricia Atkinson (Century, 2003). How vinegar turned to prize-winning wine in an uplifting tale.
Virgile's Vineyard. A year in the Languedoc Wine Country. Patrick Moon. (John Murray, 2003.) A fresh view of this fast-evolving wine region.

Classic Travel Books

Three Rivers of France by Freda White (Little Brown, 1989). Beauti-fully written (in 1952) description of Lot, Dordogne and Tarn regions.

Travels in the South of France by Stendhal, translated by Elisabeth Abbott (J. Calder, 1971). Stendhal's account of travelling in the region in the 19th century.

Travels with a Donkey in the Cévennes by Robert Louis Stevenson (1879; various editions, eg Quiet Vision, 2002). Travel journal of the lovelorn Scottish author's trip through the area.

Wildlife

Wildlife Travelling Companion France by Bob Gibbons and Paul Davies (The Crowood Press, 1992). Region-by-region rundown of the best nature-watching places.

Flowers of South-west Europe by Oleg Polunin and B.E. Smythies (Oxford Paperbacks, 1988). Bulky but indispensable guide for wildflower hunters. Oleg Polunin and Anthony Huxley's **Flowers of the Mediterranean** (Chatto and Windus, 1990) is more portable.

The Birds of Britain and Europe by Hermann Heinzel, Richard Fitter and John Parslow (Collins, London, 1991). Brief descriptions of all species likely to be seen.

Literature

The New Oxford Companion to Literature in French edited by Peter France (UOP, 1995). Open and inclusive reference work

Traveller's Literary Companion to France by John Edmondson (In Print, 1997). Gazetteer of places with literary associations, including biographies of authors associated with France.

Food and Wine

The Food Lover's Guide to France by Patricia Wells (Workman, 1999). Regional dishes, best restaurants, shops and markets from food critic of *International Herald Tribune*.

Wine Atlas of France by Hubrecht Duijker (Mitchell Beazley, London, 1997). Well-illustrated atlas, concentrating on wine and vineyards, but also supplementary information on history, architecture and culture.

Modern France

France in the New Century by John Ardagh (Penguin, London, 2000). Good overview of contemporary France by recognised expert.

On the Brink, the Trouble with France by Jonathan Fenby (Abacus, 2002). Controversial, personal and witty account of French politics and life today.

France Today edited by J.E. Flower (Hodder, London, 1993). Essays on contemporary France.

The French by Theodore Zeldin (Random House, New York, 1984). Irreverent, penetrating analysis of the French character.

Other Insight Guides

The 450 titles published by Insight Guides include comprehensive coverage of French destinations.

Insight Guides

Companion guides include *Paris, Normandy, Brittany, Loire Valley, Alsace, Burgundy, French Riviera, Provence* and *Corsica*.

Pocket Guides

Containing personal recommendations and a fold-out map, cover *Paris, Brittany, Loire Valley, Alsace, Provence, Côte d'Azur* and *Corsica*.

Compact Guides

Fact-packed easy-reference guides, cover *Paris, Normandy, Brittany, Burgundy* and *Provence*.

ART & PHOTO CREDITS

AKG London 21, 23, 24, 27R, 29, 31, 35, 38, 40, 42, 69, 70, 137T, 185, 233T, 245T, 261, 296T, 299T, 301L/R, 314T, 319
The Anthony Blake Photo Library 94, 99, 100
The Art Archive 1, 37
Ask Images/Trip 54, 142
Gonzalo M. Azumendi back cover centre, back cover bottom, 4BR, 8/9, 56, 57, 78, 83, 103, 127, 167, 227, 231, 240, 241, 243, 248, 252, 256/257, 259, 263, 265, 265T, 267, 273, 312L/R, 312T
Rosemary Bailey 62, 236T
P.H. Barret/Explorer 143
C. Boisvieux/Explorer 266
E. Brenckle/Explorer 210/211
The Bridgeman Art Library spine, back cover left, 20, 34, 41, 68, 230
Michael Busselle 92/93, 155, 156R, 213, 279
Jean-Claude Carbonne 288
D. Casimiro/Explorer 302/303
M. Coste/Explorer 297
Hervé Champollion/Cephas 52
J.D. Dallet 2/3, 5B, 6/7, 10/11, 12/13, 51, 53, 55, 71, 74, 81, 98, 104, 105, 108, 109, 112/113, 114/115, 121, 123, 124, 126, 127T, 128, 129, 130/131, 134T, 135, 136, 136T, 137, 138, 139T, 140, 146/147, 148, 149, 152, 152T, 153L, 154, 157, 159, 160, 164/165, 169, 170, 171, 177T, 178L/R, 186, 191, 197, 200, 202, 203, 204L, 205, 206L/R, 207, 219L, 251, 270, 274, 308T
Editions Clouet 44
Tor Eigeland 50, 58, 63, 192, 192T, 218T, 219R, 271, 266T, 278T
Mary Evans 19, 128T, 141, 159T, 175T, 185T, 187, 318
Christine Fleurent/Cephas 97
Michael Fogden/Oxford Scientific Films 283
B. Gadsby/Trip 82, 296
Giraudon 26, 27L, 32, 33, 36, 176, 186T, 250T, 272T, 300
P. Gleizes/Explorer 278
F. Gohier/Explorer 79
S. Grant/Trip 72
Robert Harding Picture Library front flap top, 125, 139

Pierre Hussenot/Cephas/TOP 101, 133, 182, 189,
The Hutchison Library 132
Hellio & Van Ingen/NHPA 84/85
Nick Inman front flap bottom, 4/5, 16/17, 18, 22, 25, 28, 43, 66/67, 80, 86, 89L/R, 91, 151, 151T, 153R, 156L, 158, 162T, 163, 166, 169T, 171T, 172, 173L/R, 174L/R, 174T, 175, 177L/R, 178T, 179, 180/181, 183, 188, 190, 190T, 193, 194/195, 196, 201L/R, 201T, 202T, 204R, 207T, 220, 249, 249T, 264, 264T, 274T, 276, 277R, 280T, 282, 290T, 293, 293T, 297T, 298T
F. Jalain/Explorer 4BL, 298
Marion Kaplan 46/47, 60, 96, 162, 212, 215, 215T, 217T, 218, 220T, 221, 222, 222T, 235, 238/239, 244, 253, 275, 287, 292T
J.M. Labat/Explorer 106
J.B. Laffitte/Explorer back flap bottom, 317
P. Lissac/Explorer 59
P. Lorne/Explorer 304
Mountain Sport/Trip 76/77
Oronoz Archivo Fotografico 30
Hans Reinhard/OSF 90
D. Reperant/Explorer 73
M. Rouoemont/Cephas/TOP 299
Mick Rock/Cephas back cover right, 102, 110/111, 120, 161, 217
P. Roy/Explorer 107, 223
Royer/Explorer 61
Markus Schilder/Cephas/TOP 224/225

Cartographic Editor **Zoë Goodwin**
Production **Linton Donaldson**
Design Consultants
Carlotta Junger, Graham Mitchener
Picture Research
Hilary Genin, Susannah Stone

Schings/Explorer 216
Jorge Sierra/OSF 87
Erich Thielscher/OSF 88
Topham Picturepoint 45, 48/49, 228T, 310T
A. le Toquin/Explorer 262
Bill Wassman back flap top, 2B, 14, 95, 116, 199, 226, 229, 232, 233, 234, 236, 237, 242, 245, 250, 252T, 258, 260T, 268/269, 277L, 280, 281, 284/285, 286, 289, 290, 291, 292, 305, 307, 309, 310, 311, 311T, 313, 314, 315, 320

Picture Spreads

Pages 64/65 *Top row, left to right:* Elsie Burch Donald, Nick Inman, Elsie Burch Donald, B. Gadsby/Trip. *Centre rowboth:* Elsie Burch Donald. *Bottom row:* The Anthony Blake Photo Library, B.J. Dupont/Explorer, Elsie Burch Donald, J.D. Dallet.
Pages 144/145 *Top row, left to right:* AKG London, The Bridgeman Art Library, AKG London, Labat Ferrero/Explorer. *Centre row:* The Bridgeman Art Library. *Bottom row:* J.D. Dallet, The Bridgeman Art Library, AKG London.
Pages 208/209 *Top row, left to right:* Royal Aeronautical Society, Topham Picturepoint, Aerospatiale Matra Airbus, Tor Eigeland. *Centre row:* Topham Picturepoint, Royal Aeronautical Society. *Bottom row:* J.D. Dallet, Aerospatiale Matra Airbus, Royal Aeronautical Society, Royal Aeronautical Society.
Pages 254/255 *Top row, left to right:* Bob Gibbons/Oxford Scientific Films, Manfred Danegger/NHPA, Hervé Champollion/Cephas, Konrad Wothe/OSF. *Centre row:* N. Wisniewski/OSF, Nigel Dennis/NHPA, Daniel Heuclin/NHPA. *Bottom row:* Niall Benvie/OSF, Pierre Petit/NHPA, Nick Inman.

Map Production Colourmap Scanning Ltd
© 2004 Apa Publications GmbH & Co.
Verlag KG (Singapore branch)

Index

Numbers in italics refer to photographs

A
B
C
D

F
G
H
I
J

b
c
d
e
f
g
h
i
j
k
l